Gnostic America

Gnostic America

✛ ✛ ✛

A Reading of Contemporary American Culture & Religion according to Christianity's Oldest Heresy

Peter M. Burfeind

PUBLISHED BY PAX DOMINI PRESS

Copyright © 2014 by Peter M. Burfeind
All Rights Reserved.

Publisher's Cataloging-in-Publication
(Provided by Quality Books, Inc.)
Burfeind, Peter M., 1970-
    Gnostic America : a reading of contemporary American
culture & religion according to Christianity's oldest
heresy / Peter M. Burfeind.
      pages cm
      Includes bibliographical references and index.
      LCCN 2014913105
      ISBN 978-0692260494

    1. Gnosticism- Influence. 2. United States-
Civilization–21st century. 3. United States–Politics
and government–21st century. 4. United State-
Religion–21st century. I. Title.

B638.B87 2014   299'.932
            QBI14-600138

Pax Domini Press
www.pax-domini.com
Please direct inquiries to Cyril9@aol.com

Book Design by Peter M. Burfeind

Manufactured in the United States

For Jillian, Aaron, Phoebe, Thomas,
and Vesper

Special thanks to Rita Burfeind

Contents

❖   ❖   ❖

✧ Introduction ✧

Surveying the
Cultural Landscape

Tales from the Trenches of Our Times

Easter, 2012.[1] The audience gazed on in eager expectation, sitting in the stadium seating at the newest campus of the local mega-church. A giant screen towered over them. It revealed the countdown: *four minutes forty-three seconds til the service.*

People filed in. They moved hastily to their seats ushered by well-trained worship attendants. The feeling was electric.

One minute twenty-eight seconds.

Smoke began billowing out onto the stage. Introductory music, like something accompanying a champion wrestler, came from offstage.

Three . . . two . . . one.

The show began. The praise band stormed onto the stage and churned the audience into a clapping, swaying, hand-waving throng. Images of Christ's resurrection flashed on the screen. The editing was contemporary: quick cuts, odd camera angles, symbolic images, poetry evoking Christ's resurrection, but not too much – the rules of edginess dictate you can't reveal too much, at least not yet.

Many would say the event was saturated with the Holy Spirit. For the more cynical, the event was perfectly manufactured according to every known principle of mass manipulation.

The message was revivalistic, but clothed in electronic, hip garb.

The preacher took an almost apologetic tone toward anything traditional, like the altar call or the believer's prayer, or especially the offering. Still, the content was orthodox in the Fundamentalist sense.

Then came the climax of the service. At the point where Christians have reverently received the Eucharist for two millennia, a song by contemporary Christian artist Chris Tomlin filled the building: "This is the dream / My heart is free, no chains on me / Now is the time / Now is the time for freedom / Abandoned by cold religion / My heart on fire / The walls are coming down / The walls are coming down / The walls are coming down / The walls are coming down / Yeah, the walls are coming down / The walls are coming down / Like a rolling stone."[2]

As the singer, an attractive young female, segued into the final phrase of the song, she gave out a long impassioned moan typical of the pop-vibrato style: *ooooo ahhhhhh oooo ooooo ooooo*. On cue the audience broke out into clapping and dance. The service ended.

Harold Bloom went so far as to call the scene Orphic,[3] referring to the ancient mystery cult where flutists worked initiates into an emotional froth, and then priests leveraged the emotion toward the desired goal, the vision of the mystery.

Some identify erotic or romantic overtones: the *ooooo ahhh* moaning, the impassioned surrendering, the emphasis on the heart's yearning. G. K. Chesterton is cited[4] for saying, "A man knocking at the brothel door is looking for God." That is, faith is more a matter of internal passions reaching out for transcendent, unspeakable love than a matter of external doctrinal formulas. A lonely lecher's late-night escapades are really the tugs of God on his heart. "My heart is on fire," sang Tomlin. It's a love affair with God.

In the history of the Church, there is no precedent for this sort of emotion-laden, sacrament-less, erotically-charged religiosity. There is, however, a precedent outside the walls of the Church.

That tradition is the Gnostic one.

*   *   *

After the election of President Obama in 2008, cultural elites in entertainment and politics got mystical, believing the man was something otherworldly. Can we blame them? His advent was prophesied in sacred story, at least American sacred story, which is to say, Hollywood, which has been crafting his image in our minds for years through an archetype

Spike Lee calls the *Magical Negro*.[5] The Magical Negro is the supporting black character who clarifies truth for the misdirected white hero, or the *deus ex machina*, some judge or authority figure who comes in just at the right time to be the voice of otherworldly wisdom and morality.

Through this archetype our pop culture prepared the way – like a composite John-the-Forerunner – for the sleek, cool black man with the silky baritone voice transcending our gridlocked politics: *isn't this how the movie ends?* When Obama finally came on the scene, it was as if, to paraphrase St. John, "The archetype became flesh and dwelt among us." He was, in Mark Steyn's words, "a younger Morgan Freeman, the cool, reserved, dignified black man who, when he's not literally God walking among us (as in *Bruce Almighty*), is always the conscience of the movie."[6]

Will Smith called Obama an "idea mark[ing] an evolutionary flash point in history."[7] An idea! Not an actual human being.

The Gospel according to Mark, Mark Morford that is, called Obama a "Lightworker" who can "actually help usher in a new way of being on the planet, of relating and connecting and engaging with this bizarre earthly experiment. These kinds of people actually help us evolve." At least this is the opinion of "many spiritually advanced people" he knows.[8]

And then there's the Gospel of Thomas, *Newsweek* editor Evan Thomas that is, who cut to the chase: "Obama is standing above the country, above the world. He's sort of God."[9]

The man fulfills a divine fantasy for them, the fantasy of a world where government ushers in an age in which the problems of poverty, war, and climate chaos are solved. Hollywood has been crafting this fantasy of the all-powerful government for years: what doesn't exist in the real world, and never will, they passionately, desperately manufacture in their fantasy world. If ever that fantasy can leak off the screen into reality, *wow!*

True, Obama's presidency simply fulfilled century-old progressive dreams. True, progressive ideology, like all others, is subject to debate. But to the believer, such bickering merely makes sublunary what should be transcendent: *Don't argue about ideology when here is a man who will take us beyond politics.* Politics are the stale artifacts of another time[10] otherwise known as *democratic*. *History*, after all, is fating the world toward a specific end. Evolution itself says so! So there can be no politics. There's only where God, er, History intends to take us and His, er, Its detractors, or maybe if we're "spiritually advanced" enough, *Her* detractors. *Evolve or die!*

Meanwhile, back at earth, the cottage industry on the Right documenting the obvious religiosity of the modern progressive movement is a refreshing meme. But the meme hasn't been taken to its theological roots. Ending the discussion at the birth of the progressive movement isn't enough. The deification of government and the embodiment of that divine spirit in transformative, avatar figures has a history, a very surprising history.

It's a variant of a Gnostic movement whose proper beginnings go back to the twelfth century.

*   *   *

Around 2010, when *Catcher in the Rye* author J. D. Salinger died, blogger "Nick25" waxed philosophical:

"Everyone was phony and a hypocrite, according to Holden, in J.D.Salinger's *Catcher in the Rye*. The world is seen through the eyes of the judger, who is judging primarily himself. The world is a portrayal of the person who is seeing the world. As compared to phony, is there anyone or anything who is truly authentic, in the conscious level of thought? Everything real is beyond the conscious, just as everything is fake in the conscious (i.e., beyond the subconscious world of sleep and dreaming). The superconscious state is attained by meditation, and it is there where reality resides, not here where we are writing and reading in the conscious level of thought and analysis. The conscious level dies with the body; the superconscious level does not. This is why yogis who practice meditation are not afraid of death. They go there all the time."[11]

Everyone is fake . . . the world is the product of the meaning I impose on it . . . sleep and dreaming is where the real stuff is at . . . death is release.

The blogger asks: *Is there anyone who is truly authentic?*

Authentic. The word is everywhere. It's the new *pious*, which traditionally was the proper state of mind one should have toward his deity. When God is distinct from me, my state of mind toward this other Being is that of *piety*. But what happens when my Self is God? Then the goal is *authenticity*. Being "true to my Self" replaces "deny yourself."

The word *authentic* derives from today's default pop philosophy: existentialism. In the truest sense of its own paradoxical terms, existentialism is the atheist's religion. *Authenticity*, or creating one's Self, is its chief piety. *Choice* is its sacrament. It's how creation of Self happens.

In fact, there is a whole lexicon of words we use – *authenticity, choice, freedom, Self, culture, values* – whose meanings are shaped by this atheistic philosophy. But we have forgotten the philosophical contexts in which these terms arose, so we don't question their premises.

Why don't we question the premises? Because that's how faith works. It's premises just *are*.

Faith is far from on the decline in America. It's held more fervently than ever, and its premises are more blindly adhered to and more absolutely grounded on thin air than Christianity ever was.

An atheist faith? Absolutely. History has seen the movie before, in the Gnostic movement.

*   *   *

A seventeen-year-old "genderqueer" writes in Facebook: "I have a lot to worry about . . . But who thought I would have pressure from Facebook to decide whether I am male or female. Maybe this isn't an issue for everyone, but it is for me. I'm CJ, formerly known as Chana. I'm also 'genderqueer,' which, in my case, means that I feel part-female and part-male. I'm not sure yet whether I will transition or not. . . . People like me who don't feel comfortable in the bodies in which we were born aren't sure we want to be pegged as female or male. I am just trying to decide for myself, but Facebook forces me to follow the social norm of being a male or female. . . . Some doctors are beginning to understand, and I know that my doctor does. Even some official government forms now acknowledge that gender identity isn't black-and-white, so to speak."[12]

Comfortable in the bodies we were born with.

Some, like Dietrich Bonhoeffer, would say the "we" and the "bodies" are one in the same: "Man does not have a body; he does not have a soul; rather, he is body and soul."[13] Others reject the notion, seeing flesh as distinct from our true Self, even an alien burden stifling who we really are, a prison cell to escape.

The former view represents orthodox Judeo-Christian presumptions, a presumption beginning with the creation of our flesh and the ultimate restoration and redemption of that same flesh: the resurrection of the flesh.

The latter view represents another tradition, the Gnostic one.

Gnosticism

A Neo-evangelical praise service, the anticipation of a progressive utopian age, the musings of an existentialist/New Age blogger, a young person's discomfort at his/her gender, these are spiritual artifacts of our times, detritus from the spiritual path our culture is carving out of our age. They don't stand out because no one notices the smell of the house they live in. They point to a dominant religious footprint so large no one notices it. The argument of this book is that the traits of ancient Gnosticism best explain this religious orientation.

What is Gnosticism? The Gnosticism 101 answer is, it was an ancient movement centered on esoteric knowledge. It held to a dualistic understanding of the cosmos, in which an evil, lesser god created all things material, and only those who had attained *gnosis* (knowledge) about their true Source (the higher deity) understood the bodiless Self-ness of their existence. Its salvation program was one of escape, escape of Self from materiality and this oppressive world order.

Gnosticism's major offense to traditional Christianity – to say nothing of its offense to traditional Judaism and the Western intellectual tradition in general – is its rejection of nature, nature's laws, and nature's God. The Gnostic is ever in rebellion against nature and, more to the philosophical point, natural *forms*. Such naturally-arising concepts as gender, national boundaries, the cold hard realities of economics, cultural institutions like family and church (especially its rituals), marriage, even language, are deceptive impositions, says the Gnostic, of a foreign God upon what should be the authentic Self liberated from all impositions of form, freed to transcend them altogether.

The Judeo-Christian orientation centers on created forms. God's first action was to separate the "formless and void" of creation and bring about the various species "each according to its kind."[14] After separating the elements he named them, which is to say: *language arose out of the creation of forms.* Of course, language got the whole thing rolling in the first place, when the Lord said, "let there be." Hence the sacredness given the Hebrew language by the Jew, and the sublime implications of the foundational Christian tenet: "the Word became flesh and dwelt among us."[15]

Traditional Christianity grants that these forms have been corrupted by original sin, but the whole point of its doctrine of the incarnation is that God took on human form in order to redeem these corrupted forms. The end goal of the Christian faith is a "world to come," a world with redeemed forms, a world inaugurated by the resurrection.

Gnostics reject this entire premise. The God who established forms "each according to its kind" they consider an evil, usurping god, a false tyrant deceptively thought to be the one true God, the God of the Judeo-Christian Scriptures. The true God, says the Gnostic, transcends all form, all that can be thought, all being, everything. Celebrating formless spirituality, Gnosticism rejects those formal things, peoples, and institutions marking traditional Christianity: the Church, its sacramental life, and its ministry. It despises the Jewish God and its regard for language and grammar, anything mooring spirituality to something so profane as a text.

Thus the Gnosticism 101 summary, but where things get interesting (and pernicious) is where the Gnostic movement works its program through culture, politics, and religion. Precisely because Gnosticism doesn't have marked doctrines or creedal statements, being more a "spiritual orientation," it can easily be coopted in non-religious arenas – in politics, marketing, and media – without fear of being accused of religious imposition, when in fact that is exactly what it is.

The best entrance point into this spiritual orientation is the phrase "spiritual, but not religious," which is how more and more people are identifying themselves. In 2012, WIN-Gallup International reported that in the previous seven years, the number of people describing themselves as religious fell from 73% to 60%, while those believing in God or some universal spirit stayed at 91%.[16] That's an astounding number, demonstrating the dramatic 13% move of "religious" over to the "non-religious believers" camp in six years. The trend is accentuated vastly among the young, which suggests all the energy is on the "spiritual but not religious" side.

True, some of that 13% drop includes Neo-evangelicals who recoil at the term *religious*. They've taken to the "Christianity not Churchianity" distinction, seeing in the former more authenticity. "I have the greatest admiration for the Christianity of Christ. On the other hand, I have the greatest contempt for 'Church' Christianity, or 'Churchianity'."[17] Are these Rick Warren's words? No, they belong to Laurence Oliphant, the nineteenth century mystic and proto-New Ager, and good friend of the bizarre Madame Blavatsky. Neo-evangelical cooption of this posture forces us to investigate what it is in Neo-evangelicalism's DNA leading it to become the Christian wing of the New Age movement.

On the other hand, how much of that 9% atheist crowd is truly atheist? The old meaning of *atheist* was anyone who wasn't a Christian or Jew, but who still held to some transcendent Truth. This definition dies hard, for how many atheists believe in some sort of transcendent morality, or a transcendent goal of human progress? How many of them *fanatically* embrace these goals and moralities? If one's God is that point at which doubt or skepticism ceases, one wonders if anyone is truly atheist, or if the human soul can even bear atheism.

The point is, a growing demographic of people, despite the labels, embrace a relatively unified *spiritual* posture. Alexis de Tocqueville predicted it two hundred years ago. He foresaw democracy breeding a people who believe in a divinity, but who don't put form to that divinity through doctrines, rituals, sacraments, or such.[18] The democrat fears that aristocratic institutions like the Church or academia will put a straitjacket on God, binding him with their pedantry and scholasticism. God, rather, should transcend categorization, bursting the defining strictures of any Church or institution. God should connect with us psychologically, internally, in the mysterious nether regions of the Self, in a subconscious spiritual undercurrent shared by all people.

Such is the position, said Tocqueville, a democratic people will naturally take. Fine and good. Power to the people and all that. But as a self-governing people we're obligated to investigate whence this orientation[19] arises and what it means if it truly is penetrating undetected our psychology, politics, politics, culture, and traditional religions. If it's ancient Gnosticism redux, the original "spiritual but not religious" orientation, we should at least know what we're getting into, to say nothing of applying First Amendment guidance, for a "spiritual state" is just as worrisome as a state religion.

The Waning Days of Irony and Nihilism

Gnosticism naturally rises out of nihilism, and ours is a nihilistic age. Nihilism is the view that nothing matters. Nihilism drives today's teen creed, "Whatever," whose burdensome three syllables have evolved into a languid "Whatev." Nihilism is the wrecking ball of society, an iconoclastic force tearing down traditional institutions, traditional moralities, traditional rituals, traditional habits, traditional customs, traditional grammar, traditional language, and traditional reasoning. Nihilism begins in despair and cynicism, despair because these traditions seemed to fail human aspiration, cynicism that they could have ever satisfied it in the first place. To the nihilist, every institution is run by the "powers that be," or the "rulers of the universe," by people whose only concern is control: power for it's own sake.

Nihilism often masquerades as a bitter sense of irony. Irony fits nihilism because it discharges any challenge to nihilism. Irony can cut anything good and beautiful down to size. It also raises the bad and ugly just enough to prove the high and great weren't that high or great in the first place. Irony levels everything so that nothing has meaning.

In Season Two of the 2001-2009 hit TV series *24* – a show about agent Jack Bauer's fight against terrorist plots in America – one of the main terrorist accomplices was a wealthy young blond woman.[20] In reality, for all practical purposes, this doesn't happen. But in the popular imagination, it *must* happen. It was the tribute the series had to pay to America's ironclad sense of irony.

What's the irony? It's that we all think a terrorist would be a young Arab male, but look, here's the very opposite, a typically all-American person – a wealthy, beautiful, blonde woman – who is really the terrorist. Irony puts the quote marks on phrases like *all-American*. It plants the thought in our brains: "See! You all have your ideas of what America is, but look, who *really* is the terrorist?"

But *24* was pure fantasy. Fantasy, by way of quick review, means it's not real. In reality, over and over again, terrorists are exactly what we expect them to be. That's reality. Yet, ironic Hollywood plants the question, *what is reality?* Hollywood's fantasy-fueled irony shields us from reality. It happens over and over again in the Hollywood-induced dream world so many of us live in.

Why is this sort of irony necessary? Because nihilism has taken root in the American mind. The moment any traditional institution or form or convention or custom – the nation, marriage, the Church, gender roles, freedom, the free market – is seen to have some worth or beauty or goodness (to say nothing of basic truth) attached to it, the demon of nihilism has a ready quip to deflate its pretenses. Hence the modern iconoclasm toward these institutions, their sentenced de-construction.

But the human soul cannot tolerate such emptiness, the vacuum created by nihilism. Something must fill the vacated domain. Something must be re-constructed. Hollywood understands this. At the same time they manufacture irony toward traditional notions, they craft new *fantastical* realities.

Reality, *real* reality, for example tells us that social pathologies and crime devastate our inner cities. *No*, says Hollywood. The suburbs are where all the pathology, emptiness, and loneliness are. That's the irony. Meanwhile the poor, the straggled, the homeless, and the minorities have an other-worldly wisdom, displaying preternatural inner peace as they bestow guru-like knowledge to benighted "typical Americans." That's the re-constructed replacement myth.

Or again, reality shows women as generally vulnerable, appreciating a good man in their lives. Single women and single mothers bear crushing burdens and demands from all directions. *No*, says Hollywood. Women are independent warriors, the equal or betters of men in physical competition, who shine brightest when freed from male patronage. Traditional gender roles are nihilistically destroyed, but they are replaced by a newly crafted image.

That's because the human soul cannot tolerate nihilism. Irony though fun and funny is ultimately jejune and doesn't satisfy. Hollywood cannot end with irony; it must offer new, transcendent realities, transcendent in the sense suggested by those who proclaim with wide-eyed glee, *It was like in a movie!* as if they've tapped into something more real than life. The soul enters into the dark tunnel of nihilism, but finds a light at the end of the tunnel, on the flickering projection screens, but also in the fantastical images seeping in through television commercials, in the "trending" movements of the Internet, and in the other accepted conduits of reconstructed truth.

The path from nihilism to meaning has a parallel in the history of philosophy. The most virulent, anti-Christian, atheist philosophers almost always ended up with some sort of spirituality. They *must* have some appeal to the transcendent, else they'd have no reason to lay down their philosophies in the first place. What is the transcendent, after all, but whatever I believe is true for more than just myself? That transcendency, then, soon takes on the characteristics of spirituality.

Some simply end at the irony, like philosopher Richard Rorty. But even Nietzsche, as "he assails the reason he will be enlisting," at the same time "ironizes a discourse that at the same time struggles beyond irony."[21] If modernity's most profound nihilist – who dedicated his life to assailing ironically the Logos-based foundations of Western civilization – "struggled" to find transcendence beyond irony, surely we cannot expect less from the culture he begot. The quest for truth cannot end at irony; there *must* be something beyond.

Heidegger displays the same tension between nihilism and

transcendence. He too, like Nietzsche, saw the West coming to a nihilistic end because *being*, as understood in the Western philosophical heritage, disintegrated when the Christian and classical traditions propelling that heritage ran out of steam. Heidegger also didn't leave it at that, at nihilism. In the words of political philosopher Michael Gillespie, "he believes he discerns in its depths the dawning light of a new revelation of Being." Nihilism, rather, is the "dawning recognition of Being."[22] We must go through nihilism before getting to the new understanding of Being. At that same time, we face both "utter degradation and the possibility of salvation in a new revelation of Being."[23] In other words, it's as we've been contemplating: the point of nihilistic breakdown is also the point of new possibilities.

For him, this meant becoming a Nazi, which Heidegger hoped "could be directed toward a more fundamental experience of human existence that could serve as the basis for a more authentic ethics and politics."[24] As we will see, he followed Hitler's exact understanding of himself and his fascist movement. Needless to say, these phrases – "dawning light," "new revelation of Being," and "possibility of salvation" – clue us into the truly spiritual forces at work.

American society has also followed this philosophical path from nihilism to spiritualism. In the 1960s, society's vanguards led the way. *The New York Times Magazine* put Nietzsche's epithet to a query: *Is God dead?* In the 1970s and 80s, the iconoclastic wrecking ball came in devastating cultural institutions: marriage, family, gender norms, sex norms, cultural mores. Nihilism was in full force.

In the 1990s, society turned toward irony, palpably sensed in our comedy, mores, and social interactions. The Cold War ended and the economy was blossoming, leading to leisurely yet indulgent cravings for guilty, ironical pleasures like the black comedy *Pulp Fiction* (1994) or the sitcom *Seinfeld*. Bill Clinton feeling the pain of a populace at the apex of human history was irony on steroids. Urbane snark was in. Nothing was sacred.

Then 9/11 came, along with mounting economic problems. The quest for spirituality settled in. But people aren't going to church as understood for two millennia. They're going to places suiting their spiritual-but-not-religious orientation. That might be a church – one reinvented for the new paradigms of spirituality – or they seek some other personal spiritual program: Self-help, progressive politics, some Eastern religion, or some combination of the various Gnostic programs out there.

This explains the strange, paradoxical situation we find ourselves in today: the same person who looks cynically at any traditional institution will religiously, even fanatically, hold to some cause. There are psychological and cosmic structures underlying this fanaticism as well as a particular theology (or anti-theology) undergirding the structure. That is Gnosticism, a religion in its own right and one due the same critical analysis as any other, at least in a free-thinking Republic.

A Brief Outline of the Book

This book is divided into four parts.

The first part introduces the basics of Gnosticism, with a brief outline of its mythologies, teachings, and practices. These might be interesting on an academic level, to some, but far more interesting and important is how Gnosticism works through modern spirituality, how the Gnostic traits in its ancient version echo yet today. Considerable time, then, is devoted to the Gnostic traits. Finally, a history of Gnostic movements is given taking us from the ancient world to today.

This book is not an academic treatise. It's intent is not to get caught in the weeds of different Gnostic groups or teachings. For reasons this book will hopefully make clear, dealing with Gnosticism academically kind of misses the whole point of Gnosticism, which boasts a knowledge beyond book-learning. Thus it's far more productive to deal with Gnosticism in an archetypical or heuristic manner. This approach will make sense by the book's end.

The second part explores Gnosticism in culture. It begins with the existentialist understanding of the Self and goes on to the role media and music play in the development of Self. Important in this chapter is the "practical Gnostic" view of Renaissance Hermeticism, which is to say, how magic manipulates our fantasy lives in the creation of Self.

The third part tackles Gnostic politics, finding common themes in the totalitarian movements of the modern era. The central thesis driving this part is that a specific theological outlook of the Middle Ages – millenarian, Anabaptist, Pietist, and Puritan – has laid the foundation for modern progressive politics.

Finally, the fourth part deals with Gnosticism in religion, discussing how the Neo-evangelical movement has essentially become the New Age wing of the Christian Church, and indeed has always been so.

Part I

Gnosticism 101: Its Traits and History

✧ Chapter 1 ✧

Gnosticism:
Antichrist Arising

Christianity's Archenemy

Long ago John the Evangelist wrote, "Little children, it is the last hour; and as you have heard that the Antichrist is coming, even now many antichrists have come, by which we know that it is the last hour."[1]

Little did St. John know what sort of hallmark character he was introducing into the imagination, art, and literature of the last two thousand years. Originally he was simply describing anyone who denied the two cornerstones of the Christian Creed, the Trinity and the incarnation of Jesus Christ.[2] This doctrinal understanding deflates some of the sensational mystique of the Antichrist, but in his mundaneness he becomes all the more insidious.

St. John was referring to Gnosticism, a teaching he wrote would shadow the Church throughout her days like a doppelgänger aping her across the annals of time. Addressing this trait of Gnosticism, Pope John Paul II wrote, "Gnosticism . . . has always existed side by side with Christianity, sometimes taking the shape of philosophical movement, but more often assuming the characteristics of a religion or para-religion in distinct, if not declared, conflict with all that is essentially Christian."[3]

Gnosticism is offended by the central tenet of the Christian faith: God becoming flesh in the Person of Jesus Christ. It rejects this doctrine because it rejects what flesh means for our understanding of the world.

15

Flesh allows for the possibility of different *beings*. Flesh makes *individuality* possible. Judeo-Christian creation theology begins with God's Spirit bringing order to the "formlessness and void"[4] by separating it into the various individual beings "each according to its kind."[5] He divided light from darkness, land from water, and living beings from the earth. Each created being possesses its individual existence *in matter*. After the creation God gave his imprimatur on the whole project: *It is very good*. That sets up the ethical relation between God's creation and the cosmic structures he established. Nature and nature's laws are related to ethics.

Gnostics invert this entire premise. For them, the separation of being is evil, the act of an alien god imposing multiple forms on preexistent formlessness.[6] It's the source of death.[7] The primitive formlessness – this unnameable, divine blob – reflected a superior state when everything was One. Flesh gives form to separate beings – *here is a cat and here is a dog*, etc. – and imposes walls amidst the primeval Oneness that should have remained one and indivisible were it not for the intrusion of this alien god. For the Gnostic, this alien god is what the Western tradition has called *God* since the advent of Judeo-Christian orthodoxy. It's the God of the Scriptures who imposed separateness onto the primeval Oneness. His work of dividing and separating formlessness into the various forms is the true fall, bringing forth a world full of all the various divisions.

To the Gnostic the Judeo-Christian God is not unlike the "God" of science, reason, and philosophy, disciplines seeking insight into the nature of things through contemplation of the physical universe and its divvied up properties. Their cogitations result in multiplying categories and complex definitions that help us understand nature's many properties. *Not so*, says the Gnostic. Such thinkers, usually *Western* thinkers, only build thought structures by which they impose *their* meaning on our world, tyrannically ruling us with their loftily-conceived "natural laws." Their brand of "materialistic reductionism" and "categorical thinking" – the Newtonian/Cartesian paradigm – is precisely the sort of cancer inflicting the West, a paradigm that must be replaced.

What does all this mean for me personally, from a Gnostic perspective? After all, I'm born into the individualizing materiality of flesh, imprisoned in its confines. Is there hope for me?

My birth into human flesh is my personal fall. It's the fall of a *spark* of divinity into my particular flesh. At first I deceptively believe this is *me*. This is because at my birth, the pre-existent divine spark becomes overwhelmed by flesh and falls asleep under a flesh-induced stupor. I forget I am part of the primeval Oneness. Salvation happens when I awaken to the truth: *I am not my flesh; the Oneness is my true identity, my true Self*. My true home is outside of this created order, in another world beyond the grasp of any human faculty, beyond what science, reason, or traditional religion can know, delineate, or define.

One can discern echoes of the New Age with all its *finding-God-within* hopes, and the parallels are there. New Ager Marilyn Ferguson heralded the coming new "emergent spiritual tradition"[8] in America, describing the paradigm shift in spirituality thus: "Adherents prefer direct experience – [the] 'excursion' to an inner world whose vision then infuses all of life – to any form of organized religion."[9]

She later quotes Roman Catholic theologian Anthony Padovano, who describes the current spiritual climate: "The great turmoil in the religions is caused by the spirit demanding interiority. Faith is not dying in the West. It is merely moving inside."[10]

The theme is identical in both quotes. Society is moving towards a supposed New Age of internalized spirituality. It's rejecting the forms of organized religion. The message for the rest of us? *Evolve or die.*

The implications for Christianity, or for that matter any religion, are clear. If I find God within, I don't need external mediation points, such things like texts, ministers, priests, rituals, sacraments, or any institutional form. Ultimately I don't even need a Jesus Christ, the ultimate claim to mediacy. All forms that would box God into a located presence are false and delusive, nothing more than man's attempt to manage God. Jesus Christ at best is an internal Spirit Guide, a Cosmic Guru, an archetype, a representative from the primeval Unity who helps me awaken to my inner spark and then guides me home.[11] The Gnostic tract, *The Apocryphon of James*, sets out the true role of Christ as a copilot to the Self's personal journey, recording Jesus' real message, "I tell you this, [so] that you may know yourselves."[12]

His role is not unlike that given to him by New Ager David Spangler, who describes his Christ as that "aspect of this Godhead that reaches deep into the incarnation patterns of creation and links the immanent with the transcendent, the particular with the universal . . . I think of it generically as the avatar function . . . When I first encountered it, it simply said, 'I am that which you have named the Christ.'"[13]

Self-proclaimed Gnostic Harold Bloom recognizes this Christ – a

Christ abstracted from his humanity – in America's most native version of Christianity (Evangelicalism): "The American finds God in herself or himself, but only after finding the freedom to know God by experiencing a total inward solitude. . . . In perfect solitude, the American spirit learns again its absolute isolation as a spark of God floating in a sea of space. Salvation, for the American, cannot come through the community or the congregation, but is a one-on-one act of confrontation."[14]

American spirituality eschews any idea that God can be boxed in, encountered through physical, external means, or located at specific times and places. The American God is a non-physical, abstracted Lord encountered intuitively on highly personalized terms. Jesus becomes the invisible Guide walking and talking with me on the sandy beach of life's journey, leading me onward until I'm released from this vessel of flesh. Meanwhile the flesh is something distinct from who I really am. It's a vessel, something useless at my death, fit only for the fire, which partly explains the increasing demand for cremation.

Traditional Christian doctrine centers on Christ's mysterious presence through the Church. Gnosticism, because it requires no ecclesiastical intermediary, has always strained against the Church. This is what's going on behind such phrases as, "I'm spiritual but not religious" or "I believe in Christ, but not the Church"[15] or "I believe in Christianity not Churchianity." Diana Butler Bass works with this premise in her *Christianity After Religion: The End of Church and the Birth of a New Spiritual Awakening* (2013). Meanwhile church marketing experts, recognizing where American spirituality is at, tap into it and adapt their programs to that vibe.

This anti-institutional trend in American spirituality has a heritage, and that heritage is Gnosticism. Gnosticism was the "spiritual but not religious" creed of the ancient world, a creed aptly described by Robert C. Fuller as the conviction that "the visible world is part of a more spiritual universe from which it draws its chief significance, and that . . . union or harmonious relation with this 'spiritual more' is our true end."[16]

To this end, Fuller continues, people dissatisfied with "institutional religion" seek "personal religious experience" and "associate faith with the 'private' realm of personal experience rather than the 'public' realm of institutions, creeds, and rituals."[17]

Gnosticism attracts the seeker of unbounded, unhoused, *God-outside-the-box*[18] spirituality. Gnosticism erodes the borders between different beings. It tears down the walls within which a specific *being* is defined (*form*). It blurs lines. It is *non-denominational*, appealing to a oneness said to transcend whatever is denominated, whether those be the teachings of a church body or the so-called "gender constructs." All these must be transcended.

Syncretistic

Ancient Gnosticism was syncretistic, adopting from a variety of religions, philosophies, and systems. Gnostic scholar Kurt Rudolf calls it "parasitic."[19]

In the early days of the Christian Church, syncretism attracted a pluralistic Greco-Roman culture. Syncretism is cultivated in pluralistic societies where diverse cultures live side by side. Like today the ancients saw religious diversity, and the provincialism of their own particular beliefs gave them anxiety: *Is it true that my little provincial belief is true for all people of all times?* So they sought transcendent universals to which, they claimed, not only their own particular beliefs pointed, but also those of all other particular beliefs.

Third century Roman emperor Severus Alexander (222-235) kept statues of the Lares (Roman household gods), Apollonius of Tyana (a Neopythagorean miracle worker and teacher), Christ, Abraham, Orpheus, and others.[20] Severus' tossed salad is not so different from the "spiritual but not religious" woman of today who "has a home altar that symbolizes her personal spiritual beliefs [on which] are eighteen candles, an amulet attached to a photo of her grandmother, amethyst crystals used in healing meditations, oriental incense, a Tibetan prayer bell, a representation of the Virgin of Guadalupe, and some other traditional Catholic items."[21]

Taking syncretism one step further, Emergent Church spokesman Brian McClaren recognizes the paradoxes of diverse teachings, but embraces them. He claims to be a "Missional, Evangelical, Post/Protestant, Liberal/Conservative, Mystical/Poetic, Biblical, Charismatic/Contemplative, Fundamentalist/Calvinist, Anabaptist/Anglican, Methodist, Catholic, Green, Incarnational, Depressed-yet-Hopeful, Emergent, Unfinished CHRISTIAN."[22] McClaren thrives on these contradictions, believing that somewhere in the conversation between those holding opposing opinions a story emerges in which we take part.[23]

Syncretism formats our minds against recognizing truth in specific things bounded by time/place contours, or in things articulated through propositional language. It allows us to identify meaning above and beyond the formal or physical contours of any given thing. While our mind is busy naming and identifying what we perceive are truths – everything from "there is a cat sitting there" to "this is My Body" or "this is what marriage is" – Gnosticism lifts us beyond such "imposing" of form upon our world, a world which, we remember, is the creation of a usurper deity anyways.

The Gnostic text *Thunder: Perfect Mind* is described as "an excellent example of a religious polemical stance against the power of names, labels, designations."[24] It's an entire tome whose basic gist is *I am X. I am non-X*.[25] It pushes meaning beyond the abilities of language, rendering it useless. But in exchange the Gnostic gains new, universalistic meaning transcending the limiting and miserly constraints of language.

The Gnostics mastered the syncretistic spirit, picking and choosing from the various philosophies, religions, and cults of the Roman Empire and concocting a potion saluting anything and everything it came across. There were not Gnostic schools in the sense that Plato or Aristotle had schools named after them. The different Gnostic sects didn't debate among themselves. They were tolerant of the sacred texts of other religions. They promoted a free-for-all program for self-salvation.[26]

Gnosticism holds a unique place among traditional Western categories, which forever have philosophy and religion vying against each other. Throughout the history of the West this Gnostic third force has always lurked in the shadows.[27] Gnosticism fits neither the category of religion nor philosophy. It would claim it moves beyond categories because it transcends both. It offers something superior to both, which explains its popularity in a postmodern society cynical toward both. Gnosticism offers a different path: an adventure, a journey, a way of approaching things, a way of life transcending the "old paradigms"[28] of faith and reason.

Gnosis: Inner Knowledge and the Gnostic Creation Myth

Inner Knowledge
The basic Gnostic framework is, as the rock group Police put it, "we are spirits in a material world."[29] We are spirits, or sparks of divinity, trapped in the prison cell of this material world. Our true home is outside of this world, outside all time and place designations. In modern terms we spawn from a completely different dimension. This realm the Gnostics called the *pleroma*, Greek for "fullness." The pleroma is the fullness of

Monad and the *aeons*. Monad, Greek for "one," is what we would call *God* but in reality is beyond all naming. It's the central, animating principle of the pleroma. From it came the aeons, Greek for "ages," which emanate out from Monad and fill out the pleroma. This is our true home. While on one hand we have an alien fleshly existence due to a grand cosmic error, some of us have a spark of Monad residing in our flesh, something we can potentially wake up to.

The Gnostics were anti-cosmic, an important point needing explanation. In Greek thought, *cosmos* meant the known universe, or, anything that can be known by the mind.[30] The word means "order" or "arrangement." It included all material things but also abstractions like *justice* or *piety*, anything the mind can formulate ideas on. The cosmos is the realm of *nouns*: persons, places, things, and ideas – whatever our mind puts definition to. *Noun* comes from the Latin *nomen*, meaning "name," the idea being that the diverse properties of the cosmos can be identified and named just as Adam did and the Lord himself did after separating light from darkness, sky from earth, and land from water. The *cosmos* (from which we get "cosmetic") is good, beautiful, able to be grasped by the mind, and able to be discussed with human language. Its elements are rationally arranged by a rational Mind, and rationally engaging in it involves something inherently good. Meditation on the cosmos rallies the mind to a good cause, because the objects of its thoughts reflect the intelligent, good, and beautiful Mind generating those objects. To "muse on the work of Your hands" as the Psalmist does (Psalm 143: 5) is to engage in something intrinsically good, whether that meditation results in science, poetry, philosophy, or theology.

Gnosticism was anti-cosmic, meaning they rejected as deceptive, false, and evil *all that could be known or named*[31] *by the human mind*. Gnostic scholar Hans Jonas writes, "the divinity of cosmic order is turned into the opposite of divine . . . devoid of meaning and goodness, alien to the purposes of man and to his inner essence, no object for his communication and affirmation."[32]

The human mind, the Gnostic says, is the fleshly instrument by which we impose meaning on a physical world that was a mistake in the first place. Human language is also intrinsically corrupt. Far better is an intuitive knowledge, a knowledge by ecstatic insight, a glimpse into the beyond, a knowledge of the heart rather than the mind. The word Gnosticism is derived from the Greek word *gnosis*, which means "knowledge." This *gnosis* – knowledge transcending all that can be known by the mind – is the focal point of the Gnostic quest.

The Gnostic Creation Myth

The Gnostic creation myth is really a psychological tale, feeding off the ancient view that the journey of the soul was tied to the story of the gods. Because in the ancient mind the macrocosm reflected the microcosm and vice versa, creation myths set up certain psychic archetypes which made sense of the soul's journey.

The Gnostic myth in particular begins with Monad, their "God," but not God as traditionally understood in the West, one defined by certain attributes (as in philosophy) or believed to have a name and to have done certain historical things (as in Judaism and Christianity). Again, the Gnostic would complain that such activities box God into our delineations, or box him into an insular history. Rather, the Monad is beyond all categories, beyond all names and naming, and beyond all involvement in our history. He transcends words, doctrines, names, and thought itself. Even negative theology – the sort that believes God can only be described by what he is *not* – doesn't do Monad justice.[33]

From the Monad came emanations of male and female parities, like ripples out from a stone dropped in water. The first male/female emanation proceeded to produce another male/female emanation, and so on and so forth. These parities were called "syzygies," and each new emanation was an aeon. So long as male and female were harmonized in each emanation, everything balanced out. The totality of aeons, along with the Monad, was the pleroma.[34]

Trouble began in paradise when Sophia, the female element in the last aeon, decided to create something on her own without consulting her male partner. She generated a ghastly monster known as Yaltabaoth. Ashamed of her deed, she extracted the half snake, half lion beast from her womb and hid him in a cloud. Some Gnostics called it an abortion.[35] Hidden in his cloud from the pleroma, Yaltabaoth believed he alone existed and decided to create something of his own. He created what we know as the universe. He also created our physical bodies.[36]

Yaltabaoth created 365 *archons* (powers or governors) to help him rule the cosmos. These rulers helped him set up the laws (Greek: *nomos*) governing the various orders in nature, politics, culture, and ethics. He himself pridefully declared, "I, I am a [jealous] god, and apart from me nothing has [come into being]."[37] And, "It is I who am God, and there is no other one that exists apart from me."[38]

These latter words may sound familiar to the Jew or Christian, because in the Old Testament the Lord repeats them seven times. This is why Gnostics reject Old Testament theology and its God. The Old Testament, they said, picks up the story too late, beginning only at the point of Yaltabaoth's creative activity. The Hebrews falsely believed Yaltabaoth, whom they called Yahweh, was the one true God. They misunderstood his creating as the beginning point of all things.

Throughout history Gnosticism has proposed two gods, one based in the Old Testament – a fierce, wrathful, named, provincial Deity, a bit over-involved in history, who demands blood sacrifices, rites, and rituals – and a universal New Testament God of enlightenment and love who offers freedom and spontaneity.[39] Against this classic Gnostic position the ancient Church established two of its traditions surviving to this day: the canonization of Scripture (to include the Old Testament in the biblical canon) and certain language inserted into its creeds: "according to the Scriptures" and "spake by the prophets."

In any event, Sophia pitied Yaltabaoth's human creations and cast a *spark*[40] (Greek: *spinthēr*) of the Monad in some of them, creating a duality in the human person of body and spirit, each with a source contested against the other. Eden's snake, traditionally seen as the devil, was a messenger of truth sent to alert Eve. By getting her to eat of the Tree of the Knowledge (*gnosis*) of Good and Evil, the snake hoped to provide the true *gnosis* of what is Good (the Monad) and what is Evil (the false god who made them).[41]

But alas, Yahweh cut things off at the pass, stymying the devil, and Adam and Eve's descendants fell asleep to their inner sparks under the cumbersome materiality of their physical flesh. Yet hope for salvation remained; the Monad sent Christ to give people knowledge (*gnosis*) of their true home, to awaken them to the truth of the cosmos[42] – a moment of ecstatic enlightenment and awakening[43] known as *palingenesia*,[44] or "born again experience" – and to lead them on a journey back home to the pleroma, their state of primal harmony.

Of course we misapply the myth when we take it literally. Gnostics are anything but literal. Poetry, allegory, double meanings, and surreal mindscapes are their bread and butter. Thus this myth is a psychological tale populated by archetypical aspects of our psyches. Monad is the center of our being, the depths of our true Self. The fall of Yaltabaoth is the fallen psyche, what some call the ego and its prideful ruts. The archons represent whatever it is in my personal psychological tale keeping my true Self from emerging, the bonds of the "powers that be" in my world: parents and their pathologies, Church and her doctrines, state and its arbitrary laws, global capitalism, fate, my personality, whatever. Sophia introduces the liberating role of *eros*, love erotically understood. Jesus is related to her, the otherworldly Guide who leads me home.

In this psychological tale are all sorts of characters who pepper our lives, characters abstracted from the figments of real flesh and blood personages, characters who loom larger than life as they assume the numinous mantles of these Gnostic archetypes. The Gnostic myth gives life to these archetypes but more intriguingly places them in a greater psychological narrative of self-salvation.

The archon archetype is the glowering looks of "establishment" people in society forcing me to conform to their standards. It's the uniformed police, "the man," or stone-faced traditionalists. It's the pudgy, fiftyish white man who surely runs every boardroom. It's the magical vibe conveyed by certain words or phrases – the *banks*, *Wall Street*, the *Jews*, the *system*. It's the "big X" formula used in phrases like "big business," "big oil," or "big pharmaceutical." It's Heidegger's "they." Who exactly is "the they"? The Gnostics have an answer; "they" are your masters.

Meanwhile, the Sophia archetype stands by ready to offer salvation. She peers at me through a stranger's flirtatious glance, which crafts the quickly-scribed romance fantasy, so invigorating and liberating. She sings to me through music simulating that same feeling. She embraces me with her mother's love, somatically-induced through any number of intoxicants, from the pharmaceutical to the psychological, emotional, or spiritual. Whatever she is, she defies the tyranny of logic.

Then there's the Jesus archetype, my personal Savior, the Spirit Guide who takes my hand and leads me home, who in the end is nothing more than my transcendent, ideal *me*, the unity of Monad and my redeemed Self.

Rudolf ventures straight into this psychic terrain when he comments on the difficulty in translating the Greek word for "divine spark from the Monad," *spinthēr*: "In order to make use of a uniform expression scholars have become accustomed to speak of the 'self' or 'I', . . . The 'incomparable self' in man."[45]

For the Gnostic, the *Self* is a spark of the Monad; the *Self* is God. The journey to find God is the journey to find our Selves. When we awaken to our inner Selves away from what we think we are (the ego), we find we are all part of God, or perhaps better put, a collective divine unity, the pleroma. The Self is central in Gnostic religion, even as it is central to modern American spirituality. Again Harold Bloom: "The God of the American Religion is an experiential God, so radically within our own being as to become a virtual identity with what is most authentic (oldest and best) in the self."[46] The identification of God with the *authentic Self* is a classic Gnostic construct.

Gnostic Practice

Fourth century bishop of Salamis, Epiphanius, testified of the Gnostics, "They condemn baptism even though some of them were previously baptized. They reject participation in the (church) sacraments (mysteries) and deny their value, as extraneous and introduced in the name of [the demiurge, Yaltabaoth]."[47]

This rejection of the sacraments follows Gnosticism throughout its history. True, they had some cultic activities with vague parallels to the sacraments of the Church, but no more than symbolic value, usually having something to do with the initiate's union with the pleroma or his "angel image" in the pleroma.[48] Their litanies speak the language of symbolism, uncertainties, and vagueness, as in this baptismal formula: "In the name of the unknown Father of all things, into Truth, the mother of all, into him who descended on Jesus (i.e. Christ), into union, into redemption, into the communion of the powers."[49] Or in this communion prayer: "He (Jesus) said on that day in the eucharist: '(You) who have joined the perfect, the light, with the Holy Spirit, join the angels with us also, the images.'"[50] The cryptic language is purposeful, meant to be hidden from all but the elite few, the enlightened, or the awakened.

Obviously they denied the real presence of Christ's body and blood in the sacrament just as they denied the incarnation of Jesus himself in flesh and blood (the particular doctrine that St. John described in I John 4: 3). They said Jesus only *seemed* to be human, leading to one of the names given the early Gnostics, the Docetists (from the Greek, *doceo*, "to seem").[51] Against docetic teaching already embryonic in apostolic days, both St. Luke and St. John emphasized the physicality of Jesus' post-resurrection appearances: "Behold My hands and My feet, that it is I Myself. Handle Me and see, for a spirit does not have flesh and bones as you see I have." (Luke 24: 39; see also John 20: 27.)

Irenaeus of Lyons (*d.* 202), the ancient champion of orthodoxy against Gnosticism, saw the danger in Gnostic anti-materialism for the Church's sacrament, writing, "But if [the flesh] indeed does not obtain salvation, then neither did the Lord redeem us with His blood, nor is the cup of the Eucharist the communion of His blood." He asks the question, "[When] the mingled cup and the baked bread receive the Word of God, and the Eucharist of the blood and the body of Christ is made . . . how can they [the Gnostics] maintain that the flesh is incapable of receiving the gift of God?"[52]

Gnostic premises, in other words, unraveled the Church's traditional means of contact and communion with her Lord. Herein is its revolutionary character as far as the Church was concerned: *to remove the necessity of a mediating structure negates the entire purpose of the Church*. But the damage done to the Church portends similar damage done to all earthly institutions, ultimately making sacred any act of iconoclasm both inside and outside the Church.

Certain branches of Gnosticism had a bizarre ritual known as the Bridal Chamber. If the original breach in the cosmos resulted from Sophia's break from her male counterpart, healing this cosmic breach depended on her reunion with him. Her restoration served as a model for all who would be restored to the pleroma.[53] In the Gnostic Gospels, Mary Magdalene represents Sophia, and Jesus represents her male counterpart. They were lovers – their union repairing the cosmic breach – and their kisses, as one author puts it, "produces spiritual children,"[54] the Gnostic. In the Bridal Chamber ceremony, an initiate would reenact his own reunion with the pleroma by means of a Sophia stand-in. The Gnostic *Gospel of Philip* justified the symbolism of the rite – "Truth did not come into the world naked, but it came in types and images" – and called the Bridal Chamber a symbol of "the restoration (of the pleroma, apokatastasis)."[55]

The ceremony ritualized the restoration of the union between the Father with the "virgin who descends," that being Sophia, God the Mother, the Holy Spirit. Scholars offer wide opinion on the nature of this ritual, ranging from a simple kiss of peace to a literal bridal chamber equipt with mirrors on all the walls. Here too might be placed the scandalous words of the *Gospel of Philip*, that Jesus often kissed Mary Magdalene, his lover. The sexual symbolism is meant as a metaphor, a "discovery of the spiritual self and the reunion with it."[56]

Gnostic doctrine and practice reveals several layers of syncretisim at work. Many of the terms and stories come from the Hebrew and

Christian scriptures. The idea that the material world is lacking or deceptive comes from Plato. The stark division of the cosmos into Good and Evil comes from Zoroastrianism. The Bridal Chamber ritual finds parallels in the ancient mystery cults (fertility cults that ritualized the union of father sky and mother earth). Important among the influential mystery cults is Orphism, which laid the foundation for the association of love, music, and Gnosticism. Also important in this context is Hermeticism, an ancient variant of Gnosticism which derived more this-worldly implications of Gnostic teachings.

Behind these imported concepts is the core Gnostic impulse: we are strangers in a physical world governed by oppressive forces and laws. Our bodies are bound by laws that have nothing to do with true human striving. Salvation occurs when I awaken to my true origins and begin the journey up and out of this cosmic oppression tyrannized by Yaltabaoth and his archons. Sophia and Jesus help me attain this goal. Meanwhile, completely rejected is the notion that this physical world – its laws, institutions, structures, language, or thought systems – can have any claim on my Self's journey.

✧ Chapter 2 ✧

Gnostic Traits

Naming the Demon

Gnosticism is an adventure, a journey, or a way of approaching things. It begins with a premise of namelessness, a nameless God. Its God is like the God addressed in the Orphic hymn to "Thundering Dionysus": "Universal God of many names . . . Dionysus, God among us, we honor you. Inspire us."

Of course, as we see in this hymn, the nameless God does have a name, Dionysus, and the pretense to namelessness is just that, pretense. So also with the Gnostic nameless God. At first nailing down specific Gnostic teachings seems a bit like wrestling a greased pig. Just trying to figure out how scholars define the term *Gnostic* is a game of terminological Twister.[1]

But then when we observe the common traits surfacing over and over again in Gnostic movements throughout history, we notice it most certainly does have form. It has quite nameable traits. This chapter we survey these traits, committing the sacrilege of naming, identifying, and analyzing them. Understanding these traits will help us recognize its trail through history.

These traits are: (1) God's Namelessness as a Fundamental Premise; (2) Pleromic Universalism; (3) Separateness as *the* Cosmic Evil; (4) Anti-authority; (5) Transcending Gender; (6) The Rejection of Logos; (7) The Archetypical Role of Sophia; (8) Mysticism, Ecstacy, and Palingenesia: Waking Up to the God Within; (9) Gnostic Elitism; (10) The Journey of the Self against Archontic Powers; Antinomianism; (11) Love (Eros) as Cosmic Bungee Cord; (12) The Gnostic/Magic connection; and (13) The New Age, or Emerging Paradigms.

God's Namelessness as a Fundamental Premise

We've all seen the bumper sticker spelling "COEXIST" with the symbols of different world religions. The sentiment presents the Gnostic position succinctly: *God transcends all names.*

God's name has moored Judeo-Christian theology ever since God revealed his name to Moses at the burning bush. Yahweh forbade the vain use of his name in the Ten Commandments. Sixty-six times the Old Testament uses the expression "[so and so] shall know that I am Yahweh." Hebraic theology anathematized the worship of a generic God through generic worship forms or through some wispy notion of spirituality. Likewise the New Testament Church maintained the name theology through its baptismal formula: "In the name of the Father and of the Son and of the Holy Spirit." *Invocation* grounds Christian faith and worship and by explicit definition requires a name.

By contrast the Gnostics postulate a nameless, generic God, an abstracted, unknowable, and ineffable God. The Gnostic Silvanus wrote, "[I]t is not difficult to know the Creator of all creatures [Yaltabaoth, i.e. Yahweh], but it is impossible to comprehend the likeness of this One [Monad]."[2] The Gnostic *Gospel of Truth* lifts God's name beyond the capacity of human language.[3] Church father Hippolytus of Rome (170 - 235) attests to the Gnostic worship of a "non-existent god," following the Gnostic Valentinus (100 - 160) who calls his god the "inconceivable."[4]

Gnostics set themselves apart from the named deities of the historic religions: Yahweh, Zeus, Jesus, Allah, and so on. These elemental, regional gods arise from time and place circumstances: ancient Sinai, ancient Greece, first century Judea, seventh century Arabia, etc. The true God, says the Gnostic, can't be limited by time or place, much less a name. As stated above, names delineate, *de*fine, and therefore *con*fine, placing limits on what should have no limits. They *pigeon-hole*, a cardinal sin among Gnostics because it distinguishes one thing from Other. Partisan spirit enters as those who follow one name set themselves against those who follow another. The naming of God leads to conflict and war.

Best-selling author and "spiritual teacher," Eckhart Tolle, a frequent guest of Oprah, gives a good example of the sentiment: "Man made 'God' in his own image. The eternal, the infinite, and unnameable was reduced to a mental idol that you had to believe in and worship as 'my god' or 'our god.'"[5]

And yet, he contemplates, Gnostic movements in each of the world religions have always recognized the universalistic kernel of its original teaching. He gives as examples Sufism in Islam, Kabbalah in Judaism, Advaita Vedanta in Hinduism, Zen in Buddhism, and Gnosticism and mysticism in Christianity.

Emergent Christian Samir Selmanovic shares Tolle's viewpoint, honing in on traditional Christianity's supposed idolatry of itself as a religion, commenting, "We do believe that God is best defined by the historical revelation in Jesus Christ, but to believe that God is limited to it would be an attempt to manage God. If one holds that Christ is confined to Christianity, one has chosen a god that is not sovereign." He naturally concludes the presence of Christ is "in substance rather than in name."[6]

Gnosticism's nameless God transcends all earthly delineations. The Gnostic *Gospel of Philip* reveals, "The names which are given to worldly (things) are the occasion of a great error . . . He who hears 'God' does not perceive what is firmly established, but he has perceived what is not firmly established."[7] So also with words like *Father, Son, Holy Spirit, life, light, resurrection,* and *church.* These words were introduced by Yaltabaoth's archons in order to deceive men.

A truer spirituality, says the modern Gnostic, means rejecting all pigeon-holing, especially the audacity of naming God himself. In October of 1975, a group of spiritual leaders read the following statement to the United Nations: "The crises of our time are challenging the world religions to release a new spiritual force transcending religious, cultural, and national boundaries into a new consciousness of the Oneness of the human community. . . . We affirm a new spirituality divested of insularity and directed toward planetary consciousness."[8]

A universalistic "spirituality divested of insularity" is precisely the sort of spirituality seen throughout the history of Gnosticism. Such is the Gnostic God, a generic God, a God without a name, a God abstracted from bits and pieces of the various religions. Embracing such a notion of God, says the Gnostic, is the only true remedy for the conflicts of our world, the only way we can truly "coexist."

Pleromic Universalism

The Gnostic pleroma is the totality of aeons emanating from the

Monad. It is the realm of spiritual beings, where separation has no place, where all is one. Yaltabaoth and his archons were a pale, fallen mockery of the original pleromic Oneness. Their gross materiality introduced the separation of beings, names, divisions, and all the things of the fallen material world unsettling the Gnostics. The fall of any man occurs as a spark from pleromic harmony falls into materiality. Ultimate salvation happens through gnosis, which, *The Gospel of Truth* tells us, "dissolve[s] the division, and [brings] the warm pleroma of love in order that . . . there should be the unity of perfect thought."[9]

In the end of time a final *apokatastasis* (restoration) will bring final mending to the pleroma and destroy the material world forever. All will return to Oneness as it began.

What attracts some to Gnosticism is the immediacy of this return. They don't have to wait until death for ascent into pleromic Oneness. One Gnostic calls it a spiritual resurrection possible in the present time: "Come away from the divisions (in this world) and the fetters and already you have resurrection."[10] He continues, "Nothing (earthly) redeems us from this place (the world,) but (only) the All which we are (ourselves) – we are already saved, we have received complete salvation."[11] Immediate ascent out of the divisions and fetters into the pleromic All is the Gnostic salvation program.

This program gives rise to two implications and along with these implications, a conundrum. First, if Gnosticism offers salvation free of any intervening institutions, it should be strictly personal. Second, once awakened the true Gnostic should be completely freed from *all* terrestrial concerns. The Gnostic is a stranger in a strange land and knows this world is a farce. He should embrace a radical other-worldliness of the likes of the book, *A Course in Miracles* (1976). In it Helen Schucman (1909-1981), inspired by a "Voice" she believes is Jesus, portrays the world as an illusion full of pain, violence, darkness, and sorrow. Only when everyone awakens to his origins in God and loses himself in these origins will the world cease to be.[12]

The last thing a true Gnostic should be concerned about is this deceptive world. If asked, "What does pleromic universalism imply for this world?" he should answer, "Absolutely nothing."

Still, as philosopher A. O. Lovejoy (1873-1962) observed, the human soul cannot tolerate radical otherworldliness. "The great metaphysicians might seek to demonstrate its truth [of otherworldly reality], the saints might in some measure fashion their lives in accordance with it, the mystics might return from their ecstasies and stammeringly report a direct experience of that contact with the absolute reality and the sole satisfying good which it proclaimed; but Nature in the main has been too potent for it . . . [and man] continued to find something very solid and engrossing in the world."[13]

That's the conundrum. Something always seems to call the Gnostic back into the material world. But how does this square with the quest for radical otherworldliness? On one hand, the Gnostic knows this world is an illusion and has tapped into pleromic Oneness. On the other hand, per Lovejoy's analysis, the Gnostic somehow divines implications for the created order based on his gnosis.

For instance some Gnostics ritualized the pleromic reunion through the Bridal Chamber ceremony. Some practiced property and wife-sharing communalism based on the premise that pleromic Oneness negates the categories of *mine* and *thine*: "'Love [never calls something its own, . . . It never [says 'This is yours'] or 'this is mine,'. . . ."[14] Their practices tended toward the polar extremes of either asceticism or libertinism.

But doesn't the tendency toward any of these things suggest a contradiction, a subjection to some mundane principle gnosis frees them from? If they're truly free from the body, why deny it or indulge it? Why not just let it be while they go on living a life as the Cleavers, or the Osbournes, or whomever? Why make a value judgment regarding whatever earthly mask one is wearing at all? The same could be said for every part of their program of salvation. If it's just the Gnostic and the pleromic Oneness, nothing else should be needed. *Nothing*.

Father of depth psychology Carl Jung confronted the concept of pleroma, he claims, in a vision given by ancient Gnostic Basilides. He contrasts pleroma with *creatura*. *Creatura* are the beings resulting from the disintegration of pleromic Oneness, the various distinct creations. Pleroma is "nothingness or fullness,"[15] a good mind-bending Gnostic construction. It is where distinctions cease and individuality is no more. From the pleroma Jung got his idea of the Collective Unconscious, which he says is "common to all," not unlike the ancient idea of the "sympathy of all things"[16] which was the basis of magic.

Jung himself tapped into this pleroma and found it connected him psychically with his patients. In other words, for him, pleromic universalism invaded his world and inspired ideas on how mundane existence should be understood and organized. He developed an entire practical psychology on it, meant to help patients. This should be an inconsistency for Gnosticism.

But not for Hermeticism, a more practical and relevant variant of ancient Gnosticism, especially popular in the Renaissance and resurrected by Jung in the modern era. By discovering positive implications for the pleroma *in this world*, Jung betrays his Hermeticism.

For the Hermeticists, knowledge of otherworldly divine things can help humanity's lot in this world. Grounded on the theory of the cosmic interrelatedness of all being, or *sympatheia*, the Hermeticist uncovered the secret knowledge of this sympatheia and by its secrets could wisely manipulate events. He ascends the cosmic spheres, even above its Creator (Yaltabaoth, but in this instance called the demiurge) and learns the machinations of his creative activity, all so that he can ape it and help the world along to his divinely-intuited ends. He becomes a "co-creator with God."[17]

We will return to this Hermetical idea of co-creating with God when we discuss progressivism (as well as Neo-evangelicalism[18]), only to point out here another solution to the conundrum of pleromic universalism. That is, the pleroma inspires political action, particularly of the collectivist kind. The Gnostic returns from his ascent into Oneness and is kind enough to apply his discovery to earthly politics, showing us that we are all truly one.

It's of a piece with the New Age veneration of "holism," understood either as a universalism governed by a centrifugal source (the Gnostic and Hermetic Monad) or as a universalism arising from the interrelated network of various "systems."[19] The latter view generally takes into consideration modern science and technology, fertilizing the cultural soil for mystical views of the Internet.

However it is understood, universalism is in vogue, and it strikes at the heart of, among other things, the materialistic reductionism of science, the Judeo-Christian distinction between Creator and creature, the elements of grammar, and the fragmentation of the world into self-governing nations. These are all vestiges of old paradigms and must give way to universalism. A Gnostic culture entering a new age longs for something in their world reflecting the pleromic universalism its prophets have divined.

Separateness as *the* Cosmic Evil

The Gnostic Fall began when Sophia decided to do something on her own. Yaltabaoth resulted, and through him came the material world and all its divisions. His act of creation impacted everything. It defined the fall. The creation of any individual became his own fall, when he became a being separate from other life forms.

Accordingly, flesh and matter are regarded as evil not for *moral* reasons but for *essential* reasons: they are the stuff of individuation, particularity, and separate-ness. Our vision of reality is likewise crippled, formatted in a Me/Other duality. There is *me* and there is *everything else* (Other), the various things my mind delineates through language and organized thought structures. This entire perception, says the Gnostic, is false, deluded, forever marked by "the law of individuation . . . rather than . . . a consciousness of the whole."[20]

In the above United Nations quote, the spiritual leaders spoke of "a new spirituality divested of insularity." Insularity is what happens when people and things have physical properties, when they fall into their fleshly delineations – one thing becomes an island separated from other things, thus *insular* – and for this original cosmic evil we can thank that monstrous cosmic mistake, Yaltabaoth, or more relevant to the point, the whole Judeo-Christian cosmological framework.

But the evil of separate-ness goes far beyond physical insularity. It pervades our emotional and spiritual thinking as well. Gnostic Psychologist Murray Stein describes how:

"Yaltabaoth . . . stands in contradiction to the unity and wholeness of the Self. Yaldabaoth is the principle of individuation (the ego), as opposed to the principle of comprehensive unity (the Self), and as such it is the force also behind such social imperatives as territoriality, blind nationalism, and 'ethnic cleansing.' . . . Yaldabaoth is the rigorous perfectionist in us that wishes to eliminate anything foreign, alien, or even just different. . . . The Gnostics who fixed their attention on the biblical tradition identified Yaldabaothian attributes in Yahweh, who would have 'no other gods' before him and who was a 'jealous God' who promised his chosen people specialness in exchange for ethnic purity and obedience to tribal laws. This is an attitude that we can see in every kind of provincialism, in every instance of nationalism, and in all forms of sexism.

"Yaldabaoth is certainly not . . . to be identified with the God of love of the Christian faith. And yet within even these familiar traditions Yaldabaoth shows his face: in the splintering of the biblical tradition into groups and factions – Jews and Christians, Catholics and Protestants, orthodox and reformed and fundamentalists of every stripe and doctrinal nuance, each insisting with absolute conviction on its own views and ideas and condemning all others to eternal damnation. From the pleromatic point of view, all of these certainties are tragic illusions, and all they amount to is people without gnosis banding together and reinforcing one another in common delusional systems. The Yaldabaothian splitting attitude in these groups teaches that where there are differences, there must be enemies, opposites who must battle for dominance and the right to claim all truth for themselves. There can be only one god, and he is ours, he is us. Here Yaltabaoth is ruler."[21]

That we are victims of alienation and disintegration due to malevolent cosmic forces is not foreign to modern thought. Marx placed our supposed alienation at the feet of the capitalistic system, which he said separates the laborer from the product of his labor. For Jung, the fall of Sophia and emergence of Yaltabaoth parallel the soul's lapse into "emergent psychic structures,"[22] the personal myth of my distinctness from Other. Here Yaltabaoth represents an "egoistic and anti-relational attitude,"[23] in which the soul loses connection to the Collective Unconscious from which it came.

This strain – that Western Civilization itself is a sort of mass neurosis due to our psychological disintegration, our alienation from primordial collectiveness – surfaces time and time again. Stein summarizes: "Yaldabaoth represents the ground plan of the individualistic, controlling, narcissistic ego so familiar in Western culture. What the Gnostics identified and named in Yaldabaoth is still with us, perhaps even more so."[24]

On these terms the modern Gnostic lexicon distinguishes between the terms *Self* and *ego*. The *Self* is the spark of divinity connecting us to the One. The *ego* is our *false Self* – the one formed by time and place circumstances, say, our family name, religion, or nation – which we falsely think we are. As put by Sufi scholar Llewellyn Vaughan-Lee, "The Self, not the ego, is the prime agent of transformation. The ego takes us towards separation while the Self pulls us towards wholeness."[25]

The very things defining my separateness – my body, my family, my church, and my nation – are the stuff of the Gnostic Fall. They must be overcome if I am to come to true knowledge.

Anti-Authority

In the ancient world, Gnostic communities eschewed authority structures like those of their Christian counterparts. The order St. Paul required of his congregations through the clergy and canonical traditions was not valued by the Gnostic. If the Gnostic has direct access to God, obviously he didn't need structures claiming meditation between the soul and God. Certain *leaders* (Gr. *prostatēs*), could gain authority by their charisma from time to time. Communities might gather around such teachers, but no formalized custom continued the community's structural integrity after their departure or death.[26]

"They wish the abandonment of discipline (*disciplina*) to be taken for simplicity," said Church Father Tertullian (160-225). He added, "Nowhere is there easier advancement than in the camp of the rebels, where even to be there is a merit. In this way one man is bishop today, another tomorrow, today one is deacon, who tomorrow will be reader, today a priest (presbyter), who tomorrow will be a layman. For even to laymen they commit priestly duties."[27]

Yet, setting off a paradox we see time and time again in the history of Gnostic movements, traditional authority structures yield to a new authority, one established by the personal charisma of one called *leader*. The *leader* marks Gnostic movements throughout history, from initial Gnostic *prostatēs* through the *dux e Babylon* of the later millenarians to the *Führer* himself. Contemporary Church obsession with "leadership training" feeds off the same impulse: the spiritual community cannot survive without the centripetal force of a spirit-endowed, charismatic individual.

One Gnostic, Proteus, is a good example. According to Church Father Lucian (120-180) Proteus gathered about himself a cult-like following: "[His followers] took him for a divine being (literally: god), made him their law-giver and declared him their leader (*prostatēs*)."[28] Another such cult-like leader was Marcus, "community leader, prophet and magician or priest all in one person."[29] Irenaeus, commenting on Marcus, writes in his *Against All Heresy*, "[Their leaders] claim that they have more knowledge than all others, and that they alone have attained the greatness of the knowledge of the ineffable power."[30]

Gnosticism holds to that paradox we see over and over again in modern life, where anarchy against traditional authorities – Church, state, family – gives rise to a groveling submission to another leader. Donna Minkowitz gives an honest behind-the-scenes look at this tendency, writing about her leadership role at a gay rights rally: "This is a movement that celebrates anarchy, but I am one of its leaders. That's just one of the paradoxes that make the gay movement the sweet impossibility it is . . .

I am the 'bus captain,' and the title makes me feel like a gentle but masterly authority figure."[31]

While at the same time eschewing establishment authorities, the Gnostic accepts the new leader's claim to transcendency. In a Gnostic climate, personality cults are not only possible, *they define social or political arrangement.*

Transcending Gender

If separate-ness characterizes the primordial cosmic evil, Eve's cleaving from Adam, the separation of genders, is one of the fundamental evils of our world. It is, as the Gnostic Bogomil sect put it, "alien to identity, imposed by the devil."[32]

Gnostic Elaine Pagels writes how the story of the separation of Adam from Eve "describes how we, as human beings, became separated – alienated from our spiritual selves, how we become literally 'dis-integrated.' Thus the myth shows how we have lost consciousness of our spiritual potential and consequently of our innate need for spiritual growth."[33]   The male/female division provokes all divisiveness and disconnectedness, divisions among races and nations, divisions of all sorts.

Of course, the fleshly sexual organs making men men and women woman are just more things to be transcended for those reconnecting with Monad, himself called the"androgynous Father"[34] by the *Gospel of the Egyptians*. Rudolf summarizes, "for the Gnostics bisexuality is an expression of perfection; it is only the earthly creation which leads to a separation of the original divine unity."[35] Gnostic communities stressed gender equality and affirmed the role of women as priests, prophetesses, and ministers. This was the true source of St. Paul's polemic against female ministers in his letters to the Corinthians and to Timothy. Throughout the history of Gnosticism, this transcending of gender figures prominently.

The tendency is accelerating.

In 2009 Swedish parents made news when they let their two-year-old child "Pop" determine his/her own sexuality. They kept Pop's gender a secret to all but the few who changed his/her diapers, believing it "cruel to bring a child into the world with a blue or pink stamp on their forehead." Mimicking feminist *gender-as-social-construct* dogma, they added, "We want Pop to grow up more freely and avoid being forced into a specific gender mould from the outset."[36]

The idea is being pushed in international Law. The Yogyakarta Principles, presented to the UN in 2007 as a charter for gay and gender identity rights, declares in its preamble that "gender identity" refers "to each person's deeply felt internal and individual experience of gender, which may or may not correspond with the sex assigned at birth, including the personal sense of the body."[37] It later declares in its Principle 3: "Each person's self-defined sexual orientation and gender identity is integral to their personality and is one of the most basic aspects of self-determination, dignity and freedom."[38] Sixteen states and Washington D. C. reflect The Yagyakarta Priniciples.[39]

One wonders what the practical effects of such laws would be. Could a peeping Tom enter a women's locker room claiming his "self-defined gender identity" was a woman? That was Robert Domansky's defense when in 2004 the 48-year-old cross-dresser entered a girls' locker room in a Pennsylvania high school dressed as a cheerleader. Or when the city of Portland's gender identity law permitted a cross-dressing sex offender to enter a female locker room while little girls were present.[40]

Gnostic spirituality sets a person's physicality against his inner spark, his true Self. As the genderqueer in our introduction said, "People like me don't feel comfortable in the bodies in which we were born." The physical body is nothing more than a vessel, a shell, an illusion bestowed upon us by Yaltabaoth deceiving us to think we are something we aren't.

This discussion reveals confusion about authentic feminism. Is feminism a *celebration* or a *transcending* of unique female attributes? On one hand, as in the above incidents, those things defining female sexuality are to be transcended and ignored. On the other hand, embracing the feminine in our spirituality is one of the trademarks of modern Gnosticism. By this they mean we should quit being so logical and linear in our thinking and more intuitive and feeling-oriented. Or is it sexist to say women are illogical, capricious, and do everything based on feeling? Therein is the paradox.

Ultimately the Gnostic believes female illogicality (or intuition, pending on one's perspective) and capriciousness (evidently a woman's prerogative) constitute a superior way of knowing, bestowed upon us by Sophia. These ways of knowing can belong to a person not by virtue of his sex organs, but by virtue of his self-determination, provided he is willing to wake up from his patriarchally imposed patterns of thinking. When elementary school teachers discourage boyish competition and force boys to participate in traditionally female activities, the purpose is to introduce the boys to their true Self, their superior inner Sophia.[41]

The Rejection of Logos

The Gnostic *Gospel of Truth* describes the "knowledge of the living book" whose letters "are not vowels nor are they consonants, so that one might read them and think of something foolish, but they are letters of the truth." The things of truth, it continues, "surpass every form (and) every sound."[42] Rather, it proposes, not the ears but the nose picks up the fragrance of the Father's gifts, the nose being a metaphor for the intuition of the heart.

The idea that truth transcends the written word permeates Gnostic texts. The Gnostic *Exegesis of the Soul* lays down a teaching which sounds a lot like the trend in contemporary Christianity against catechism-learning in favor of nurturing "hearts that pump for Jesus" or some such: "[I]t is by being born again that the soul will be saved. And this is due not to rote phrases or to professional skills or to book learning."[43]

It's not anti-intellectualism, the Gnostic would say. It's trans-intellectualism. Like the elements of creation, the elements of language are things the Gnostic transcends. Truth is "inaccessible to the human mind" and incommunicable through mundane means.[44] Rational discourse cannot relay knowledge. The truth takes us beyond the edge of the word, into the mysterious, silent wilderness beyond its borders. Here mythology, symbolism, allegory, paradox, and sometimes undecipherable babble rule. Gnostic writings are cryptic, poetic, and mysterious. Hence the opaque nonsense we regularly come upon in Gnostic writing. The Sufis in particular cloaked their thoughts in non-discursive, non-rational writing forms – the romantic love tale for instance – and even dance, believing direct knowledge of God rendered futile all "book-learning and theological subtleties."[45] The Sufi asks questions like, "Why is the sound of an onion?"[46]

The Gnostic *Gospel of the Egyptians* reveals this nugget: "And the throne of his glory was established in it, this one on which his unrevealable name is inscribed, on the tablet . . . one is the word, the Father of the light of everything, he who came forth from the silence, while he rests in the silence, he whose name is in an invisible symbol. Hidden, invisible mystery came forth iiiiiiiiiiiiiiiiiii eeeeeeeeee oooooooooooooooooo uuuuuuuuuuu eeeee eeeeeeeeeeeeeee aaaaa aaaaaaaaaaaaaaaaaa ooooooooooo oooooooooooooooo."[47]

We've run across this insightful line before in our introduction, with our peek into the climax of the mega-church service. The Gnostic climax cannot come under the management of human language.

This view of language follows their view of physical nature. What is language, after all, but words describing actions and properties possible only in a physical universe set up in time/place contours? Because *word* denotes *being*, the multiplicity of *beings* begets the multiplicity of *words*. *Word A = Thing A* and not *Thing B*. But if multiplicity and division of being are seen as perverse, a truer religion whose quest is the nameless God needs no names or words. In the words of Schuyler Brown, "There can be no one-to-one correspondence between language and external reality."[48] Thus thought the ancient Gnostic, as well as his modern counterpart, as aptly put by Marilyn Ferguson: "Words and sentences have given us a false sense of understanding, blinding us to the complexity and dynamics of nature. Life is not constructed like a sentence, subject acting on object." She concludes, "Language frames our thought, thus setting up barriers."[49]

Or as Paul Davies puts it,"We can say that just as creation is the 'dualitude' of an original unity, so language is the refraction into parts of what is in principle a whole."[50]

Adam's first assignment from God – naming the animals – marked the consummate evil. But then how typically male – patriarchally logical, phallically linear. With such patriarchal strictures, we close ourselves off from the fullness of what may be relayed to us; our "canonicity entails a closed system, to which only texts passing scrutinizing, standardized tests gain access." Such is the conclusion of one author, who rather celebrated the "mixtures [involving] paradox, puns, and other features of lived experience."[51]

This explains the current antipathy against grammar. Peter Elbow's influential grammar textbook suggests grammar "makes it almost impossible to achieve that undistracted attention to your thoughts and experiences as you write that is so crucial for strong writing (and sanity). For most people, nothing helps their writing so much as learning to ignore grammar."[52]

English Professor David Mulroy, fighting a losing cause on behalf of grammar, describes the "righteous struggle" of modern grammarians whose arguments are "couched in rhetoric reminiscent of political campaigns for civil rights or against censorship." He recognizes the revolutionary, cosmically sweeping posture of his opponents.

The results are an abysmal comprehension of language. Administering an in-class study, Mulroy asked his students to paraphrase the prologue to the Declaration of Independence. He elicited a variety of responses, only a few of which captured even the gist of Thomas

Jefferson's prose. Most were radically off, for example, "People must have true facts to back up their thoughts on a god if they are different from the thoughts of the majority."[53]

Many of the responses veered into Gnostic sentimentality, unbeknownst to the students of course, who simply fell back to their default spiritual cocktail of warmed-over Nietzschean thought, New Agerism, and existentialism.

Some examples: "Mankind is in a state of separation. There will come a time when all will be forgotten, and man will be one with mother earth." Or "Cut your earthly bonds and wear the mantle of Nature and God. Wield the power and declare justly your ascension from man's law. Then all shall bow before your might." Or again, "I think it means that people should look at their own morals. They should follow the laws of Nature and Nature's God, but also in their own way follow their own morals."[54]

At a minimum the paraphrases reveal a student body preoccupied with the Self, as if the objective writings of another are mere window dressing for their own personal musings. Of course this is deliberate. It goes hand in hand with the Gnostic preoccupation with the Self as the true locus of meaning. The meaning of another (like Thomas Jefferson) and the student's sort of blur together in an impressionistic haze of random stream-of-consciousness thoughts.

Here should be placed the discussion on gay marriage, which is not about the gay lifestyle but about violence done both to language and to an institution, particularly the meaning of the word *marriage* and what it means for society. A society rooted in a respect for nature acknowledges the role flesh plays in defining sexual identity and compatibility. It rests on the biological reality that egg and sperm create baby. Last we checked, the determining factor in one's gender was whether he produced an egg or a sperm.

But through the ministrations of Gnostic iconoclasm, fleshly distinctions are illusory, the product of Yaltabaoth's mistake. And any linguistic forms institutionalizing this fleshly compatibility are illusive as well. The term *marriage* and all it means for society are there by human convention alone, *corrupt* human convention.

As Gnosticism takes over society, marriage goes from being about the fleshly compatibility of male and female to being about the union of two abstracted Selves transcending gender. Gender itself is no longer a biological reality but a construct of personal "Self-identification." Of course, the only way to arrive at this understanding is to deny the actual physical form of the male and female bodies. To deny what is obvious – what biology tells us about male and female compatibility – doesn't lend itself to, we might say, a naturally-flowing development of language.

Instinctually we recoil at such denials of nature: a spade is a spade. Such is the basis of tradition and traditional views of marriage. Tradition is the "distillation of centuries of human experience,"[55] which is without a doubt the basis for a traditional view of marriage. Gnostics rejoin with an *a priori* rejection of tradition, human experience, and instinct. These things only institutionalize natural arrangements, which are at root inherently corrupt, the creation of our usurper deity. Whatever violence, then, is done to tradition is redemptive in and of itself. There has always been a strain in Gnosticism that sacralizes iconoclastic violence, its founding violence being Sophia's redemptive abortion of Yaltabaoth.

Donna Minkowitz gives us a peek into this inherent violence and iconoclasm with an insider's perspective on homosexual love. Her words look obnoxious at first, until we understand them according to the above Gnostic reading of her position. (By the way, she's writing these words in the context of positively comparing her sexual experiences with the charismatic experiences of Christian believers, mainly women, at an event in Toronto, for whom "it's impossible for the Torontans to go into spasm without knowing it's a sign that God loves *them*.")

She writes, "I take sex as a sign of radical disobedience. Though I believe I'm obeying the Sublime One when I have sex, I also feel intensely that I'm fighting back, that each caress is a blow of sorts. But who is it a blow against? It's a whack at all the forces that want to deprive me, want me to be untouched, unpetted, caged in. I understand these forces in political terms, as the social interests that don't want women, or lesbians, or people in general to feel sexual ecstasy. There certainly are social forces that ache to lace us up, but it's odd that I should identify with the forces in my own head that want to shield me, hold me back. . . .

"I love disobedience as much as I love sex itself, the rebel-god who topples earthly rules. Sexual chaos fights the 'principalities and powers' St. Paul warned about, 'the rulers of the darkness of this age, the spiritual hosts of wickedness in the heavenly places.' Religious-right people love this verse and quote it all the time because at bottom their religion is, like mine, a Manichaean [i.e. Gnostic] one."[56]

Those that do not face up to this sentiment do not understand the visceral hatred and potential for justified violence aimed at tradition and its representatives. It is justified because it's the acting out of a grand cosmic battle. The Gnostic feels caged in, and autoeroticism, with the pretext of an "Other" stand-in (*any* other), is his key out of that cage.

Again, "iiiiiiiiiiiiiiiiiii eeeeeeeeee oooooooooooooooooo uuuuuuuuuuu eeeee eeeeeeeeeeeeee aaaaa aaaaaaaaaaaaaaaaaa oooooooooooo oooooooooooooooo."

Language is violently overthrown. It cannot be about *reflecting* the natural order, but about *manipulating* our perception of the natural order according to the Gnostic myth. Thus the politicizing of language, the violence done to language by Political Correctness. Minkowitz' sadism, or the violence of sodomy, or the injustice done to children in broken families, or the violence of abortion, must be accepted as unfortunate collateral damage in the greater cosmic battle. And so, by fiat marriage shall be redefined as "Two adult Selves who love each other."

Of course, the alert will note that with this new sentence, a whole new regime of boundaries, delineations, and constrictions enter, all deserving violent overthrow just as much as the previous ones. Why only "two" and not "three"? Why not everyone in one big pleromic orgy, like Woodstock, or like the tangled lines of illegitimacy and step-parentage making up the modern family? Or why "adult" and not "any age" as NAMBLA is pushing for?[57] Why must love be a component, as the "asexuals" are now asserting?[58] We end up on a slippery slope. When the boundaries of words are transgressed, the effects on our society parallel the cacophony of vowels we saw above, or the cacophony of interpretations of the Declaration, the complete breakdown of order, a return to chaos and formlessness. But again, this is the Gnostic quest, to return to that time before Yaltabaoth imposed his institutes on the original Oneness.

The word for *word* in Greek is *logos*. *Logos* denotes more than what *word* means to us. In the Greek mind it denoted rationality itself, *reason*, *argument*, or *discourse*. It comes from the Greek verb *legein*, meaning "to arrange in order." From *logos* we get logic, and we get other derivatives like all the studies ending in -ology, meaning "study of." *Logos* fuels what we normally consider knowledge to be. We go to school and take classes ending with -ology, and at these classes we learn a body of knowledge governing its particular branch.

Gnosticism undoes traditional ways of viewing knowledge. Traditional knowledge comes to us objectively from the outside and needs a medium like a teacher or a book, or some experience with the natural world, some observance coinciding with the actual, physical world.

Traditional knowledge comes to us *extra nos*, from the outside. Gnostic knowledge [*gnosis*] cannot be something coming to us from the outside because the external world is essentially evil and deceptive.

Again from the *Gospel of the Egyptians*: "Really, truly, iEa aiO, in the heart, who exists, u aei eis aei, ei o ei, ei os ei (or: (Son) forever, You are what you are, You are who you are)! This great name of yours is upon me, O self-begotten Perfect one, who is not outside me."[59]

Our Tourette's-inflicted Gnostic friend hasn't the discipline to organize much in this mess, but the one thing he's got down is, *whatever it is, it's not outside of me.* It's from the inside, from the heart. It's intuited, felt, or experienced on a level rendering the humble word wholly unsatisfactory. Wayne Dyer's Self-help book *Real Magic* gives seven tips for finding that magic within. His seventh tip? "You can go beyond logic."[60]

With the breakdown of Logos and language comes the breakdown of rational discourse. In the past a rational argument had potency insofar as it was logical, concise, and true to basic rules of propositional thinking. Now rational argument is *ipso facto* corrupt.

Those who take their Gnosticism through feminism will speak of the patriarchalism of the whole rational enterprise: to speak rationally is to think like phallo-centric males or write literature that is "boring in its pointedness and singularity."[61] (A=B, B=C, C=D, therefore A=D. How linear! How phallic! It's a linguistic rape! Etc.) This is the position of the Ecriture Feminine strain of literary theory.

The one who takes his Gnosticism through the New Age speaks of rationality as the mode of thinking in the Age of Pisces. The above-mentioned Ferguson lauds the Hopi and Chinese for their "nonlinear" language.[62]

In any event, using words with meaning and arguments with logic are things to move beyond in our current postmodern world. On these terms the tongues-speaking charismatics were ahead of their time. Through a Gnostic reading of current culture, we live in an entire society of tongues-speaking charismatics.

The deconstructionist movement suits this understanding of language, accelerating its decline. Deconstructionism claims all language is a mask hiding the power politics of the person saying it. One's words only reflect what he is as a flesh-bound, particular individual confined by gender, race, and other physical delineations. They are a "logocentric prison" we must get out of and discover life beyond the edges of language, as in Michel Foucault's *silence*, or in "the fiction of the invisible space" between words. Words and their accompanying thoughts are borders beyond which we "fumble, fall, bruise ourselves [and] enter the labyrinth and become entangled in paradox, parody, and negation."[63]

Schuyler Brown is describing Gnosticism but gives an excellent primer on deconstructionism when he writes, "Language does not mirror the outer world but interprets it, and no interpretation is uninfluenced by the interpreter. 'Objective' reality finds expression in language as a creation of human consciousness."[64]

In short, Gnosticism does not outline its program with arguments or systematic teaching. It traffics in non-rational, supra-rational, trans-rational, and even irrational speech. Human language is not something to be used respectfully as a way to construct civilized life. It's something to be toyed with during the passing interlude of this world's existence, something to be de-*construct*-ed.

The Archetypal Role of Sophia

The above-quoted Brown sees contrasting paradigms of knowledge set up between Christ the masculine Logos and Sophia the feminine personification of Wisdom: "Gnostics and orthodox seem to be guided by two different root metaphors. . . . The masculine Logos replaces the feminine figure of Sophia." Alluding to a theme we'll cover in a bit, he continues, "In the Gnostic reading of Scripture, sexuality, not speech, is the root metaphor. The beginning of the cosmic process is not the divine word but an act of autoeroticism."[65] This autoeroticism refers to Sophia's breach of the male/female pairing in the pleroma: she conceives without her consort's approval.

In any event, she represents a "critique of religious rationalism."[66] She's the archetypical challenge to the logocentric orientation supposedly established with Christianity's patriarchal beginnings. What marks this orientation? Dogma, rituals, a focus on externals, the establishment of clergy to enforce discipline, the idea of canonicity, all rooted in us/them, true/false, orthodoxy/heresy distinctions. Sophia represents not just a new god, but new paradigms of thinking.

Specifically her critique has three components:

First, by being Yaltabaoth's mother, she stands above the one most people consider God. She's a higher God. The God of this world is merely the product of her bad choice, after all. Irenaeus recounts how Gnostics invoke certain spells as they ascend back into the pleroma through the various archontic spheres, needing to bind the archons guarding the gates at each sphere. When at last they meet Yaltabaoth himself, the final gate, they say, "I am a vessel more precious than the female who formed you. If your mother is ignorant of her own descent, I know myself, and I am aware from where I am. And I call upon the incorruptible Sophia, who is in the Father, and is the Mother of your mother."[67]

Modern Gnostics interpret this archetypically. If Yaltabaoth is the foundation of both rationalism and religious dogmaticism – cancers on the Western heart – Sophia is the beginning of a restored view of God. Understanding this point clarifies the *God-is-dead* sentiment of the nineteenth century. It's not that *God* doesn't exist, but *God as we have historically understood him in the West* has been replaced by a superior understanding. Put another way, *Yaltabaoth is dead*, and the religion replacing him yields to a truer spirituality so *other* and *beyond* traditional religious categories it requires a reoriented lexicon and new paradigms.

God-is-dead proponents like Nietzsche, Heidegger, and the existentialists divined transcendent meaning, else they wouldn't have philosophized in the first place. In the words of Heidegger, *God-is-dead* "is no atheistic proposition, but the formula for the basic experience of an event in western history."[68] That event is the changing orientation away from religious dogmatism and rationalism.

Most supposed secular humanists, both of the past and present, don't deny God; they deny God *as traditionally understood*. Their atheism or agnosticism is actually a very earnest faith in Sophia, not so named of course – we're beyond names – but a metaphorical Sophia, the fount of a reoriented cosmic perspective.

Second, Sophia's desire to fix what she damaged serves as a model for us all. Unlike her deformed son, she recognized the need to change course. She shows how we can be restored through Christ, her counterpart with whom she became reunited. The ancient Gnostic demonstrated this reunion through the Bridal Chamber ceremony. Obviously this ceremony no longer exists, but it does at a metaphorical level. It's the *love-will-save-us* theme permeating modern thinking, love understood as the breakdown of divisions but really nothing more than "the reintegration of the masculine with the feminine . . . symbolized by the sexual act."[69] Sex as a non-procreative symbol of restoration is Sophia's heritage to our culture.

Finally, Sophia serves as a principle of *The Feminine*. In 1993 members of several mainline Protestant Churches attended a "Re-Imagining Christianity" conference in Minneapolis which included a "Milk and Honey" ritual dedicated to Sophia, seeking to tap into their inner female. Pursuit of the Divine Feminine has long marked the New Age. Its roots stretch back to Gnosticism.[70] The Gnostic will claim traditional Christianity deprecated The Feminine through its negative views on Eve and on the fallen soul (which is seen as feminine), whereas Gnostics present a more positive view of The Feminine principle in our soul.[71]

This feminist element pervades modern spiritualism. In the popular book, *The Shack* (2007), God the Father appears as a black woman. Could he have appeared any other way, given where we are at spiritually and culturally? Only two things have a numinous enough quality to house the Father's appearance in a human character: woman-ness and blackness. The black element is the culmination of several decades of American literary and cinematic myth-making, the *Magical-Negro* archetype referenced above. The woman element comes straight from Gnosticism.

Richard Smoley explains in *Forbidden Faith* (2006), "much of the present enthusiasm for Gnosticism comes from those who perceive the God of the Bible (both Jewish and Christian) as unsalvageably patriarchal and who feel much kinship with his demotion in the Gnostic myths to the status of [the self-serving Yaltabaoth]. For women (and men) who still identify with Christian values but reject the institutional establishment, the welcoming of Sophia back into Christian theology represents a way to transform Christianity from within."[72]

Mysticism, Ecstacy, and Palingenesia: Waking Up to the God Within

Among the influences on Gnosticism were antiquity's version of secret societies, the mystery religions. These influences included initiation rites, secret handshakes, graduated levels of involvement, and finally an elitist division between the "initiated" and "uninitiated."[73]

Mystery cults centered around local deities like Cybele, Atargatis, Astarte, Demeter, Isis, or Dionysus, inspired by the fertility myths associated with these characters. Initiates ritualized the annual death/renewal cycle of the seasons, believing participation in these rituals procured immediate resurrection, an event experienced ecstatically or mystically. Rituals included blood baths, sacrifices, castrations, orgies, the sacred marriage (*hieros gamos*), or ecstatic vision of the *secret thing* (the mystery), something engineered through various techniques. Prevalent was the use of musical instruments – tambourines or the flute-like *aulos* – to whip initiates into a frenzy. Second century satirist Lucian mentions the use of dance.[74] Even alcohol and drugs were used to achieve the ecstatic state.

The Dionysian mysteries (related to the Orphic mysteries) staged orgies. The orgy ritualized love binding multiple souls together as one. The cult of Astarte practiced ritual prostitution, a rite rooted in the sacred marriage. The Syrian cult, devoted to the goddess Atargatis, involved a bizarre rite demanded of the initiate. After a period of penitential self-flagellation and self-castration, the candidate ran through the streets, threw his severed penis into a randomly-selected house, and took as his permanent dress the clothes of the house's female occupant.[75] The cult of the Great Mother also included emasculation rites in which the priest assumed female dress and grew his hair long. Bisexuality, transgenderism, the Divine Feminine, extreme attitudes on sexuality, the mystical program, all these traits reverberate in Gnosticism.

The role of mystical vision, gnosis, ecstasy, rebirth, or illumination in religion is a fascinating topic. Christianity has always wrestled with movements claiming the ability to ascend into divine mysteries through mystical technique. These programs passed on from the mystery cults some version of the sacred marriage, elitism, and the moment of ecstatic, beatific, or mystical insight. When these movements occupied the fringes of Catholic Christianity, some (like the Spiritual Franciscans or other mystics) dabbled dangerously close to heresy, others (the Cathars or the Free Spirit movement) embraced full-throated Gnosticism.

What is the fine line between so-called orthodox mysticism and heretical gnosis? It depends on one's perspective.

Medieval Christianity, following the Neoplatonic mysticism of Origen, Evagrius, and Pseudo-Dionysius, staked claim on a safe, modified form of mysticism by anchoring it on the Church's earthly symbols. Meditation on the sacrament, for example, could lead to mystical vision.[76] Medieval scholar David Knowles highlights the "doctrine of mediated illumination and spiritual knowledge conferred by the sacraments and by angelic ministration" passed on from Neoplatonism to medieval Christianity.[77] We think of Thomas Aquinas' famous mystical vision of Christ during mass.

But then we also think of not-so-famous Theosophist Charles

Leadbeater (1847-1934), who described his vision at the moment of consecration: "At the moment of consecration the Host glowed with the most dazzling brightness; it became in fact a veritable sun to the eye of the clairvoyant, and as the Priest lifted it above the heads of the people I noticed that two distinct varieties of spiritual force poured forth from it." So powerful was the force that neighboring society itself was affected by it.[78]

Leadbeater invokes Lord Buddha in the same treatise, showing his hand. But this only amplifies the fuzzy line between orthodox and heretical mysticism. What exactly is the difference between Leadbeater's experience and that of Aquinas, both of which centered on the sacrament?

Some emphasize doctrinal distinctions. Historian of love Denis de Rougemont classifies two types of mysticism: *unitive* and *epithalamian*. Unitive mysticism – shared by Gnostics and Neoplatonists – holds possible the fusion of the soul to the Monad: the two become one. Epithalamian mysticism prefers the language of marriage between the soul and God, maintaining the "essential distinction between creature and Creator."[79]

Or is this a distinction without a difference? Rougemont notes how difficult it is to isolate the two traditions historically. He untied the Gordian knot by focusing on the role of *agape* versus *eros* in mysticism, the former orthodox and the latter Gnostic (a distinction we will pursue further in a bit). But then he mentions how the mystic Meister Eckhart, seemingly orthodox in his emphasis on *agape*, was condemned by a papal bull for the "unitive mystical" belief that "We become completely changed into God and are converted into Him."[80]

This ambiguity leads other Christian theologians to reject mysticism altogether. Mysticism, they argue, begins with the mistaken premise that "sin is creatureliness."[81] In other words, for the mystic, man's limited, finite perspective prevents ascent into infinitude. The beginning of the mystical ascent calls the seeker to look beyond, even to deny, his limited creatureliness. Christ's call for one to deny himself is not because he is sinful, but *because he exists*. Only when he annihilates his creatureliness through the ascetic disciplines can he ascend into infinitude. Late medieval mystic Johann Tauler spoke in these terms, delighting in the moment when "the created nothing submerges in the uncreated nothing."[82]

Rather, these anti-mysticism theologians argue, sin is an *ethical* breach between Creator and creature. Salvation seeks not the dissolution of the creature into the Creator. It centers on the gracious work of

Creator upon creature. The creature ends up not dissolved, but restored. Yes, there will exist a "fellowship of I and Thou,"[83] but this can only happen so long as Creator and creature remain distinct. Communion, not union, is the goal.

That all being said, this whole discussion is pedantic, because by the standards of current American spirituality, no one cares. Half of Americans are claiming mystical experiences to varying degrees. We're beyond doctrinal subtleties. The floodgates are opened. However one wants to define it – unitive, marital, psychological, ecstatic, experiential, divine, annihilative, transcendent – whatever it is, it's claimed by one out of two people. To decide that Bob's "oceanic feeling" at church supercedes John's "dissolving into light" at New Age camp ignores what's really going on.

And what is going on? Our culture has embraced an understanding of salvation going back to the mystery cults, one centered not on the validity or truthfulness of a teaching, but on the *enthusiastic* experience, an experience ranging anywhere from holy barking to benign sensations of personal wellness, but each an experiential happening nonetheless.

Aristotle used the term *entheos* (Gr. *full of god*) to describe the experience of mystery cultists induced by music, dancing, drugs, or sex. Since then the term *enthusiasm* historically and theologically refers to the experience of God's presence through internally-induced techniques. This understanding in turn has guided one particular understanding of *palingenesia*, or "rebirth," an ancient concept embraced by Jesus in the New Testament and understood today by many as some sort of personal frisson induced at church camp, or wherever.

Scripture centers rebirth on the Church's baptismal and catechetical ministry. St. John's Gospel emphasizes rebirth "by water and the spirit" (John 3: 5) while St. Peter relates it to the word. (I Peter 1: 23) Palingenesia was externally, not internally, induced.

For the mystery cults and their enthusiastic heirs, palingenesia was wholly an internal affair, something manufactured through various techniques leading to that personal experience. These techniques, observed Aristotle, "induce such a heightening of consciousness in a man that he would be receptive to the god who came to be united with him. Such a person was then an [entheos], an enthusiast."[84]

Without a doubt this is how Americans increasingly understand salvation, which is why Harold Bloom used the term *Orphic* to describe

American religion.   We've adopted the enthusiastic, experiential understanding of palingenesia.   Meanwhile the possibility for an ecclesiastical, sacramental understanding really doesn't even compute.

What is the nature of this enthusiastic rebirth?   One author describes it as "the 'great rush,' the flash of white light or moment of illumination that takes over the body completely and that can . . . change the course of a person's life."[85]   After describing his own experience of "dissolving into light," the same author musters mystics from across the ages to justify his experience: "The same sort of turnaround occurs with classical 'oceanic' experiences, such as have been reported by Jakob Boehme, William Blake, Teresa of Avila, and many other[s]."[86]   Charles Wesley famously felt his heart strangely warmed during his experience.

Physicist Fritjof Capra details his experience: "I 'saw' cascades of energy coming down from outer space, in which particles were created and destroyed in rhythmic pulses; I 'saw' the atoms of the elements and those of my body participating in this cosmic dance of energy; I felt its rhythm and I 'heard' its sound, and at that moment I knew this was the Dance of Shiva."[87]

Charles Lindbergh, eighteen hours into his famous flight, chronicled his own "awareness spreading through space, over the earth and into the heavens, unhampered by time or substance." He reports a feeling of weightlessness, as if separated from his body. Behind him the spirits of family and friends filed through the fuselage giving him "messages of importance unattainable in ordinary life." He added, "Death no longer seems the final end it used to be, but rather the entrance to a new and free existence."[88]

Natural man needs palingenesia of this nature, said the Gnostic, because he is born in a state of drunken sleep, and would die blissfully unaware of his true origins from the Monad were it not for the possibility of being awakened.[89]   Today poets, prophets, mystics, and artists – the crazier the better – are best suited to awaken us, for the likes of these have tapped into the dream life of the pleroma.   "Sleep," a hymn of the archetypical poet-musician Orpheus proposes, will "bind us in invisible chains." But dreams are the "Source of oracles."[90]   Seen as melancholic in ages past or even as madmen to some, today the poet-artists are the prophets of our Gnostic religion. They have dared to venture into the dreamland of the reborn imagination and have come back with images, both visual and audible, to show us the way.

Gnostic Elitism

Gnostics were and remain elitists. Palingenesia was not for everyone. Not everyone had the same endowments. Not everyone had received the divine spark. Some received the spark and were keenly aware of it; these were the *pneumatics*, or, *spiritual ones*. Some had received the spark but had to be helped along in discovering it; these were the *psychics*, or *natural ones*. Others had no hope for salvation, the *earthly ones* (*hulikoi*).

The medieval incarnation of Gnosticism, Catharism, likewise had a twofold division among its followers between the *Perfecti* (the *perfect ones*) and the *Credentes* (the *believers*). We see the same elitism in the medieval heresy of the Free Spirit, which distinguished between the *Little Church* of Rome and its own *Great Church* comprised of its own members, those who achieved deification through gnosis.[91]

Over and over we see this trait in secret societies, communistic movements, and spiritual programs. Each has its frozen chosen. This is the true source of progressivism's elitism, the likes of which we will see in philosophers Auguste Comte and John Stuart Mill.

But what about the previous point on transcending divisions and separateness? Isn't separating humanity into classes one of the great divisions of history? Here we see one of Gnosticism's ugliest tendencies: *they can hold the paradox by denying the essential humanity of fellow human beings*. Humans, understood as individual flesh and blood beings, were created by a monster. Consequently no particular human *as a flesh and blood creature* has inherent value. Rather, true humanity is understood as those who have received the inner spark of the Monad. And these are all one.

So all who have the inner spark are one. And what of those that don't have the spark? Technically they're not the same species. They are dust and destined for dust. They haven't developed to the next great stage of human evolution, from mere matter into emerging light beings. They haven't "achieved a cognitive state that empowers a more coherent understanding."[92] Like children, they think in linear, causal, black/white terms, not holistically as an adult might.

Understanding Gnostic elitism explains one of the great conundrums of modern philosophy, an inconsistency pursued by political philosopher, Leo Strauss. He rightly pointed out the inconsistency of various modern philosophers – particularly from the social sciences – who proposed sweeping theories said to explain the totality of human behavior, while somehow exempting their own philosophies from their sweeping generalizations. The paradox goes as follows:

Philosopher proposes Theory X to explain why everybody's minds and brains work the way they do.

But (we would respond) *does Theory X explain why your brain thinks the way you do, particularly how it thought up this dumb theory?*

Essentially their answer is, *No. I am of a unique character and special in the history of the world.*[93] *I have been granted an insight that lifts me above everything, to see what's really going on.*[94]

Oh. OK.

Strauss' critique nailed it. It remains the intellectual scandal to modernism. The problem is, no one cares, because philosophy has moved into Gnostic terrain where all thinking is divided into two camps: the enlightened elite who know the big picture, and the regressive masses thrashing around under the paradigm of a previous intellectual tradition, the sort in which the likes of Leo Strauss excelled.

The French Revolution, communism, and Nazism each believed itself the vanguard of a dawning new age. They each claimed a position for their version of the *new man*, gloriously evolved individuals who had glimpsed into the very cosmic truth of where history was marching. For the French Revolutionary, that cosmic truth was *liberty and the brotherhood of man*; for the communist, *the triumph of the proletariat*; for the Nazi, the German *Volk*. Those that shared their enlightenment were one with them. The rest were of a lesser species, non-human, fit only for the guillotine, the showers, and the gulag.

The more benign, but no less pernicious, manifestation of Gnostic elitism in today's world is progressivism. Progressives believe they have unique insight, a secret gnosis, into the cosmic end toward which society must *progress*, and their cosmically-ordained task is to lead their benighted fellow citizens toward this end. Progressive attitudes about the unconvinced may not be as murderous as those of the communist or fascist. Nevertheless they amount to a sort of *evolve-or-die* mentality.

Human evolution obviously plays a role in this thinking. Human evolution proposes we will develop into new beings. If that evolution is slow, no harm no foul. What do I care if some being eight million years from now is a species distinct from me? But if evolution is believed to operate in shoots and fits, as Peter Russell proposes in his *The Awakening Earth: The Global Brain* (2008),[95] then perhaps we are in the midst of an evolutionary fit right now. This is exactly what Will Smith thought

Obama would be, an "evolutionary flashpoint." Those shoots, fits, and flashpoints may be part of the natural progression of evolution, or they may be catalyzed by science and technology toying with our genes. Presbyterian ethicist and minister Rev. Mark Douglas, resurrecting the ideas of Jesuit theologian Pierre Teilhard de Chardin, suggests God is directing humanity to an evolved "transhumanism."[96]

In best selling author Eckhart Tolle's, *A New Earth* (2008; featured in Oprah's Book Club), all the classic tropes of modern Gnosticism come marching out – the rejection of religion in favor of spirituality, the antinomianism and iconoclasm, the awakening to new consciousness, the disavowal of material delineations, etc. The last line of his book ought to terrify us. He writes, "A new species is rising on the earth. It is arising now, and you are it!"[97]

The question each of us should ponder is, "What if I am not *it*?"

The Journey of the Self Against Archontic Powers: Antinomianism

Irenaeus refered to a Gnostic sect, the Carpocratians, who were "so abandoned in their recklessness that they claim to have in their power and to be able to practise anything whatsoever that is ungodly (irreligious) and impious. They say that conduct is good and evil only in the opinion of men."[98]

Such recklessness proved to the Gnostic how free he was from all the binding laws set up by Yaltabaoth and his archons. Echoes of Gnostic freedom reverberate in Nietzsche's philosophical treatise *Beyond Good and Evil* (1886) and – his philosophy laying down the foundation for postmodern relativism – introduce a convergence between our times and ancient Gnosticism.

What exactly is antinominianism?

By convention the Gnosticism 101 summary will always include *Gnostic antinomianism*. By this is meant Gnostic rejection of moral codes, especially in regard to sexuality. But the issue is more complex, and we have to investigate ancient psychology to understand what's at stake.

For the ancients, the soul reflected the cosmos and vice versa. Psychology was the flip side of cosmology. The myth of what happened in the cosmos was directly related to what went on in the soul. In the *Timaeus*, Plato argued the soul resided in the head and concluded the universe is round because the head is round. The only reason the head is attached to the body is so it doesn't roll around on the ground, a gravitational dilemma evidently avoided by the universe.

This macrocosm/microcosm sympathy is the basis of astrology. The ancients believed the soul entered the body through various cosmic influences, represented by the sun, moon, planets, and stars. On the way down its descent the soul picked up certain character traits – based on the position of the various spheres – and these traits dictated the fate of that individual because, as ancient philosopher Heraclitus said, "Character is fate."

But there's more. The elements of the cosmos – the things dividing the cosmos up into time and place, everything from the heavenly bodies down to the rocks and trees, but also days, months, and years – took on spiritual qualities. Animating spirits called *daemons* lurked behind these things of place and time. The sum total of these animating spirits – the hierarchical network of daemons – constituted the cosmos.

These animating spirits populated the ancient imagination in any number of ways: the sprites and nymphs of Greek myth; the personified Ideas of Middle Platonic philosophy (Sophia's origin); the genii, numina, and manes of Roman piety; the angels and demons of Hebraic religion. They were seen as ethically neutral, capable of either good or evil.

Psychologically, each man's soul had a place in the cosmos and was placed under the tutelage of certain daemonic beings based on his situation in time and place. The quest of any ancient philosophy or religion worth its salt was to provide an answer to the question of how the human soul should relate to this daemonic reality of the cosmos. Generally there were three answers to this question.

Platonism, Aristotelianism, and Stoicism argued the soul should adjust itself and relate favorably to the principles of the cosmos by yielding to the hierarchy.[99] For them the question is, *what is according to nature?*

Christians saw the world as invaded by fallen angels, Satanic powers subjugating the world to their influences. For them the cosmos is not evil, but it's corrupted by this reign of demons. Christ came to regain the dominion Adam lost – the kingdom of heaven – realized in the "world to come." The Christian casts a sanctified vision on the fallen creation, hopes in its redemption, and through faith sees its original beauty.

The Gnostics reject the possibility of redemption.[100] Any product of this world order – the creation, our bodies, the societal and political systems – came about by a grand cosmic error. They can disregard such things completely. For them the daemonic spheres are a large prison house with multiple layers of walls and gates, and each individual spirit is locked away in his bodily cell at the center. Upon awakening to the knowledge from whence he came, the Gnostic begins his ascent out of his cell. Gates and doors open up for him with each new Gnostic insight, little Gnostic keys attained through enlightenment. Eventually he ascends out of the prison cell of the cosmos altogether and enjoys pleromic bliss. Thus, a major attraction of the Gnostic salvation program was "salvation from astral determinism, because they regarded fate as demonic."[101] And this salvation began with a total rejection of the demonic world order, which went way beyond orthodoxy's understanding of demonic powers to include the entire created order.

The Gnostic sect, the Cainites, believed they could not "be saved in any other way, except that they pass through all things."[102] What things? The gates and doors, those things laid down in law by the "angels who created the world."[103] These were the same spirits who gave Moses the Law, or who dictated fate through astrology, or who set up the laws of nature. Gnostics predicated redemption on the enlightened discovery of their freedom from all restraint, moral or psychic. These were the keys opening the doors, their liberation from all order, moral and other.

Yaltabaoth's 365 archons governed these gates and doors.[104] They oversaw all the systems of the world and established the laws and principles governing these systems. For this reason Gnosticism was antinomian,[105] meaning it was anti-*nomos*, *nomos* being the Greek word for *law* or *principle*. Yaltabaoth was the chief Law-giver. *Nomos* includes, but means more than, the Ten Commandments. *Nomos* denotes the governing principles of the world, both in nature and in society.[106] It's Latin counterpart is *institutum*,[107] cluing us to the affinities of modern anti-institutionalism with Gnostic antinomianism. It includes all the written and unwritten rules of *the system*, whatever system that may be, from the solar system to the political system. It includes natural order itself, such arrangements dictating, for example, the unwritten societal rules of what femininity, masculinity, and marriage are.

Each commandment of the Decalogue codifies the principle of individuation and separation, thereby sanctifying whatever entity is set apart from the other. The Lord and his name are separated from all others and only should be served, not taken in vain. His Sabbath day is separate from all others and must be kept holy. My person, wife, properties, and reputation are my own and ought to be protected. To the Gnostic, these laws sanction a system, for example, of private property. Or of parental authority. Or of the sanctity of bodily life. Or of marriage. Or of worship preserved for a named, local deity. These laws offend because of their fundamental premise: *the only thing bringing about individualized properties like life, wife, and land is Yaltabaoth's flawed creation.*

Abusing St. Paul's grace-centered theology, the Gnostics claimed to be completely free from all *nomos*, and this antinomianism led to the shiftlessness and sexual immorality described by the apostles in their epistles. (II Peter 2; Jude; Revelation 2: 20) It also led to communalism and wife-sharing, for their Gospel brought them to a pre-Law point of existence, back to a primitive age when there was no law, only an Eden where all things were shared. This at least was the position of the Gnostic Carpocratians.[108]

Today's Gnostics likewise always butt up against nature and nature's laws like battering rams, insisting nature should not dictate anyone's place in the world, as in the forced argument that femininity, masculinity, and marriage are not natural but social constructs. Their archons take new forms: the Church, culture, the state, or whoever perniciously controls language and cultural institutions, overseeing the cosmic constructs by which they maintain power. The Gnostic must deconstruct this cosmic architecture and all its arbitrary conventions to be liberated. Put another way, he must break open the archontic gates binding him to the dominant paradigms of thought.

In Christian circles the code word for archontic evil is "legalism" or "Pharisaism," which upon inspection is often nothing more than the denigration of standards in morality, doctrine, or worship. Robert E. Webber summarises the attitudes of younger Evangelicals after giving two examples of "legalism" (one of which included a pastor telling a young woman that she would have to stop sleeping with her boyfriend before she could be a Christian), "[There is] one word that I have heard over and over again from the twenty-somethings – *authentic*. They want to be real Christians in a real world – not phony Christians in a world of their own making. To achieve this goal, they know that they must break from the legalistic bondage of a spirituality defined by external rules and embrace the true meaning of freedom in Christ."[109]

Breaking free of the legalistic bondage, such is the stuff of the Gnostic antinomian salvation. Of course, the Occupy Wall Street movement took the cake on the antinomianism front. For them, *Walmart* or *Wall Street* or *The 1%* are the archons. The very mention of such phrases conjures up something uncannily evil for those who believe they are imprisoned in a multinational capitalistic system. *Halliburton* has a similar effect on those convinced the world is governed by military-industrial overseers. The *Koch brothers* of course are the puppetmasters duping Middle America to be conservative against their better interests. The simple word *big* prefixed to any concept *archontifies* it. Gnostics always need these archontic characters, some word or idea looming large, dark, oppressive, and controlling in the collective mind, something to rebel against to give their lives meaning.

Take this random example from a blogger in the *comments* section following a political essay on energy: "Forget gas economy . . . the oilers are gonna be sure to make their profit . . . start knee cappin'/head blastin' some of these big shots with their fingers in the pie . . . ceo's, cfo's x's and o's with their theivery hiding behind make believe cost increases,etc, supply and demand, free enterprise, bs democracy, and their control freak so called keep the peace bunches . . . they're just the same as any thief, dope dealin' cartel, they lie, they cheat, they steal and they're protected by a bunch of ********* with black robes, thick ass law books, and of course the almighty fraternal protectorates of the police and the military . . . I wonder how well these big wigs are truly protected . . . not as well as some might believe . . . ."

The comment parades forth all the usual archontic suspects: oil companies, CEOs, supply and demand, free enterprise, democracy, judges, the police, and the military. These are the rulers of the system, a system the commentator believes is inherently corrupt. Not only rulers, but ruling principles – like supply and demand, or democracy – are hopelessly corrupt. He suggests the positions of these entities aren't so secure, hinting at some sort of revolution.

Such is the fantasy-infused perception of the Gnostic, particularly when he applies the dark/light formatting of his mind to politics. His opponents are not flesh and blood people. They're abstracted archetypes animated by the characters in the Gnostic myth, ready-made evil stock characters sitting on Hollywood's shelf, or drab-grey oils blended on the palette of our cultural myth-makers for the sole purpose of shading in the contrasting dark haunts on the canvass of our imagination. The idea that any of these characters could actually be human with blends of good and evil cannot be. They are two-dimensional personifications of evil itself, only suitable for "head blastin'." Moreover, the possibility that the author himself, after toppling this evil system and gaining power, would fall for the same corrupting impulses, is also impossible. He's on the side of light; the powers are on the side of darkness.

Anyone insisting "it can't happen here," to use Sinclair Lewis' eponymous phrase for his novel exploring how totalitarianism might arise in America, needs to peer into the above quote and wonder what it portends that more and more Americans are engaging our world with thusly-formatted minds.

Love (Eros) as Cosmic Bungee Cord

A certain sort of sexuality, non-procreative in nature, appears throughout the history of Gnosticism. The word *buggery*, a synonym for *sodomy*, derives from a group of medieval Gnostics known as Bogomils, a descendant of the early charismatic sect, the Messalians. The same non-procreative understanding of love fueled Socrates' celebration of pederasty in the *Phaedrus*. Or again, there is the Gnostic practice of *coitus interruptus* which we see in its various permutations, as in tantric sex practices and in the sex practices of the utopian Oneida Community.

For similar reasons the Gnostics condemned marriage. The Apostle Paul had the Gnostics in mind when he warned against those who forbid marriage and command abstinence from foods "which God [i.e. the evil Yaltabaoth, in the mind of the Gnostic] created." (I Timothy 4: 3) Later third century Marcionite groups believed marriage fulfilled the "work of Satan."[110] Irenaeus likewise testified to this Gnostic impulse: "Marriage and procreation, they maintain, are of Satan. Many of [their] followers abstain from [meat]."[111] This rejection of marriage, along with vegetarianism (because vegetables are food not produced by sexual intercourse), follows the Gnostic stream throughout history.

Sexuality per se isn't forbidden. Irenaeus attributes sexual license to Simon Magus, whom ancient Church tradition decreed the first Gnostic. Simon took up with a prostitute named Helen. Irenaeus summarizes: "[Simon believes] they should as free men do what they wish: for through his (Simon's) grace are men saved, and not through righteous works. Nor are works just by nature, but by convention (*accidens*), as the angels who made the world ordained, in order to enslave men by such precepts." Irenaeus goes on to cite Valentinian Gnostic justifications for license as "repaying to the flesh what belongs to the flesh."[112]

Erotic overtones mark Gnostic spirituality throughout its history, from the medieval Free Spirit movement to the Children of God cult in the 1960s. Mystic G. I. Gurdjieff (1866-1949) fathered eight illegitimate children and sought liaisons with adepts he knew to be married. One of his students defended him: "All his strange and often repellent behavior was a screen to hide him from people who would otherwise have idolized his person instead of working for themselves." Some suggest Gurdjieff may have been a follower of the Sufi "way of blame," which believed the "most elevated group" of adepts purposely hid their goodness.[113]

If salvation rests on liberation from moral order, the Gnostics demonstrated their freedom by their libertine sexual attitudes. Some Gnostics sects were downright X-rated in their rites. The Barbeliote Gnostics believed the spark of a man resided in his sperm or in a woman's menstrual blood. Their rites included intercourse, but prior to consummation, the discharge was collected in the hands of the man and woman. They ate it saying, "This is the body of Christ, and this is the Passover; hence our bodies are given over to passion and compelled to confess the passion of Christ." Similarly at a woman's menstruation period, the substance was taken in the hands of the man and woman, and eating it they said, "This is the blood of Christ."[114] These emissions were not allowed to escape, but were collected in the hand lest they became united and generated more sparks falling into evil material existence. If conception did occur, the fetus was aborted, and according to one early church father, eaten sacramentally.

Gnostic defenders claim these accusations are slanders made by institutional powers maligning Gnosticism in the eyes of the public. But what are they afraid of? The Gnostic is free from this world's Creator, Yaltabaoth, and all his morality laws. Worse, procreation replicates the primal evil, the creation of evil flesh. As one contemporary Gnostic "reverend" writes, "There is a current that goes against having children in the history of Gnosticism. . . . [I]f humans are imprisoned here then we shouldn't take part in that imprisonment. 'I have sown no children to the rulers of the world,' is in keeping with this view."[115] Indeed it is!

To compound the problem, children stifle one's journey of Self-discovery. Explaining his inspiration for the movie *Revolutionary Road* (2008) starring Leonardo DiCaprio and Kate Winslet, director Sam Mendes said, "[The movie] deals with this idea . . . that you somehow find yourself living a life you hadn't quite expected and certainly one that you didn't really want to live." The movie climaxes with the wife getting an abortion to combat suburban ennui. Thomas Hibbs comments, "Pregnancy is the great evil in the film, the enemy to be defeated." Why? "[B]ecause the presence of children punctures the world of perpetual adolescent fantasy to which the main characters are devoted." Hibbs' analysis recalls Justice Anthony Kennedy's justification for abortion: "At the heart of liberty is the right to define one's own concept of existence, of meaning, of the universe, and of the mystery of human life."[116]

For new Gnostics seeking to escape mundane reality for their self-absorbed worlds of light and authenticity, sex resulting in demanding children must be replaced by new paradigms of sex. It's rather about the transcendent feeling connecting two Selves on a higher plane.

Marilyn Ferguson lauds the advent of "new-paradigm relationships" that are more about "shared psychic intensity" than sexuality. Some Gnostic-minded Americans, she says, flinch at this new understanding. "For many people, giving up the idea of exclusive relationships is the most difficult paradigm shift in their own transformation." In a footnote she quotes a sociologist's study suggesting monogamous marriage is outdated and needs to be expanded to include "relationships with others, possibly including various degrees of sexual intimacy."[117]

Where does this emphasis on a non-procreative, anti-marriage love come from?

The English language doesn't delineate the various nuances of the word *love*. The word is used with everything, from high school infatuations to the spouse of a sixty year marriage, from hot dogs to God. The Greek language allowed for a bit more nuance, especially in its differentiation between *eros* and *agape*. Of these two, orthodoxy coopted the latter and Gnosticism the former.

Agape in Christian terms is defined by God's sacrificial love for humanity, displayed in the giving of his Son unto death. This sacrificial love works the love a Christian has for his neighbor: *love creates a neighbor where before there was none*. It restores the original order in which the entire flow of life itself is one of self-giving: the Father giving of himself for the Son, the Son giving of himself for man, man giving of himself for woman, and woman giving of herself for her child. This self-giving happens at the bosom point. After the Fall, the same self-giving goes on, but now – as typified by the crucifix – through suffering, hence, *passion*, which comes from the Latin for *suffering*. Love, in Christian terms, involves real *gut-wrenching*[118] agape: Christ spilling out his guts on the cross; a woman wrenching her insides to give birth; a man working in the coal mines or going off to war to protect and provide for his family.

Gnosticism is the negative image of everything just stated. First, the whole idea of *neighbor* is nullified. The creation of one who could be a neighbor was not only the work of a usurper deity, but a fundamentally corrupt action: *there should be no neighbors because we should all be one as we were before Yaltabaoth started dividing everything up!* With the annihilation of ego upon which salvation depends also goes the annihilation of Other, or neighbor. Neighbor along with me joins the collective pleroma and thus must be dealt with by a new understanding of love, erotic love.

Likewise is self-sacrifice – fathers sacrificing to provide and protect; mothers giving birth – simply a continuation of Yaltabaoth's creative activity, a *pro*creation. Love resulting in procreation and its demands is an obnoxious notion. It continues Yaltabaoth's error.

What then is love to the Gnostic? *Eros* more closely approximates what they mean by love. Eros is erotic love, or romantic love. This sort of love defines the Romantic period, a longing and yearning for some intangible *out-there* thing transcending anything this earthly existence can offer. The ultimate *out-there* thing is Monad, our Source. It makes its appearance to us as Sophia, setting the table for a whole literary and philosophical history of Divine Female love motifs.

Because nothing in this physical world can satisfy one's erotic longing for his source, the true Gnostic always suffers. He too has passion, but passion as we understand it today, the passion of love, the suffering of yearning fulfilled in the ecstacy of orgasm. The ecstacy is where it's at – a spiritual moment really – certainly not the resulting physical occurrence: sperm bursting forth to germinate egg.

The above-quoted Donna Minkowitz aptly describes such love: "Love without inequality. Pleasure without restriction. Vulnerability without exploitation. To me, to most of us, gay love means all these things and more – an ecstatic knowledge, almost a *gnosis*, that sex is possible outside of the horrifying thickets in which the rest of the culture has hedged it. And that we ourselves can get to it! Visions of a totally satisfying oral bliss, what Ginsberg called 'caresses of Atlantic and Caribbean love,' the mind-stealing kisses of 'human seraphim,' a physical joy beyond the bounds of anything most people experience, almost beyond the bounds of desire itself, my God! no wonder people fear us! But they should not fear. They should open to the Ultimate, as we have done."[119]

Sex resulting in children is obviously what nature has bestowed on us, something biology classifies as the operation of the *reproductive system*. If a "culture" is "hedging" sex with this "horrifying" reality, it's because culture is formalizing something quite natural, kind of like the way culture hedges drivers to speed limits on mountainous curves because nature has a few horrifying things to say about centripetal force, which among other horrifying things tethers our planet to the sun. But through the Gnostic myth, nature is the work of Yaltabaoth, something to liberate oneself from.

In any event, this notion of love – mystical ecstacy as sublimated orgasm – runs deep in literary and philosophical history, going back to the Orpheus myth, then through Socrates and Plato, to the Neoplatonists and Gnostics. It's shared by Christian mystics. We see it among the Romantic poets and philosophers. It drives modern pop and rock music.

It's ultimately rooted in what we might call the *cosmic bungee cord* view of love in the ancient world, in which love is the spiritual searcher's magnetic draw to his Source, Monad. It's like a spark descending from the Monad through the pleroma on a bungee cord. His fall is a process of individuation whereby his spark takes on all sorts of fleshly designations, falling through one archontic sphere to another – the stellar and planetary influences – until he reaches the nadir of his existence, a flesh and blood human falsely believing himself to be defined by gender, ethnic, religious, cultural, and personality designations. The walls are up, the very rudiments of hate setting up a world of *We's* and *They's*, ego and *Other*.

But for the Gnostic the bungee cord is a two way process; what goes down must go up. The slumbering spark awakens. He learns of his origins in the Monad, and Sophia appears ready to guide him home. Suddenly all the things he thought were real are deceptive frauds. He cares only for the return home. He cares only for Sophia, his new love. This love tugs and draws him upward and outward in an ascent only consummated at death, when at last he will reunite with the pleroma.

The Neoplatonist philosopher Plotinus meditates on this sort of love when he asks, "What is this intoxication, this exultation, this longing to break away from the body and live sunken within yourselves? All true lovers experience it. But what awakens so much passion?"

He answers, "[O]nly those reach it who rise to the intelligible realm, face it fully, stripped of the muddy vesture with which they were clothed in their descent . . . and enter in nakedness, having cast off in the ascent all that is alien to the divine. There one, in the solitude of self, beholds simplicity and purity, the existent upon which all depends, towards which all look, by which reality is, life is, thought is."

He continues, "Seeing with what love and desire for union one is seized – what wondering delight! If a person who has never seen this hungers for it as for his all, one that has seen it must love and reverence it as authentic beauty, must be flooded with an awesome happiness, stricken by a salutary terror. Such a one loves with a true love, with desires that flame. All other loves than this he must despise and all that once seemed fair he must disdain."[120]

Romantic poets and philosophers continue the theme. First there's the descent on the bungee cord – the evil of separation, the disintegration of humanity, the alienation of the human spirit. "All relationships," said Hegel, "are tearing themselves apart." For Schiller this fragmented humanity was the cause of mental illness. But then things bounce back, as love pulls the soul back to its source. "Love is the bond and the sanction which connects not only man with man, but with everything that exists," said Shelley. Hegel adds, "In love the separate does not remain, but as something united and no longer as something separate."[121]

Christian agape is an other-directed love unrelated to how one feels or what's going on internally. It's formalized expression through, say, charity organizations or the institution of marriage can be ploddingly, drudgingly participated in and still be effective. But this harkens back to a time when *duty* was a component of love and seen as good. It lengthened marriages, protected women and children, strengthened communities, and gave some hope for the poor.

Gnostic love is entirely inner-directed and has little to do with the object of that love.

Exhibit A is the adulterous affair, whose whole point is love without sacrifice or commitment for the actual person. Gnostic love scorns a real flesh and blood person: that person is a stand-in for something deeper going on, the subject's love for love. Hollywood traffics in Gnostic love. They cut off the story right before the real agape-oriented stuff is required, right before the lovers get married and have to deal with actual issues. Sacrifice as a component of love has long left the equation of American love, replaced by utopian ideas of romance and eroticism.

Exhibit B is how love for humankind has replaced love for actual humans. John Lennon left his first wife behind at the train depot on his way to go to India and write songs about love. *All you need is love!* (I'm sure that sentiment was a great relief to his estranged son Julian.) This is the love inspiring the moral preening about an expanding welfare state. It's not love for actual people who in reality end up soul-sapped and dependent on a cold bureaucracy. It's rather a love for an abstraction, an idea, that is, the idea of a pleromic collective, that we are not individuals but bound toward one another, including an abstracted "the poor." One can be self-satisfied not by the old pagan observation of Christians – "See how they love one another" – but by the newest ascription, "See how I voted!"[122]

What agape sees as the necessary consequence of true love – the begetting of others, the begetting of neighbors, the begetting of one's wife, one's children, the begetting of one who calls upon my self-sacrifice – the Gnostic sees as corrupt.

In any event, to set the table for further discussion, we emphasize three things about Gnosticism and love. First, Gnostic love was a concept pregnant with symbolic meaning as reflected in its spiritual marriage and sex rituals, symbolizing the reunion between "one's lower aspect with its Lightworld prototype."[123] Second, love or the spiritual marriage had nothing to do with procreation, and in fact procreation was seen as the perpetuation of an evil, something to be aborted. Here, Sophia's dismissal of Yaltabaoth after his conception serves as the prototypical abortion. Third, central to Gnostic love was passion, understood as the suffering that the lover undergoes as part of his healing process, of leaving this evil material world behind for the journey into cosmic bliss.

The Gnostic/Magic Connection

We saw how ancient cosmology was related to psychology. The ancient cosmos was populated by a hierarchical network of spirit beings called *daemons*, which bore influence on the individual soul. The magician was a practitioner of the art of manipulating the network of demons. By influencing one demon, through the network, he could manipulate other areas, like tugging at one part of a web to effect a reaction at another part. He influenced a point in the demonic network through certain secret words and phrases, or spells. Christianity's arch-nemesis Simon Magus was a magician. The posture of the magician is ultimately Gnostic: if the world is the product of a usurper, then the world may either be avoided altogether – how the ascetics interpreted it – or tinkered with.

This is how some, like Renaissance scholar Francis Yates, see affinities between modern science and Gnosticism. Yates is particularly interested in the role Hermeticism played in the rise of modern science. It was the Hermetical posture toward nature, she argues, or "magic as an aid to gnosis,"[124] which laid the revolutionary foundation from which modern science arose.

One of the fathers of the scientific revolution, Francis Bacon, nicely echoes this Hermetical posture: *Nature, to be commanded, must be obeyed.* It's all about technique. The goal is subjugating nature. *How* do we gain mastery over something? *How* do we manipulate our world? The Hermetical magician manipulates and uses nature to his own advantage, whether good (white magic) or bad (black magic). This posture revolutionized the ancient model, possessed as it was of far more humility before nature and its divine order. The Hermetical posture toward nature by contrast allows for the sort of tinkering modern technology does, because the *divine* in *divine order* is cast as a usurping fraud. He is freed from the laws of nature, freed to master them in turn.[125]

So far so good. While there are some cases, like tinkering with genes or DNA, where the ethics of "playing God" enter, much of modern technology is simply a footnote on the invention of fire, the wheel, or the alphabet, hardly usurpations of the Creator. But then we can't forget: cosmology is related to psychology. The Renaissance magicians were far more interested in the psychological side of this equation, and for this reason, doubled as the world's first psychoanalysts, or, tinkerers of *human* nature. The magician influenced not only cosmic realms through his manipulations, he also manipulated the troubled soul and released it from cosmic influences. Marsilio Ficino's medical treatise, *De vita libri tres* (1489), attempted to do this for those suffering from melancholy and stands as a signpost for the Self-Help times to come.

The Hermeticists also understood the role of music in magic. Given the saturation of music in all areas of modern life, their viewpoint is illuminating. If love is the cosmic bungee cord drawing the soul back to its source, and if the archons are impeding the way, music might unlock these archontic doors. The magician will learn its erotic secrets. Ficino played a lyre emblazoned with an image of Orpheus for good reason. Just as Orpheus pacified the powers of this world order with his song, so can the magician-musician change the constitution of the world – set up as it is by the powers that be – through the wise manipulation of melody and harmony. Likewise can he help the trapped soul during his ascent out of his pathologies.

Obviously music can have positive or negative effects on the human soul, but can music change society? The Camarata – a group of Florentine Neoplatonic humanists – said "yes," and opera was the result. They paved the way for the likes of Jimi Hendrix, who said, "through music, you can hypnotize people . . . and when you get them at their weakest point, you can preach into the subconscious minds what we want to say."[126] His goal was put bluntly in a 1969 interview with *Newsweek*,

"Definitely I'm trying to change the world."[127]

Giordano Bruno (1548-1600), the Renaissance philosopher whose work *De vinculis in genere* (1590) laid out the basic connection between magic and love, particularly how the magician can manipulate the masses by understanding the erotic bonds in the human psyche, put it this way: "Magic action occurs through . . . sounds and images which exert power over the sense of sight and hearing. . . . Passing through the opening of the senses, they impress on the imagination certain mental states of attraction or aversion, of joy or revulsion. . . . Sounds and images are not chosen at random; they stem from the occult language of the universal spirit. . . . With regard to sounds, the manipulator should know that tragic harmonies give rise to more passions than comic ones . . . , being able to act on souls in doubt."[128]

In other words, the collective mind of any society is saturated with images (or *phantasms*) fueled by the passions and loves of its people. These images are situated in a grand network and cross paths with a wide variety of icons. The master magician can tug at one part of the network and effect something at another part. He uses both sound and visual images in the manipulation of masses. A melody here, a harmony there, conjoined with some logo or archetype, all these conjure up images which can be leveraged to specific actions. It's magic.

Coupled with the modern use of marketing – the manipulation of branding for products, the control of narratives by political campaigns – we truly live in magical times, the blurring of the border between Disney World and reality. Rational discourse is less and less about cogent or logical ideas in the same way that the purchase of a product is less and less premised on useful information. It's all about manipulating the images, or conveying thoughts through archetypical shorthand, and tinkering with these abstracted ideas in the fantasy life of the individual.

The New Age, or Emerging Paradigms

The term *New Age* is prejudiced by decades of wackiness associated with it. Then again, as a *Christianity Today* article observed, "[T]he New Age label itself [has fallen] away. Like Baptist and other churches disowning their denominational identifiers to present themselves as 'community churches,' postmodern New Agers would rather not be encumbered by the pigeonholing of the New Age name."[129]

No longer, the article continues, is the New Age using traditional verbiage to describe its program – we're all beyond language and pigeonholing now – but it's using phrases like "emerging mainstream." We would expect modern Gnostics of all stripes to disown words and names: it's what they do. But what exactly is the New Age? What is the Gnostic view of how history goes forward?

A traditionalist view of history is developmental: things build off of what precedes it; the wisdom of the past is passed on to future generations. But that implies respect for institutions involved in passing on the past such as family, society, culture, traditions in the Church, and state rituals.

In the Gnostic mind, however, these institutions are all creations of Yaltabaoth, systems of this false and evil world he must transcend. The Gnostic understanding of history thus moves from *developmental* to *revolutionary*, or using the newest phrase, *emerging*. Developmental *builds* off the past; revolutionary *revolts* against the past; emerging *transcends* the past. *Revolutionary* and *emerging* have similar ends but differ in means, the former willing to force the issue, the latter believing that minds will change first by the gentile tugging of Gnostic avatars, and then by an avalanche of societal change.

This interest in history at all, of course, presumes an involvement eluding more radical, otherworldly Gnostics. But Hermeticism, or "proletarian Gnosticism"[130] allows for such involvement through mechanisms we'll explore in our section on politics.

Today's Gnostics are closer to this proletarian variety, and so believe we are at the threshold of a new age. The code word most suggesting such thinking is *paradigm*.

Thomas Kuhn introduced the word in his *The Structure of Scientific Revolutions* (1962). Marilyn Ferguson popularized it in her New Age work, *The Aquarian Conspiracy* (1980). Those attracted to *paradigm* talk generally believe there is an imminent revolutionary *shift* in the lodestars guiding how people think, a spiritual reorientation. It's not just a change of opinion; it's a change in the psychic architecture by which those opinions are made.

History itself is divided into periods reflecting supposed paradigmatic change. Common to each of these periods is the pretense of a new, world-historical way of thinking, a new age. The very terms of historical nomenclature display over and over again the rotting corpses of periods considered imminently paradigm-shifting at the time. What is remarkable is how this nomenclature smacks of Gnosticism: *Middle Age* (transitional period leading to a revolutionary, third millennial age);

Renaissance (new birth); *Enlightenment* (as opposed to the darkness of the Dark Ages); the age of *Radical Revolution* (uprooting the status quo). These terms don't suggest developmental change or reformation of cherished institutions.

From John Stuart Mill's thinking that "the times [are] pregnant with change" and how a revolution was taking place "in the human mind and in the constitution of human society"[131] to Robert Schuller's *New Reformation* (1982), over and over we see this strange and steadfast insistence on the dawn of great change concurrent with the author's own age.

The most humorous example is from an author contributing an essay on *The Apocalyptic Vision in America* (1982). His tome is a dispassionate review of all the new age thinking occurring in the nineteenth century among the various revivalistic groups. He rightly identified how these revivalistic groups were fueled by their millenarian views of society: *Christ was coming to establish his kingdom on earth!* But then without irony he writes in a final chapter, "I believe with great conviction that our own age is in fact different from previous ages. . . . Such predictions are now based on a scientific observation rather than on religious inspiration."[132]

What he failed to realize is that he was in perfect consort with the revivals of the past. Precisely where he failed to see the "religious inspiration" of his own thinking, he was perfectly in tune with Gnostic currents today.

Conclusion: Cur Deus Homo?

The incarnation of God in human flesh is the most powerful affirmation of physical creation ever given. That doctrine governs all of Christian theology: Jesus Christ is the bridge, or Mediator, between God and man. The Church is the post-ascension extension of this truth.

Because Gnosticism locates the process of salvation internally, it is the mother of those heresies claiming the Church is ultimately unnecessary. Throughout history, there have been movements outside the Church claiming not to need the Church. They claim salvation comes through intuition, through inner feeling, or through a personal experience of the Holy Spirit. These movements are all part of the Gnostic family tree.

Writers sympathetic to Gnosticism say the Church tyrannizes or monopolizes an experience open to all (or at least the elite) without any mediation. The Church puts forth, says one author, a "transitional object"[133] through which contact with God must be found, just as the medieval Church said "outside of the Church is no salvation." The transitional object includes such things as dogma, rituals, or sacraments. By inserting the transitional object, the Church gains political power: it controls access to God.

Such authors may take heart, for by droves people are casting off the transitional object and all institutional churches. Already in the 1990s, a study revealed a third of Americans hold to the statement "people have God within them, so churches aren't really necessary."[134] More recent studies suggest this figure has expanded, as younger people tend more toward this "spiritual, but not religious" creed.

Marilyn Ferguson predicted it: "[T]he heretics are gaining ground, doctrine is losing its authority, and knowing is superseding belief."[135]

✧ Chapter 3 ✧

The Underground Stream

A Brief History of Gnostic Movement

Christian orthodoxy early on recognized the threat Gnosticism posed and quickly disposed its most offensive teachings. The Church reaffirmed ecclesiastical order against Gnostic anti-authoritarianism, emphasized the incarnation against Gnostic deprecation of the flesh, codified its belief in "the resurrection of the flesh" in the Apostles' Creed, affirmed orthodox cosmology in the Nicene Creed (confessing the Father to be Maker of "all things visible and invisible"), and canonized the Scriptures, guarding it against any popular preference for Gnostic gospels and confirming the inclusion of the Old Testament. Theologians like Irenaeus tackled the heresy in depth, establishing the orthodox defense against Gnosticism. Meanwhile, Gnosticism itself dissipated, went underground, or embedded itself psychically in other movements, awaiting a new dawn in a later era.

These are the facts of the situation more or less. Not much debate exists regarding these facts, save one: those sympathetic to ancient Gnosticism deny the existence of a true Christian orthodoxy guarding the standards of Christ's religion against Gnosticism. They see orthodoxy as one of many sects which triumphed over others, each having as good a claim to authentic Christianity as orthodoxy.[1]

Gnosticism Runs to the Hills

In 313 AD, when Constantine legalized Christianity with the

71

Edict of Milan, orthodox Christianity attained another weapon in her arsenal: the state. Over the next two centuries – the age of the great councils – Gnosticism declined as a threat. The Church issued a host of statutes against its teachings.

Morris Berman describes the period: "[E]xperience with the 'god within' was effectively closed off." In his words, Christianity in the late ancient world became "cocooned," typified by the "frozen body, and a frozen God" in the "stiff iconography of Carolingian art." He concludes about this era: "Having had several centuries of intense and turbulent interiority, the *psyche*, Jewish as well as Christian, was exhausted. [Interiority] did not get revived until the . . . rediscovery of the Self in the eleventh and twelfth centuries. And this rediscovery was the next episode in the history of countercultural . . . experience."[2]

It's a historical cliche – a Dark Ages when only ignorance prevailed – yet ancient religiosity did settle into a pretty monochrone Christian orthodoxy. Still, Gnosticism lurked in the margins, in various enthusiastic or charismatic movements popping up here and there. Sufi Idries Shah's interpretation of this period is typical: "When temporal powers, that of the State or of religious leaders who are in fact disguised power-seekers, becomes supreme, as often occurs in most communities, this inward religion, the Gnostic one, has to go underground, and may remain for centuries as a parallel stream, waiting to come to the surface again." During this period, inner experience became "locked within [the Church's] teaching or sacraments."[3]

Several modern Christian movements center their historiography on these outlier enthusiastic cults, holding to the "Great Apostasy" thesis of Church history. Accordingly, shortly after the apostolic age the Church embraced paganism to ever-increasing degrees.[4] Meanwhile, true Christians ran for the hills. As such, true Christian history should not be sought in the decrees of the organized Church, or in the writings of the Church Fathers, or in the creeds and councils. It should be sought in the rejected sects and alienated groups, hidden in the ghettoes and hinter regions, in the margins of society, falsely maligned in the condemnations of the councils, always persecuted.

Disparate groups hold to this view because, depending on their particular bugaboo with standard Church history, they find the early Church far too ritualistic, sacramental, or dogmatic. Fundamentalists identify infant baptism and the real presence in communion as marks of apostasy; Seventh Day Adventists deplore the rise of Sunday as the Lord's

Day; Jehovah's Witnesses and Mormons object to the doctrine of the Trinity, novelly conceived, they say, in 324 AD; liberals bemoan the supposed rise of an all-male clergy and the freezing of doctrinal license. Rejection alone unites these disparate groups, for among the rejected groups one will hardly find even a hint of a unified doctrine.

The one group who can honestly embrace this history are the Gnostics. Those especially from more Neo-evangelical or Fundamentalist traditions bark up a dangerous tree when they cheer reports how the true, alienated Christian groups eschewed rituals and sacraments while pursuing more spontaneous, enthusiastic, and charismatic programs. The complete report reveals these outlier sects to be marked also by feminism, anti-Trinitarianism, Gnosticism, and a host of other beliefs.[5]

Let's consider the Euchites, also known as Messalians. They were a charismatic sect arising in the mid-fourth century, claiming an experiential baptism of the Holy Spirit. Enthusiastic, in the tradition of ancient mystery cults, they hoped for an indwelling of the Godhead through the Person of the Holy Spirit. They denied the Trinity and were libertine in their morals. They didn't take regular occupations, occupying themselves with constant prayer – the intensity of which they believed brought them into union with God. They denied the effectiveness of baptism and communion. Several orthodox synods banished the sect, and they retreated to Armenia.[6]

In Armenia another sect known as the Paulicians carried the Gnostic flame in the mid-seventh century. The Paulicians taught two Gods, one of the material world and one of the spiritual. They rejected the Old Testament, the sacraments, the ecclesiastical hierarchy, rituals, and the incarnation of Jesus Christ. Jesus Christ they considered an angel. Their places of meeting were called *prayer houses*, not churches. The Paulicians were embroiled in the politics and affairs of Byzantium in the last centuries of the first millennium, fueling the iconoclastic controversies marking this period. Constantine V (718-775) had settled a large group of them in Thrace, and from their center in the city of Philippolis, they continued as a thorn in the Church's side.

The Bulgarian Church also harbored Gnostic activity. Founded in the seventh century, the Bulgarian Church was predominantly anti-Rome, and when the Roman Church imposed disciplinary rules regarding the use of the Latin rite and scripture, Bulgarian monks rebelled. Attracted by the asceticism of the Paulicians, they united with them and adopted some of their doctrines. Persecution drove them west toward the area of Philippolis, where they were first called *Bogomiles*, a translation in Slavonic of the word *Messelian*. Busy trade routes connected Philippolis to the west, and this Gnostic cult found its way into Western Europe, where it resurfaced as Catharism.

These sects show their Gnosticism in their rejection of formal sacraments for direct contact with God. Also witnessed is Gnostic dualism, the belief in two gods, one for the spiritual world and one for the material. The rejection of the Old Testament, rituals, and the incarnation of Jesus Christ likewise show echoes of Gnosticism.

Church-Sanctioned Forms of Gnosticism

While these outlier sects and groups were running to the hills, Gnosticism coopted the Church in two areas: Neoplatonism and monasticism.

Neoplatonism

Neoplatonism, a form of Plato's philosophy contemporary with Gnosticism, fascinated several church fathers especially around the Egyptian city Alexandria. Theologian A. D. Nock had this third century philosophy in mind when he described Gnosticism as "Platonism run wild."[7] The Platonists first commandeered the term *Gnostic* ("one who knows").[8]

Two themes from Platonism help us understand the Gnostic cosmological framework, highlighting where Christianity's defenses were weakened for Gnostic intrusion. One theme is Plato's doctrine of Ideas articulated in *The Republic*, in his "Allegory of the Cave." The other is the cosmology found in his *Timaeus*.

In the "Allegory of the Cave" (*The Republic* 514a-520a) men are tied to seats at the nether end of a dark cave. They're facing the far wall with their backs to the cave's opening. Behind them a fire casts light on the wall. Between the fire and their backs, men carry statues of animals and other things back and forth, casting shadows of these statues on the wall. For those sitting there, this is the only truth they know, a shadow of a copy of what is real. Eventually someone descends and liberates a man. As the man ascends, he learns the truth, about the statues, about the fire, about the passageway. When he reaches the opening, the man cannot bear the light; his eyes must adjust. Soon he sees what were formerly mere shadows of statues, real animals. Eventually he glimpses the sun itself. He sees the light! If he returns to share his discoveries with the other prisoners, he's seen as a madman, doubted.

This allegory sets up the spirit/matter dualism characteristic of Platonism. Material things are illusions, mere shadows on the walls subject to constant change. By nature we are imprisoned to the illusions of this world. But by ascending the ladder of intellection we may attain a vision of the Truth. More to the point, we leave material things behind and see the spiritual truths behind them. It's the sort of intellection related to ecstatic seeing-the-light insight, or mysticism. These spiritual truths behind the changing material things patterned on them, Plato called *Ideas*.

Plato's dialogues (Socrates conversing with key characters) suited the process of intellection, the graduating ascent of the mind climaxing in a moment of intellection. The philosopher leads the discussion, a madman slowly leading students up the ladder of intellection as he discharges whatever patterns of false opinion impede the soul's ascent. This Socratic method, the key opening bonds of ignorance, works to free the soul during its laborious ascent. Soon the student gains ecstatic insight, the vision of pure Ideas, the essence of things.

Gnosticism carried over Platonism's view that matter is a deceptive shadow, but it took the idea one step further. For the Platonist, the mind could reach into the realm of Ideas and come back with articulated truths. The Gnostic put even these Ideas under Yaltabaoth's reign, and so he needed to ascend higher, into the pleroma, beyond what even the mind could know.

Plato's *Timaeus* (c. 360 B.C.) codified many of his themes in a semi-religious myth, for example deifying Eternal Being – the sun from "The Allegory of the Cave" – and dubbing the lesser beings *daemons*. Because of the absolute incommunicableness of matter and spirit, Plato introduced the *demiurge* (Gr. *builder*), a secondary divine being emanating from the Eternal Being tasked with creating material things based on patterns of Ideas in Eternal Being, like a master craftsman using an architect's blueprints.

Plato's *Timaeus* attracted Christian thinkers, who saw echoes of the Father and Son in the Eternal Being and demiurge. From it also came the fundamentals of Neoplatonism, articulated by Plotinus (204-270) in his *Enneads*, his student Porphyry (234-305), and Iamblichus (245-325), who developed theurgy as a magic intended to help the soul on its ascent out of multiplicity into the One.

The Neoplatonists called Plato's Eternal Being, in Greek, *to en*, meaning "the all" or "the one." The demiurge they called the *nous* (Mind) of the One. Here is their main departure from Gnosticism: where the Gnostics saw their demiurge, Yaltabaoth, as an abortive mistake, the Neoplatonic demiurge stands in friendly relation to the One. For the Neoplatonist, cosmic dissipation into individuality was part of the plan, not a mistake. Getting back to our cosmic bungee cord metaphor, Neoplatonists posited an eternal "emanation and return" of the One into many and back into the One. Neoplatonism still held to Plato's matter-spirit dualism, but unlike the Gnostics, matter was more *deceptive* than *evil* for the Neoplatonist. The demiurge as evil, not part of the plan; matter as evil, not something to be worked with; Gnosticism was a radical Platonism, a "Platonism run wild."

Neoplatonism taught something akin to the Gnostic ascent experience. The soul's journey begins when it realizes the multiplication of being is an illusion. As one looks inward, away from material things, he contemplates increasingly pure essences of things. He climbs the ladder of being until he glimpses the Light of pure Unity itself, the One.

This classically mystical program for salvation attracted Christian theologians such as Origen (185–254) and Clement (150-215), Alexandrians who worked Neoplatonic themes into their theology. Clement, called the "half-Gnostic," even preserved a Gnostic text for us.[9]

Pseudo-Dionysius the Areopagite stands out among others as the theologian most responsible for transmitting mysticism to the Middle Ages. Dionysius lived and wrote in the late fifth and early sixth centuries, taking the name of St. Paul's convert who notably worshiped "the unknown God." (Acts 17) Neoplatonism fueled Dionysius' mystical theology. To his writings the medieval mystical tradition owes its ideas on negative theology (where God is seen beyond all being and knowing), the nine hierarchies of angelic beings, the illuminating power of sacraments, and angelic mediation.[10] Later Hermeticist Marsilio Ficino approvingly called Dionysius' theology the summit of Platonism,[11] and through Dionysius' Neoplatonism he synthesized Christianity with Jewish Kabbalah.

Monasticism

Monasticism arose partly in reaction to the laxity settling in the Church around the third century. The Church was wrestling with whether she should be a "community of saints" or a "hospital for sinners." Deciding in favor of the latter – around this time confession, penitence, and absolution developed as "second baptisms" – she left behind members who sought the perfectionism implied in the creedal statement "*one* baptism [*i.e. not two!*] for the forgiveness of sins." To use a phrase echoing across the annals of Christian history from the perennially disgruntled, *they wanted something more.* They wanted self-sacrifice. They got it in the monastic movement.

In the third century, persecution by the Roman Empire still siphoned a great deal of Christian yearnings for sacrifice, for the "intense desire for self-surrender."[12] But when Christianity became legalized in 313, hordes of former pagans entered the Church. Becoming a Christian was too easy, and the monastic movement was off and running furiously.

Western monasticism per se began when a certain Castor from Apt (40 miles north of Marseilles) founded a monastery. He petitioned eastern monk John Cassian for advice on the rules for monks. Cassian responded with his *Institutes*, which became the foundation for *The Rule of St. Benedict*. John Cassian in turn looked back to Origen for inspiration as well as a solitary ascetic named Evagrius (345-399).[13] Evagrius's mystical theology reflected the Egyptian variety of Christian Neoplatonism,[14] in the monastic tradition of Desert Father St. Anthony.

Athanasius' *Life of Anthony* (c. 360) recounts Anthony's ascent experience giving us a taste of the Gnostic as well as Neoplatonic cosmological vision: "'Anthony, arise! Come forth and see.' And when he lifted up his eyes he beheld a vast and hideous shape, reaching to the clouds, and other winged beings which strove to rise. [Yaltabaoth and the archons] And as they rose the monster stretched forth his hands to catch them, and if he could not then they soared aloft, untroubled for the future. And Anthony knew that he looked upon the passage of souls to heaven.'"[15]

The monster Yaltabaoth guards the way, but through contemplation the mystic gains ever-advancing apprehension, lifting him from the corporeal to the incorporeal, into ultimate fellowship with the Holy Trinity, at which point prayer becomes a wordless, mental act. The process finds kinship with Plotnus' *Enneads*, which posits the ultimate fusion of the soul with the object of its contemplation: knower and known become one.[16]

Cassian, more comfortable with the Pelagian theological position which allowed an important role to the human will, set aside Augustine's doctrine of grace. He also laid down his monastic version of the "Apostate Church" thesis. When the apostles died, he suggested, believers got lukewarm; newcomers did not freely give up their property as did those in the primitive Church; yet, some Christians wanted to observe apostolic, communitarian practice, and so sprouted monasticism.

In the monastic movement we decipher Gnostic impulses in its tendencies toward negative theology and in the beyond-the-word impulse of its mystical wordless prayer. Doesn't the very institution of monasticism suggest elitism, a two-tiered division of the Church into the truly committed and those less so? In the end we wonder if monasticism became the formalized expression of the yearning for perfection and the communitarian ideal which, precisely because such things are impossible, led to the psychic conundrums not only breeding later more radical communalistic movements but also the Reformation itself. We will explore this thesis in greater detail.

Even Sophia sneaks in through one of monasticism's heroes, Boethius. This sixth century monk – one of Dante's twelve lights in heaven, who stands "at the crossroads of the Classical and Medieval worlds"[17] – sired the medieval scholastic tradition. His widely read *Consolation of Philosophy* introduced the woman *Philosophia*, Boethius' "physician" and "nurse in whose house I had been cared for since my youth." He describes her thus:

"She was of awe-inspiring appearance, her eyes burning and keen beyond the usual power of men. She was so full of years that I could hardly think of her as of my own generation, and yet she possessed a vivid colour and undiminished vigour. It was difficult to see her height, for sometimes she was of average human size, while at other times she seemed to touch the very sky with the top of her head, and when she lifted herself even higher, she pierced it and was lost to human sight."[18]

Gnostic imagery resounds. Lady Sophia reaches down from the Unknowable One, guiding us in desperate moments. True, here she is still *Philo-Sophia*, the "loved wisdom," a friendly sort of *philos* love, like receiving a beloved old-time friend. Sophia comes in her full, Gnostic glory, however, as *Ero-Sophia*, the erotically-adored Wisdom, in the Islamic mystical tradition known as Sufism and in the Cathar movement.

Sufis, Cathars, and Troubadours: the Cult of Eros

In Gnosticism, eros is a longing for reunion with Monad. Sophia, representing Monad, is the object of eros, the Lady beckoning us to a love truer than anything human physicality could provide. Some Gnostic sects ritualized the erotic yearning through a Sophia stand-in and embraced sexual license. Other sects cherished abstinence, disavowing marriage.

These are classic "cosmic bungee cord" understandings of love. Love draws the Gnostic out of this world and its mundane arrangements like marriage. Sex is a means to transcendence.

In the Middle Ages these ideas manifested in three movements: Sufism, Catharism, and the Troubadour movement. Understanding their role in Gnostic history lays the foundation for the nineteenth century Romantic period, which obviously had related themes.

In upcoming chapters we'll draw out certain themes and relate them to specific topics – the relationship between eros and both magic and music. Here we introduce them as historical movements.

Sufis

Sufis were Islamic Gnostics. They arrived at their Gnosticism through a mystical tradition current in Persian Baghdad, which had in turn received the esoteric tradition from a body of exiled Syrian monks. These were the monks who translated the works of Aristotle into Arabic between 750-900.[19] Through them Aristotelianism eventually found its way through Spain back into the West. Their Aristotle had a Neoplatonic flavor, cluing us not only to Sufism's roots, but also to the nature of the Aristotelianism received by the later scholastic movement.

Sufism reflects several Gnostic themes. It is, as described by Sufi master Ibn El-Jalali, "truth beyond form."[20] Sufi knowledge was yet another Gnostic claim to transcend arguments, dogmas, or scholastic discourse, a secret knowledge not governed by the "tyranny of words."[21] Answers aren't given from the outside through external channels. Rather, recalling the role of the magician, Idries Shah describes how the "Sufi . . . must make [secrets] develop within the disciple." He continues, "Sufism is something which happens to a person, not something which is given to him. . . . Rumi calls upon the scholastic, the theologian, and the follower of the false teacher: 'When will you cease to worship and to love the pitcher? When will you begin to look for the water?' Externals are the things which people usually judge by. 'Know the difference between the color of the wine and the color of the glass.'"[22]

Formalized studies analyzing the external world cannot convey truth, so the Sufi employs non-rational devices like jokes, stories, poetry, music, and dancing. Through these techniques the master prods the seeker to find truth within. Their famous dancing technique, the "whirling dervish," is said to bring them "into affinity with the mystical current."[23] Their great storytelling and poetry (like *1001 Arabian Nights*) not only helped midwife Western literature, but fit their esoteric purposes: their romances were Gnostic allegories.

Using a line of reasoning elusive to anyone not homed in on the way Gnostics think, Idries Shah proposes, "Among those directly influenced by Sufism we can name at random Raymond Lully, Goethe, President de Gaulle, and Dag Hammerskjold of the United Nations."[24]

He adds: "Scholasticism and mysticism are opposed to one another. But the Sufis gave rise to, among others, a school of each. Were these Moslem schools? No, they were Christian, associated with the Augustinians and St. John of the Cross, as Professor Palacios and others have established. From being an Oriental mystic, the Sufi now appears as the antecessor of Catholic mystics and philosophers. Let us add a few more facts. The coffee which we drink was traditionally first used by Sufis, to heighten awareness. We wear their clothes (shirt, belt, trousers); we listen to their music (Andalusian, measured music, love songs); dance their dances (waltz, Morris dancing); read their stories (Dante, Robinson Crusoe, Chaucer, William Tell); employ their esoteric phrases ('moment of truth,' 'human spirits,' 'ideal man'); and play their games (cards). We even belong to derivations of their societies, such as Freemasonry, and certain chivalric orders."[25]

Shah finally lists St. Francis of Assisi, Albert the Great (teacher of Thomas Aquinas), and even William Shakespeare (whom he claims was a sheik: Sheik Spear) as remarkable Sufis.

When I first read these words, I was incredulous. Albert the Great, Shakespeare, and Dante were Sufis? Coffee was a Sufi drink? How could any credentialed scholar make such claims? But, quite frankly, the type of scholarship gaining credentials is limited in the Gnostic world. Gnostics, Sufis, and the like laugh at book-learning scholarship, so consumed as it is with categorizing and delineating. Gnosticism bursts labels. It glories in surreal, undefined meaning.

Anyone could be a Sufi because, as Shah says,"Sufism is an adventure, a goal of human perfection attained by reviewing and awakening within humanity a higher organ of fulfillment, completion, [and] destiny. . . . The Sufi does not need the mosque, the Arabic language, litanies, books of philosophy, even social stability. The relationship with humanity is evolutionary and adaptive."[26]

Catharism

While Sufism transmitted Gnostic spirituality from Baghdad to

Spain south of the Mediterranean, Christian Gnosticism worked its way from Armenia and Bulgaria to southern France in the north. Trading networks extending from eastern Europe to the west helped Europe's southern markets to thrive, and among the goods and ideas arriving in southern France and northern Italy lurked the dualistic Gnostic teaching known as Catharism (or Albigensianism).

Gnosticism flourishes in cosmopolitan areas where a leisure class has time to dabble in boutique spiritualities. Southern France and northern Italy fit this description. In particular, the Languedoc province in southern France became ripe for alternative spiritualities. Its mental climate was "hostile to the sacred," possessed as it was of an "ironic indifference" about ultimate truths.[27] Europe's discovery of the Self is said to have begun here.[28] The thriving cloth and leather trade increased the wealth of the area, and with the increase of wealth came sophistication and gentility especially among the nobility.

Languedoc – an area where Jewish communities thrived and Spain, just to its south, remained under Muslim control – bred a tolerant people. The marriage laws remained liberal despite the growing control of the Church in other European areas over marriage custom and laws. Here, Catharism grew rapidly, claiming millions of adherents.[29]

Catharism differed somewhat from its ancient Gnostic forbears. Their adherents didn't author new revelations set beside the canonical Scriptures: gone were the elaborate mythologies. Their gnosis occurred through a ritual known as the *consolamentum*, a baptism of the Holy Spirit through the laying on of hands, a ritual inherited from the Bogomils similar to the Messalian practice discussed earlier.[30]

Catharism fully embraced Gnostic dualism based on Jesus' teaching that "A good tree cannot bear bad fruit, nor can a bad tree bear good fruit." (Matthew 7: 18) For the Cathar, good and evil do not come from the same God. The good God created spiritual, invisible, eternal things. Another being created material, visible, corruptible things. That other being was either a lesser god coeternal with the true God, or the fallen creature of the true God named Satan.

The Cathars held the docetic view of both Jesus and Mary: Christ only *seemed* to be human, and Mary was an angel from heaven who only *seemed* to be human.

This divine status given to Mary originated from a general Mariolotry going back to antiquity. It's a Gnostic idea. Mary, so the sentiment went, represented the Divine Feminine, Sophia. She's also related to the Holy Spirit, the Person of the Trinity most often expressed in feminine terms. Montanism, an ancient charismatic sect, set Mary and Christ up as gods besides the one God. The Montanist prophetess Priscilla claimed Christ came to her in female form, blurring together Christ, Mary, and the Holy Spirit. The Church always had to temper an undercurrent of Mary worship from boiling over. The *Koran* even references the angelic position given Mary by Coptic Gnostics, lumping her with Christ as personages not to be deified.[31]

Like the Gnostics, the Cathars were elitists. They had two levels of involvement: the believers (*credentes*) and the "good Christians" (impugned by their opponents as *perfecti*, "the perfect ones").[32] Their *consolamentum* ritual turned a believer into a good Christian. It was a "supplement to [baptism] which did not suffice for your salvation."[33] In the *consolamentum* the human soul reunited with its heavenly, angelic counterpart, or the Holy Spirit. The "Word of illumination" came upon him. But before this ascent experience, the initiate underwent a forty day fast (the *endura*), renounced the material world, sexual relations, and any food product resulting from sexual relations (i.e. meat and dairy products). After committing to these criteria, the candidate received the transforming grace of the *consolamentum*.[34]

Catharism flourished for awhile until the Church crushed it in the Albigensian Crusade (1209–1229), beginning serious use of the Inquisition. If Catharism would continue, it would have to go underground. Some suggest that this is exactly what happened, that Catharism went underground but reemerged allegorically through the tropes and love songs of the troubadours.

Troubadours

Those minstrels of love poetry, the troubadours, set Western literature on a new course. They were the first to move away from the classical tradition of the Latin tongue and pen literature in the *romance* languages (from *Roman*) of French, Portuguese, and Italian.

Arabist scholar Maria Rosa Menocal contends the troubadour movement continued the tradition of Sufi love poetry. Sufi romances entered Europe, she argues, through translation centers in Spain and in Italy, where Arabists like Holy Roman Emperor Frederick II (1194-1250) established the University of Bologna as a center of Arabist activity. Evidence of Arab-love even lurks in the writings of the conservative Dante, who allowed a position for Muslim philosopher Averroes in

Limbo. (He still put Mohammed in hell.) Or again, the mystic Bonaventure translated Mohammed's *The Book of the Ladder*, an account of Mohammed's ascent into heaven. Influences from Arab culture clearly left an imprint on the twelfth century Western psyche.[35]

One can imagine Cathars recognizing kindred spirits in Sufism. One can also image them noting how Sufis slyly plant esoteric teaching in their love stories. It's natural to wonder, as many have, whether the troubadour movement was sublimated Catharism, a Gnostic spirituality allegorized in romantic poesy. Themes of love, passion, and death mark troubadour poetry. The idea is, our entrapment in flesh parallels our entrapment in earthly institutions like marriage. Calling us from above, from a source transcending this world's forms, is eros. Eros calls us home, to Monad. Sophia appears through the Lady, the object of troubadour adoration, and beckons. Poetry and the romantic song work mystical union with her. They are hymns he offers to Sophia through the pretense of a real, superior woman, for instance, the lady of a manor.

True for both the Cathar and the troubadour, the worst thing would be a consummated union with the lady, thus the vow of chastity. Like other mystical traditions, the retention of sperm drives the mystical program as the lover suffers, always pining away for a union he cannot have until death, allegorized in the unattainableness of the real woman he forbids himself from having. Such longing is divine allegory: "This pain of longing is the most direct road back to God. . . . Within the heart the Beloved speaks directly to the lover, leading us through the fire of our own transformation."[36] Fleshly union would ground the lover's transcendent love, demanding a more mundane love if, God forbid, a child resulted. It would anchor the soul to the earth, limit his ascent.

The status of Beatrice in Dante's imagination fits troubadour sentiments exactly. First beheld at the tender age of nine, the real flesh and blood Beatrice eventually became an ideal, Dante's Sophia guiding him through the spheres of *Paradiso*. Though they never came together – troubadour love can never be consummated! – Dante wrote of Beatrice, "The moment I saw her I say in all truth that the vital spirit, which dwells in the inmost depths of the heart, began to tremble so violently that I felt the vibration alarmingly in all my pulses, even the weakest of them. As it trembled, it uttered these words: Ecce deus fortior me, qui veniens dominabitur mihi ['Behold, a god more powerful than I, who comes to rule over me']."[37]

Philosophically, Catharism and the troubadour movement both

idealized the woman and the virtue of chastity. Both had the kiss of initiation. In practice there are striking similarities as well. Both the troubadours and the Cathar Pure, like the Messalians above, were wanderers, wandering from castle to castle in pairs. Troubadour poetry borrowed from the Cathar liturgy. Both deplored marriage as a stifling imposition of convention by the corrupt Roman Church, the Cathars even calling it "the oath of fornication."[38] Many of the castles frequented by the troubadours also housed adherents of the Cathar heresy.

From Sufism, Catharism, and the Troubadour movement the Western World inherited its ideas on feelings and emotions, particularly the idea that they are a truer insight into truth than rationality or formal tradition. The Romantic period of the nineteenth century, called *romantic* for reasons which now should be clear, resurrected interest in the troubadour movement. This period gave us the passionate music of Beethoven, the love operas of Wagner, the Transcendental movement, the Gnostic poetry of William Blake, and the nationalistic movements in politics. Uniting all these phenomena is the idea of passionate love for something transcending status quo forms of reality – i.e. mundane life – and the willingness to suffer passionately for that love.

Radical Politics: The Pursuit of the Millennium

Around the time the troubadours and Cathars were working with eros, a monk believed himself to have been visited by the Holy Spirit in the form of, not surprisingly, a woman.[39] His name was Joachim of Fiore (c. 1132 – 1202).

A Cistercian monk, mystic, and student of the book of Revelation, Joachim became the first of many to divide history into three eras corresponding to the Holy Trinity. He is the original New Age prophet, believing the last Age of the Spirit to be the coming millennium promised in the book of Revelation. During this final age, no Church would be necessary. People would have immediate contact with God.

Each age had its dominant figure. Abraham defined the first age; Jesus, the second; and Joachim identified a *dux e Babylone* (leader out of Babylon) for the third age whose advent, he believed, arrived in 1260. Preceding these figures of the past were forerunning precursors like John the Baptist. We can see where this is going: Joachim claimed to be the anointed precursor to the coming *dux e Babylone* of the Third Age.[40]

Political philosopher Eric Voegelin identifies Joachim as the father of all modern totalitarian movements. He argues Joachim's program is ultimately Gnostic, laying down the historical precedents for modern radical politics, all rooted in the millenarian understanding of history taught by Joachim.[41]

Radical, from the Latin for *root*, literally means "to uproot." Current society – its culture, its political arrangements, its socioeconomic classes, even its language – must be wholly uprooted, says the radical, and replaced by a new and perfect age. There can be no compromise or political accommodation of diverse interests united loosely in a federation. Rather, the millenarian mind, like the Gnostic, is set in light/dark contrasts. Everything leading up to its moment is systemic darkness and oppression; everything it promises to inaugurate is lightness and perfection. Joachim's millenarian doctrines laid the foundation for wholesale radicalism rooted in a mind formatted in light/dark contrasts.

A series of radical cult leaders after Joachim gained followings throughout the Middle Ages. Usually their followers consisted of poorer urban dwellers awaiting a coming new age where class divisions would cease and all property would be shared as in days of the apostles. Such groups believed Joachim's "Age of the Spirit" had arrived and God had endowed his special Elect with unmediated spiritual contact. They and their charismatic leaders were God's hand in history working his divine will. Of course they rejected the Church and its ministry precisely because of its claims to mediate between God and man.

True, the Church's ministers often *were* rank political opportunists who leveraged their positions for ill-gotten gains. Yet, history allows for two kinds of reformation, radical or conservative. The Lutheran Reformation and the American Revolution are examples of conservative reactions. Both respected received tradition and sought to fix or enhance it.

Not so the millenarians. Only radical change could do justice to the coming new millennial age. Thomas Müntzer, Andreas Karlstadt, the Zwickau prophets, and Anabaptist groups constituted the Radical Reformation which represented this other response to the corruption in the Church. Their radicalism played out in everything from the Peasant's Rebellion led by Müntzer to the separatist tendencies of the Anabaptist groups. Such groups were iconoclastic, rejecting everything the institutional Church represented: its ministerial order, its book-learning, its sacraments, and its rituals. They were charismatic and informal in worship because earthly forms could not house the immediate contact with God they claimed. Like the Gnostics these groups were also given over to personality cults, as charismatic leaders emerged and claimed the divine status of *leader*.

Normon Cohn's *The Pursuit of the Millennium* (1970) recounts the radical movements in the Middle Ages preceding the Radical Reformation. He takes them back to the source, to Joachim, showing how his millenarian doctrines laid the foundation for later communitarian revolutions.

More to the point is why this is so. Millenarianism assigns the same moral perfectionism attained by the believer to society as a whole. Personal perfectionism becomes a political program. Where traditional original sin doctrines help the more conservative Christian bodies adapt to various corrupt political systems – society is not any more perfectible than any human is – the millenarian denies original sin, believes in the possibilities for holiness, and translates these possibilities into social movement. Sacraments and their liturgical cradle, being so much ritualistic hypocrisy, fall short of the call for internal purity. Consequently radical politics has always been a good fit with anti-ritualistic permutations of Christianity.

The Reformation

If Martin Luther (1483-1546) represented a more conservative approach to received tradition, it's because he believed novelties set the Church off course. He didn't care to have another moral reformation cleaning up the greed and sexual immorality in the monasteries. Perfectionism wasn't his aim. He had more profound concerns questioning the very foundations of the monastic movement.

A monk himself, Luther's soul became the battleground for the psychic energies demanding monasticism in the first place. He *wanted something more*. He sought perfection. His mind was formatted in the light/dark contrast marking every perfectionist.

Confronting these psychic factors, he eventually became alert to the revolutionary, ultimately Neoplatonic, postures monasticism introduced into the Church's theology. Eventually he curtly concluded, "It would have been better for the church if [the ancient Neoplatonist philosopher] Porphyrus with his universals had not been born for the use of theologians."[42]

What exactly were these postures monasticism shared with Neoplatonism? We focus on three here.

First was the idea that physical properties and the flesh are accidental, incidental, deceptive, or even evil, at least something to be mortified in order to experience mystical ascent. The strange flagellant movement of the Middle Ages, in which adherents whipped their own flesh as part of their personal piety, took anti-flesh tendencies in monasticism to the extreme.

But it also led to more acceptable forms of asceticism, like celibacy and abstinence from foods. St. Paul had Gnosticism in mind when he warned the young pastor Timothy, "Now the Spirit expressly says that in latter times some will depart from the faith, giving heed to deceiving spirits and doctrines of demons . . . forbidding to marry, and commanding to abstain from foods which God created to be received with thanksgiving by those who believe and know the truth. For every creature of God is good." (I Timothy 4: 1-4)

That last statement clues us in on Paul's meaning: *Gnostics* believed the creation was *not* good, and his position is clear. A program of asceticism regularly eschewing the gifts of the created order – marriage and foods – cannot be the lynchpin of the life of faith. The trend toward celibacy in the Church attests to a revolutionary, certainly anti-Hebraic, posture settling in the Church, a movement feeding from the same anti-flesh ideas from which both Neoplatonism and Gnosticism fed.

Second, the above-proposed question whether the Church was a hospital of sinners or a community of saints only makes sense in a Neoplatonic context, which allows for the possibility of an elite corps of perfected individuals set against the regularly-sinning, run-of-the-mill Christians. For those who believed themselves elite, Neoplatonism best accommodated the stark light/dark formatting of their psyches. The quest for God could only be satisfied in radical action: joining a monastery, selling all one's possessions, going on a crusade, sitting on a column for thirty-nine years, flagellating oneself, imposing upon oneself whatever purgatorial program one feels will do the trick.

Meanwhile, over and over again the ideal clashes with reality. Sexual immorality and concubinage among medieval clergy and monks, and the constant need to cleanse monasteries of greed and heresy, proved St. Paul's more reality-based position regarding asceticism to be correct. (Cf. I Corinthians 7; Colossians 2: 20-23; etc.) The quest for perfection is ultimately a utopian project leading to a dreary cycle of moral reformations and revivals. The range between imperfection and perfection has no clear point at which one can say "I'm there!" There's always something more. *Have you really given up everything? Do you really love everyone with Christ's love?* If the Church truly is a community of saints understood in terms of perfect personal sanctification, heaven would be empty.

Hence the psychic need for Purgatory, a remedy in the next life for what cannot be attained in this life. C.S. Lewis remarked, "Our souls demand Purgatory, don't they?"[43] Well yes, of course they do, else Plato, whoever launched the Orphic Mysteries, and the Pythagoreans wouldn't have invented it. These sublime observers of the soul's deep mysteries knew and understood its needs. The Church – the Western Church at any rate – accepted their observations and accommodated their ideas on Purgatory.

Luther also confronted these psychic factors but concluded the monastic program abandoned the Gospel. Perhaps because his soul was formatted in such stark light/dark contrasts, his embrace of radical action didn't rise to the occasion of the soul's truly deep darkness. As he penned in one of his hymns, "Death brooded darkly o'er me. Sin was my torment night and day; In sin my mother bore me. But daily deeper still I fell; My life became a living hell, So firmly sin possessed me."[44]

Luther's poetry, almost pathological to modern ears, fit the times. If in previous eras the inner life was ignored, by Luther's day it had come roaring back, evidenced by the host of Gnostic and mystical movements peppering his period. Luther encountered it as well but came to the seminal conclusion: *the inner life is a dead end.*

Third, Luther's critique on Neoplatonist influence affected his understanding of which canonical authorities would determine Christian doctrine. The quick gloss of the issue is, Luther and the Protestants were for *Sola Scriptura*, but the Roman Catholics were for Scripture and Tradition. This is unfortunate and ridiculous. Lutheran doctrine appeals amply to the historic canons of the Church, the ecumenical creeds, and Church Fathers. The Lutherans embraced the historic liturgy with slight modifications. Luther's real reformation was his rejection of Neoplatonic mysticism as a component in Scriptural exegesis and doctrinal formulation.

C. S. Lewis spoke of the psychic need for Purgatory: *we demand it, don't we?* As far as an observation about human psychology goes, he's probably correct. The ancient world's best minds came to his conclusion as well.

The next question is, do the psychic speculations of humanity's best minds determine orthodox Christian doctrine? If the answer is *yes,* it's because they have access to divine truth *psychically*. Traditional Judeo-

Christian teaching permits access to divine truth only to a specific body of prophets and apostles who received revelations not through inner psychic means, but through clear, external, angelic manifestations of God's messengers. Their writings became the canon.

Another strain of Judeo-Christian thought, through the ministrations of Neoplatonism, allowed for certain spiritual adepts to ascend into the mind of God and procure new revelations internally. Wasn't this the Pentecostal promise? "Your young men shall see visions, Your old men shall dream dreams." (Acts 2: 17)

The Alexandrian "half Gnostics," Clement and Origin, took this position, using the above-quoted passage to justify a school of interpretation known as the allegorical method. (Origen, *De Principiis*, ch. 7)[45] Allegory grants the "spiritual" exegete a more "spiritual" meaning of the text than what the text plainly says. The plain meaning, like the elements of creation or the elements of language, is a lower, corporeal meaning, something to be transcended. Rather a higher meaning sort of hovers fuzzily above the actual words: *Don't you know that the deeper meaning of Moses crossing the Red Sea was his abandonment of ignorance? Of course you don't, because you're too fleshly.* Far better suited to arrive at the true transcendent meaning of the text were the spiritually-attuned saints, the sum of whom became subsumed in the numinous expression, *the Fathers* or *Holy Tradition.*

Luther rejected the allegorical method. The Church shouldn't receive some ancient father's interpretations as sacred just because he, the pious mystic, could claim a more spiritual interpretation than what the text actually says.[46]

But something deeper is going on. Long ago Irenaeus saw how the Gnostics "ascribe whatever they recognize themselves as experiencing the divine Logos!"[47] Such is the natural solipsism of every Gnostic: *If I feel it, it must be a universal truth whose source is the divine, monadic truth.* If the psyche truly can tap into transcendent truths – because according to Neoplatonism the soul is capable of doing so – its insights would be glimpses of what Luther called the "uncreated [as opposed to incarnate] Word,"[48] the supra-incarnate Christ (the Logos), the Neoplatonic Nous (or Mind), the animating Spirit flowing through all being. Those elite, psychically-attuned mystics can focus their spiritual antennae and claim to hear the voice, if garbled, of Christ himself. When they return from their mystical heights back into mundane flesh to let us plebs in on their insights, surely they have earned the title of *Angelic Teacher.*

Didn't this happen to St. Paul when he got caught up in the Third Heaven? Is this not the very nature of inspiration itself? And shouldn't we expect similar revelations today?

Perhaps so. The Pentecostal passage quoted above has inspired many a charismatic movement. Thomas Aquinas is said to have had an ascent experience during mass, an experience of a supra-sacramental Christ. He stopped writing and considered everything he had written in the past to be straw. Why write when the mystical experience reveals truth to be a beyond-words beatific vision?

Yet, St. Paul quite capably returned from his experience and wrote a significant part of the Scriptural canon; as did Moses, Isaiah, and Ezekiel; or Peter, James, and John after the transfiguration of Christ. True, Paul referred to the "inexpressible words" (II Corinthians 12: 4) he heard, but the point is they still were words. They were words too sacred to speak. This is in sharp contrast to St. John of the Cross's transcending-all-knowledge visions which rendered "all that he knew before" to be "worthless" because "his knowledge so soars that he is left in unknowing."[49] Definitely the canonical authors believed their words to be something more than "straw," rather the very form of truth itself, and Paul referred to "all that he knew before" in his Scriptural training as a Pharisee.

Again, we're talking about a fundamental revolution. Here the revolution is in how knowledge is revealed, from a more Hebraic tradition of angelomorphic revelation to the Neoplatonic ascent into wordless bliss. The latter smacks of Gnostic beyond-the-Logos impulses.

At heart an Old Testament scholar, Luther championed a more Hebraic, less Neoplatonic, approach to biblical interpretation suggesting his awakened recognition of Gnostic influence on the tradition of biblical interpretation. To this day, between the Roman Catholic and Reformation parties, the former has for about a millennium been far more willing to dabble in esoteric spiritualities and Gnostic trends, evidenced, among other things, by their wide divergence from the more conservative Eastern Orthodox Church. Mariolotry, Purgatory, papal universalism – all ideas setting them apart from the East – are ultimately rooted in Gnostic themes.

As far as practical effects of the Reformation, perhaps the most radical was the end of the two-tiered salvation program – monks and laymen. For over a thousand years Christianity maintained the symbiotic relation between the two in its developing doctrines: the latter prayed and did good works for the former and the former gave alms to the latter. But things are pushed to ridiculous extremes when the former need merely to go through the motions of faith without even understanding its basic forms, while the latter can accrue such an overabundance of holiness that their surplus can be sold in the form of indulgences. True, we get St. Peter's Basilica out of the bargain, but Christians should be forgiven if they are a bit skeptical.

What Luther nailed (*eh hem*) was that there's gold in that there guilt, in that space between the demands of perfectionism and the reality of human capabilities. It's the wizard's spell of do-gooders of all ages: show the perfectionist vision to the subject *vis a vis* his own lackluster ability to attain it, inducing a swirling maelstrom of guilt and despair – a sense of pending apocalypse resulting from the subject's inadequacies – and then in the midst of his turmoil propose how, for the small price of a cup of coffee a day, he can take care of the problem.

Luther's insights explain why the "Bridges to Nowhere" of all ages – from the Pyramids to St. Peter's Basilica, from the Hoover Dam to the disastrous programs of Johnson's war on poverty – have been tolerated by subjects whose hard-earned cash has been stolen to build them at threat of something worse than gunpoint: the threat of damnation. People do not part with their cash to get nothing in return. But *nothing* looks quite lovely when coupled with the promise of salvation from pending apocalypse or the appeasement of guilt. Of course, the fantasy only works so long as the salesman is believed. And the salesman is believed most certainly when he is seen as a messenger from God. Swipe out this pretense and the salesman loses his magical claim on the subject's soul and wallet.

Luther did precisely this number on John Tetzel, the papal legate sent to sell indulgences (a propagandist and marketer if ever there was one), and the Reformation was off and running. Against Tetzel's magic Luther applied traditional orthodox doctrine to perennial psychological questions left confusingly answered, and the rest is history. The Reformation began.

In later years the Lutherans turned their energies to the Radical Reformers, to men like Thomas Müntzer (1489-1525), Andreas Karlstadt (1486-1541), and Ulrich Zwingli (1484-1531). The Radical Reformation misapplied Reformation teachings and took a path recognized in the earlier millenarians. They rejected ritualism, ministerial order, and the use of sacraments. They were enthusiasts and embraced a mystical theology more in the tradition of late medieval mysticism (as reflected in John Tauler and the so-called *German Theology*) than the original Lutherans. Accordingly, "man's inner nature again [attained] intrinsic value as the locus of revelation," and people had a renewed interest in "union with God."[50] The Lutherans described how such enthusiasts "sit in a dark corner doing and saying nothing, but only waiting for illumination."[51]

This wing of the Reformation, in addition to laying the foundation for later Lutheran spiritualist Johann Arndt and through him the Pietists,[52] fostered the more Bohemian Anabaptist movement. The Anabaptists, though typically pacifist and seclusive, were culturally iconoclastic, rejecting involvement in civil society and harboring dreams of communalistic communities in the millenarian tradition. Occasionally their millenarianism erupted in bloody political movement.

In terms of the psychic terrain we've been mapping, the Lutherans were simply dealing with another permutation of monasticism in the Radical Reformation. Monasticism is to Roman Catholicism what revivalism has become to the Evangelical heirs of the Radical Reformation. Both provide an outlet for those who seek "something more" from the Christian faith.

Just as the medieval monastic movements needed constant reformation, so has Evangelicalism ever needed new revivals and new movements. The stumbling block in both cases is humanity, the problem original sin poses to it, the chasm between the reality of human imperfection and the idealistic belief in human perfectibility.

Modernity's Labor Pangs: Before the Scientific Revolution

Hermeticism scholar Ioan Couliano (1950 -1991) has a different take on the Reformation, defending the Neoplatonic developments in the Church not from a Roman Catholic perspective, but from the perspective of Hermeticism. He believed a "breath of liberal air had been circulating in the Renaissance Church" because of Hermeticism, and "[f]ar from appearing as a liberal movement, the Reformation represented, on the contrary, a radical-conservative movement within the bosom of the Church. [The Reformation] aimed to reestablish in the world a Christian order it believed the Catholic Church . . . was unable to maintain."[53]

Through Hermeticism, Gnosticism eventually synthesized with Lutheran doctrine, spawning the Pietistic movement of the seventeenth century. Paracelsus (1493-1540) – a Renaissance doctor, alchemist, general occultist, and proponent of Hermeticism – influenced the thought of

Johann Arndt (1555-1621), the Lutheran theologian whose widely disseminated book *True Christianity* inspired Pietist founder Philipp Jakob Spener (1635-1705). Pietist Heinrich Müller (1631-1675), revealed the Gnostic tendencies of the Pietistic movement when he called the font, pulpit, confessional, and altar "the four dumb idols of the Lutheran Church" which denied the "inner power of Christianity."[54]

The Pietists were not unlike the Anabaptists, rejecting ministerial order and book-learning for feelings of the heart, lay-directed small groups, and individualism in spirituality. Paracelsus' words, "Let us depart from all ceremonies, conjurations, consecrations, etc., and all similar delusions, and put our heart, will and confidence solely upon the true rock,"[55] certainly rang true with Arndt, who wrote, "Our worship in the New Testament is no longer external in figural ceremonies, statutes, and obligations, but rather inward in spirit and truth, that is, in faith in Christ."[56]

Likewise was it with the Pietist movement that the flame of millenarian utopianism continued to flicker. Again, perfection of society follows the perfection possible through *true Christianity*. Lutheran theologian Johann Valentin Andreae (1586-1654) penned a utopian novel, *Christianopolis* (1619), which envisioned a "Christian social order" founded on "platonic-communist" principles.[57] When the Thirty Years War demonstrated the futility of religious dogmatism, it's effect was similar to that of World War II on the Western conscience: people were ready for something paying less attention to dogma, and putting more emphasis on the inner life.

The Pietists' fingerprints can be seen in later German Romantic philosophers Immanuel Kant, Arthur Schopenhauer, and G. W. F. Hegel, all of whom we will meet again.

But what of Paracelsus' Hermeticism?

Hermeticism derived the core of its teachings from the writings of the "thrice-great Hermes," or Hermes Trismegistus. He took his place among the notable pagans of the so-called *prisca theologia*, who included Zoroaster, Orpheus, Pythagorus, and Socrates. He is, according to an Orphic hymn, the "Good Shepherd, priest and sage, celestial messenger of a thousand skills."[58] The Hermetic work *Asclepius* had some readership in the early Middle Ages, and early advocate of the scientific method Roger Bacon (1214–1294) called Hermes, "the Father of Philosophers."[59]

When Renaissance patron Cosimo de Medici discovered writings attributed to him, the *Hermetica*, he ordered his pet scholar Marsilio

Ficino to set aside his projects on Plato (whose works were recently discovered) to translate the *Hermetica* instead. The *Hermetica*, so it was thought, anteceded and therefore superceded even Plato. Medieval scholars dated the *Hermetica* to about 1000 B.C., some claiming it could be dated back to Noah. When classical scholar Isaac Casaubon (1559-1614) discovered the true milieu of the *Hermetica* to be second or third century Alexandria, its pretense to distant antiquity ended and so did its influence.[60]

But a century or so before, Ficino completed his translation, and the first of sixteen editions from 1471 to the end of the 1500s began a wide diffusion of the *Hermetica* throughout Europe. Hermeticism would dominate the philosophical landscape of the fifteenth and sixteenth centuries.

The story of Hermeticism in the Renaissance is the story of magic and astrology ultimately based on Neoplatonic and astrological presuppositions. Ficino's medical treatise *De vita libri tres* (1489) propounded a cosmos comprised of three worlds: the Intellect of the World, the Spirit (or Soul) of the World, and the Body of the World.[61] Translating forward Plato's breach between Eternal Being and the material world, he too divined an unbridgeable chasm separating the Intellect of the World and the Body of the World. The Spirit of the World mediated between them, much like Plato's demiurge. The Spirit of the World was how the Platonic Ideas (from Eternal Being) gave life and spirit to the World Bodies. It was a fine and subtle substance, a luminous veil, descending into the physical bodies of the material world.

The stars were also composed of this same substance, explaining why magic and astrology were useful, for the spirit in each material thing was subject to stellar influences. In the human body as well, every part had a correspondence in the Spirit of the World subject to manipulation by those who understood its stellar properties. If degeneracy maligned one part of the body, the magician could provide healing by manipulating things in the Spirit of the World. This manipulation happened through various talismans and spells.

More to the point, astral magic is a program of escape from material fortune and destiny. If certain stellar influences fated one's personality to be sanguine, choleric, melancholic, or phlegmatic, astral magic introduced the possibility of escape from these personality ruts.

The fifteenth through the seventeenth centuries show a popular acceptance of the occult which even Shakespeare's plays reflect. But as we saw, when scholars discovered the true dating of the *Hermetica*, Hermeticism lost its luster. Robert Fludd (1574 - 1637), one of the last proponents of the *Hermetica*, became the object of a scathing attack by Marin Mersenne (1588 – 1648) in a commentary on the book of Genesis, in which he dismantled magic and laid the philosophical groundwork for his friend Descartes to usher in the Scientific Revolution.[62]

Science would seem to be a sort of anti-gnosis, or anti-Hermeticism. It focuses on the observable details of the physical world, not on inner knowledge. Accordingly some would see in science a triumph over Gnosticism's mysticism and magical inclinations.

Renaissance scholar Francis A. Yates disagrees, claiming Hermetical and Gnostic adjustments in cosmological understanding actually laid down the foundation for the scientific revolution. The real revolution, she argues, began with a *change of will* effected by the discovery of the *Hermetica*, a reoriented posture toward nature preparing the way for the scientific revolution. It was not with science, after all, but with Hermeticism that man became, in Yates' words, "no longer only the pious spectator of God's wonders in the universe, and the worshiper of God himself above the creation, but Man the operator, Man who seeks to draw power from the divine and natural order."[63]

Ancient and medieval thinkers saw nature as an emanation and reflection of God's good order, something to be contemplated for the good of the soul. Hermeticism anticipated the scientific revolution with its view that nature should not be *passively* contemplated but *actively* mastered. And more interesting, and more to the heart of the Hermeticist, *human* nature could be mastered. This shift in perspective began not with the scientific revolution, but with the Hermetic and Neoplatonic philosophers of the Italian Renaissance.

Like the proponents of science, the magicians looked at nature as manipulable, something to be controlled for the good of humanity. What science calls gravity Hermeticism calls a demon, but if both act with perfect consistency, what's really the difference? The point is not the mysterious source of these daemonic forces and laws of nature; the point is they can be manipulated for the good sake of humanity.

Both science and magic require a philosophy of the cosmos in which "all is One" and acts in perfect consistency manipulable through knowledge of math. In both science and magic an operator can only manipulate nature so long as A will lead to B on a consistent basis. If results are the only goal, what difference does it make what invisible forces cause those results? Modern science still subjects the vast majority of the universe to dark matter, of which they know very little, and they're still in the dark about gravity's properties.

Both the magicians and the scientists saw math as the key to understanding the universe. Here, the magicians were drawing off the mystical understanding of number inherited from the Neopythagoreans. The scientists rejected this course, but Yates writes, "Renaissance magic was turning toward number as a possible key to operations, and the subsequent history of man's achievements in applied science has shown that number is indeed a master-key, or one of the master-keys, to operations by which the forces of the cosmos are made to work in man's service."[64]

In other words, it's not so much *how* the math is used, as it is *that* it is used, wherein the "change of will" occurred at the end of the Middle Ages: from faith and reason to math.

Hermeticism fueled a change in posture toward the natural order, a change fueled by two specific doctrines Hermeticism shared with Gnosticism. First, they both held to the absolute separation between the material world and the world beyond (called the pleroma by the Gnostics or the Intellect of the World by Hermetic magicians). Second, they both believed the human soul was part of the divinity of the world beyond. If our true Selves are part of a divine world beyond, then they stand above the demiurge of this world. The human Self stands above this world's Maker, in a position to ape his creative acts and even take the reins of creative activity from him, to make the world a better place.

Man as magician is a theme emerging repeatedly in the history of esoteric doctrines, including ancient Gnosticism. Upon observation of a modern world full of electricity, machines, invisible waves, and mass information encoded in a chip, or as we see pollsters and marketers manipulate masses and project the future based on statistical analysis, or again as we engage our fellow human beings through the various electronic media – like living manifestations of the Hermetical Spirit of the World: humanity abstracted from materiality – we wonder if magic is no longer noticed because we are so very immersed in it at every turn.

Science and Gnosticism

Francis Bacon (1561 - 1626) , the father of experimental science, testified to the new posture toward nature, calling it in his words, a "study of nature with a view toward works." He knew such a view was the posture of "the alchemist . . . and the magician." His problem was that they had "scanty success."[65] He proposed the empirical method as a more successful strategy. It was not about ends, but means.

The connection between science and gnosis is tempting. The Latin word for the Greek *gnosis*, after all, is *scientia*, prompting Francis Yates' suggestion, "Is not all science a gnosis, an insight into the nature of the All, which proceeds by successive revelations?" She notes how Descartes fell into bouts of Gnostic ecstacy in his writing.[66] But at this point the analogies end. The methodologies of science run in opposite directions from the Gnostic path. Science focuses on external, observable, quantifiable data; it is materialistic. By contrast gnosis rejects the external for inner knowing; it is anti-materialistic.

Still, in the final analysis, gnosis is less in opposition to science as it is its doppelgänger, or in Jungian terms, its shadow. In other words, Gnosticism is what *must* happen when science dominates. That's because science so separates the material from the spiritual that neither side can speak to the other. Thus, if any discussion of the spiritual can ensue, it must be in trans-rational, that is, Gnostic terms.

The Theory of Evolution is ground zero for this situation. Until Darwin, theology, science, and philosophy could generally all play nice together in the same sand box. They could do so because they saw the cosmos in monistic, not radical dualistic, terms. None took an *a priori* rejection of God, leaving only a material world. Plato's philosophy naturally developed into monotheism centered on his Eternal Being, Aristotle needed his Prime Mover, and Newton was a devout believer. How many scientists doubled as priests? Religion likewise always had room for philosophy so long as it remained a handmaiden of theology. The holy grail of medieval scholasticism was that *highest theology* which would harmonize philosophy and theology.

With the rise of Hermeticism and its Gnostic assumptions, however, the material and spirit worlds experienced what became an unbridgeable fissure after Darwin. Today serious talk of God in the laboratory is banned, precisely because of the radical breach between the material and spiritual realms.

Evolutionary biologist Richard Lewontin lays the current state of science down with brutal honestly: "We take the side of science . . . because we have a prior commitment, a commitment to materialism. It is not that the methods and institutions of science somehow compel us to accept a material explanation of the phenomenal world, but, on the contrary, that we are forced by our *a priori* adherence to material causes to create an apparatus of investigation and a set of concepts that produce material explanations, no matter how counterintuitive, no matter how mystifying to the uninitiated. Moreover, that materialism is absolute, for we cannot allow a Divine Foot in the door."[67]

Lewontin nails it. Science today holds to an *a priori* dedication to materialistic causes in the universe. It must content itself with only the physical world. If there is a non-physical world – the source of ethics and teleology – science keeps its hands off the subject. The "Divine Foot" must remain in that world to which science makes no claim. The moment it attempts to do so, it ceases to be science. Let's face it, what do atoms randomly colliding together have to do with whether I should love my neighbor or whether the world should progress into a collectivist, enviro-friendly wonderland? Attempts to connect the two, to say the least, are somewhat entertaining for those of us who can comfortably rest in God's active role in creation.

But the evolutionists have the last laugh, because they reinsert the Divine into the equation through Gnostic means. Steve Martin, whose 1970s comedy routine betrayed incisively the exact cultural mood of his era leading to today's Gnosticism, put it best: "It's so hard to believe in anything anymore. I mean, it's like, religion, you really can't take it seriously, because it seems so mythological, it seems so arbitrary . . . but, on the other hand, science is just pure empiricism, and by virtue of its method, it excludes metaphysics. I guess I wouldn't believe in anything anymore if it weren't for my lucky astrology mood watch."[68]

Science as it has come to be understood (interestingly, it used to be called *natural philosophy*, i.e., one of several philosophies playing in the sand box) forces a paradoxical dualism onto our thinking from which the only real winner, spirituality-wise, is Gnosticism. The traditional religions have been deemed unscientific, unprovable, and impractical as far as the material world go, so the only tradition making sense is the one having nothing to do with the material world, Gnosticism. Gnosticism cannot be disproved because it's said to transcend the very instrument by which we go about proving or disproving in the first place, the mind.

Practically speaking, the Gnostic can be schizophrenic about Truth. Cognitive dissonance becomes perfectly normal. His fissured psyche can embrace science and mathematics as the governors of the material realm; at the same time he can have his own private religion, never granting his religion a "Divine Foot" in the door of his scientific thinking. Robert Runcie, Archbishop of Canterbury from 1980 to 1990, took this position: "[Religion has] nothing to do with the rational part of your mind." Only with such a posture did he have "a way in which [he] could hold together a fundamental skepticism with religious devotion."[69]

Meanwhile Gnosticism allows for the scientist to harbor vibes traditionally associated with religion, like the reality of something the ancients called a *telos* (the *end-to-which* the world is progressing, a goal of human development) or ethics. An evolutionary standpoint should lead to a nihilism of the most arbitrary kind. Evolution tells us various species, including our own, routinely rise and fall without any rhyme or reason. So long as materialism is absolute, there cannot be a *telos* to this world. Matter will randomly do what matter will do, and T. Rex will not hesitate to kill a competitor T. Rex on his way to eating some inferior species into extinction, or at a minimum, the universe will not hesitate to hurl a meteor into our planet.

But very few are willing to assume a true nihilism. Morality sneaks in through the back door, and this through a Gnostic framework.

Leo Strauss calls this the "fundamental dilemma . . . caused by the victory of modern natural science."[70] It's the clash between science which is now by necessity non-teleological – its materialism provides no discernable end goal at a metaphysical level – and what Strauss calls the "teleological science of man," or a course of philosophy which aims to answer what man's ultimate purpose is (involving ethics, politics, natural law, and so on). Put another way, science should be purely descriptive, describing *what is*, yet somehow modern thinkers sympathetic to atheistic evolution still find *prescriptions* based on science.

Thus does sociology become the Bible for multicultural dogma and for the inauguration of social programs. Thus does environmental science prescribe government regulation of industry. Thus does progressive political thought, well, happen, and not just happen, but happen with fanatic adherence.

To a traditionalist, this is cheating. The secularists claim the mantle of science, celebrating how we're not answerable to a nonexistent God – the world is materialistic and has no purpose or goal – and then they bludgeon us with our duties toward whichever moral end they conceive, claiming all along their view is supported by science, when in fact, all science really does is declare *what is*, never prescribing *what should be*. Somehow they find in those randomly-colliding atoms unassailable truth that carbon-based energy is evil, or that I have the transcendent right to secure someone else's money to pay for my sexual reassignment surgery.

The movie *Lorax* (2012) provides a good example of cheating. This preachy animated film – based on the Dr. Seuss book – portrays a world where evil capitalists make money off of the eradication of all trees. During the movie, one of the evil capitalists sings "How bad can I be?" because the world is all about survival of the fittest and he's just doing what comes naturally when he exploits. As he says in the second verse, "There's a principle of nature / That almost every creature knows / Called survival of the fittest / And check it this is how it goes: / the animal that eats has got to scratch and fight and claw and bite and punch, / and the animal that doesn't, well, the animal that doesn't winds up someone else's l-l-lunch . . . I'm just sayin'"[71]

Well, yeah, he's just sayin' what anyone but an utter moron would be sayin', classic Darwinism, which everyone knows is perfectly rooted in science. Is the movie suggesting schools teach something other than evolution? Of course not. That's what morons do. What then? Therein is the inconsistency.

At one point, creationist Duane Gish brought this inconsistency up with philosopher of science Michael Ruse, essentially telling him, "You don't play fair!" Ruse eventually agreed. "Evolution came into being as a kind of secular ideology, an explicit substitute for Christianity." It is "a full-fledged alternative to Christianity, with meaning and morality."[72]

"Meaning and morality" derived from randomly colliding atoms? Absolutely! How so? Nancy Pearcey in her book *Total Truth* (2004) gives a good review of how science forces a round peg into a square hole. This is where the entertainment begins.

Introducing our first performer, evolutionary psychology, which claims our genes deceive us into thinking there is a higher morality in order to get us to behave well with others. Evolutionist Robert Wright wrote in *The Moral Animal*, "our genes control us." And "We believe the things – about morality, personal worth, even objective truth – that lead to behaviors that get our genes into the next generation." But in the end, "Free will is an illusion, a useful fiction."[73]

Unfortunately this methodology ends up merely justifying as moral whatever *is*, because by definition whatever *is* is exactly where evolution has placed us. This would make moral, for example, such things as rape – as when biologist Randy Thornhill and anthropologist Craig T. Palmer argued that rape is "a natural, biological phenomenon that is a product of the human evolutionary heritage"[74] – or infanticide.[75]

It's quite the conundrum. The world evolutionism gives us opens the door for monsters – rape, baby-killers, Social Darwinism, tyrants, etc – to enter. Yet, even labeling such things *monsters* is a construct enjoyed by those with a different orientation than that which evolution gives us. In other words, a believer is free to say rape is wrong because God says so. The honest evolutionist should at least admit at some level that the only thing standing between us and these monsters is our psychological affirmation of God, that our human nature needs God or else we'll fall into a nihilistic chaos. Even Napolean Bonaparte acknowledged, "Religion is excellent stuff for keeping common people quiet"?

But a religion constructed on purely psychological grounds is a house of cards, and so is the morality derived from that religion. Therefore, because the evolutionist knows the ruse religion is and how firmly morality is grounded on thin air, he has an urgency to discover a new source of transcendence. At least this is true for those who enjoy and want to perpetuate the safety of a residual Judeo-Christian ethical system where, among other things, rape is wrong.

The above-quoted Robert Wright thinks he's discovered transcendent morality. He suggests we can, *without God*, "correct" what our genes have built into us by natural selection, especially if they go against his goal of "brotherly love."[76]

But how such an ideal can coexist given the determining forces of our genes eludes us. What power in us is supposed to correct what our genes have given us, when our genes have determined everything *we* are? Again, the only possible solution is a Gnostic one, a *beyond-logic-and-rationality* solution which imposes a dualistic understanding of humanity on us. There is the *we* of the material world – what we think we are according to the dictates of our evolved physical bodies – and then there is the *Self* of the Gnostic myth, the aspect of us that transcends what nature has given us or what can be known. This *Self* has the power to strive against the genetically-fated *ego*. And evidently this transcendent *Self* exists else these supposed evolutionary scientists wouldn't appeal to this gene-transcending *we*, which against all empirical evidence embraces brotherly love.

But where does this gene-transcending *we* come from? Again, we're in Gnostic territory here. They just know it's there; the elite intelligensia just know it, even if it has no logical, rational, or scientific foundation whatsoever. Likewise they just know rape is wrong, or they just know Social Darwinism is wrong.

Let's bring in our second performer, Tim Radford of *The Guardian*. Radford reviewed famous atheist Richard Dawkins' watershed book, *The Selfish Gene* (1976), on its thirtieth year anniversary, summarizing its conclusion on how morality works: "In the hurly-burly of life and death, altruism becomes not just desirable but inevitable, even in vampire bats; hawks and doves have no choice but to coexist; there become good reasons why populations always more or less seem to keep in step with resources; and male and female sexual behaviour naturally proceeds towards the spendthrift and cautious strategies we observe today."[77]

Where do we begin with this reality and logic-defying statement?

Populations keep up with resources? That may be true . . . until it isn't. Because I'd love to see the ironclad scientific law, with formulas and all, governing this supposed truth. Gravity has that luxury. Every time we drop something, it falls to the ground. But if the world evolved in such a way that every species until the human one kept up with resources, and then the human one did not, then, by definition, is this not simply more evidence to factor into our analysis? The world also evolved to a place where a meteor smashed into it. Hey, things happen. Anomalies happen. But the theory of evolution doesn't really grant us the luxury of throwing a flag on nature's actions: *Hey, you can't do that!* To such protests, nature says . . . actually, nature says nothing, which is sort of the point, but if it did say something, it would say, "Watch me."

Altruism becomes desirable? But evolutionism isn't about what we should desire. It's about what *is*, where we are at this random point in evolutionary history. Focusing on desire naturally leads us to ask the question, *why are there so many people who could care less about coexisting and sharing resources?* Clearly desiring *not* to coexist and *not* to share resources is just as much a product of evolution as doing so, and evolution, again, offers no tools by which we might evaluate one choice as better than another.

When Radford says it's *inevitable*, he would appear to be on firmer evolutionary ground. Evolution has made it inevitable, for example, that rocks fall to the ground. But then this brings up the same question, "If it's so inevitable, why isn't it happening?" Rocks always fall to the ground but people clearly don't always coexist. Laws of nature with as many anomalies as our non-co-existing planet provide are not exactly laws.

Which brings us to his ultimate purpose and paradox hidden in that pearl of a phrase, "no choice but to coexist." That is, by evolutionary fate the world *will* one day coexist. Just as the rock will end up on the ground, so you, dear reader, will coexist on Radford's terms, but it will just take some time. It's what evolution has fated you to do, so you might as well accept it. Your free will, again, is an illusion.

If nothing else, this thought gives justification for massive government overreach in our lives, because in Radford's imagination, government is the primary instrument of evolution. When government regulates your life, it's just doing what's inevitable, what evolution says should be happening. Freedom is an illusion because evolution gives you "no choice but to coexist." But what if I want to exercise my freedom not to coexist? *No*, he implies, *you don't fully understand what evolution is fating you to think, so we have to do the job for you.*

Yet, the true reality of our world stands: most people don't coexist, and if anything, Darwinism has given a pretty accurate explanation for wars, the fighting over resources, the poor, and so on. These things have gone on not just in the West, but all over the world as long as we've known. When Social Darwinism arose in the nineteenth century as a natural followup to Darwinistic evolution, who could deny the far greater sensibility of this development over against Radford's dream of coexisting? It's all survival of the fittest, just as Darwin said. It's exactly where evolution put us and exactly what we observe.

So why isn't this Social Darwinistic understanding of reality just as good an explanation as Radford's? Because Radford is a Gnostic. He just knows the true course of evolutionary history, where it's leading. He's one of the enlightened avatars of evolutionary fate shepherding all of us toward the peaceful new world. The facts must be forced to fit his inner gnosis about the world.

But more is going on here, and the Gnostic angle actually has a specific history.

That is, the Social Gospel quickly arose to counter Social Darwinism. The Social Gospel in turn developed into the progressive movement. These first progressives believed humanity could transcend evolutionary determinism, *but they could do so because they still believed in God, the Christian God(!), at the time.* They could insert God into the equation and with his sanction fight the implications of Social Darwinism. But then through eventual historical and philosophical forces – all Gnostic – the *implications* of God being in the equation stayed while *God himself* was removed. The *Gospel* part of *Social Gospel* was taken out and replaced by a suffixal *-ist*. The implied divinity of the whole project has remained. (More on this in our chapter on the true religiosity of progressive politics. Needless to say, Hegel and his Pietism play a crucial role in this process.)

Even Dawkins cannot keep himself pure of these divine yearnings and all but mouths the Gnostic creed when he remarks that our genes "created us, body and mind," but then he turns around and concludes, "We have the power to defy the selfish genes of our birth."[78] But how do we construct the notion that *selfish* is evil when we're beyond good and evil, and where does this power come from if our genes determine all our human faculties of "body and mind"? The power comes from somewhere beyond our bodies and minds, precisely the place outlined by Gnostic spirituality: *beyond good and evil there is, strangely, a Something... anything but the Christian God*!

We should be forgiven if this looks an awful lot like mysticism. Some scientists cut to the chase, introducing the third performers in our pageantry of paradox. Biologist George Wald believes the universe brought about intelligent life because it "wants to be known." Or again physicist Freeman Dyson echoes the sentiment, "It almost seems as if the Universe must in some sense have known that we were coming."[79] Back to Richard Dawkins, who wondered if perhaps alien life forms deposited life on earth![80]

The conundrum ironically leads to absolute fantasy, something no different than the role scientists say religion plays. Religion, says the sociologist, equips us with an explanation for what cannot be explained. Enter Dawkins' aliens, essentially an updated version of the ancient gods.

Of course, aliens are the fabrication of a thought experiment still lacking any evidence, a product of faith, absolutely no different than the place gods have had in history. The "Fermi Paradox" has never been answered. Physicist Enrico Fermi asked why there is no evidence of aliens, if indeed there are trillions times trillions of solar systems to the nth degree. By conservative estimates there should be some evidence of species who have evolved to a point of long-distance space travel millions of years prior to us. Our sky should be teeming with aliens! But there is nothing. Fermi asked *why?* Most answers to the conundrum border on the mystical – aliens haven't introduced themselves to us because we're not evolved enough – yet the *Occam's Razor* answer no one wants to give is, *Because they weren't made.*

More interesting is the psychological question: why the desire for aliens fueling alien mythology? Why this "visionary projectile hurling from the unconscious depths of the information age"?[81]

It's because aliens are the perfect characters in the Gnostic myth, satisfying two specific, if opposing, Gnostic yearnings. On one hand they're transcendent beings waiting for humanity to evolve so they can contact us, as in the movies *Contact* (1997) or *Star Trek* (*First Contact,* 1996). Like the Jedi masters in *Star Wars* they are the evolved elite. They are Sophia or Christ characters waiting to lead us out of our war-stricken, poverty-laden, environmentally-unfriendly world. On the other hand they're archons, instruments of Yaltabaoth, secret monsters controlling the fate of our world. *The Invasion of the Body Snatchers* (1978) and *Men in Black* (1997) fit this mold.

Most interesting is E. Michael Jones' psychological explanation in his fascinating *Monsters from the Id* (2000).[82] Aliens represent our ignored consciences haunting us on the silver screen, and nothing more. The alien from *Alien* (1979), designed by HR Giger, for example, is an aborted fetus. (In light of Giger's portfolio and biography, it's creepily remarkable.) In any event, Jones points out the dangerous terrain the West entered once it embraced scientific absolutism and shoved all metaphysical questions into the Gnostic realm beyond the realm of rational discourse, leaving the material world without moral law.

The word *monster* is derived from the Latin *moneo*, meaning "to warn." A monster, in the ancient understanding, was the embodiment of some ugly crinkle in the natural order, something portending doom after societal forces had gone awry. Teratology, based on the Greek parallel to *monstrum* (*tera*), studies freakish anomalies like two-headed snakes. The sight of such things signals, say, leakage of toxic material in the ecosystem. It warns a nearby community of hidden, scary things.

Today's atheists, so confident in their scientific certainty, bask in the assurance that the world is evolving to a point of brotherhood, coexistence, and love. It's inevitable, they tell themselves. It's science, they uncuriously insist. They're actually making a monumentally important wager about human nature and the future itself. They're betting that, once the West becomes unanchored from its Christian ethical foundations, the evolutionary currents will carry us to safe harbor at paradisiacal islands. They're betting we can retain the dignity of the individual, human rights, the love of neighbor, the rule of law, and respect for free will without the forms of Christian teaching and dogma.

The bet is that there's no such thing as original sin, a natural inclination in human nature leading to monstrous, barbarous, and uncivil behavior. Given the evidence of barbarity across the globe, one has to consider such a bet against remarkable odds, to say the least. Adrift from the Judeo-Christian ethical anchor, we seem more to be headed toward the Bermuda Triangle, ignoring the flotsam of other cultures who've ventured there before us: fascist German, communist Russia and China, the Middle East, pre-Christian India and Africa. When modern progressives are incapable of making the argument that the practice of sati in India, or the treatment of women in the Middle East, or the cannibalism of ancient Americans is evil – as seems to be increasingly the case (because given their philosophical foundations it *must* be the case) – the monsters have arrived.

If Jones is correct, we've been witnessing on the silver screen these warnings from the Id, these monsters crawling out of the pit of moral anarchy: zombies heralding the mass inhumanity and incuriousness of group-think; vampires representing the soul-sucking eroticism of electronic phantasms; aliens embodying the reptilian, mysterious, but potentially cold and vicious, allure of highly-advanced thinking. If these vibes translate into reality, as they have for countless cultures in the past and around the world today, we can't say we weren't warned.

The Romantic Movement: The Revenge of Nature

Francis Bacon established the wizard's spell for man's mastery over nature in his famous quote, "Nature to be commanded must be obeyed."[83] That mastery came to be applied to all fields, not only physics, biology, and chemistry, but also politics. If *physical* nature can be commanded by first being understood, why not *human* nature, and human *societies?* Thomas Hobbes (1588-1679) reduced human yearning to a Newton-like formula – men by nature seek pleasure and avoid pain – and built his political philosophy from there. If the physical scientists could harness the nature of electricity to give the light bulb, why can't we harness the natural urges of humanity for orderly society?

This scientific view of social organization posited man as a rational animal who rationally and predictably submits to political conventions in exchange for protection from violent death. Mere *matter-in-motion*, a cog in the societal machine, an entity motivated by self-preservation, nothing more than desire for comfort and avoidance of death motivates him. He is the stuff of democratic society, the majority, the mass, the bourgeois, the standard of conformity, the one who defines convention.

As Leo Strauss put it, quoting John Locke (1632-1704), the first modern political thinkers constructed the world on solid, but low ground,[84] solid because the new politics worked with sound reasoning – who likes death? – low because the question remains unanswered, *Once my right to life is guaranteed, what should I live for?*

Jean Jacques Rousseau (1712-1778) pursued these questions. Rousseau's variegated experiences with the underbelly of human nature gave him a perspective eluding Hobbes' or Locke's more optimistic appraisal of the possibilities of human nature for civil society. "Rousseau was forever being dislodged from the society that his mind examined and condemned," Jacques Barzun wrote. "He was in effect outside it, because he had passed through so many of its artificial niches."[85]

He saw the unfairness of priests and noblemen whiling away their time while peasants toiled beneath them. The peasant, unable to pursue meaningful existence, suffered under the suppressing network of feudal traditions and customs. Hobbes and Locke attempted to place man within the laws of science, but Rousseau observed more powerful motives at work than mere fear of death or desire for pleasure, these forces being emotion and feeling.

With Rousseau arose the myth of the *noble savage*, and the modern world inherited its *back-to-nature* proclivities. By *back-to-nature* is not meant roughing it out in the woods, but rather the avoidance of the suppressing excesses of artifice in conventional society. The opening famous line of his great work, *The Social Contract* (1762), sets the tone: "Man is born free; and everywhere he is in chains." What for Locke and Hobbes were social arrangements protecting citizens from death were for Rousseau chains binding the free spirit.

Rousseau began the modern hunt for the *authentic Self*. He contributed to what we will refer to as the *postmodern creed*. Its protagonist is that beastly human spirit bound by no convention, who does as he wishes, and lives in a raw state of mysterious humanness.

The *noble savage* in the modern mind has worn several different masks: bohemians and bikers, beatniks and mountain men, hippies and Indie rockers. There's Herman Hesse's *Steppenwolf*, the wandering wolf alone in the steppes, a metaphor of the alienated. There are those choice phrases peppering the opening song in Hollywood's iconic tribute to beatnik culture, *Grease* (1978): "Their lips are lying only real is real / we got to be what feel / Conventionality belongs to yesterday / This is the life of illusion / What are we doing?"[86]

The myth of the *noble savage* answers the myth of the *rational animal*. The *noble savage* resurrects and embraces troubadour passion, saying, "Why should I submit my natural urges to *conventionality* just because I fear pain and death? Why should I give up who I am for the sake of societal peace? Maybe I'm quite happy to experience pain and die for the sake of something higher than mere preservation of life!"

This *something higher* could be anything: one's national identity, his gender or race, or his sexuality. Whatever it is, there can be no rationality behind it: it's a "mystery of the spirit"[87] on a quest against the submission of *me* to artificial convention. As Rousseau said, "True happiness . . . is felt, and it is felt the more the less it can be described."[88]

Hobbes and Locke on one side, and Rousseau on the other, began the schizophrenia in the Western mind referenced above in our discussion of science. On one side was the observable facts of science, concerned with matter which could be quantified and put on a grid, and man in turn is also a bit of matter in motion whose actions can be predicted by the science of politics. On the other side is a human nature whose mysterious yearnings transcend what science can know, something akin to the Gnostic *spinthēr*.

Immanuel Kant (1724-1804) codified the schizophrenia, dividing the cosmos into two worlds, the *phenomenal* and the *noumenal*. The phenomenal world is everything our senses perceive; the noumenal world includes only what intuition grasps, the *thing-in-itself*. Between these two worlds lies a chasm Kant can't bridge, and didn't. Science, facts, and sensory data reveal a world determined by physical properties and the laws governing these physical properties. Intuition reveals a universal world of the mind. Rousseau's emphasis on feeling and emotion prepared the way for this renewed acceptability of intuition.

Kant spawned the subsequent German philosophy of the 1800s and opened the doorway into a world beyond the material world, his noumenal world. Kant, Hegel, Marx, Schopenhauer, and others surveyed the noumenal world, each attempting to map its mysterious terrain by discovering its meaning through such capitalized (thus divinized) abstractions as *History* (Hegel and Marx) or *Will* (Schopenhauer), which they believed directed the course of this world, giving a *telos* for a world denied by science.

From this intellectual milieu comes the materialistic determinism that marks Marx. He offered one answer to the paradox of science mentioned above, that science offers no prescription but only describes the external world. The external world (Kant's noumenal world) offered no prescriptions for the direction of the cosmos – a *telos* – but the phenomenal world most certainly suggested prescriptions for those adept enough, like Marx, to understand its mysteries. These were the *Idealists* – the above-mentioned Germans – who descended from the noumenal world to inform us of the inner truth, the *telos*, of the material world. This period is known as the philosophical era of German Idealism.

Rousseau's reaction against eighteenth century rationalism also gave birth to the Romantic movement of the 1800s. Art, poetry, and literature give evidence of a marked emphasis on all the wild but beautiful impulses of nature.

With Romanticism, Gnosticism fully came out of the closet. Paul Davies explains how (in *Romanticism and the Esoteric Tradition*, 1998), pointing out the various intersections of the Gnostic myth and Romantic ideas. Both Romanticism and Gnosticism, for instance, see the individual as the protagonist in his own heroic journey of Self-discovery, ever seeking, after a rebirth experience, to find his way out of this oppressive veil of tears and artifice we call earth.

His journey begins as he realizes the artificiality of this world, that even his individuality is nothing less than a product of what John Keats (1795-1821) called, recalling the Hermetic luminous veil, the "veil of soul-making." Explaining what he means, Keats adopts the Gnostic line: "There may be intelligences or sparks of the divinity in millions – but they are not Souls till they acquire identities."[89]

Similarly, Samuel Taylor Coleridge (1772–1834) speaks of the "outlines, and differencings by quantity, quality and relation" and the "birth-place" as those things defining the "relative individual," calling it "an alien of which they know not." Again, separation from Other constitutes the fall; our individuality is the primal evil.

Language too, composed as it is of elements reflecting the divided elements of the world, suffers the same fate as the individual, because the "very words that convey [our individuality] are as sounds in an unknown language."[90]

What, then, of poetry, so central in Romanticism, which is a product of language? Again, poetry is the perfect vehicle for a true unveiling of the hidden truths of the cosmos, just as it was for the Sufis and troubadours. It's perfect because it isn't sequential, or logical, or linear. Rather it's the "collapse of language." As Davies puts it, in italics, *"language only moves close to the Unity when its sequencing function is frustrated and it collapses, closes in on itself."*[91]

On account of this world's veil of tears, one seeks to return to the world of light. He experiences rebirth – palingenesia – by remembering from whence he came. His soul takes on wings and begins the ascent. As it rises, the soul discovers a personal figure on the horizon to guide the way, his Sophia, and again, eros is the passion driving the flight. "Eros has taken the guise of Woman," Rougemont writes, and adds the words of Romantic poets Goethe – "The Eternal feminine leads us away" – and Novalis – "Woman is man's goal."[92]

At that point, there is a moment of "oceanic feeling," described by Wordsworth as a "harmony and deep power of joy," adding, "We see into the life of things." This is the "chink in his cavern" that Blake described in his *Doors of Perception*.[93] This is the gnosis. "Error, or Creation, will be burned up, and then, and not til then, will Truth or Eternity appear. It is burnt up the moment Men cease to behold it."[94]

Our American contact with this philosophical stream came through the Transcendental movement. The Transcendentalists likewise believed they were pioneers in the frontier of the noumenal world, from which came transcendental ideas to which each lone Self had unmediated access. Their Self-reliance was not classic American rugged individualism so much as the power of the Self to transcend worldly conventions into higher truths. Thoreau's work *On Civil Disobedience* (1849) spelled out the justification for bucking political laws for truths transcending conventional laws, most notably in his case, the laws supporting slavery.

The iconoclastic posture of these Romantic thinkers helped bring about some of the bloodiest periods in human history. If the system is seen as artificial – and the Self alone is true to nature – justification settles in for radical revolutionary change.

Emerson's speech before the Phi Beta Kappa Society at Cambridge, England (1837) laid it out: "We will walk on our own feet; we will work with our own hands; we will speak our own minds . . . . A nation of men will for the first time exist, because each believes himself inspired by the Divine Soul which also inspires all men."[95]

Such inspiration can justify revolution, a revolution beginning in the consciousness, something he encouraged in his essay *Nature* (1836): "So shall we come to look at the world with new eyes. It shall answer the endless inquiry of the intellect. – What is truth? and of the affections, – What is good? by yielding itself passive to the educated Will. . . . Build, therefore, your own world. As fast as you conform your life to the pure idea in your mind, that will unfold its great proportions. A correspondent revolution in things will attend the influx of the spirit."[96]

In the name of a human nature imbued with divinity, the Romanticist (or Gnostic, or Hermeticist, or Millenarian, or Pietist, or Revivalist, or Transcendentalist, or Idealist) believes himself to be on the side of angels representing the forces of divinity for change. If God is in me, using me as a co-worker in his directing of History, I can ascribe divine qualities to my political aims. I can justify a crusade, and if my personal theology calls for conforming "your life to the pure idea in your mind," then a "correspondent revolution in things" is justified.

The Romanticists with their esteem of nature – like the environmentalists of our own day – would seem to be the opposite of the Gnostics, who said the natural order is evil. But this ignores how monumentally *un*natural the ideas of the Romanticists really are. Rousseau wrote a book on education entitled *Emile* (1762) even as he horridly raised his own five children. Many attributed the massacres of the French Revolution to Rousseau's ideas. Marx's idea of the inevitable triumph of communism over capitalism – after sweeping up thirty to forty million dead in its ideological broom – has itself been assigned to the dustbin of history. In America, Transcendentalist Amos Bronson Alcott set up Fruitlands as an ideal utopia. It lasted about eight months. The Ripley's Brook Farm lasted a bit longer, three years. Transcendental ideas of education – seeing it more as an opportunity for children to express themselves – have resulted in an education system universally acknowledged a disaster.

The flotsam of ideological movements that became shipwrecks litters the stream of modern history. Those movements most claiming to be in accord with nature end up being monumentally unnatural or anti-nature. The Idealists would claim they have glimpsed at the true gnosis concerning the inner workings of nature. But what ultimately exists is a split between the real world and their ideological interpretation of the world so unstable that attempts to fuse them together over and over again prove disastrous.

The Death of God and Triumph of the Self

Romanticism and German Idealism whirled about in the turbulent thought period of the 1800s when Charles Darwin introduced some scary questions. If *Homo sapiens* is a random slice in an ever-evolving world, alone on this world, with no direction from above, no standard to guide his behavior, what can we possibly understand about the point of human existence? Previously, philosophers needed God – not necessarily the Christian One – as a foundational postulate for their philosophies. God gave us rights. God gave us our natures. God lurks behind History. The Divine had some role. But if the Theory of Evolution was correct, God's harrowing last stand as the foundational cause of the universe finally came to an end.

The Theory of Evolution conjures up the Gnostic in everyone, as we've seen, because it proves absolutely correct the materialist presuppositions of our world. Given infinite time and space, it may have taken trillions of attempts to the nth power to produce a world with life on it, but here we are. Holes or gaps in the theory will be filled as new facts arise, but no one fears such facts will demand the rejection of the theory. The theory itself may evolve but the element of God can never be allowed as a material cause. Some calculable force at some level *must* be discovered, therefore *will* be discovered. God must be given a nice burial, and humanity must go on without him.

A true materialist should conclude life is meaningless. Evolution calls for a survival of the fittest, the rule of the strong, the herd, the adaptive, or whatever. But can the human spirit tolerate this standpoint? It's terrifying to consider a "trillions to the nth power" universe in which I'm essentially a nonentity. Throughout philosophical history humanity has not tolerated this radical conclusion. As evolutionary psychologist Daniel Kruger wrote concerning this very issue, "We're not designed at the level of theoretical physics."[97]

Human nature demands meaning to its cosmos. But the Theory of Evolution nullifies meaning through traditional means – reason or revelation. Neither Aristotle's reasonable argument for a first cause nor Scripture's revelation of the creation have any merit. Meaning must be introduced through trans-rational, trans-religious, non-traditional means. The orientation best-suited to this conundrum is that of gnosis.

Enter Steve Martin's mood watch, as worthy a metaphor as ever for contemporary Gnosticism. More specifically, meaning enters into a meaningless evolutionary world in two ways.

First, as we've seen, the German Idealists claimed to intuit direction in the evolutionary unfolding of history, a *telos*. Here they located divinity in capitalized abstractions like *History*, as in the expression "the judgment of History." This project inspires those today who fuse evolutionary theory with spirituality: they tend to speak of good things *emerging* as part of the evolution of humanity. Each successive age is directed by some divine force. We earthlings cannot empirically quantify where things are progressing, but those with knowledge (gnosis) and an uncanny perception just know there's change in the air – evidently some can smell it – a spirit directing the world to emerge with a new consciousness.

A second way that meaning returns is through the doctrines of the Self. Our understanding of the Self owes its patronage to, in order, Nietzsche, Heidegger, the early psychologists, the existentialists, and the Self-help gurus. Concluding God is dead, for them only the Self remained. *So I'm a blip in the "trillions to the nth power" universe, what does this mean for me? How can I, a nonentity, give some meaning to my meaningless existence.*

Here it would appear the above-mentioned philosophers operated under truly nihilistic presuppositions, but they really didn't. Their writings are pocked with all sorts of judgments of what should and should not be. Nietzsche proposed his *superman* as the answer to the nihilistic problem. He loathed the *last man*, that conformist herd animal blindly yielding to artificial convention.

His loathing is one thing – anyone can loath – his loathing driving an entire revolutionary philosophical movement is quite another, something akin to my taste for Rocky Road ice cream becoming the lodestar of all future thought. Obviously Nietzsche believed his thought to be something more than a matter of taste, but rather some insight into transcendent meaning. He was re-reading Emerson's *Self Reliance*, after all, before launching into his masterpiece, *Thus Spake Zarathustra*.[98] And let's remember that Zarathustra was himself the founder of Zoroastrianism, one of the feeder streams of Gnosticism.

Gnosticism best accommodates the need for meaning after the triumph of the Theory of Evolution because it sets up the cosmos in an absolutist, dualistic framework. On one hand the material world is random and meaningless, and all attempts to find meaning *through* this system (through theology or philosophy) are muted. On the other hand meaning can exist in a transmundane realm, *outside* of this system, a meaning mediated not through revelation or rationality, but to which each Self has direct access. Nietzsche's teachings on the Self, even if the above-mentioned scientists didn't realize it, are the true source of their justification for morality beyond the dictates of our genes.

✧ Chapter 4 ✧

The Fullness of Time

Gnosticism Today

The drift towards Gnostic spirituality continues apace. "Spiritual but not religious" gains new converts daily. In a 2009 study, the Barna Group concluded that "By a three to one margin (71% to 26%) adults noted that they are personally more likely to develop their own set of religious beliefs than to accept a comprehensive set of beliefs taught by a particular church."[1] *61% of Neo-evangelicals agree with that statement*, and the tendency to hold to that view increases among those under twenty-five (82%). Poll after poll yields the same result: people feel themselves less and less tied to religious institutions and are more inclined toward personal spirituality. (This is related to a similar anti-institutional trend found in other areas, something outlined by Robert Putnam's book *Bowling Alone* (2001) about the American drift away from community engagement in general.) As far as Christianity is concerned, books like Ken Ham's *Already Gone* (2009) point out the alarming drop in allegiance among youth. Clearly we are in the midst of a seismic shift in the spiritual landscape, and all indicators point toward this Gnostic spirituality.

Why now? What are these forces?

Globalization is one explanation. Globalization highlights the provincialism of one's own denominational thinking, so the globally-minded seek more universal expressions in their thinking, a commonality with others. The old attitude was, even if one person in all the world held to it, the truth was the truth. During the great debates on the Person of

Christ it was *Athanasius contra mundum* ("Athanasius against the world"). Or at least we got Galileo's *Eppur si muove* ("and still it moves") after recanting his theories on a heliocentric galaxy to save his hide. No longer. The provincialism of one's beliefs is proof, not so much of one's untruth, as it is of every else's truth. *How can I alone be right*, is the sentiment. So everybody's religion is thrown in one big universalistic soup: *we're all on the same page, even if we're using different terms*. Athanasius' *contra* must take a hike.

Then there's an explanation rooted in political philosophy: democracy breeds Gnosticism. That great observer of American culture, Alexis de Tocqueville (1805-1859), speaks of the natural drift toward personalized religion in democratic societies: "[R]eligions ought to have fewer external observances in democratic periods than at any others. In speaking of philosophical method among the Americans I have shown that nothing is more repugnant to the human mind in an age of equality than the idea of subjection to forms. Men living at such times are impatient of figures; to their eyes, symbols appear to be puerile artifices used to conceal or to set off truths that should more naturally be bared to the light of day; they are unmoved by ceremonial observances and are disposed to attach only a secondary importance to the details of public worship. Those who have to regulate the external forms of religion in a democratic age should pay a close attention to these natural propensities of the human mind in order not to run counter to them unnecessarily."[2]

By now we should recognize the Gnostic code words such as "external observances," "subjection to forms," "artifices," "ceremonial observances," and "external forms of religion." Tocqueville's prevision of American religiosity is decidedly of a "spiritual but not religious" bent. But why would American democracy lead to Gnostic impulses? Tocqueville suggests, "Everyone [in America] shuts himself up tightly within himself and insists upon judging the world from there. The practice of Americans leads their minds to other habits, to fixing the standard of their judgment in themselves alone."[3]

Tocqueville observes how one's place in a political body informs his religious perspective. Historically this is certainly true. Political institutions – the Romans or the medieval kingdoms for instance – grounded their founding in sacred myth: *they are not random rulers but have been set up by the gods*. Tocqueville proposes something similar in democracies. The rule of the people is grounded in the sacredness of their position, their aggregate Will and each particular Self: *the people have spoken!* The superiority of Self – along with the collective Selves of others (the pleroma) – over form nicely fits the Gnostic impulse.

A third sociological or psychological explanation is given in Paul Vitz's *Faith of the Fatherless: The Psychology of Atheism* (2000), which recounts the uncanny relationship between some of modernity's leading thinkers and their relationship, or lack thereof, with their fathers. His Freudian analysis[4] aside, Gnosticism *is* iconoclastic against traditional institutions, chief of which is the family. Perhaps seeing Gnosticism as the cause of this iconoclasm puts the cart before the horse. Perhaps the breakdown of the family is the cause of Gnosticism. For instance, what happens when more and more families are headed by single or divorced mothers? How easily can a traditional religion promote a heavenly "Father" when the only "father" many Americans know is a deadbeat loser that abandoned them? Or what sense of self will one have if, to use John Lennon's choice phrase about his son Julian, he had "come out of a whiskey bottle on a Saturday night"? Illegitimacy breeds not only social pathologies, but a sense of alienation, a cynicism towards one's physical place in the world. Is it just a coincidence that the replacement of "patriarchal" religion with "matriarchal," Gaia-centered spirituality coincides with the replacement of traditional father-led families with mother-headed families?

A fourth reason is related to our bodily chemistry. Psilocybin, the drug we know as *mushrooms*, induces mysticism. It's been called the "god drug." LSD induces similar hallucinations. Aldous Huxley, famous for his experiments with subjects under the influence of LSD, claimed he never understood the meaning of "God is love" until under its influence. "I learned from LSD about alternative realities – and suddenly all bibles made sense." He believed that "drugs, not evangelists" would bring about the "long-predicted religious revival."[5] To the user, LSD causes forms to blend and blur together, bringing about a glimpse into what is believed the essential unity of the cosmos. In a post-1960s culture of drug-use, the role of "mind-expanding" pharmaceuticals sets the gold standard for what is expected on a spiritual level. Religion is no longer a matter of truth, but about personal experience and wellness.

This discussion of LSD leads to a fifth explanation for the rise of contemporary Gnosticism, and that's the drug-like character of electronic media. Back in the 1960s, some called the computer the "LSD of the business world."[6] Steve Jobs' dabbling in LSD is well documented.[7] In *Techgnosis: myth, magic, and mysticism in the age of information* (1998), Erik

Davis suggests that it's no coincidence Silicon Valley is in California, land of wacky New Age Gnostic dreamin'. He writes, "One of the great paranoid rumors of the 1960s was that the freaks were going to pour LSD into the water supply; it may turn out that digital devices and media machines wind up dosing the population, infusing an undeniably psychedelic mode of cognition into the culture at large. Moderns pry open Huxley's mental 'reducing valve' and let in the networked Mind at Large."[8]

So immersed are we in technology that it's difficult to evaluate the psychological effect certain things have on our soul. Long ago theologian Tommaso Campanella (1568-1639), in a discussion on magic, denied that "such forces and materials [as used in magic could ever] be such as to capture a human soul."[9] Lots could happen, but no ghost in another machine was possible! The idea was too farfetched. Yet that's exactly what we run into time and time again over the course of a typical modern day, the capture of human souls in telephones, televisions, and radios. We spend more time with disembodied souls in mechanical devices than we do with actual flesh and blood people. How does this affect our anthropology, our understanding of man as man?

It readies us for the idea of human consciousness abstracted from the physical person. The Internet takes things to a whole new level, collectivizing disembodied persons on a mass scale. Back in 1922 Jesuit priest Pierre Teilhard de Chardin (1881-1955) proposed his noosphere, the third and final phase of evolution after the geosphere and biosphere, in which mind replaces body as the locus of existence. Today proponents of the "global brain" carry his torch. (See "Google Consciousness"!)

Both Gnosticism and modern technological marvels abstract humanity from the physical, the latter by electronics, the former by subtle doctrines of the spirit. With little surprise, people spiritualize their electronic experiences. MIT psychologist Sherry Turkel interviewed 450 teens and twentysomethings, hearing them describe their laptops and smart phones as places of "hope" and "where sweetness comes from."[10] The Net becomes a new metaphor for God.[11] It's a remedy to depression (that it itself produces!), a place where one can literally create a new Self, or avatar. One college student described to Turkel how his real life is "just another window [and] usually not my best one." Gnostic spirituality is well-suited to a generation where the real world of "global" this and "global" that loom as oppressing forces stifling the development of my authentic Self, while there at my fingertips is a portal into another world transcending the grey real one.

Finally, there is the historical reason. In 1945, just months after the bombing of Nagasaki and Hiroshima, the Gnostic Nag Hammadi texts were discovered.[12] The mystically-minded everywhere didn't ignore the optics: *science and rationalism only brought World War II and the A bomb; was the Divine moving history in a new direction, away from the paradigms of the past?* The Nag Hammadi texts were read, translated, and diffused to the academic world, and since then their influence has crescendoed. Carl Jung recognized much of his own depth psychology in Gnosticism. Hans Jonas found existential philosophy in Gnosticism. The ancient movement helped Eric Voegelin explain modern totalitarian political theories. Finding parallels in Evangelicalism, Harold Bloom used Gnosticism to help explain the "American Religion." New Agers obviously found an ally. A Gnostic church was even established, the *Ecclesia Gnostica Catholica*, of course in California.

Gnosticism is the new kid on the block and solicits interest. One may have never heard of Gnosticism per se, but it pervades our popular literature and through that our imagination. Dan Brown's *The Da Vinci Code* (2003), for example, was entirely based on a Gnostic reading of Christian history. Accordingly, Church authorities suppressed the Gnostic texts because they revealed how Jesus was Mary Magdalene's lover and together produced a line of descendants reaching down to our own day. Throughout her days, the institutional (read *evil* and *patriarchal*) Church has been engaged in a campaign to suppress the truth of Christ's descendants. Tellingly, the lead female protagonist was named Sophie.

This reading of history is regular fare on the History Channel, the nightly news, and in the magazines that come out every Christmas and Easter with *new* understandings of this or that sacred doctrine of traditional Christianity. A quick perusal through a book store will reveal any number of "lost books" of the New Testament, which by and large are from this Nag Hammadi collection. This historical perspective hangs in the air like a miasma, breathed by people who, based on the other factors listed above, already have tendencies toward Gnostic spirituality.

Thus the perfect storm: globalization and the yearning for transcendence, the sacralization of the Self bred by democracy, the abstracting of humanity worked by technology, the cynicism toward traditional institutions fostered by the breakdown of the family, and the novelty of a seemingly more authentic expression of Christianity. These forces synthesize with movements in culture, politics, and religion, and a

Gnostic reading of contemporary society illuminates the movements of our times. In religion, the popularity of New Age spiritualities, but more interestingly the trajectory Neo-evangelicalism has taken, falls under this banner. In politics, the progressive movement has clear kinship with Gnostic impulses, especially given the evidence of its medieval roots.

But we begin with Gnosticism in our popular culture.

Part II

Love Sick:
Gnosticism and Culture

✧ Chapter 5 ✧

The Postmodern Creed

America's Secular Religion: The Postmodern Creed

During the last decade, a spate of anti-religion books came on the scene. Secularism seemed to be on the rise. Books like Richard Dawkins' *The God Delusion* (2008), Christopher Hitchens' *God is Not Great* (2009), and Sam Harris' *The End of Faith* (2005) openly attacked faith. Along with declining church attendance, such evidence suggests America's growing secularism. Yet, as we've wondered periodically, *can the human spirit maintain a true secularism?* A truly secular culture would be amoral, non-transcendent, and truly materialistic. Yet American culture is not any of those things, not one bit. Spiritualism is as potent as ever, but it's sublimated in non-religious, even atheist or secular, ways.

In this second part, we investigate this sublimated religiosity as it pertains to culture, through what might be dubbed the *postmodern creed*. The postmodern creed is the default psychological mode programmed into our DNA, formatted into our minds through the various cultural channels. The following is a generalized version of the postmodern creed:

I am an absolutely free Self, born randomly in the body I have. My body – which is my possession but is not essentially me – places me in a given situation in which I inherit certain values from my parents, from the church I grew up in, from my country, and from my culture. As I get older, I begin to break free from these values and, either I begin to discover who I really am, or I decide to create who I will be. I may have a crisis of identity at some point during this period, but I eventually must be me. This I do by making my own choices of what I will be, choosing my own politics, my own church, my own styles, my own music, my own sexuality, even my own gender; etc. Whatever it is that defines who I am, such things must be freely chosen by ME. I understand life as a journey whose paths are Self-chosen. If there is some "out there" divine entity guiding me as I choose my path, it will communicate to me internally, personally. Along this journey, I may be assisted by certain gurus, both human or not so human. Or not.

In the creed, certain themes predominate. The distinction between Self and body is primary. Our bodies fate us in many ways. Focus on Self offers a chance to be free from the dictates of body. *Choice* enters here. Choice is the *sine qua non* of the postmodern creed. True freedom entails that I – as something distinct from my body – determine to choose what defines who I am. The lifelong process of me defining or discovering who I am given the body I have is the journey.

Reading the postmodern creed, many will think, "Well of course that's the way it is. How else could it be?" And that's exactly the point. *How else can it be?* statements are religious statements, uncritically-accepted statements, statements of faith, creedal statements. Hence, postmodern *creed. How else can it be?* statements suggest that, if there were other ways that it could be, these would be something akin to heresy, to be determined by the tribunals of our various media.

How did we get to this point? Where did the postmodern creed come from? And what does it have to do with Gnosticism?

Existentialism: The Default Pop Philosophy

The postmodern creed comes from a single philosophy, existentialism, whose current triumph over all other philosophies proves how embedded it is in our cultural habits. This was the heart of Allan Bloom's point in *Closing of the American Mind* (1987). Americans use all these words – *rights, values, Self, commitment, relationship, culture, choice, authenticity*, etc. – ignorant of the heavy philosophical freight these words carry.

Philosophy has argued itself out of the possibility of being argued, and this because of the Gnostic character it assumed. Traditional philosophy rested on the premise that propositional truth (the notion there is an objective meaning and inherent logic to the universe) could be discussed. The presumed existence of some Divine Other introduced a lodestar, as it were, to which all participants could situate their claims.

Darwin destroyed the need for *any* divinity, and so destroyed philosophy's historical assumptions. With him the universe lost all inherent logic save that of randomness, chaos, and meaninglessness. Gone now is the presumption of a meaning true at all times and in all places. Our randomly evolving ball of chaos could take any number of trajectories, all just as meaningless as its current form. Under such circumstances, philosophy *must* lose its luster, just as it has. The possibility for discussion is also lost. Like a philosophical *survival-of-the-fittest*, what remains are competing power plays by various philosophies, each vying for supremacy. This is the heart of the postmodernist critique on philosophy.

The triumph of Darwinism is what formatted the Western mind to believe all thought is a blind quest for power. Ralph Waldo Emerson forecast the age to come when he wrote, "A foolish consistency is the hobgoblin of little minds." That is, only a small mind seeks a consistent, inherent logic to the world. With one fell swoop he sabotaged the entire philosophical enterprise and prepared the ground for Darwin's revolutionary discovery.

After Darwin, philosophy should have packed up its toys and gone home, signing off with something like, *"We gave it our best, but we failed. You're on your own now, humanity."* As it happened, "being on your own" became a philosophy of its own right, with prescriptions just as earnest, moral, and teleological as anything leading up to it. Today's postmodern-creed-in-a-nutshell, "be yourself," replaces the philosophical "know thyself" or the theological "deny yourself." It remains our current philosophy, our default philosophy, a philosophy just as accepted, religiously so, as those in the past. For this philosophy we can thank Frederick Nietzsche.

Frederick Nietzsche (1844 – 1900) clarified the new course for Western philosophical history given Darwinism's new realities. He famously declared on behalf of Western thought, "God is dead." An honest philosopher – the type so honest he becomes insane (which he did) – he charted the most realistic course philosophy could take us.

The great question for him was, *Without gods to guide our ways, what now?* Nietzsche hoped for new gods to arise in the world. The old gods were projected deceptions propagated by great men of the past who by sheer force of charisma and character bedeviled others into following them. After Darwin shattered those myths, the new gods would be those courageous folk who gave up childhood fantasies about God and became their own gods.

Nietzsche helped midwife the Self as the focus of the postmodern creed, the true modern God. The Self is modernity's answer to the soul. What's the difference?

The soul finds meaning only in relation to an objective divinity. The soul calls upon us to deny our Selves, which in antiquity meant the bodily passions. The soul calls us to submit our Selves to something higher and transcendent. The happiness of the soul depended on doing such things.[1]

The Self, by contrast, is the core of an onion. Like onions we have layers of influences telling us what we think we are. We're born in families with a family name, a family tradition, a family religion. We're raised in the customs of that family, ritualizing us into the sacred character of the family. The same with our country, the one that raises us. Likewise also the Church. These three were the traditional pillars of spiritual formation. Happiness rested on the healthy integration of these three pillars.

Happiness erodes as the onion's layers fall away from the core. The Theory of Evolution can take the blame. When one believes his own experience has no meaning – that everything is *random*, to use the popular expression – he becomes cynical about who he is as defined by his birth in a random family, a random country, and a random church. One by one the layers of the onion fall away, leading to dread despair, precisely the emotional culture breeding Gnosticism.

The postmodern creed is the hallmark of the adolescent experience. Adolescence itself is something of a modern invention, a creation of the last century as a result of child labor laws and compulsory education. In the leisureness of adolescence – while mom and dad put food on the table, while his state-sponsored schools provide cutting edge facilities and technology, while the government underwrites his financial security and health care – the American undergoes the great journey of Self-discovery or Self-actualization. His science classes and progressive education convince him there's no meaning to the world, at least at a religious level. He's learned to become cynical of his Indian-killing, slave-trading, environment-destroying, women-subjugating country. Meanwhile his church becomes hopelessly outdated, something he's growing out of. And his parents, themselves brought up in the same postmodern creed, enable their teen's feelings with sentiments like "You can't force him to do anything or he'll hate you." No parent wants to be the archon!

And so the layers of the onion fall away. He comes to that

Nietzschean rite of passage: *How will I define what I am? Who am I?* He comes to the core of the onion, to that core of his being, the location of his *authentic Self* stripped of all foreign impositions of family, Church, and state, which only awaits his personal discovery for it to emerge fully in a glorious *coming-of-age* experience.

The only problem is, onions have no core.

At the threshold of his existence, standing with his back to the artificial past and his face toward absolute darkness, he finds his life, his very Self, to be a blank canvass. He is the artist. He must create who he will be and what will have meaning for him. Guiding his behavior are not commandments from Mt. Sinai or ideas of moderation from artificial society, but *values* generated by his own Self, whose value exists solely in the extent to which he is committed to them. What matters most is not any sort of divine end or goal of all things, a *telos*, but the Will. *Willing* alone makes meaning, not the *object* of that will. A *telos* is outside of me, a *that-to-which* I am going. A Will is inside of me, a mysterious *that-from-which* my life's pursuits spring. If the *that-to-which* (God) has been removed, all that matters is the *that-from-which*, and the *that-from-which* is my Self making choices.

Hence *values* and not *morals*. *Value* is an economic term. Economics is the science of human choice: value is determined by the strength of one's choice for any particular good or service, known as *demand*. Something has value if it is chosen; increased value parallels the *commitment* of that choice.[2]

As an ethical construct, the same applies. The term *morality* needs an objective standard for guidance; it exists as a standard even if no one holds to it. *Values*, on the other hand, exist only as they are chosen and committed to. Take away choice and commitment, value disappears.

Nietzsche emphasized the Will as the source of meaning for each individual. The freight of that term has been taken up in today's age by the term *choice*. For the American, *choice* is sacred. *Choice* allows me to define who I am going to be. *Choice* is essential to Self-development. *How can I be what I am truly meant to be if I cannot make my own choices?* If Nietzsche is the father of the religion of the Self, *choice* is his initiation sacrament.

The philosophy of existentialism advanced Nietzsche's project. The existentialists were not so concerned about the internal essence or logic of the world as they were about the simple reality of *existence*, an existence whose meaning is authentically created only by a freely-choosing

Self.

This quest for *authenticity*, ever present today, is the gift of philosopher Martin Heidegger (1889-1976). To live *inauthentically* is to live by some image imposed on the Self, perhaps by parents, the Church, or the culture. *Authentic* living is the goal, wherein we face the absolute meaninglessness of the world (going through the so-called *existential angst*) and nevertheless freely choose a course of action, which may change, but must at all times be freely chosen. The philosophy of existentialism imposes upon us the jitter-inducing task of living not by images imposed upon us from the outside, but by our own choices.

Discussing this point of absolute meaninglessness, Allan Bloom suggests a difference between European and American nihilism.[3] European nihilism is pessimistic. Nietzsche's philosophy proposes dreadful things. It takes one to the abyss of his being. It's a tremendously confounding, depressing, scary, and confusing time. All the more was nihilism scary for the Europeans because they saw what it resulted in, fascism. In a complete breakdown of cosmic order, humanity seeks an Orderer, and any Orderer will do so long as they give some structure. Europe saw where this led.

For the optimistic American, on the other hand, the nihilistic point is exciting and thrilling, a time for wonderful Self-development and growth. The Self can be the Orderer, right? It's an optimistic nihilism.

Bloom suggests our American approach hasn't taken Nietzsche seriously. I would suggest that *Harold* Bloom's insight helps understand *Allan* Bloom's observation: American nihilism takes on an optimistic flavor because there's a light at the end of the dark tunnel: Gnostic spirituality.

To help move us along toward this light we go to Hans Jonas.

Existentialism and Gnosticism

Gnostic scholar Hans Jonas couldn't ignore the connections between existentialism and Gnosticism. He writes, "When, many years ago, I turned to the study of Gnosticism, I found that the viewpoints, the optics as it were, which I had acquired in the school of Heidegger, enabled me to see aspects of Gnostic thought that had been missed before. And I was increasingly struck by the familiarity of the seemingly utterly strange."[4]

Central to his thesis is that Gnosticism is a nihilism of the same variety as existential nihilism. He calls them cousins.[5] Nihilism, which

Nietzsche recognized "stood at the door" in his day, was invited in and offered a seat by the existentialists.[6] But the beginnings of nihilism, says Jonas, go back to the seventeenth century, to Pascal, to the dawning realization – come to fruition with Darwin – that as individuals we are cast alone in a vast sea of cosmic silence, adrift without any mooring, certainly without any immediate divine hand to guide us. Man is only a "blind accident."[7] But unlike the rest of nature, man has self-knowledge. He can see himself as separate and distinct from the sum of arbitrary, blind cosmic forces. We're back at that unbridgeable chasm we saw in our discussion of science, between the individual as a physical being who is part of, and product of, the physical world, and himself as a mind with self-knowledge believing he has power over the physical world, over what Jonas calls the "community of being."

Enter the fissured mind, the cognitive dissonance. My physicality tells me I'm X, Y, and Z. Meanwhile my mind recognizes me as a distinct Self in potential conflict with what my physicality says I am. "Estranged from the community of being in one whole," he writes, "his consciousness only makes him a foreigner in the world, and every act of true reflection tells of this stark foreignness."[8]

Here enters the nihilism signaling the intersection of Gnosticism and existentialism: "Gone is the cosmos with whose immanent *logos* my own can feel kinship, gone the order of the whole in which man has his place. That place appears now as a sheer and brute accident."[9]

The belief that God has created me in my body with inherent dignity – something made in his image, to be redeemed – is replaced by such questions that Pascal asked, *Why am I here and now, and not there and then?* Man finds himself lost in the "little prison-cell in which he finds himself lodged, I mean the (visible) universe."[10] As the Gnostics said and the existentialists picked up on, even sharing the same terminology, the Self is "thrown" accidentally, arbitrarily, and randomly into this world.[11]

The intersection of Gnosticism and existentialism, says Jonas, is not just a shared mood, a shared sense of "homelessness, forlornness, and dread."[12] It goes deeper; it effects what we have been calling a *telos*, an end and purpose to our existence here, to our politics and ethics, to how we construct civil society and civil discourse. "With the ejection of teleology from the system of natural causes, nature, itself purposeless, ceased to provide any sanction to possible human purposes."[13]

We get no clues from nature about what is ethical or what is the best political system! Nature and nature's God are rendered impotent and, as we'll see in a moment, even evil. Furthermore, just as we highlighted above, "Values are no longer beheld in the vision of objective reality, but are posited as feats of valuation. As functions of the will, ends are solely my own creation. Will replaces vision; temporality of the act ousts the eternity of the 'good in itself.'"[14] That is, *will-from-which* replaces *end-to-which*.

Jonas notes how Pascal could at least believe in God, albeit a transmundane God, a hidden God not discerned in his creation. Pascal was a Christian, but only in the sense suggested by the wager named after him: *Pascal's Wager*. He chose Christianity merely, almost cynically, because given the two situations – God not existing or God existing – the latter choice granted a greater reward (heaven) for choosing it than the former (annihilation), also a greater threat (hell) for not choosing it than the former (annihilation). But beyond this cynical reasoning, God had no affirmative grounding in the created order. The created order only reveals a game of blind power, of survival of the fittest. On these terms Pascal was more Gnostic in his thinking. Later thinkers dumped Pascal's embrace of the Christian God but kept his cynicism, a cynicism far more in keeping with both existential philosophy and Gnosticism.

Jonas points out how both existentialism and Gnosticism arose at similar times in their respective ages, the latter in post-antiquity and the former in post-Christian times. Both times are times of Empire-decay, when the spiritual assumptions and foundations of society crumbled precisely from the sort of cynicism Pascal injected into modern thought. What did third century Rome offer against economic turmoil and barbarian invasion, save a series of blundering and competing politicians, each more power hungry than the previous? What does the modern Western world offer against economic turmoil and the threats of China, or terrorism, save another series of blundering leaders, who seem only motivated by the lust for power?

Thus if the world truly is a reflection of a transcendent being, such a being cannot be much more than the world made in his image: arbitrary, mindless, and power-hungry. The world reveals nothing but "unenlightened and therefore malignant force, proceeding from the spirit of self-assertive power, from the will to rule and coerce. The mindlessness of this will is the spirit of the world, which bears no relation to understanding and love. The laws of the universe are the laws of this rule, and not of divine wisdom. Power thus becomes the chief aspect of the cosmos, and its inner essence is ignorance."[15]

For the Gnostic, the god of this world is a mistake, the product of Sophia's disharmony with her male counterpart. He's something we don't have to worry about because our inner spark – the Self – is above him.

For the existentialist, the god of this world is the projection of a fissured and broken psyche, giving rise to religion and philosophy. It's the source of inauthentic living, also something we don't have to worry about.

In any event the cosmos, as a reflection of whatever God, becomes alien to us and no longer venerable. Yet the cosmos continues to oppress us with its laws, like the laws of nature. Jonas again: "[Cosmic] law, once worshiped as the expression of a reason with which man's reason can communicate in the act of cognition, is now seen only in its aspect of compulsion which thwarts man's freedom."[16]

The cosmic reason (Logos) so beloved of Plato, the Stoics, and Christian philosophers is replaced by cosmic fate, an oppressive law put into effect by God and his archons. If according to ancient notions, one's place in the cosmos was best served by conforming his reason with the cosmic reason – so that he *acted as part of a rational whole* – for the Gnostic such an endeavor was merely *playing a part*, or in existential terms, *living inauthentically*. Ultimately the laws of the cosmos were set up by demons, by Yaltabaoth and the archons. Today, the demonic is seen more metaphorically: natural, political, and moral laws are uncannily evil precisely in their overshadowing bigness, spawned from the very *structures* and *systems* of the world, whatever exerts its invisible control over us. They are power-based, hypocritical, and artificial. They "thwart man's freedom."

Their laws must be subverted if I would be saved. Here enters Gnostic antinomianism. Be it for Gnostic or existentialist reasons, I must confess *the God of this world system and all its laws dead . . . dead to me*. Or as Jonas puts it, the God of this world has "ceased to be divine for us and therefore to afford the lodestar for our lives." God, as traditionally understood, is liquidated.[17]

For Nietzsche, "God is dead" was not a blanket confession of absolute atheism. It was a reorientation, a change in paradigms in how we view the cosmos: *the Judeo-Christian theological structure marinaded in ancient philosophy must come crumbling down!* If by "God is dead" Nietzsche merely wanted to say the universe is composed of matter alone, everything's random and chaotic, and there's no meaning to life, the most consistent thing he would have done is put his pen down and do whatever the hell he wanted, enjoying his affair with Wagner's wife and whatnot.

But he didn't.   He continued to write, and right there lurks the transcendent wisdom he wished to impart, and right there also lurks the spiritual light at the end of the tunnel.   In Europe the fascists and communists discerned this light on their terms – hence the dark cynicism associated with their nihilism, the darkling of their light – but in America we discern that light in our own New Agey sort of way.   In both cases the *posture* is Gnostic.

Salvation for both the Gnostic or the existentialist begins when he rejects the laws associated with the traditional orientation, when he comes to that moment – for the Gnostic, the moment of gnosis; for the existentialist, the existential moment – when he chooses no longer to live a role, the role given by the powers of this world system, but rather to free himself and be, as existentialist Jean-Paul Sartre said, "nothing but his own project," where "all is permitted to him."[18]

But what exactly is that salvation? Here is where Gnosticism and existentialism part ways, precisely because of the paradox we've been seeing. Gnosticism saw invisible forces at work in its dualistic posture: both Yaltabaoth and Monad were real entities. Salvation for the Gnostic entailed a rebellion against Yaltabaoth's powers, yes, but this yielded a true gnosis into one's origins in Monad. Existential dualism by contrast is more radical. The world system with its competing power plays is utterly indifferent, and upon knowledge of this indifference, there is literally no light at the end of the tunnel. None![19] One's awakened knowledge, or gnosis, of the artificiality of this world's systems yields a series of moments in the dread reality of present existence, each one of which I am aware, but each one marching forward toward death.

What then does the existentialist do with this dreadful gnosis?

Jonas falls back on Heidegger's observation that "facing our finitude, we find that we care, not only whether we exist but how we exist."[20] In other words, whatever are the paradoxes we see cropping up again and again – with the evolutionary scientists listed above, with Nietzsche, with the existentialists – the reality is there's something in us not allowing us to slip into a complete "let us eat, drink, and be merry, for tomorrow we shall die." No matter how hard we try, we can't turn off the light at the end of the tunnel. Something in us knows that, sure, our evolution may have fated us to rape, but still rape is wrong. Sure, blind power quest may be the nature of the world evolution gives us, but still somehow we sense a brotherhood of man.

Yet, where does the light come from given the metaphysical

foundations so firmly darkening the tunnel? Jonas puts it this way: "Between that Scylla and this her twin Charybdis, the modern mind hovers."[21] On one hand anyone with a brain knows we're here by blind, evolutionary fate and traditional religion is a fairy tale; yet on the other hand the radical implications of this – rape is justified – force us to posit transcendent meaning. We're falling in the abyss pretending we're standing on firm ground, hoping the abyss remains bottomless! Of course, as the communist and fascist movements showed us, it isn't bottomless, and the smack is pretty awful. Scylla and Charybdis exact their toll.

Jonas concludes his essay wondering, "Whether a third road is open to it – one by which the dualistic rift can be avoided and yet enough of the dualistic insight saved to uphold the humanity of man – philosophy must find out."[22]

He answered his own question by the analogy he set up in the first place, the parallels with ancient Gnosticism. Western thinkers flirted with the hopeless variety of existentialist nihilism, but ultimately embraced Gnostic nihilism, which offers a light at the end of the tunnel, evidenced by all the existentialist thinkers who embraced Gnostic spiritualities – Heidegger for fascism, Sartre for socialism, Camus and Kerouac for Buddhism – establishing the precedent for the modern embrace of politics, Self-help, and the New Age as religion substitutes.

That, indeed, is the "third road."

From Existentialism to Psychology and Self-help

Depth psychology sprouted from the same philosophical soils giving rise to Nietzsche's philosophy and existentialism. Depth psychology claims to investigate the deep, inner workings of the Self, the aspects of our Selves lurking in the shadows of our early childhood, in the recesses of our unconscious. Depth psychology abetted the Self-help programs invading the cultural scene from the 1950s on, anticipated already in Ralph Waldo Emerson and Norman Vincent Peale. People, preoccupied by their Selves, seek solace for their pains through programs assuming the philosophical baggage associated with the Self. This pursuit of the Self's healing leads us straight into Gnostic territory. As Gnostic scholar Gilles Quispel wrote, "the discovery of the Self is the core of [Gnosticism]."[23]

Sigmund Freud divided the person into an *ego* (the conscious *I*), the *Superego* (the voice of our parents; the drive for perfection), and the *Id* (the pleasure principle; basic primitive drives). His fissure of the psyche became easily adaptable to Gnostic dualistic ideas, a fissure marking American culture throughout. Again, "I am not comfortable in my body." Or there's Barack Obama's identify crisis, trying to decide if he'd go with his black part or white part. Freud gave scientific credence to the fissured psyche, naming its components. All that remained was for someone to evaluate them: the Superego represents the impositions of foreign elements into Me (the voice of authorities; the archontic powers of the Gnostic myth); the ego is "Me in the world" trying to live as a social being (the slumbering spirit needing to be awakened); the Id is my connection to the primitive past, where my true authentic longings lurk and only need to be awakened, related to erotic desire (the awakened *spark* from the primordial Monad; the true Self).

Freud's influence cannot be denied, but far more important, far more interesting, and far more enduring, is Carl Jung. Carl Jung founded analytic psychology, a psychology more open to the spiritual than Freud's more strictly scientific approach. Jung's psychology offered a light at the end of the dark tunnel, and key to his intellectual development was his Gnosticism.

Quispel writes, "Jung really thought that familiarity with Gnostic imagery and Gnostic experiences helped uprooted man to solve his psychological problems."[24] In 1916, Jung wrote his *The Seven Sermons to the Dead written by Basilides in Alexandria, the City Where the East Toucheth the West*. Apparently Jung was visited in his dreams by the ghost of Basilides, an ancient Gnostic whose preached sermons Jung transcribed. In these sermons he introduces Abraxas, the God beyond good and evil. When the Nag Hammadi texts were discovered, one text was dedicated to him. Jung, an old man at the time, proclaimed, "All my life I have been working and studying to find these things, and these people knew already."[25]

In short, Jung was a Gnostic.

This is the same Jung ubiquitously peppering the pop cultural landscape: the Jung who influenced the Star Wars movies, as Bill Moyer's famous 1988 interview with Joseph Campbell revealed; the Jung who gave the terminological universe of the *complex* as invoked in the 1955 James Dean classic *Rebel without a Cause*; the Jung invoked by the Marine in *Full Metal Jacket* (1987) explaining to the colonel why he bore on his helmet the phrase "Born to kill" while wearing a peace button: "The Jungian thing, sir"; the Jung whose theory of personality types was incorporated into the Myers-Briggs Type Indicator, the popular personality test; the Jung whose ideas of a Collective Unconscious led Nobel prize Physicist Wolfgang Pauli to believe that his mind was linked to the universe,[26] enabling him to make his discoveries in physics; the Jung whose term *synchronicity* found its way in the title of Police's 1983 best-selling album (the album that knocked Michael Jackson's *Thriller* off the top of the charts); the Jung idolized by TV psychiatrist Dr. Niles Crane . . . or by Batman archnemesis Dr. Jonathan Crane (no relation), aka, the Scarecrow (itself a Jungian archetype); the Jung on front cover of *Sergeant Pepper's Lonely Heart Club Band* . . . that Jung. He was a Self-identified, *bone fide* Gnostic.

Jung identified the unconscious – the hidden Self[27] – with the divine spark of the Gnostics. The hidden Self in turn is part of a collective whole, the Gnostic pleroma. At birth we lose touch with this collective, and so it becomes unconscious.[28]   This he called the Collective Unconscious, something we have to wake up to.   Meanwhile the individuated, slumbering Self – absorbed in delineations made possible only by one's physicality, his physical birth in a family (such as gender, ethnicity, nationality, religion, etc.) – is the ego. The ego lives life in the world with a *persona* – Latin for "mask" – a mask we put on as we play our roles in the society. If the ego does not reacquaint itself with the unconscious Self, it will fall into a variety of neuroses, a fissured psyche, and a sense of alienation.

We get shadows and glimpses of our Collective Unconscious through certain archetypes found in dreams, artwork, or in reoccurring themes in religion, literature, legends, fairy tales, and myth. These archetypes connect humanity together collectively, which is why similar themes are found in the mythologies of diverse peoples, or why similar symbols appear in the dreams of all people. Related is Jung's idea of synchronicity, where similar events concur having no causal link. For example, someone is thinking of a word while driving just as he comes upon a street with the same name.

Jung commands a huge role in our ongoing metaphor of the dark tunnel. Freud and the existentialists assumed a metaphysics rooted in evolution, *everything is random and meaningless*. Their posture was, *the dark tunnel is there; how should we live given the ultimate meaninglessness of our existence?* They pretended no light, only a way of surviving the darkness. Jung – at least a young Jung – operated under these same assumptions, but he still introduced parallels to Gnosticism and opened the door ever so slight to transcendence. At first, however, he only saw in the Gnostic myths mere psychological projection – "man is just projecting his own illusions on the patent screen of eternity"[29] (a view inherited from Feuerbach through Freud). These illusions might curiously seem to be universal to human experience, but to discern anything transcendent in them would flirt with something science says is off limits: the Divine. Later in life, Jung made the leap. Again Quispel: "All his life he had rummaged in the collective unconscious, but now he had forced a breakthrough from the soul to the cosmos . . . it is the experience of the fullness, the pleroma, of Being that matters."[30]

He broke on through to the other side!

After that Jung told Quispel, "[T]he concept of projection should be revised completely." Jung had "left the limitations of the psyche and found in the cosmos meaningful correspondences." Others took note of Jung's breakthrough. The "prosaic and rectilinear" (i.e. scientific) psychologist Erich Neumann, after Jung's coming out party regarding the transcendent Self, found peace just before his death in a "'Self field' outside of the psyche, which created and directed the world and the psyche, and manifests itself to the ego in the shape of the Self."[31]

Jung's associate C. A. Meier worked with the eros themes pervading Gnosticism, which found their way into psychology through Freud's Id and his work with the libido. In doing so he resurrected Renaissance Hermetical ideas, such that "the circle of Love which originates in God, pervades the universe and descends to matter and Chaos, but returns in human Eros to its source."[32]

Jung's *breaking-through-out-of-the-psyche-into-the-cosmos* coming out party even had its effect on hardcore physicists, for instance the above-mentioned Wolfgang Pauli, who told Quispel, "This negative theology, that is what we need. As Schopenhauer said, [God] cannot be personal, for then he could not bear the suffering of mankind. This is it, the Unknown God of Gnosis."[33]

Pauli's love of Jung's Gnostic ideas metaphorically represents science willing to allow the spiritual back into the discussion, laying the foundation for New Age understandings of science. He, a leader in the field of quantum mechanics, understood how science itself had pushed the limits of rectilinear, logical, and mathematical reasoning – *how can light be a wave and particle at the same time?* – and he was more than willing to grant Jungian psychology (i.e. Gnostic spirituality) the domain of all things spiritual. "The psychology of Jung points to a deeper unity of psychical and physical occurrences."[34]

This foundation brings us to today. Jung's idea that individually we are part of a collective not only fuels progressive political aspirations but more importantly gives divine sanction to the archetype. The archetype is the fingerprint of the Divine in our collective psychology, by which it speaks to each of us individually, drawing us together as one. The archetype finds its way in our myths and dreams. Our myths, in the modern world at least, are without a doubt conveyed in our various media, the most popular sources being television, movies, music, and the computer. Here is how divine sanction can be given, for example, to the Internet. If mass peoples drift in a certain direction as reflected by their Google inquiries, surely this is the impetus of the collective, which itself is the Divine. "Google Consciousness" is more than a cute metaphor.

Our movies, television, and music also take on divine characteristics. They are the light at the end of the tunnel. As far as the postmodern creed is concerned, they work meaning in that abyss we discovered at the onion's core, the abyss of our being. They introduce us to the collective archetypes, and more profoundly they give us insights into the pleroma, a very vision of the Divine even as these archetypes are common to the human experience. As we, in turn, draw these archetypes into our own lives – shedding those false masks given us by family, Church, and state – we take part in a divine, collective, thing. We become transformed. We incarnate the archetypes. We become transformed by our media. The process is almost magical.

Or alchemical.

Alchemy, the Postmodern Creed, and Personality Tests

Jung looked back to medieval alchemy as a forerunner of his own psychology. In alchemy, he said, "I had stumbled upon the historical counterpart of my psychology of the unconscious. The possibility of a comparison with alchemy, and the uninterrupted intellectual chain back to Gnosticism, gave substance to my psychology."[35]

The alchemical challenge was to turn base metals into gold. The alchemist purportedly could rarefy certain vapors from the base metals (lead, for example) and from this rarefied vapor form gold. It was a process of dividing and reuniting.[36] This he did with the help of the Philosopher's Stone, a mythical stone whose meaning has been interpreted both exoterically and esoterically. Jung interpreted it psychologically.

Base metals represent the "sheer ego consciousness"[37] of a hidden Self trapped in bodily existence. Gold on the other hand represented the "ego's rediscovery of the unconscious and reintegration with it to forge the self."[38] The subversive element of the alchemist – his discovery, hidden from church authorities – was that the process was truly an inner process, the "projection of the internal" state of mind. Upon coming in contact with the stone – his internal gnosis[39] – the alchemist could effect literal change in his soul, from the leaden soul he was born with to a golden soul.

Medieval alchemy was of a piece with the general "Self-actualization" or "Self-help" magic marking the occult in its more respectable permutations. Accordingly, the cosmos was seen as ruled by cosmic forces alien and menacing to our individual spirits. Its network of demonic rulers can and should be triumphed over. This can happen for the magician. The magician, knowing the cosmos' true nature, is enlightened to its inner workings. He can manipulate it to his and the world's advantage. In astrology for example, the heavenly bodies are stellar and planetary influences – the Gnostic archons – binding and fating us to certain personality traits. Through astrology we can triumph over the dictates of stellar fate, healing our alienated psyches.

In its updated Jungian version, whatever binds us to certain ways of thinking, those influences shaping the ego, are the archons. My birth into a family name, a religion, within the borders of a certain nation are as random as my birth under the influences of a random array of planets and stars. My first task, then, is to awaken to the influence of these bonds in my life, unlock them, burst through the prison doors, and find true freedom, the freedom of the unbounded Self. As we do this, we take part in the alchemical process: we rarefy our hidden Self from the base materiality of our flesh; we learn to recognize the false ruts and neurotic patterns of our ego.

Enter the personality test, the navel gazing drill without which any spiritual formation seminar would be incomplete. With its help, like the Philosopher's Stone, we discover the ruts and neuroses preventing personality growth. Wholeness is possible as the therapist lifts us from our personality habits into new, healthier habits. The personality test functions essentially as the horoscope did for the astrologer, but with some scientific accreditation. Jung wrote his *Psychological Types* in 1921, and his theories influenced the popular Myers-Briggs personality test, the Keirsey Temperament Sorter, and the Socionics model. Meanwhile the Enneagram with its nine personality types has Sufi origins, of which "the fundamental idea behind [its personality types] is that each person has a core fixation around which the 'false personality' or 'ego' is constellated."[40] G. I. Gurdjieff explains further: "Essence is the truth in man; personality is the false."[41]

There is the masked me (*persona*) and then there's the real Me (Self). The real Me can tinker around with the masked me and make it whatever I want. The masked me is composed of all those things impressed upon the real Me by family, Church, and state. Such things are falsified, delusory. Healthy growth demands I recognize this fact.

But back to Jung. If we use the alchemical process as a metaphor for personality development, and work in Jung's ideas on the archetype, we can understand the role media plays in pop culture. *Pop* is short for *popular*. *Popular* is whatever majorities of *people* trend toward, and that, in turn, is said to be the acting out of the collective, even the working of the Divine itself.

Alchemically understood, the archetypes and symbols we see in our collective mythologies – on the screens of movies, television, and the computer – are lifted from our collective unconscious and reflect divine, primitive properties. As we are filled with these images, they have the power to lift us from our provincial, ego-based existence, the existence we define by our birth, our country, and our church, and allow us a taste of the collective, the emergence of our hidden Self, which in turn we take back into our mundane existence, reintegrating our ego and our Self. This turns the TV, the movie, and the Internet into a sort of spiritual exercise, even a communion event, a sharing of the various, archetypical myths by a mass of people, all through the medium of a *light device* peopled by electronically conveyed *light beings*, the characters crafted from the various collective archetypes.

Music has the same power, as Joscelyn Godwin writes, "[Music] contains all the requisites for a path of spiritual development. It offers transformative experiences for the body, the emotions, the intellect, and the soul, as surely as the Hermetic tradition does."[42] This we leave for a later discussion, but here we explore the role media has in our alchemical process, particularly in our fantasy life.

✧ Chapter 6 ✧

Mass Media and Phantasms

Giordano Bruno and His Hermetical Magic

No greater spiritual or philosophical system in all of history puts into context the alchemical power our media have on us than that given by the Hermeticists, those Renaissance Gnostics who adopted the ancient cosmological structure, filled it with Gnostic characters and themes, and then worked with it magically. The semblances between today's mass media and the work of Renaissance Hermeticist Giordano Bruno (1548-1600) are uncanny. They need to be explored.

Media is powerful. It manipulates us in ways we should at least be prepared to call magical. No discussion of modern cultural changes can honestly occur without a discussion of mass media and its effects in our psyches, be it in television, movies, print, music, or the Internet. This is a given.

What is not a given is *why* mass media has such power. The answer to this question is without doubt *spiritual*. Use of that word is deliberate according to the Hermetical understanding of the spirit. Mass media operates in this spiritual realm, a realm it populates with fantasy characters playing out themes the media manipulates to some end.

We get a sense of the spiritual dimension when a tragedy hits the airwaves. People will send millions of letters of condolence to the victims; they'll travel hundreds of miles to offer help and comfort; they'll cry together with total strangers. They'll exhibit behavior once reserved for family members, neighbors, or the community. By contrast they often don't know or care about equally tragic events in their actual physical proximity. Mass media has reinvented the Biblical *neighbor*, lifting it from the physical to the abstract, to the realm of fantasy. We are more drawn to distant abstractions of tragedies than to tragedies going on next door, even in our own families or homes. This denotes a very tangible, real, and spiritual revolution, a change in our very core.

There's more . . . much more.

Orthodox Christian teaching grounds its doctrine of love in the teaching that God's creation is good, but fallen. Christian charity calls the believer to look upon someone caught in his fallen condition with compassion and address his need. Quite literally he is to "love his neighbor," *the one nearby him in his physical proximity.* The parable of the Good Samaritan, answering the question, "Who is my neighbor?", is all about physical proximity. The Levite and priest in the parable, in obedience to Hebrew Law, walked out of the range of physical proximity to what they thought was unclean, a corpse, the beaten-up man. The Good Samaritan didn't abstract what he saw through the lens of national pride or misunderstood Hebrew Law, but acted with compassion to what lay before him.

In terms of the Gnostic categories we've been working with, Christian love, or *agape*, is premised on the denial of Self for the sake of Other. It's premised on the separation of beings so despised by the Gnostic.

For the Gnostic, love is something entirely different. We're back at our cosmic bungee cord metaphor, the view of love shared by Neoplatonist and Gnostic alike. Love is an internal yearning for the source of one's being, the Monad. It's a feeling of longing, forlornness, suffering, even sickness, paralleling erotic love or infatuation. Far from a denial of Self, it's an absorption *in* Self. It's not *com*passion for Other (neighbor) but *passion* for the Higher Self, the One. Other (neighbor) is a flesh and blood cosmic mistake. What have I to do with him?

Metaphysically, Christian *agape* is premised on the reification of abstractions: particular beings – from particular trees to particular people – are embraced as good and redeemable in themselves. "The works of the Lord are great, studied by all who have pleasure in them," says the Psalmist, meaning that meditation leads one not to abstractions but to the thing itself in its glorious "is"ness.

In the Neoplatonic/Gnostic system, by contrast, the abstractions are what matter and the particular thing is accidental, incidental, an illusion, even unreal, or in the Gnostic case, corrupt. In this case, love is an internal yearning for higher and higher abstractions up the hierarchy of being: it is *eros*. In the former case, love is directed toward an external object: it is *agape*.

So far, so good. Much of this is by way of review. But the concept needs development.

According to ancient philosophy, as we saw in Plato, body and soul (or mind) were so distinct and separate that they were incompatible/ One of the big conundrums was, *how can the body pick up sensory data and formulate it into universal and transcendent ideas?* For instance, the eye picks up data – greens, browns, and shades – but how this data translates into *tree* is a mystery, particularly if the soul – the thing that gives us the idea of *tree* – is completely distinct from the body.

The child eyes a tree and measures it with his thumb and forefinger. He jokes, "That tree is an inch big!" The tree increases in size from his perspective as he extends his arm. Closer to the eye, the tree will theoretically be reduced to nothing. Yet we know mentally the tree to be about forty to sixty feet. On ancient philosophical terms this is the conundrum.

Renaissance poet Giacomo da Lenino wrestles with the conundrum on another level, "How can it be that so large a woman has been able to penetrate my eyes, which are so small, and then enter my heart and my brain?"[1] In short, how does the soul communicate with the body?

The answer given by several ancient thinkers – philosophers and doctors – was the *spirit*. The spirit mediated between soul and body, assembling data from the body into images for the soul. The spirit was of the same substance as the stars, a subtle substance that "approximates the immaterial nature of the soul, and yet it is a body which, as such, can enter into contact with the sensory world."[2] It was a sort of luminous, filmy substance, sometimes called a veil. Only through this spirit can the body convey its data to the soul. When I see a tree, my eye doesn't hew down the tree and transport it to my cognitive faculties. It takes the image, converts it into a phantasm, and transmits it to the soul for contemplation.

The process is the same for the ear. The soul doesn't receive the sounds we call words; these are incommunicable to it. The sounds must be converted to phantasms before the soul comprehends them. Consequently, "everything that reaches [the soul] from the body – including distinct utterances – will have to be transposed into a phantasmic sequence. . . . *It follows that the phantasm has absolute primacy over the word.*"[3]

Enter the "beyond the Logos" trait of Gnosticism discussed above.

This theory of human cognition explains why Hermeticists respected Egyptian hieroglyphics and symbols in general. The more divinely-attuned Egyptians bypassed the realm of earthly sounds and words for phantasmically-based images more closely approximating the divine knowledge of the soul.

We're back at Plato's *Allegory of the Cave*. The phantasm represents several things going on. It's related to the material, sensory faculties of our bodies because the image conveyed approximates the thing we physically see or hear. But it's related to the soul because the image conveyed is an abstraction of *treeness* under the word we hear as the sound "tree." We ascend out of the cave as we realize the tree *we see* is not real (to be distinguished from the tree we *know*, which most certainly *is* real). Both it and its name are transitory and changeable.

Meanwhile – here is where eros enters – because the Idea of *tree* comes not from its materiality (from what is seen) but from Eternal Being – Monad, Father, my Source, or whatever we would call God – the phantasm of *tree* gets wrapped up into my internal yearning for my Source. I develop a "love for wisdom," a *philosophia*, for the beings making up the cosmos, a love involving contemplation of the nature of the tree. Not only the tree, but my heart is filled with longing for all the innumerable phantasms of nature, all of which eventually lead up, through hierarchical levels, to the Monad, the highest being, where all things are one. Meanwhile the material objects are stand-ins for the Ideas, mere pretexts upon which the mystical ascent begins.

Because the spirit was seen as feminine, the chief phantasm was the feminine, the Divine Woman, Monad reaching out to us through Sophia. Muslim poet Bashshar ibn Burd back in the eighth century identified the spirit as a woman to whom he had dedicated his poems. He was put to death for his heresies. He wasn't unlike Boethius, to whom *Philosophia* also appeared as a woman.

Grammatically speaking the identification works. In Hebrew *ruah* (spirit) is feminine, as is *sophia* in Greek. As linguists know, the feminine gender generally covers the abstracted version of its more concrete, masculine counterpart (eg. *inimicus* (m) "enemy" and *inimicitia* (f) "enmity"). The feminine is the abstract, precisely the realm of the spirit, Neoplatonically understood. By the Middle Ages the femininity of this mediating, abstracting spirit was expressed through the "[i]dealization and even hypostatization of woman."[4]

This idealization, we saw, translated into the erotic love poetry of the troubadours (stemming from Islamic Sufi poetry) as well as the rejection of marriage by the medieval Cathars. No earthly form (like marriage) can institutionalize love for a divine abstraction. A real woman stands in as the expression of the feminine phantasm – she is a "pretext"[5] – and the love song allegorizes the soul's passionate longing for its Source. Her image is a phantasm quite detached from the actual person. Her image is a phantasm in the poet's unconscious, which in turn is an aspect in his own Self he yearns for. No real woman could ever fulfill the longing, so the lover must always live in a state of suffering, of unfulfilled longing. This explains the connection between melancholy and love sickness in the Middle Ages.

Meanwhile, the phantasm begins to take over the subject, who is consumed with the phantasm to the point of self-destruction, or rather, to translation into the phantasm itself: "Metaphorically . . . the subject has been changed into the object of his love."[6]

Put another way, infatuation, the passion of love, is a form of narcissism resulting in, as it did for Narcissus, self-annihilation.[7] Bruno allegorized the process through the Greek myth of Actaeon and Diana. Actaeon is hungry, and while hunting he comes upon a naked Diana, seeing her glory. She turns him into a stag for his crime, and his dogs devour him. The hunter becomes the hunted just at the point he perceives the Divine Woman. He is consumed, but his self-destruction is the cost of divine ecstasy, the sight of the Divine.[8] Physically, self-destruction manifests in base love sickness, the profane eroticism of those who don't know what's really going on. For those in the know, the Gnostic, erotic self-destruction yields divine delirium and mystical ecstasy. For those in the know, love resulting in death is its proper use.

The process anticipates Jung's *anima/animus* archetypes. *Anima* (feminine mind) and *animus* (masculine mind) are the chief archetypes by which the human being – *anima* for the man and *animus* for the woman – is reintegrated with the Collective Unconscious.

For the man, reintegration involves four stages, named after four archetypical women: Eve, Helen, Mary, and Sophia. Eve represents man's understanding of Woman as the object of desire; the woman merely satisfies a need. As far as love is concerned, here man loves the woman as the means of procreation. Helen personifies the Woman of achievement and accomplishment, perhaps a reflection of man's own powers; at any rate by casting these traits onto her, man is beginning the reintegration. Mary represents man's ability to project onto Woman internal spiritual capacities, albeit still in dogmatic form. Sophia symbolizes full reintegration, the adoption of intuition as a means of true knowing beyond any dogmatic framing. Man finally learns that true eros is directed not toward a physical woman and procreation, but toward God herself/himself.[9]

Therein enters Sophia into the realm of fantasy. She represents the mystical union of Self (the male Self) and Woman, the reintegration of the person.

For women, the process is a similar four stage process, but Hermes is the Man. Hermes was the mediator between the gods and man in Greek myth, the messenger of the gods, representing the spirit's intermediary role between body and soul. (Here we also see why Hermes was the patron of the writings attributed to his inspiration, the *Hermetica*.)

The question is, is this lovesickness, this death of Self through its reintegration with the phantasm – Jung's animus/anima reintegration – a good thing or a bad thing? For some in the Renaissance, it was dangerous, a malady. The melancholic person needed remedies to assuage his love sickness, for instance having his head wrapped with the menstrual rags of an aging hag, as sure a cure to the modern sex addict as could be imagined.

To the Gnostic, however, melancholic suffering is salvific, a living out of Christ's call, "whoever loses his life for My sake will find it." In losing his life, he gains life through the phantasm, through reintegration with Sophia. Like Christ, the loss of life calls for suffering, or *passion*. We still retain two senses of this term, the romantic and the cruciform. Only according to a Gnostic framework are they related. In the romantic context, the passion one undergoes in his longing for the Woman is Christlike, exactly aligning with the quest to take up one's cross on the path to salvation. When Bruno was put to the stake for his heresies, it was a fitting end, so typical for the one who like Actaeon has glimpsed the divine. It's the mark of his divine integrity. As Ioan Couliano writes, "In every witchcraft trial – and I believe Bruno's was one – the passion of Jesus was repeated."[10]

Back to the myth of Actaeon and Diana. Bruno describes the ecstatic climax of the reintegration of animus/anima – the self-destruction symbolized by Actaeon being devoured by his dogs – as a point at which the soul leaves behind phantasms, the spiritual realm, and lives purely as a soul-being, contemplating heavenly things having no earthly counterpart. This is the gnosis. This is the return to Monad, as he writes: "he contemplates [the whole horizon] as being one thing, he no longer sees distinctions and numbers according to the diversity of the senses. . . . He sees [the] origin of all numbers, all species, all causes, who is the *monad*, true essence of all being . . . [T]his monad – nature, the universe, the world – derives from the other monad, which is divinity. The latter is reflected and beheld in the former, like the sun in the moon . . . . This one is Diana, the One, the entity, the truth, intelligential nature in which the sun and the splendor of higher nature shine."[11]

Bruno claimed to have had this experience, to have died completely in terms of his earthly existence and enjoyed the heavenly vision. As such he "considers himself a religious leader" like St. Paul, Zoroaster, or St. Thomas.[12] It was for this claim he was executed by the Inquisition and has become a hero to all anti-Church movements.

Couliano comments: "If he sought to be the apostle of a new religion, Bruno no doubt accomplished that wish. His name influenced the spirit and the voice of many a freemason, freethinker, revolutionary, materialist, or anarchist of the nineteenth century." But Couliano also notes, "[he] has become the prophet of a religion of which he would never have approved . . . . He, the most antidemocratic of thinkers, winds up as a symbol of democracy!"[13]

This is one of those mysteries in the history of Gnosticism, something we'll explore further in our discussion on politics: *why does Gnostic spirituality so often turn into a political movement?* Bruno eschewed democracy but was a "fanatic believer in world empire."[14] He hoped Queen Elizabeth, like the moon goddess Diana, would replace the pope, himself symbolized by the sun, as the head of Empire. The image is powerful, cosmic, and quite relevant: the feminine spiritual orientation will replace patriarchy.

Bruno's anti-democratic divergences most certainly abide. But for now we keep our focus on these divergences in terms of *culture*, not politics. To explore more deeply we look at the role of the magician.

The Magician

According to Gnostic elitism, some were in the know and others weren't. As far as the passionate quest for Woman went, the Gnostics were in the know about what was going on. They embraced the passion, the suffering, and ultimately longed for death. They had achieved the

Sophia point in Jung's schema. Those not in the know, however, were fated to stay at the lower levels, ever to see women as objects of desire, or idealizations of their own prowess, or whatever. But as a phantasm, that baseline of desire resides in every human. (Jung identified the first stage in women's reintegration with animus as Tarzan, the type of physical power.)

Furthermore, a Gnostic's gnosis about the mysteries of the cosmos – that it is a creation of a false usurper – places him in a superior relationship to the created order. Enter the tinkerer again, or the magician. The magician knows the workings of the cosmos, and rather than submitting to them in quiet contemplation and awe – *awe for Yaltabaoth? Not him!* – the Gnostic can manipulate and engineer the created order in a way better than Yaltabaoth, by aping Yaltabaoth and doing what he did, but doing it better. At least that's the case for white magic . . . good magic.

In this matrix stands Bruno, the Gnostic, whose work *Of Bonds in General* (1590) fascinatingly and frighteningly assesses how social control works. His manual on magic is the psychological counterpart to Machiavelli's political treatise *The Prince* (1532). Couliano comments, "Without being aware of it, the brain trusts that dominate the world have been inspired by it, have put Bruno's own ideas to practical use."[15]

Couliano goes on to suggest, while no modern politician would adopt the principles of *The Prince*, all of them have coopted the magician's "methods of persuasion and manipulation" as outlined in Bruno. In short, he writes, "the magician of *De vinculis* is the prototype of the impersonal systems of mass media, indirect censorship, global manipulation, and the brain trusts that exercise their occult control over the Western masses"[16]

The magician's task is to understand the phantasy life of the subjects he's trying to manipulate. Their phantasy life takes place in that subtle, luminous, veil or film that is the spiritual realm, of the same substance as the stars. As any individual appropriates his part of the spiritual realm into his own life, the phantasms arise as the mediators between his bodily senses and his soul. These phantasms in turn – being part of, as it were, a single sheet of "subtle spirit" – are arranged in a great cosmic network, each one in sympathy with, or in correspondence with, all other phantasms.

Love is the binding force of the network, the power setting up the networks in which the phantasms are arranged. On what basis, after all, do the phantasms exist but that the subject has a desire for some thing or person he has abstracted into a phantasm? Desire brings phantasms to life. The magician, by working one area of the network, leveraging the power of love related to one phantasm, can influence a corresponding phantasm, and thereby manipulate the subject who possesses that phantasm. The magician's greatest trick is to make the subject believe he is acting from his own resources, totally unaware he's being manipulated by a master magician.

To get to this point, the magician must know his subject, understand his yearnings and his loves. "Like a spy wanting to procure material for future erotic blackmail, the magician must collect all the indices that permit him to file his subject under some classification or other."[17]

Mass manipulation, easier than individual manipulation because more generalized, requires the manipulator to know the demographics of his subjects. In the end, however, Bruno describes how all desires can be reduced to love, to eros: "that is why the Platonists called love the Great Demon, *daemon magnus*," he wrote. Eros, in turn, is understood positively and negatively, as both what the subject yearns for and what he despises.

Here's the kicker: "Magic action occurs through the indirect contact . . . through sounds and images which exert their power over the senses of sight and hearing." These "sounds and images . . . stem from the occult language of the universal spirit."[18]

Understanding how different harmonies affect different souls, for example, is critical in the quest to control him. So also with images. But lurking behind both the sound and the image is the phantasm. That is where the trap is truly set, where the chain is secured, where the bond is set.

Because "love rules the world," as Bruno says, and is "the foundation of all emotions," the magician must free himself from the capacity to be set in bonds, from love. That's his uniqueness, what separates him from everyone else. He knows the game. "He who loves nothing has nothing to fear, to hope, to boast of, to dare, to scorn, to accuse, to excuse himself for, to humiliate himself for, to rival, to lose this temper over. In short, he cannot be affected in any way."[19]

He's the tinkerer, playing with the emotions of his subjects while feigning emotional commitment. He embraces the faith of his subjects while never fully quite committing himself to the ultimate bondage of that faith. While painting on the fabric of their fantasy life a beloved vision for them to imagine, he's "just sitting here watching the wheels go 'round and 'round." He's like our scientists above who know that the world is really about rape and the law of survival, but for the less intelligent it's important for them to hold to the myth of world brotherhood and morality, to keep the world together.

What exactly is the bond and how does it work? Intuitively we know. It's the crafting of a beautiful, abstracted image in our fantasy life for which we yearn. It enters us "through the door of the imagination."[20] Many are the bonds, from man to woman, man to man, man to child, and so on.

Ioan Couliano concludes his study of Bruno's *On Bonds* by noting that magic continues today as the "magician busies himself with public relations, propaganda, market research, sociological surveys, publicity, information," and so on. Today technology works in the realms of the human phantasy life: "Electricity, rapid transport, radio and television, the airplane, and the computer have merely carried into effect the promises first formulated by magic, resulting from the supernatural processes of the magician: to produce light, to move instantaneously from one point in space to another, to communicate with faraway regions of space, to fly through the air, and to have an infallible memory at one's disposal."[21] The magical tools may have changed, but the fundamental power of magic, the erotic bonds governing "intersubjective relationships," remain universal, the same today as it was in the Renaissance.

Curiously, Couliano cannot decide whether this magical control over mass societies is good or bad. After all, what is good or bad in this context? Our instincts are to say all human control by whatever means is bad. But if all human relations are marked by erotic bonds, and "human society at all levels is itself only magic at work,"[22] then what remains to determine is not whether manipulation will occur or not – it's impossible for it *not* to occur! – but whether manipulation will occur for good or for ill. That's the difference between white magic and the dark arts, and of these two, Couliano can't decide which form Western society has assumed, but in the end, he writes, he'd prefer the "magician State" to the "police State."

The police State, he writes, is doomed to fail because it exerts its control superficially, externally. It's ultimately a "jailor State"[23] imposing a "system of restraints" to control its population. The subject obeys out of fear and force, not because of any internal desire.

The magician State, by contrast, conjures up in the subject the "illusion of liberties," and manipulates by "a science of metamorphoses with the capacity to change, to adapt to all circumstances, to improve."[24] It "expects to develop new possibilities and new tactics." It masters the Hermetical art of getting the subject to act a certain way while all along believing he is in control of his actions.

Couliano – a Romanian who grew up in the Eastern Bloc, received political asylum in Italy, and ultimately was murdered by communists at the University of Chicago – wrote his survey of magic and eros in 1987 when the Cold War was coming to an end. From his perspective the jailor State was superior in a superficial sense in its battle with the West because the magician State, instead of using its magical abilities to "hypnotize . . . the advancing cohorts of police,"[25] was too busy exhausting its energies on the transformation of its own society, like a collective Narcissus self-obsessed with its own issues not noticing the bear creeping up to the river's edge. But he believed the future belonged to the magician State.

In the end, however, Couliano's preference for the magician State is more about means than ends. For him, the end and purpose of the state – something that could be established through "knowledge of intersubjective relationships [i.e. erotic magic]" – was a "homogeneous society, ideologically healthy and governable." In such a state, the leaders are magicians "instructed to produce the necessary ideological instruments with the view of obtaining a uniform society."[26]

But isn't a "uniform society" that's "ideologically healthy and governable" the same goal of any totalitarian state? Of course it is. Couliano shares the same ends with the jailor State. He only wants to secure them through different means. The difference is whether the human will is affected internally, so that the subject operates under the "illusion of liberty," or whether that will is directed through coercion.

This is a stunning admission revealing the heart of how a Gnostic thinks. Bruno and all his Hermetical magic could be either profoundly arcane or poppycock. It's irrelevant. What's more interesting is how Couliano and others interpret him, how they view the world if they believe Bruno was on to something. They believe the world is dominated by spiritual and erotic forces controlling all human relationships. While most people submit before these laws unknowingly, the awakened magician can manipulate others toward a "homogeneous [or 'uniform'] society." Meanwhile the rest of us live under the "illusion of liberty" or the "myth of morality" or whatever. All the while we believe we own the transformation of ourselves unto self-identified ends, when in actuality these ends have been manipulated by the magician.

What's most ironical, however, is the paradox this dynamic introduces. Essentially, the Gnostic magician assumes the role of Yaltabaoth! He knows that everything in this physical world is an illusion, that interpersonal relations are all governed by a network of erotic forces, and that these oppressive laws keep us in subjection. This is the way it is; this is the way of the world; this is the way of the world's god. And there's no chance of salvation in terms of an essential liberation from these cosmic forces. So long as people are flesh, that's impossible. But he alone, the Gnostic, stands above this cosmic framework, aping its god in order to assume his powers. He ends up manipulating the world through the same erotic laws governing the world used by Yaltabaoth and his archons!

He'll set out on his "long march through the institutions" and change the institutions from within. He'll take control of capitalism's black magic powers – marketing – and use it on behalf of his own political "messaging." He'll take possession of religion's powers over the mind and repackage them to his ends, all the while saying he's not religious.

Not to fear, however, because he understands the ultimate goodness of "a homogenous [or 'uniform'] society, ideologically healthy and governable."

Because really, what the world needs more of is ideologically governable people. Scary.

All the World's a Stage

The Gnostic realizes all the world is a stage, and we are all actors. This is the motto of the Globe Theatre, home of Shakespeare's plays: *totus mundus agit histrionem* ("the whole world plays the actor").

Shakespeare's theater was so named because of ancient psychology, reflecting the same cosmological architecture embraced by Bruno but more specifically by another Hermetical thinker, Giulio Camillo (1480-1544). His treatise, *The Idea of Theater* (1544), proposed that the whole world is a stage into which our souls have fallen through the various planetary spheres. In our fleshly existence we merely play a part. On those terms, Shakespeare is the magician.

Shakespeare's plays constituted not only the external drama of various personality types clashing, but also the internal drama of the mind, as in Hamlet's soliloquies. There, the spectator is granted a seat in Hamlet's mind, itself a reflection of the cosmos. It is, literally, the globe, but the globe, like the Platonists told us, is a reflection of the mind and vice versa.

Throughout his plays this interplay between the external and internal worlds goes on, as when, in the tragedy *Othello*, the storm augurs the demise of the protagonist's interracial marriage. Something is rotten in the external world at the same time something is rotten in the psychological drama of the hero's mind, and interesting the role that eros (romance) plays in Shakespeare's tragedies!

In one sense, Shakespeare grants us a seat from his perch, as spectators watching all the sad or silly (tragic or comic) drama unfold on the stage of this world's physical existence, to see how eros blinds the players and affects their behavior. We get to play Gnostic, to be in-the-know about the goings on of the world, all the while detached from it. But this analysis ignores the role catharsis plays, for the rules of Gnostic elitism don't allow all of us to be detached magicians like Shakespeare. His plays suck us in. Their themes, archetypes, and characters attach themselves to our spirits, which is what catharsis is. As we vicariously see ourselves in the characters, we face our own emotions and are moved to action, the ultimate magic trick! From the poet-magician's perspective the lure has been set. Shakespeare is like the manipulator working the marionettes operating the various characters with the deftness not of his fingers, but his poetic genius. Meanwhile we wonder who the true marionettes are, the players on the stage or us in the seats.

Shakespeare blossomed under Queen Elizabeth, the Sophia type, the representative of a new age of spiritual reorientation. She was the virgin, after all, the head of a religion against Rome, the Church of England. She was a counterpart to *Maria Beata* (blessed Mary), being *Eliza Beta*. Leading an expanding and confident British Empire, she represented the possibility of a new political order.[27] As we saw, this did not escape the notice of the Hermeticists.

Many people don't or can't read Shakespeare. Time has made his language abstruse, neutralizing his powers. But he laid the foundation for the relationship between artist and spectator, between manipulator and manipulated. He admitted as much through Prospero, the magician in *The Tempest*. In this last of Shakespeare's plays, many of the Hermetical themes crop up, for example the idea that a magician manipulates the unfolding drama of a situation to work things out to his advantage. Prospero begins the play in exile on an island but manipulates events to secure a ride home, where he receives a dukedom.

His concluding epilogue has been interpreted as a fitting sign-off for the Bard, who upon retirement believed his days of magic were over: "Now my charms are all o'erthrown, And what strength I have's mine own . . . my ending is despair, Unless I be relieved by prayer, Which pierces so, that it assaults Mercy itself, and frees all faults. As you from crimes would pardon'd be, Let your indulgence set me free."[28]

His was a different age. European minds dabbled in magic but remained grounded in Christianity. Shakespeare knows he's manipulating and casting charms on his audience, but in the end he begs *their* pardon, that they might set him free from the allurements of being the magician. Like Pascal, the comfort of Christian faith is too powerful to subvert with magic's enticements. The magician, the poet, the scientist, and later the political theorist may set sail from the mainland of Christian orthodoxy, and like Prospero they may be exiled on intriguing islands of magical insight, but ultimately their grounding, their Christian foundation, called them back home.

No longer. The ships of the spirit left European shores and didn't return home. They set up shop in the New World, a land not under the assumptions of the old, a land where the magician need not apologize to his subjects.

Which brings us to today. Hollywood obviously assumes the role played by the magician, at least in theater. Hollywood works in new charms added over the four hundred years since the Renaissance. In particular, the postmodern creed and the Jungian archetypes have given modern theater an almost dogmatic flair, yielding a bizarre maelstrom of psychological stresses with their own subset of magical influences on us.

The movie, *The Truman Show* (1998), directed by Peter Weir and starring Jim Carrey is especially instructive, because the lines between actors, spectators, and directors are so fuzzy. Truman (played by Jim Carrey) was taken as a baby and placed in a completely manufactured world. His mother, his neighbors, even his wife are all actors who work on a set, a set Truman believes is his home town. Unbeknownst to him, Truman's life is broadcast throughout the world via hidden cameras. It's the ultimate reality show based on Truman's daily dramas.

The producer of the show, Christof (played by Ed Harris), is the magician, operating all the characters affecting Truman's life like a manipulator of marionettes. At the same time he manipulates Truman's world we see he's also manipulating the spectators in the movie, who watch Truman on the screen and themselves are frequently panned with their glossy-eyed, wonder-filled, hypnosis-like expressions.

Recognizing the existential postmodern-creed plot line with its Gnostic archetypes is an interpretational chip-shot given the Gnostic foundation we've laid. Michael Brearley and Andrea Sabbadini do the yeoman's work: "[Truman is a] prototypical adolescent at the beginning of the movie. He feels trapped into a familial and social world to which he tries to conform while being unable to entirely identify with it, believing that he has no other choice (other than through the fantasy of fleeing to a far-way island). Eventually, Truman gains sufficient awareness of his condition to 'leave home' – developing a more mature and authentic identity as a man, leaving his child-self behind and becoming a True-man."[29]

True to Gnostic form, it is memory of a woman – the girlfriend of his youth played by one of Christof's actresses who ends up falling in love with Truman; later she broke onto the set and tried to tell him the truth; she's a Sophia figure – that draws Truman toward his awakening. He triumphs over the manipulations of Christof; the spectators in the movie cheer him on. Alas! All's well that ends well!

Or does it?

Because . . . are those spectators watching the movie *Truman* any different from those spectators *in* the movie, who played such an integral part in the plot, who themselves were portrayed by the movie as manipulated just as much as Truman? And are the producers who produced the movie manipulating us through the movie's storyline any different from Christof? One wonders whether, like Shakespeare through Prospero, Hollywood through Christof is broadcasting their role as magician, only doing it without asking our forgiveness.

But this brings us back to Bruno's principle that the magician, in order to set the lure on his subject, must have faith in the erotic bond he is using, or at least make us believe he has that faith. The existential subplot of *The Truman Show* is itself a magician's charm feeding our own yearnings, but it goes undetected because Hollywood believes its own magic. We leave the movie thinking, "Whew! Good thing Truman found his own authentic Self and was freed from illusion," and we conclude this was Hollywood's ultimate message, a message we believe is good and true, and a message we believe Hollywood believes as well.

But never do we wonder whether we've just been manipulated to believe this existential narrative arc is an ultimately good trajectory in the first place. And the fact that we do not wonder such things, that we accept it without thinking, is the setting of the lure. We can't evaluate and delve into things we cannot see. It's a blind spot, and eros blinds us.

It's remarkable to what extent Truman's authentic Self was a nonentity. What did he have to fall back on once he discovered his entire world was manufactured? Nothing! Truman came to the core of his onion and found nothing: no family, no Church, no society, nothing. What then, exactly, are we cheering at the movie's denouement? The poor guy is falling in the abyss! *No, no, no.* We have to understand the role eros has in this narrative. The memory of the Woman, the love for the Woman, is why we cheer. That is Truman's salvation. His authentic Self is wrapped up in the Woman. Neither Jung nor Bruno could craft a more apt plot line to express their ideas.

Movies have to end eventually, and so they can't delve into the boring part of Truman's new existence when he and his lover have to negotiate issues like, "How are we going to raise our children, Truman? Your entire experience on child-rearing was manufactured. You have nothing to contribute." And Truman theoretically will have to agree, going on in a sort of slavish existence with his wife. Magic is deflated when the mundaneness of reality enters the picture. Reality is the perennial enemy of Gnosticism.

This magical dynamic drives so much of what Hollywood offers. They leverage the postmodern creed – the existentialism marinaded in Jungian archetypes – and by so doing reaffirm the myth in their subjects, which in turn sets them up for further manipulation. The postmodern creed dominates Hollywood myth-making, too many movies to number. The plots always involve some character living in a situation in which he's not able to be his authentic Self, or be with the woman with whom he is *meant* to be (who said Hollywood isn't religious?), or else, negatively, is caught in his circumstances and cannot break free, so he develops certain neuroses. Redemption occurs when he breaks out of his situation and becomes who he is meant to be, or in the negative example, the one who cannot break free becomes the villain of the movie (as in the case of the Marine in *American Beauty* (1999), a homosexual who cannot accept who he is and it leads him to murder).

In the movie *Titanic* (1997), directed by James Cameron, the main female character, Rose, is trapped in a conventional engagement her parents set up for her. She is mildly (almost sleepily, as in a daze) accepting of her lot, until she meets the uncouth Jack, a male Sophia figure. Jack is real. Jack is authentic. He's not stuffy and conventional.

He's an artist, a romantic. Jack awakens her. Jack leads her through a journey of Self-discovery, winding through the labyrinth of what so many have seen as a metaphor of modern life, the *Titanic*. Like Yaltabaoth's world, it is peopled by those who live under its various illusions – illusions about class, about marriage, about gender. Even religion's hopes are rendered illusory as we watch the gentry sing the Navy Hymn, offering petitions for safety we know will be unanswered. Meanwhile the various archons, those governors of the established order (represented mainly by the butler of Rose's fiancé), try to prevent their love.

Eventually after sex with Jack, she is set on a new course. But like something out of the Globe Theatre, where the drama unfolding inside the individual parallels the external drama, the climax of their love anticipates the crackup of the Titanic. So it must be, for authentic erotic love will always set modernity's assumptions on a collision course. The death of Jack – death and love are always related in the Gnostic myth (marriage being entirely too mundane, earthly) – becomes redemptive for Rose, something Christlike. She will now live her life being truly free, having found her authentic Self. And behold at the end how she becomes the emblem of the liberated woman, flying planes, doing whatever she feels.

In the *divided-and-then-united* alchemical sense, Rose underwent transformation. Her better Self was abstracted from her sleepy, leaden ego, united with Jack, and then through the death of the latter she lives on carrying Jack with her, a Jungian fusion of anima/animus, a golden soul. It's an entirely spiritual dynamic, symbolized at the end of the movie when she as an elderly woman casts her treasured necklace into the ocean. Her last physical hold on the earth is cast away, and later she dies, being reunited not with her husband, but with Jack.

We move to another 1990s classic. We recall the role *choice* has in the existential narrative. Without choice, no one can truly participate in the great journey of Self-authentication. The movie, *Saving Private Ryan* (1998), nicely works this theme into its plot line and serves as an excellent primer on how contemporary culture applies the existential narrative to a rather difficult subject, the reality of war. Steven Spielberg contrasted his own film with World War II films of the past: "as a youngster I got the impression that war was something to be glorified, to be looked at with a kind of awe."[30] The older war movies glorified the cause, usually defined in patriotic or humanitarian terms; meanwhile the erotic or authentic aspirations of the characters didn't add up to, in Bogart's famous words, "a hill of beans."

Spielberg opted for something different. Even if Captain Dale Dye, the Marine employed to help the actors understand the Soldiers' ethic, understood "that people sacrificed to serve their country in the military,"[31] Spielberg didn't convey this in the movie. Dying for one's country played no role in the movie. In the early part of the film, death was nothing more than senseless and random slaughter in the name of some meaningless or incomprehensible principle.

Choice, however, ennobles death. At a dramatic point in the movie, each of the main characters makes the choice to dedicate himself to one random act which would define himself, that is, *saving Private Ryan*. That was a cause that could redeem the death we knew was coming, not because Private Ryan meant anything, but because each Soldier made the choice.

But the choice is not quite the redemption. That's the sacrament. As with all sacraments, it's the grace conveyed that finally matters, not the means by which that grace comes. The sacrament of choice is the means by which the grace of eros comes. Just before the moment arrives when most of the characters died for their choice, while waiting to ambush the German army in the town, the Soldiers discover an old phonograph with a recording by Edith Piaf in it, *Tu es Partout*. Piaf's voice echoes through the broken-down, drab-grey town like eros' call amidst our broken world. It's full translation can only do justice to the incredibly erotic and Gnostic undertones – especially in its placement in the movie. It's all but a Gnostic hymn:

> we loved each other tenderly
> like we loved all lovers
> then one day you left me
> ever since I've been desperate
> I see you everywhere in the sky
> I see you everywhere on the earth
> you are my joy and my sun
> my nights, my days, my clear dawns
>
> you are everywhere because you are in my heart
> you are everywhere because you are my happiness
> everything that is around me
> even life does not represent you
> sometimes I dream that I am in your arms

and you speak softly in my ears
you say things that make me close my eyes
and I find that marvelous

maybe one day you will return
I know that my heart waits for you
you can not forget
the past days we spent together
my eyes never stop searching for you
listen well, my heart calls you
we can love each other again
and you'll see life would be beautiful[32]

Here sings the lonely lover, yearning for reunion with lost love. The lover is discerned everywhere. Is it God? Is it the lover? He is everywhere because he is in her heart, yet life cannot fully represent him. Rather, in those quiet moments, in her dreams, the lover appears. One day they may love each other again, in a beautiful world, in a beautiful life. That is the redemption of the Soldiers who made the choice to sacrifice themselves for the random act of saving Private Ryan. Shortly after the song most of the Soldiers met their deaths. Eros climaxes in the destruction of Self, presaged by the discussion two of the Soldiers had during the song, one joking about wanting to commit suicide and the other telling an erotic story about a buxom teacher in his high school.

From erotic love as "a hill of beans" to love as "you are everywhere, [where] my heart calls you" in fifty-six years, a fitting metaphor for our own cultural history!

A less subtle Gnostic theme in cinema is from the *Star Wars* series, based on Jungian archetypes which in turn were rooted in Gnosticism. Gnostic themes dominate. The entire galaxy is under the magical control of the Empire (Yaltabaoth and his archons). Certain individuals, the Jedi (the spiritual ones), are an elite group which, endowed with magical abilities, are in tune with the force (the inner spark; the Self; made up of a collective of former Jedi, similar to the pleroma). When awakened to their potential (moment of gnosis), certain gurus (Christ figures; Obi Wan Kenobi) lead them through the stages of initiation until they join that elite group, tasked with the job of liberating others from the oppressive powers of the empire. Once again, the external drama of the Empire parallels the internal drama of Anakin Skywalker. Without reintegration of his "dark side" (Darth Vader), what Jung termed the shadow archetype, both Anakin and the entire galaxy will be lost. Obviously we all know the end.

Finally, there is the Gnostic movie series *par excellence*, *The Matrix* trilogy (1999-2003). The world of *The Matrix*, like that of the Gnostic, is dualistic. Computers have taken over the bodies of humans and, in order to keep them alive and happy, have plugged their minds into an imaginary world. Each human mind believes itself to be living a contented existence in twentieth century America, but in fact, the bodies attached to these minds are being used by the computers as batteries to fuel their own computer world.

Neo, the protagonist, is a Christlike figure ("the one") who frees minds from the imprisonment created by the computer world. He's aided by mystics, prophets, and adepts who possess secret knowledge of the way things truly are. As minds are freed from this computer-induced sleep, they discover the real world, an underground world dominated by the city Zion. Before a final battle scene, the city of Zion erupts in a frenzied celebration of dance and music, engaged in a ritual that finds parallels in the orgiastic rites of the mystery cults. The image is powerful. The world of the computer is false, deceptive, and conventional (typified by the grey-drab conformist dress and look of the antagonists). The world of Zion is primal, authentic, and expressive. The movie presents what we think to be real as fake, meanwhile offering what amounts to a rave in the sad underbelly of an industrial park as real. Ravers everywhere can rest content – their lifestyle has been sacralized.

The interesting thing about *The Matrix* trilogy is, it's sort of a reverse Gnostic myth. In the ancient Gnostic myth, the body is free in what appears a typical existence in this world, while the mind is imprisoned and needs to be awakened. In *The Matrix*, it's the opposite. The body is imprisoned, and the mind is free in what appears to us a typical existence. In the Gnostic myth, the freed mind ascends into heavenly light. In *The Matrix*, the gnosis is chthonic, a descent into subterranean regions. Curiously, where the traditional Gnostic salvation was seen as more heavenly, a flood of light for instance, *The Matrix* reveals some sort of strange goings on about our postmodern age in that, living in underground cities is seen as more salvific – a Zion – than the old shining "city on a hill" Zions of the past.

Communicating with the Light Beings

Let's take things to the next level, the manner with which we communicate with movies or TV, because it's almost uncanny. Wide-eyed, with torpor, I sit in front of the portal, assuming a rather odd, unhumanly pose. I don't engage it, or converse with it. It's a one-way form of communication. I hardly apply the skills of a logician to test its non sequiturs, feats of superhumanness, or impressionistic storylines. I might offer a weak "Like that would happen . . ." now and then.

Still, many people think it can and does happen. Of course aliens exist. Of course corporate board rooms routinely trade human lives for marginal profits. Of course the CIA was probably behind the Kennedy assassination. How many of us have the opinions we hold because of media, not even news media, but *fictional* media? How many of us unthinkingly accept the media's archetypical shorthand, their two-dimensional characterizations of real life people?

It speaks to an odd formatting of our minds. One reason the Dark Ages are called dark is because the world and vision of a typical denizen of that age consisted of a ten-mile radius around the castle. A peasant or knight had little to no knowledge of other cultures, religions, ideas, or peoples. But our own "Light Ages" give us a ten-foot radius around our flat screens and computers, and we have our own lack of knowledge about anything beyond this world of light. We think we know truth and reality, but what we really know is an archetypical presentation of truth. The Light-Being enters my soul, works in the Hermetical realm of the spirit, and builds a fantasy reality, shaping the very contours of my normality. It's truly a magical event.

Many people have a better relationship with the Light-Being – we watch 34.5 hours of television a week[33] – than they do with their own neighbors. The lines between my Self and the Light-Being become fuzzy. Gone are the physical parameters giving rise to *neighbor*.

This is why we get so personally invested in stories hitting the airwaves. We lose our perspective, falling in love with phantasms and images. We become easily manipulated. We might have a neighbor with a child down the street struggling to survive because he doesn't have a job. We might say *"Get a job!"* and we might be right. Or we might help him because we know his circumstances; we live near it. At least that's what neighborliness used to mean. On the other hand, some celebrity will speak plaintively about the poor, brown children of Timbuktu to the emotive melodies of a piano, and off we go running to our checkbooks. That money could be going anywhere, but it doesn't matter. We felt so good doing it.

But this is among the many myths these forms of media craft in our fantasy lives and then exploit. Poor, brown children half way around the globe are lodged in our fantasy life, and caring for them constitutes the epitome of love. The American church leader or politician or high school senior who can add to the monthly newsletter or his resume that picture of himself surrounded by poor brown people, heaven itself isn't worthy of such as these. It's a piety arising from the bits and pieces of trendy ideologies. Whatever those ideologies are, the archetype has been embedded in our fantasy life, and the magician has a ready-made myth to leverage for his ends, usually the generation of cash flow.

This is just one of many myths. There are many others. We've already brought up the archetypes about aliens or government, or the CIA. But what about others? What about images of men as chiseled, reckless heroes, or images of women as urbane, sexually liberated beauties kicking the asses of men twice their size? Or what about the variety of other archetypical characters, the other-worldly child who speaks simple wisdom; the teen girl love interest who inspires the angst-ridden teen boy, or vice versa; the monstrous outlier character who is just misunderstood; the homeless, fey character screaming a truth no one will hear?

On the negative side, the archontic myths persevere as well. These are those dark figures in finance and business who place profit above everything, even at the risk of mass death. We all know that this is what goes on behind the scenes in board rooms everywhere because, well, because why? Because we all have experience sitting in corporate board rooms? Of course not, but we are granted a fantastical seat in such movies as *Unstoppable* (2010), based on a true story about a runaway train. There, we learn that the major factor determining what measures the CEO will take to stop the train is how a mass-casualty crash event will affect stock prices. There's actually a character who figures that information out in about a half hour's time. In any event, this is why these movies say "based on" true events and not "a true story." They add their Hollywood flourishes, and those flourishes are almost always rooted in Gnostic archetypes.

On and on we could go with the various types animating the silver screen. All of these are absolute fantasies, crafted as fantasies and developed in our souls as fantasies. In reality they rarely exist. They are figments of our imaginations and hopes, reality deconstructed and re-constructed according to the dictates of the manipulators. Yet every time we declare about some person or event – "It's like a character/scene out of a movie!" – we betray an unprecedented formatting of the human soul: fantasy has become more real than reality.

Human souls are complex. Movies and television literally remove a dimension from the three-dimensionality we expect in the human person. They remove physicality from the person, sucking him dry of his flesh and blood. Meanwhile the archetypes are granted full authority to communicate their cargo into our souls. Soon our choices are dictated by the craftiness of a show's engineers. We become two-dimensional characters ourselves. Our lives, our manners, our styles, our clothing, and our attitudes become scripted, and we believe such an existence is more true than reality.

Repeating almost verbatim these sentiments, media scholar Jane Stewart, introducing the "female trickster" archetype, writes, "[Movies] can be modern day mythmakers activating new archetypal images in the culture. Together, sitting in the dark, we can change our lives and update ancient mythology. Mythic figures like Aphrodite and Hermes are not simply characters but psychic energies that come alive through the medium of film. For instance, when we go to movies and identify with images of women appearing in film, we are not only observers but participants in the making of myths about the feminine sensibility we live by."[34]

Working the alchemical formula perfectly, media targets us precisely at the eros points in our soul, those areas of Self-absorbed longing, where we long for this or long for that (a character trait, a desirable personality, a product, etc.). It attaches itself to that longing, making us feel more alive, as we vicariously live our ideals through the medium. It's a pure magical moment according to the very terms set up by the Renaissance Hermeticists. My only contribution to the process is when I wave the magic wand known as the remote control. But who is controlling that magic wand?

Later in her essay on the female trickster archetype, Stewart observes (in a celebratory sort of way), "Archetypes on the big screen come alive in society as audiences take them home. . . . When we watch a movie, identifying with a female protagonist and her dilemmas, the archetype is at work. As we're enjoying the heroine, crying or laughing in the dark, we're also taking her into our hearts and minds – and letting her change us. We feel smart, clever, and good. The next thing we know, she's in our workplace, pulling the lever in our voting box, and making different choices down the street at the local store."

How a woman making choices based on images manipulated by some behind-the-scenes crafter of archetypes – who very well may be a man – accords with the view that she is making rational choices as a free individual eludes us. Of course, if all the world is governed by magic, it doesn't matter. Better to be manipulated by Stewart's archetypes than by patriarchal archetypes embedded in "the system" because, well, Stewart just knows they're better. She's a Gnostic.

A far more healthy engagement with media is given by Julie Gunlock. She humorously describes the magic going on with the media's alarmist fixation on the "hidden dangers" in our homes: "It's weird. I sometimes fall for it. I know I shouldn't but sometimes . . . only once in a while . . . I forget and fall into the alarmist trap. These news anchors seem so eager to protect me, so gallant, with such nice hair and skin. They look like they smell really good and take care of their teeth. They are genuinely concerned for my kids. I think they like me. I bet they'd want to hang out. . . . And then I snap out of it and remember that this is all part of the plan to freak me out so that I will welcome, even demand, the guiding hand of government."[35]

Snapping out of it and reconnecting with reality is exactly the remedy to magic, manipulation, and hypnosis. Sadly, this might be asking for too much. Adults prefer to be raptured by some silly sit-com while their children beg to revel in their physical humanity: play a game, play catch, wrestle, whatever. But not to fear. The children will soon be transformed into similar zombies as well. They'll become obese. They'll lose their creativity. They'll plug into the fast, bright lights of the box, whatever box that is, a realm of exciting prospects where you can leave your humanity behind and become an avatar, a god of your own world. And when the box turns off, and they return to the mundane realm of human existence formerly known as God's creation, they become bored, lethargic, and depressed, as only Yaltabaoth's drab-grey world can be.

Melancholy

Is America love sick?

Sometimes Occam's Razor helps explain phenomena: the simplest explanation is the true one. Is depression on the rise among all demographic groups, even pre-schoolers (!), due to this media revolution? Is it a coincidence that "mass unhappiness"[36] demanding the new tools of psychology came hand in hand with the proliferation of mass media, in the 1950s? 34.5 hours doing anything is an awful long time. That's literally a third of our waking hours, a third of our lives lived in an imaginary, fantasy world of "technological ecstasy."[37] And this doesn't factor in the amount of time spent on video games, plugged into music, or time spent social networking. This world of light – of fast-paced, flickering fun – is exciting, all the more because it works with erotic themes, beautiful people, exciting plots.

Then we turn it off: *have to feed the dog, have to buy groceries, have to eat, have to go to the bathroom, have to get that stink off my skin and take a shower.* Care of the body, the mundane, intrudes on my world of light. It's depressing.

History has seen this movie before. In the Middle Ages they called it *melancholy*, and the explanations for it from Renaissance doctors of the soul are surprisingly relevant to today.

According to the reasoning of the Renaissance Hermeticists like the above-surveyed Bruno, melancholic personalities (which he claimed he was) are more in tune with the spirit world than the body. They are more prone to *vacatio*, that habit of leaving the body behind to drift into the realm of thoughts, imaginations, and fantasies. Thus they're more likely to be artists, poets, thinkers, philosophers, scientists, and generally speaking, geniuses. It's the classic personality type of the moody artist.

Couliano hints at something we all suspect, that "this melancholic epidemic can be explained also by a secret solidarity between the patient and the sickness, since the yearning for 'useful suffering' [affects] all those who, for one reason or another, were not satisfied with what earthly existence can offer. They had bumped against its confines."[38]

In other words, they were depressed *because they wanted to be*. It was part of their salvation, their "place of sweetness," their passionate longing to leave the "confines," the prison cell, of this boring, dull world behind. To give up their depression would be to give up the possibilities of a world of light, or of sound, and accept life in the mundane world. The melancholic artist or thinker type, far from needing to be cured of his love sickness, secretly craves his depression and embraces it even as he embraces his imaginary world of light and eros. To embrace one is to embrace the other.

As Vaughan-Lee notes in the context of Sufi ideas on love and longing, "Longing can so easily be misunderstood as a psychological problem, even a depression. One who suffers it can feel rejected and isolated, not realizing that longing is the greatest gift because it does not allow us to forget Him whom the heart loves."[39]

Saturnine is a synonym of melancholic because it was believed such a person possessed of a saturnine nature received his soul while Saturn ruled the zodiac. Saturn was the most distant then-known planet. It was the closest to the divine realms.   Thus the saturnine, melancholic personality type had the greatest propensity for phantasmic ideation. Phantasms filled his spirit and stayed there longer. In the medieval mind, this astrological framework explained why melancholics tended on one hand toward sloth, apathy, cowardice, indifference in relationships, and that medieval soul disease known as *acedia*. On the other hand, it was most often the type of the artist, genius, and those given to contemplation and abstract reasoning. In short, it was the personality type of those most prone to *vacatio*, the "separation [i.e. vacating] of the soul from body."[40] This led on one hand to carelessness regarding the body and its relationships, but also to a greater aptitude for phantasmic activity, which is to say, contemplation of divine things, or to use the Romantic term, *imagination.*

The artist or scientist is closest to the apex of the chain of being, therefore most likely to ape God (or Yaltabaoth) in creating alternate and presumably better realities. Media expert James Bowman wrote shortly after the debut of the James Camaron's movie *Avatar* (2009), "Recently, Internet chat forums on the film's fan sites have been clogged (one was closed after more than 1,000 posts) by viewers reporting feelings of depression and despondency after seeing the movie. On one site, a discussion called 'Ways to cope with the depression of the dream of Pandora being intangible' featured myriad fans recounting just how repulsed they were . . . by the reality of life on Earth after witnessing the phosphorescent beauty of Pandora."[41]

He quotes a *New York Times* writer presuming to speak for scientists, who upon immersion in the 3-D world of *Avatar* "enters into a state of ecstatic wonderment, [and has] the urge to leap up and shout: 'Yes! That's exactly what it's like!'"

That's dangerous stuff, but no wonder people are depressed. If the scientist in cahoots with the artist – both melancholics – are able to craft into our fantasy life not just reflections of our realities, *but actual new realities,* and then claim that these are "exactly what it's like," who wouldn't be depressed when his own mundane existence in no way approximates "it"?

Studies confirm the link between Internet usage and depression. "[T]he computer is like electronic cocaine," says Peter Whybrow of the

Semel Institute for Neuroscience and Human Behavior. The Diagnostic and Statistical Manual of Mental Disorders has added "Internet Addiction Disorder" to its list of addictions. In a University of Maryland study a student confesses, "I clearly am addicted." "Media is my drug," says another. Of course, as with any addiction, the driving force is the vicious cycle of mania and depression. Studies regularly find a connection between frequent Internet or video game usage and depression. "[T]he more a person hangs out in the global village, the worse they are likely to feel. Web use often displaces sleep, exercise, and face-to-face exchanges, all of which can upset even the chirpiest soul."[42]

Meanwhile studies emerge on the depression of Facebook users.[43] The urge to keep up with a multiplying brigade of electronic Joneses, who every hour casually toss aside reports of their latest exciting escapades while I'm doing dishes and changing diapers, crafts another sort of fantasy existence. But that's what it is, fantasy. Teens are burned out on social media, which might explain Facebook's loss of popularity among teens. They understood the fantastical game: it's all about crafting a persona and keeping up with it. Young users admit to crafting several personas. If Freud introduced the fissured psyche, could he ever have foreseen the multiplication of psyches in today's world? But according to the postmodern creed, this is all justified. It's all a game, really, this art of crafting the persona. My authentic Self lurks behind my screen like the magician as I craft my personas in the fantasy world of Facebook, and these in turn bait the various victims and subjects I wish to manipulate: the opposite sex, those in my peer group, those who share my interests. For once I can play the part of Christof, or Shakespeare, or James Cameron.

But the devil exacts his pound of flesh. Along with embracing the role of the magician must come melancholy, as the Hermeticists knew. Hence the depression.

In the spirit of moderation, part of being human means taking vacations into escapist fantasies. But as Bowman notes, "the difference between a neurotic and a psychotic was once defined by saying that the former built castles in the air and the latter lived in them."

What distinguishes our day of fantasy is the illusion we can live in these places for real. Today we're beyond the crafting of a fantasy life into our imaginations. We're at the point of saying, "Enough! It's time to quit talking and make the leap into this world!" Fun diversion now becomes urgent mission. And that inspires strong emotion, particularly that of depression when, in fact, we learn that this fantasy world can never be attained.

Martin Luther had an expression he used to describe the soul-disease of this navel-gazing, Self-obsessed, fantasy-making, depressed personality: *incurvatus in se*, or "curved in on oneself." He often had to deal with the melancholic Melanchthon, himself a man of the Renaissance who dabbled in Hermeticism. Luther's remedy was a life lived *extra nos*, "outside yourself," a life lived through love of neighbor and in the faith of the Church. The expression *incurvatus in se* aptly fits our own day, as we behold a population slouched over their electronic devices, curved in on their own little passions, curved in their own Selves, ignoring others, ironical and irreverent about forms and formalism.

On these terms, "sit up straight!" at the dinner table is not just manners. It's soul medicine.

Marketing, the Art of Memory, and the Retention of Sperm

Conformity is the goal of marketing: *get as many people as possible to buy a given mass-produced product.* Yet, the default posture of America is the existential postmodern creed: *I choose my own path as I create my Self and break free from the conformist rules.*

How do these two paradoxical aims square? The solution has been the systemization of the postmodern creed in modern marketing: *Each person must find his own path, learn to be authentic, go through his existential moments, break free from the bonds of family, Church, and state, and product X will help him.*

Generally such marketing aims to convince me that, by purchasing a certain product, I'm not joining millions of others who are also doing so. Rather I'm making choices and crafting my authentic Self.

Again Bruno's psycho-social model helps explain the spiritual process going on in a typical commercial. The marketer is the magician worming his way into the subject's onion core. He plants the idea all the while convincing the subject his choice is freely made.

Here, Bruno's eros comes in, the most important tool in the magician's kit. Sex sells. In the typical car commercial, for example, we all know what's subconsciously going on: if I buy that car, it will improve my sex appeal and attract the type of woman in the ad. Again, the likes of Bruno spent a lifetime analyzing the various erotic baits, according to the multitude of demographic variables. So also Madison Avenue. Not everyone is seduced by porn stars. The attracting types are many, but whether it be a sex kitten caressing a Corvette or a stately soccer mom smartly driving her Chrysler Town and Country, the erotic bond is intentional.

During its *Chevy Runs Deep* ad campaign, Chevy ran an ad promoting the Malibu. Two 35 - 45-year-old couples are going out. Spandau Ballet's 1983 hit *True* is playing on the radio, and the three passengers begin singing. Suddenly the driver turns down the song so that the others can hear the wonderful sound of the engine as he explains its fuel efficiency. His annoyed, very normal-looking wife in the passenger seat turns up the song and spunkily sings the song again in the driver's face as if to say, "take this!" Something reaching into the core of the target audience (my demographic, which is why it sticks out in my memory) is more true than a porn star caressing a Corvette. The ad works various charms, each of which feeds off the others. Spandau Ballet was the sound track for any number of infatuations in that circa forty-year-old demographic, recalling good feelings of youthful eroticism.

Meanwhile, there sits the Chevy Malibu, whose wonders are oddly slighted in the commercial, overwhelmed by Spandau Ballet. Yet the bigger point of the ad campaign is *Chevy Runs Deep*. The writers of the ad are crafting the fantasy that Chevy runs deep in our psyche. It lurks deep in our fondest memories, in that cauldron of fantasies along with Spandau Ballet and that age of youthful eroticism. *Yeah, I could imagine going back in time, being in love at the age of 14, listening to Spandau Ballet, and in the background of that memory see a Chevy in my driveway. And yeah, how nice it would be to resurrect that memory, especially when placed in an updated, hip, cool, urban context with beautiful people.*

As far as the beautiful people are concerned, the ad is peopled by four characters, two of whom are two-dimensional and beautiful (the woman almost out-of-place, a twentysomething amidst forty-year-olds; she says nothing in the commercial), while the two driving the plot are attractive enough, but far more real. The two male/female pairs conspire to manipulate the rarefaction process in the viewer's soul. The real characters with whom we identify draw us in. The beautiful characters are the wallpaper of a possible existence. They are what is possible if only I purchase a Chevy Malibu.

Marketing is big business and a well-crafted ad demands huge resources. By some estimates, car companies spend thirty billion dollars on marketing. That's two million cars that need to be sold just to cover marketing! Borrell Associates estimates total spending on ads in 2011 was $238.6 billion, an enormous figure. Such money would not be spent if it weren't effective.[44]

But again, *why* is it effective, and more interestingly, *how* is it effective?

Back to Bruno. In hermetical terms, phantasms are how sounds and sights are communicated to the soul. They dwell in the spirit, translating sensory data to the mind. Insufficient as the word is, the hieroglyph was preferred as a heightened form of communication, something the more spiritually-attuned Egyptians knew.

One of the implications was that memory was enhanced though the instrumentality of the phantasm. Couliano writes, "The Art of Memory is a technique for the manipulation of phantasms, which rests on the Aristotelian principle of the absolute precedence of the phantasm over speech and of the phantasmic essence of the intellect."[45] St. Thomas, building off Aristotle, recognized that images were easier to remember than concepts or logical sentences. Later Renaissance thinkers worked their ideas of theater into this quest for memory, for the theater builds an entire phantasy world of the mind on stage, accessible to all spectators, something more visually memorable.[46]

By contrast the Egyptian hieroglyph restricted perception only to the wise. Art historian André Chastel describes how the hieroglyph keeps "the spirit in a state of tension propitious to a kind of meditation close to ecstasy."[47] They take things to the next level beyond the phantasms, closer to the intellect. They are mysterious, understood only in the mind's eye.

Whether theater or hieroglyphic, however, the power behind them is the same: eros. They exist because erotic desire gives them being. So long as erotic desire pulsates in the heart of the subject, his phantasy world will be vivid, active, and ripe for manipulation. So long as the image is fueled by eros, the subject's memory will retain the image. An ad campaign is useless unless the net result is that Product X *runs deep* and memory of its wonders activates at just the right time. Of course, the corollary is also true: when erotic desire is deflated, the life drains from the phantasms and from my memory.

Hence the importance of the retention of sperm, something normally connected to mysticism – as in tantric sex – but used by the magician-marketer. As Bruno wrote, "Ejaculation of semen releases the bonds, whereas its retention strengthens them." Or again, "Cupid's bonds, which were strong before the mating, were dissipated after the moderate ejaculation of semen, and the ardor was diminished even though the attractive object did not cease to be."[48]

The idea is that erotic (or romantic, or sexual) climax is a form of mystical ecstacy. In the context of the world of phantasms – each of which exists because of desire – each phantasm has life the greater the desire for it is held in a suspended state. So long as the desire is held in that state, the magician can exert control over the subject, like a woman playing "hard to get." The trick for the magician is to sublimate that erotic energy toward the desired action, to engineer an ecstatic climax in that same action. Orgasm becomes sublimated in the purchasing of a Chevy Malibu.

And again, even if eros is the "great demon" and Woman is the prime example of what we desire, this doesn't preclude other desires. Climax and ecstacy can occur in any number of contexts, and ejaculation is probably too profane and blunt a metaphor. Still, at least at that metaphorical level, the parallels exist. Worked in my phantasy life are various desires, crafted by the marketers, those modern magicians. They linger deep in the subconscious, dormant phantasies that only await the appropriate moment. A simple swoosh, golden arches, four interlocking rings, two capitol G's facing each other and interlocking, these are modern hieroglyphics, serving the purpose exactly described by Bruno and the Hermeticists regarding magic. They, combined with the phantasms crafted through all the stagecraft, are manipulated to effect the magical result: my purchase of the product, the ecstatic moment.

Unhealthy habits, debt, the marital conflict following debt, and the inevitable depression only underscores the need for more. It's the life of the melancholic leveraged for profit, for Prospero's dukedom.

Erik Davis nicely puts it: "A baroque arcana of logos, brand names, and corporate sigils now pepper landscapes, goods, and our costumed bodies. A century ago, advertisements were almost exclusively textual, but today's marketing engines now saturate the social field with hieroglyphics to an extent never seen before in human history."[49] He calls it "the corporate colonization of the unconscious."

Sigmund Freud's nephew, Edward L. Bernays (1891-1995), considered the father of public relations and marketing, was part of that pool of progressives gathering around the Wilson administration. In every sense he exemplifies Bruno's description of the magician, specifically in that role of engineering a uniform culture, as in, a uniform culture around a political program or a unified subculture around, say, a clothing style. He christened the art of *propaganda* before the term became bad.

In his book *Propaganda* (1928), Bernays channels Bruno: "There are invisible rulers who control the destinies of millions. It is not generally realized to what extent the words and actions of our most influential public men are dictated by shrewd persons operating behind the scenes. . . . In some departments of our daily life, in which we imagine ourselves free agents, we are ruled by dictators exercising great power. A man buying a suit of clothes imagines that he is choosing, according to his taste and his personality, the kind of garment which he prefers. In reality, he may be obeying the orders of an anonymous gentlemen tailor in London."[50]

Like Verbal Kint's statement about Keyser Söze in *The Usual Suspects* (1995), "The greatest trick the devil ever pulled was to convince the world he didn't exist." The ultimate trick of the magician is to convince us we are making the purchasing decision, not knowing we are marionettes operated by the manipulator.

This is not meant to be a critique on capitalism or the free market, which arguably is simply what naturally happens when people are set free to pursue their ends in a rational manner. But it does shed some light on how some run their critiques *against* the free market. For them, Bruno's observation stands: everything is magic. Everything in this world is under the control of dark systems and powers who exert their control in our lives. No one is truly free. The marketers are those tools of big business who have learned how to manipulate Yaltabaoth's systems to their own profit advantage. It's *black* magic.

For them, the only defense against black magic is *white* magic, which is magic utilized to engineer the "uniform society." This was Couliano's exact position. White magic can conjure fictions and phantasms effecting more appropriate ends, the menu of progressive goodies. And that is how things are framed: *all is magic, the only question is whether it's black or white magic.*

Thus the critique on the free market or capitalism is framed not in rationalistic, debatable terms but in "white magic vs. black magic" terms: capitalism's very forms of support – reason and nature – are just phantasms crafted by black, profit-seeking magicians to deceive the masses. Any argument based on reason or nature, then, must fall on deaf ears. Where the proponent of the free market is appalled by the progressive's intrusion on people's freedoms, the progressive is on a completely different wavelength. To him, freedom is an illusion, a phantasm, a word bandied about by capitalists to bedazzle others into believing they are really free. No one, after all, is truly free anyways!

A traditionalist critique would grant that there is such a thing as rationality and that it can be mustered against the influences of magic. Rationality reinserts the possibility that anyone so mesmerized by the phantasms crafted in his imagination can be literally talked off the ledge with actual words (not symbols), logic (not archetypical abstractions), and linear thinking (not phantasms): *no, that car won't give you great sex*.

That is the answer to the above critique of marketing: *free will*. This is why a republic of free individuals needs those old habits of critical and analytical thinking. That and a few of the old republican virtues.

The New Prophets

We've referenced the paradox in several places, but it deserves reiteration: how are the likes of Hegel, Marx, Weber, or the evolutionary biologists able to posit grand schemes that explain how and why everything works, but somehow believe themselves to be exempt from those behind-the-scenes operations?

Gnosticism as outlined by Bruno's understanding of magic is the only reasonable answer: *it's because those thinkers have been granted to see the bird's-eye view of the cosmos, to see the wizard behind the curtain*. Why them and not others? Because of Gnostic elitism: some are granted the vision; others aren't, certainly not those theologians, rationalists, and slew of philosophers who littered the past.

In his reference to the Actaeon and Diana myth, Bruno describes how Actaeon was killed for the crime of seeing with his eyes the "naked truth." After receiving the vision, his dogs kill "him in his aspect of social and common man, freeing him from the ties of the perturbed senses, from the carnal prison of matter." The *vision* consumes him. He dies to this world and its illusions. Only death can fully free the one under the spell of magic. To wake up to it is to cease to be human as typically understood. No longer does Actaeon, or the Gnostic, need phantasms. He sees "naked truth" in the mind's eye freed from "the carnal prison of matter."[51]

In terms of ancient psychology – where mind and body are mediated by spirit – this vision of naked truth occurs solely in the mind. This was the ultimate *vacatio*. In this world everything is one, *even time*. Past, present, and future are "not separate and distinct," but "everything is there *sub specie aeternities*. [Under the aspect of eternity.]"[52] Consequently the Gnostic not only has the capability to know *what essentially is*, but also *what will be*: he is a prophet.

Hegel or Weber, then, are not philosophers in the usual sense adding their two-cents worth to the body of developing philosophy. They are prophets whose ideological gnosis has given them a vision (toward which other philosophers could only grope) of what things are *really* like.

This claim, to have glimpsed into the ultimate truth and know history's true course, marks Gnostic movements throughout history. The millenarians of the Middle Ages certainly fit this bill, but so did the above-mentioned Romantic philosophers who claimed knowledge of the true course of history. Today the habit is picked up by "futurists" like business guru Peter Drucker (1909-2005), who reflected his Pietist upbringing as well as his Gnostic vision when he wrote, "[Mankind] needs the deep experience that the Thou and the I are one, which all higher religions share."[53]

The habit is also picked up by those prophets of doom in the environmental movement. In 2011, the secular and more sane Christian world had a sporting time witnessing the antics of Harold Camping, the radio preacher who predicted the world would end on May 21. Of course the world didn't end as it never does for these types. But then let's be fair. What's good for the goose is good for the gander. History did not produce the predicted triumph of the proletariat. The world hasn't ended by overpopulation or mass starvation. And we're still awaiting that environmental disaster, be it the ice age or global warming.

Maybe Jesus was on to something when he said, "Of that day or hour no one knows."

✧ Chapter 7 ✧

Phantasmic Sound

The Revolution of Phantasmic Sound

In the early 1990s I ran a summer program for children in Milwaukee's inner city. Occasionally we would pile into our church van and venture out on field trips. During one rather lengthy drive, the burning question was, *What music would we play?* The children had their favorite stations, and I had mine, but on this trip I decided to play classical music. It would be their introduction to some culture, I reasoned. It might also put them to sleep.

The trick worked. At one point, I turned the channel to another station, and one of the children said, "Turn that back. That's peaceful."

A charming enough episode, until we consider who was playing on the radio: Wagner. Specifically it was one of those quintessentially Wagnerian Wagner pieces, the type leading to riots, the type arousing passion like few other composers had ever done in history, the type the Nazi's used to inspire *Volk* pride among the Germans.

But that day Wagner's music became a lullaby.

What happened? Without doubt it is the advent of pop music and its subsequent descent into greater and greater levels of soul-smashing intensity. We hardly notice what shocked parents in the 1950s. With each new year, music pushes our sensitivities to such new heights that we can hardly imagine the likes of Wagner inspiring anything but a long nap.

This chapter is an extensive investigation into this issue of music. Unlike any other period in history, music pervades our culture. Where in

174

the past music was almost always an event, today we can literally live our lives with our personal musical score. As we study music and its relation to the spiritual history we've been contemplating, we see that music's powerful role in modernity cannot be separated from the philosophical and spiritual milieu of our day. The music forms embraced by any given period of history provide a window into the soul of that era. If we are truly in a period of Gnostic spirituality, does our music reflect that? Absolutely it does.

It does so precisely in the way that Bruno identified, as the audible version of the phantasm. Couliano describes Bruno's magic: "Magic action occurs through indirect contact . . . through sounds and images which exert their power over the senses of sight and hearing [which] stem from the occult language of the universal spirit."[1]

From its mass ubiquity to its character of being sonic wallpaper to any number of situations of modern living, music permeates our souls to our core. It's impact, along with television and other visual media, cannot be denied.

Music and the Cult of Eros

In *The Republic*, Plato addresses the subject of music because he knew its impact on the body politic. As passions are to the human soul, so is music to the body politic. And as reason must tame the passions, so must the rational elements in the body politic tame music. Music should be censored for the good of the political body.

He writes in *The Republic* (lines 424b-c): "there must be no innovation in . . . music contrary to the established order . . . . [The overseers of the Republic] must beware of change to a strange form of music, taking it to be a danger to the whole. For never are ways [modes] of music moved without the greatest political laws being moved."[2] He recognized something that Jimi Hendrix recognized: if you can change the music you can change society.

Aristotle (in his *Politics* Book 7, chapters 5-7) gets so analytical as to delineate how different modes – Lydian, Dorian, and Phrygian – affect the hearer. The Lydian mode induced grief; the Dorian, contentment; and the Phrygian fills the soul with enthusiasm. (Chapter 5) He also classifies the different effects of rhythm, some generating violent behavior, others generous behavior.

Concerning the education of youth, he too recognized the influence and effects of music on the mind, particularly its ability to mesmerize and fascinate it. Precisely for this reason he wanted to use music in education. Youth, he notes, don't pay attention to anything unless it's agreeable – we might say entertaining – and therefore music should accompany learning, music being one of the few things youth are interested in.

Aristotle understands music has unavoidable corrupting influences, which is why he counsels the careful management of music. He fears unrestricted access to music will result in stifled maturation – delayed development – or that it will render the body unfit for war, even effeminate. For these reasons, he concludes, music should be embraced by the young, but judged by the old.

Can music make a person effeminate? Aristotle thought so, especially when used with the flute, which he believed was an immoral instrument because it inflamed the passions. It was fine for animating the soul, but was a hindrance to instruction.

Aristotle knew the corrupt use of the flutes by the mystery cults. Playing in the enthusiasm-inducing Phrygian mode, the flute-player was an ingredient in the mystery cults' initiation rites. The frantic playing – along with ecstatic dancing – worked the initiate up into a frenzy signaling possession by the deity.

The Romans – far more stoic, masculine, and reserved than the Greeks – after conquering the eastern half of the Mediterranean world reaped the fruits of their plunder, including the music of the Greeks. For some, that accommodation was the beginning of the end. Ammianus Marcellinus lamented in the late fourth century that the libraries were empty, meanwhile instruments were in high production. And the Roman Lucian in the late second century writes surprisingly current words, if *flute* is replaced by *guitar*:

"My dear fellow, can a man who has had the benefit of an education as well as a little traffic with philosophy, who strives after the better things and has familiarity with the ancients – can such a man sit down and listen to flute music and watch an effeminate man strutting about in woman's clothes, imitating amorous females with his lewd singing?"[3]

The ancient fathers of the Church held similar views. Clement of Alexandria (c.150-c. 215) commented how the pagans "foolishly amuse themselves with impious amusements . . . occupied with flute playing, dancing, intoxication, and all kinds of frivolity."[4] He and others understood the corrosive effect certain music had on Christian doctrine and morals. In particular, he writes, "let love songs be banished far away."[5]

He goes on: "Temperate harmonies are to be allowed. But we are to banish as far as possible from our robust mind those liquid harmonies. For, through pernicious arts in the modulations of tones, they lead persons to effeminacy and indecency. But serious and modest strains say farewell to the turbulence of drunkenness. Chromatic harmonies are therefore to be abandoned to immodest revels, and to ornate and tawdry music."[6]

Christian historian Henry Chadwick believes Clement was thinking of the Gnostic sects "among whom there would probably have been much less sense of inhibition and restraint."[7] He references the *Acts of John*, a Gnostic text, which was intended to be sung during a ritual dance.

Clement's remarks introduce us to the fascinating relationship between music and eros. In fact the Gnostic cult of eros maps out the psychic terrain of Clement's love songs and explains its magical powers in our culture today. We recall Chesterton's quote: "Every man who knocks on the door of a brothel is looking for God." At some deep level, unfulfilled yearning and lust impelling a trip to the brothel equates with the search for God. Gnosticism gives us the tools to understand what Chesterton meant.

Gnostic love is *romantic* love. Simply understanding the history of this word *romantic* is a primer on Gnostic movement over the past 800 years. Somehow or another, a word initially meaning *based on the Roman language of Latin* (i.e., French, Italian, etc.) has come to describe those nineteenth century champions of intuition and transcendentalism in art, poetry, music, and philosophy, precisely these forefathers of contemporary Gnosticism.

The original meaning of *romantic* is understandable when we realize the first literature in non-Latin (i.e. *romance*) languages was the love song of the troubadour. The second meaning is a bit more difficult to surmise, but clearly the Romantic era poets saw something in the troubadours' love songs they liked and connected with. Understanding their attraction is crucial to understanding the role music plays in today's world.

Predecessors of Eros: Orpheus and Platonism

One of the feeder streams of ancient Gnosticism was the mystery cult known as Orphism, based on the mythological character Orpheus.[8]

Orpheus was arguably the first troubadour.

Orpheus, whom Ovid calls the "bard of the Thracian mountains," wooed his beloved Eurydice with his golden seven-stringed lyre. Shortly after their marriage, Eurydice was bitten by a snake and died immediately. Orpheus descended down into Hades and begged its ruler to release her soul. To convince the god of the underworld and his wife Persephone, Orpheus so lugubriously played his lyre and sang his song of woe that it was granted Eurydice to follow Orpheus out of the underworld, provided he didn't look back upon Eurydice until they reached the upper world. Just as Orpheus reached the upper world, he looked back, not realizing Eurydice had not yet left the underworld. Immediately she disappeared, recalled to death. In grief Orpheus retreated to the mountains of Thrace, scorning the advances of women, turning to pederasty, and spending his days pacifying nature with his lyre. Angry, the Thracian women attacked Orpheus with stones, but he disabled them midair by his song. Finally, so frenzied were the women that their shrieks and frantic Bacchic music drowned out poor Orpheus' music. Lost in the cacophony of sound, stones no longer heard Orpheus' music and began hitting him. Animals previously placated by his song likewise turned on him, and he was downed. And in his death he and his beloved Eurydice finally "walk together side by side."[9]

Orpheus stands in the pantheon of ancient heroes along with Abraham, Moses, Homer, Socrates, and Hammurabi. He is the father of music, a prophet, a character whose story was allegorized in the ancient and medieval worlds. His story sprouted the notion that poetry and music are divinely-inspired forms of knowing, that music is a key releasing the grip of the powers (archons) on the world. Orpheus' music can unlock the doors on the soul's ascent. It quells the forces of death itself. Orpheus began what became a long and subtle history in the West of the association of love with enchantment, music, and ultimately death. One can see why Orpheus was the patron saint of opera among a group of sixteenth century Florentine Neoplatonists who sought to change society through music.

What is the connection to Plato?

Orpheus bestowed to the West the idea that love is the binding virtue of the universe, bringing order out of chaos, by which a soul is drawn to its Source. To his pupil Musaeus (identified with Moses in some early Christian sources) Orpheus passed on the teaching that "Out of One all things come into being, and all things will return to the One."[10] Other ancient movements fleshed out this general concept according to their own understanding, most especially the Neoplatonists and the Gnostics. But common to each of these systems was the idea that from the One (the Monad, God, Eternal Being, the Father, etc.) multiplicity came into being, and but for the love that binds the multiple beings to their Source, multiplicity would dissipate into an absolute, atomized chaos. The return to the One is precipitated on love – the cosmic bungee cord – a magnetic draw deep within our souls pulling us from our particularity and distinctiveness back into our primal unity.

An Orphic poem describes the soul's journey: "Exploding from the Great Soul, souls reel and writhe, seeking each other in space. From planet to planet we fall, crying for home in the abyss, we are your tears, Dionysos. Mighty one! God of Freedom! Bring your children back into your heart of singing light."[11]

Or again we hear the painful cry of the lover: "I am a child of earth and of starry heaven, but my race is of heaven. This you know. I am parched and perishing.   Give me cold water from the lake of memory."[12]

The lover's intense, passionate longing is enthusiastic love, an internal love for an abstraction, a wispy feeling for *something-out-there* that is really a projection of *something-in-me*, my own Self. Inner gnosis occurs when we realize the chasm between *something-out-there* and *something-in-me* disappears.   Enlightenment cannot be satisfied by some external journey, but only internally. There is an old Sufi tale about an adept who, driven by love for this *something-out-there* goes out on a long journey to find the truth, only to find at his destination his own Self. True love pulls us toward the One (Monad) from which we came, to whom we have access through our inner Selves.

Denis de Rougemont (1906-1985) describes the nature of this sort of love:

"[Plato describes] a kind of frenzy or delirium which is neither conceived nor born in a man's soul except by the inspiration of heaven. It is alien to us, its spell is wrought from without; it is a transport, an infinite rapture away from reason and natural sense. It is therefore to be called enthusiasm, a word which actually means 'possessed by a god', for the frenzy not only is of heavenly origin, but culminates at its highest in a new attainment of the divine. . . . Such is Platonic love. It is 'a divine delirium,' a transport of the soul, a madness and supreme sanity both. A lover with his beloved becomes 'as if in heaven'; for love is the way that ascends by degrees of ecstasy to the one source of all that exists, remote from bodies and matter, remote from what divides and distinguishes, and beyond the misfortune of being a self [or better put in our context, an ego] and even in love itself a pair."[13]

The forlorn Platonist or Gnostic is ever in passionate love with the Source of his being, of which the Platonist has remembrance and the Gnostic has the spark. As Rougemont points out, echoing Bruno, the Divine Source became personified in the Divine Female figure, whether that be the Divine Woman of the druids, the Philosophia of the Platonist, the Sophia of the Gnostics, or the Velleda of the Germans.[14]

Into this program the Gnostics added abhorrence of the material world. This is his *passion*, or suffering. The forlorn lover suffers, as Orpheus did, scorning the advances of earthly desires, ever keeping his heart set on that which this earth can never even approximate, not earthly marriage, not earthly food, not earthly privileges. This world isn't just broken or deceptive; it's full of active evil forces (the archons; Orpheus' suitors) trying to pull the Gnostic from his journey home, from his lover.

The Orpheus myth explains the role music has in the Gnostic ascent. For good reason Ficino played a lyre with Orpheus painted on it. Paralleling developments in music leading to the birth of opera, he believed music had the ability to change the world. Artists following the path of Orpheus could "by fashioning our perceptions of the sensible world and by his privileged access to its secrets [be] able to act on it and change it," writes John Warden in an essay on Ficino and Orpheus. This was because music is the truest revelation of the inner truth and unity of the cosmos.[15] By learning its secrets one could gain a magical control over the world's future. "Nothing is more effective in natural magic," said the Renaissance magician Pico della Mirandola, "than the hymns of Orpheus."[16]

The Sufis and Love Poetry

The above description of Gnostic love, with its passion and forlorn longing, its pain, its heartbrokenness, parallels our Western understanding of romantic love. This is not a coincidence.

Rougemont describes romance: "[Lovers] imagine that they have been ravished 'beyond good and evil' into a kind of transcendental state outside ordinary human experience, into an ineffable absolute irreconcilable with the world, but that they feel to be more real than the world. Their oppressive fate, even though they yield to it with wailings, obliterates the antithesis of good and evil, and carries them away beyond the source or moral values, beyond pleasure and pain, beyond the realm of distinctions – into a realm where opposites cancel out."

He continues, describing the classic love story of Tristan and Iseult, "Tristan and Iseult do not love one another. . . . What they love is love and being in love."[17]

Two things we notice in his description of romantic love. First is its power to lift us "beyond good and evil," its power to lift us out of the mundane rules governing such things as the institution of marriage, rules like, "Thou shalt not commit adultery." The adulterer doesn't care about rules because he possesses a more sacred love transcending the marital contract. *What are these laws*, says the Gnostic lover, *but Yaltabaoth binding our transcendent yearnings and deluding us to believe love can only be contained by marriage?*

Second, romantic love centers on abstractions, not on the concrete where distinctions occur. It is "beyond the realm of distinctions." The flesh and blood person is a pretense. Romantic love has no room for the quotidian regiment demanded by marriage. A flesh and blood person may symbolize higher love, but actual care for a material person – a "til death do us part" sort of human care and devotion – is impossible. What matters is the transcendent image, the phantasm. With haste adulterous lovers dispense with each other when the affair comes crashing down. What held the affair together was the illusion of transcendence, which is it's enticement.

In this transcendence Sophia works her magic, and here romantic love and Gnosticism intersect. We look again at Sufi mysticism – its role as a bridge linking ancient Gnosticism to medieval Catharism and the troubadour movement. Through their romantic poetry and story-telling the Sufis perfected Gnostic love themes and transmitted them to the twelfth century Cathars. In the language of passionate longing they cloaked their Gnostic mysticism.

Llewellyn Vaughan-Lee describes the divine side of passionate longing: "Within the heart, lover and Beloved unite in love's ecstasy. The wayfarer begins the journey with a longing for this state of Oneness. The longing is born from the soul's memory that it has come from God. The soul remembers that its real home is with God and awakens the seeker with this memory. The spiritual journey is a journey that takes us back home, from separation to union. We have come from God and we return to God."[18]

Here is the Orphic as well as Platonic theme of "remembering the

Oneness from which we have come." Here also is the perfect image of the forlorn, lost lover, ever "longing for this state of Oneness."

Traditional religious categories cannot do justice to this sort of spirituality, says the Sufi. The Gnostic is always beyond language! Only the mystical language of love will suffice.

Sufi master Dr. Javad Nurbakhsh describes the spiritual journey of the forlorn Gnostic lover in a poem: "The speech of Love is beyond words and their meanings. For Love, there is another language, another tongue. . . . Love speaks in a language unknown to ordinary men."[19]

For this reason the Sufis perfected romantic poetry and story-telling. Hakim Nizami (1141-1209), a medieval sufi master, was Persia's leading poet. He is famous for two romantic tales, *Layla and Majnun* and *Khusrau and Shirin*. Both underscore the theme of suffering and death for the sake of love. They were allegories of divine love in which "a spiritual seeker's quest for union with the Beloved is an endeavor that leads to the annihilation of the limited identity of the love in the infinite being of the Beloved."[20]

In this "quest for union" – Jung's alchemical union of animus/anima which the love story allegorizes – words and talk are merely "bankrupt chatter." Yet, trans-rational means of communication such as story-telling, poems, jokes, quips, even dancing, and certainly music, all had their place. Such things lift us out of the mundaneness of *brain language* into a truer *religion of the heart*.

As far as Sufi music and dancing are concerned, medieval Sufi master Abu Hamed Mohammad ibn Mohammad Ghazzali (1058-1111), describes the importance of music for Sufis, "who by [music and dance] stir up in themselves greater love towards God and . . . often obtain spiritual visions and ecstasies."[21]

Shah describes the power of music in its magical context: "The moral ascendancy, or the magnetic personality, which the Sufi attains is not his goal but the by-product of his inner attainment, the reflection of his development."

Shah goes on describing this "magnetic personality," which along with miracles the Sufis use as part of their developmental progress toward truth. Such supernatural wonders, Shah comments, are merely the products of a highly emotional state: "When the magician is trying, shall we say, to move a person or an object, or influence a mind in a certain direction, he has to go through a procedure . . . to arouse and concentrate emotional force. . . . When present-day followers of the witchcraft tradition in Europe speak of their perambulation of a circle, seeking to raise a 'cone of power,' they are following this part of the magical tradition."[22]

The inadequacy of objective rationality, the importance of symbolism and poetry, the inner quest, the role of the heart, the use of magic and miracles, the personal perfectibility of the human subject, and the use of non-rational forms of communication like music and dance, these are all areas where Sufi passed on the Gnostic tradition. Important for our purposes here, in our discussion on music, Sufism helps explain the ultimate mysticism behind romance, the true spiritualism behind Clement's "love songs." The bridge between medieval Sufism and today is the eros ideology outlined by both the Cathars and the troubadours.

The Church of Love and the Religion of Love

The Church of the Cathars was sometimes referred to as the Church of Love. The Latin word for love, *amor*, inverts *Roma*. What a clear contrast, said her sympathizers, between the simple, humble, pure spirituality embraced by the Cathars and the pompous, ritualistic, wealthy, and powerful Church of Rome.

But why love?

Orphism through Platonism had passed into the ancient melting pot of ideas the cosmic bungee cord understanding of love: love draws the individual to his Source out of multiplicity, out of materiality into the One. The Sufis showed that this love is erotic. Sophia the Divine Woman is the object, the feminine principle of the cosmos superior to this world's God. The soul will be restored through her. The Cathars replaced Sophia with Mary, their "symbol of pure saving Light."[23] The Cathars retained the Gnostic kiss of peace, which, as we saw among the Gnostics, "produced spiritual children." Love was an allegory of the soul's reunion with the Monad.

Whether in parallel with or as a result of Sufism, Rougemont describes the invasion of the cult of eros in Europe at the beginning of the twelfth century. This century witnessed a flurry of Gnostic revivals through mysticism, Catharism, and new forms of poetry all using the language and tropes of eros. It dominated not just Gnostic spiritualities but more acceptable Christian mysticisms. It was the energies of this period that encouraged the development of Mary adoration, says Rougemont. He points to a specific date for the rebirth of the cult of eros, 1118, the year that Abelard and Heloise met, whose love story is among the most famous in Western history.[24]

Love poetry was troubadour poetry. No less than Frederick Nietzsche claimed Europe "owes so much and, indeed, almost itself" to the troubadours. "Love as passion is our European specialty," he claimed in *Beyond Good and Evil*.[25] From medieval figures like Dante (who modeled his own poetry on troubadour forms) to modern figures like Ezra Pound (who translated its poetry), the troubadour movement has continued to fascinate poets, philosophers, and cultural commentators. The troubadours brought a new topic in a new language. That language was non-Latin (i.e. Vulgar), and that topic was love. They introduced the *canzone*, the poetic love-song, "making its link to both music and moving emotion its defining characteristic."[26]

The rules of this "religion of love," as the troubadour movement was called, were several. First, their poetry always involves illicit love between a lesser man and the perfect symbolic stand-in for Sophia, a superior woman. (The ladies often took over the administrative duties of the manor when their husbands were off on the crusades. This left them alone with a variety of inferior courtiers, among whom were the troubadours.) Second, the lover-poet's beloved is generally an "impossibly beautiful" ideal. Third, the lover is repeatedly rebuffed; his proposals are eternally met with an answer in the negative. Fourth, the suitor is repelled by evil enemies such as spies sent by the husband or gossips. Fifth, in "the rebuff of the lover's frustration and subsequent pain lies his redemption and the power and beauty of love." Sixth, the lover's love is ritualized in a feudal arrangement; he becomes the vassal or servant of his beloved, swearing eternal fidelity to his Lady, bestowing, however, a loyalty that is forever unfulfilled, but is sealed by a kiss. Traditional forms of the feudal rite are reinterpreted erotically.[27]

Rougemont sides with Maria Rosa Menocal's argument for the Arab roots of troubadour poetry, focusing on the spiritual atmosphere of the twelfth and thirteenth century. If they are correct, and if this era truly was a "summer of love" for the Western world due to Sufi influence, then what was one movement for the Islamic world – Sufis writing romantic poetry allegorizing their yearning for Sophia – became two movements in the Europe, the troubadours and Catharism.

More to the point, Catharism and the troubadour movement are the beginnings of the existential postmodern creed, with all the same Gnostic archetypical characters.

First, love is the gnosis. Once awakened to love's call, the soul rebels against any institution which would formalize love or box it in according to certain rules, as ecclesiastical marriage or the arranged feudal marriages would. Then the soul allegorizes his antinomian rebellion in a cosmic myth. The institutional Church and its God, or the feudal arrangement, become the demiurge and his archons, in modern speak *the establishment* or *the system*. These are those forces keeping Lover from Beloved. Just as the Beloved is a truer goal than one's own conventional wife, so is the God (Monad) beyond this world's God (Yaltabaoth) a truer and more authentic source of the soul's life. And just as true love needs no formal structure like marriage, union with this truer God needs not be mediated by the Church. The program is "spiritual, but not religious." Finally, God is feminized, as he meets us through Sophia, the object of the troubadour's poetry, the Lady. Of course, all along the language used to express this love is a trans-rational one, generally taking on a poetic and musical form.

Romanticism and Music

That, of course, is precisely the mystery and beauty of music, its trans-rationality. "Music expresses that which cannot be put into words," said Victor Hugo. Aldous Huxley agrees, "After silence, that which comes nearest to expressing the inexpressible is music." Beethoven called it a "higher revelation than all Wisdom and Philosophy."

Martin Luther too called it "one of the most magnificent and delightful presents God has given us." But his caveat, along with the ancients and Church Fathers, was that the Logos should be preeminent over music. Music can carry the Logos. Like a beautiful wine glass, music can add sublime highlights to the content it carries, beautifying the experience of sipping it. But the old Sufi *know-the-difference-between-the-color-of-the-wine-and-the-color-of-the-glass* they understood in opposite terms: Logos, not gnosis, is the content.

Today's cultural Gnosticism sides with the Sufis. Bob Dylan momentarily became a born-again Christian in the late '70s. Asked in 1997 of his views on God and religion, he replied, "Here's the thing with me and the religious thing. This is the flat-out truth: I find the religiosity and philosophy in the music. I don't find it anywhere else. Songs like 'Let Me Rest on a Peaceful Mountain' or 'I Saw the Light' – that's my religion. I don't adhere to rabbis, preachers, evangelists, all of that. I've learned more from the songs than I've learned from any of this kind of entity. The songs are my lexicon. I believe the songs."[28]

Songs . . . that's his religion, and he doesn't need organized religion. He believes the songs. Dylan's born-again, seeing-the-light conversion was of a piece with his generally Gnostic outlook. He fits nicely into the Romantic tradition, the bard whose lifelong iconoclasm against the conventions of the day unlike few others inspired a counter-cultural movement.

Even Gnostic namelessness makes its way in his explanation for why he gave up his birth name, Zimmerman, and assumed the name of Romantic poet Thomas Dylan: "You're born, you know, the wrong names, wrong parents. I mean, that happens. You call yourself what you want to call yourself. This is the land of the free."[29]

Just a mistake of the cosmos, a fallen spark in a random body, named by the "wrong parents." Such is the pretense of the modern Gnostic, the marks of the postmodern creed.

But what of Dylan's Romanticism? We've already touched on Romanticism as a philosophical movement, but how does Romanticism fit in the spiritual chain linking back to ancient Gnosticism in terms of music?

For the Romantics, intuition and feeling were far better suited to discover transcendent truth than reason and the senses. Such things as the arts were far more suitable for the challenge of finding transcendent truth than reason, science, or dogma.

And of the arts, music played the central role.

Romanticism deliberately drew from the troubadour tradition. The troubadours celebrated romantic love, forbidden love. They were the classic type of the forlorn lover, pining away for a transcendent beauty, something unattainable in this life. If the troubadour movement truly sublimated Cathar (medieval Gnostic) spirituality with its focus on transcendence devoid of institutional, ecclesiastical mediation, the Romantics deliberately sought to pick up where they left off.

Immanuel Kant and Arthur Schopenhauer

If Rousseau surveyed the territory later peopled by the Romantics, Immanuel Kant paved the way, felling trees and laying the pavement. Felix Mendelssohn called him the "All-Pulverizer,"[30] because like few others he destroyed philosophical structures built by his predecessors.

Accepting David Hume's skepticism regarding what can be truly known by the mind – i.e., nothing; everything we sense is but the "illusion of realism"[31] – but wanting to preserve some role for absolutes and universals, Kant took a vintage Gnostic step and divided the cosmos into two worlds, the noumenal and phenomenal world. The phenomenal world includes whatever reason or the senses experience. The noumenal world includes whatever reason or the senses cannot know. We know the noumenal world exists, but it will always be framed by categories our subjective minds impose on it. Thus, objective knowledge of this world is impossible, an illusion. What we think we know is nothing more than our minds imposing order on our surroundings and making us believe our experience is universally true. Yet, objective reality abides. How, then, can it be known? Again, we're back to trans-rationality, to ways of knowing beyond the Logos.

Hume's skepticism led to atheism, but Kant was raised by Pietists and said he was a Christian to his dying day. "I have found it necessary to deny knowledge," he said, "in order to make room for faith,"[32] echoing Pietist emphasis on personal experience and faith as opposed to rationalistic doctrine. As a good Pietist, Kant undermined those institutions claiming authority to manage objective knowledge, like the Church with its theologizing, science with its factualizing, or philosophy with its rationalizing. Yet, one could experience his noumenal world through non-traditional means of knowing such as faith or intuition.

Arthur Schopenhauer (1788-1860) took the Kantian ball, ran with it, and applied it to music. Awed by Kant's philosophy, his paeon to it reveals his *palingenesia*, or gnosis: "Kant's teaching produces a fundamental change in every mind that has grasped it. This change is so great that it may be regarded as an intellectual rebirth. It alone is capable of removing the inborn realism that arises from the original disposition of the intellect . . . . In consequence of this, the mind undergoes a fundamental undeceiving, and thereafter looks at everything in a different light. But only in this way does a man become susceptible to the more positive explanations that I have to give."[33]

Only by changing our way of understanding objective truth, only when we undergo an intellectual rebirth regarding how the truth is known, will we be properly prepared for what he, Schopenhauer, had to teach us about music.

And what did he have to teach us? What did he add to the discussion Kant began?

Kant argued for a plurality of being in the noumenal world, which is simply to say he acknowledged a diversity of unknowable universal absolutes and truths. Schopenhauer disagreed with Kant. For him, plurality still implies differentiated things, things that have meaning only in the phenomenal world of senses and experiences. Our brains slice and dice everything up into categories and forms because it's trapped in materialistic ways of thinking, as matter alone gives distinction to things. In a non-material world, there should be no distinctions at all.

Rather, "everything must be one and undifferentiated" in the noumenal world, which is "a single, undifferentiated something – spaceless, timeless, non-material, beyond all reach of causality – inaccessible to experience or knowledge."

Thus we are all one in the noumenal world, an inner world encased in the phenomenal world, which then becomes illusory upon discovery of this true inner world.[34] It's Monad and the pleroma redux.

How do we connect to this oneness? Through the Will, a current we tap into during acts of sex, art, and music, things which induce what amounts to a gnosis. Concerning sex, Schopenhauer writes: "If I am asked where the most intimate knowledge of that inner essence of the world, of that thing in itself which I have called the will to live, is to be found, or where that essence enters most clearly into our consciousness, or where it achieves the purest revelation of itself, then I must point to ecstasy in the act of copulation. That is it! That is the true essence and core of all things, the aim and purpose of all existence."[35]

The act of copulation, but also art, connects us to the noumenal world as expressed in pure Will. Of all the arts, music was preeminent: "[Music differs from] all other forms of art in that it does not depict phenomena . . . , but is the direct expression of the Will itself and thus pits the metaphysical against the physical things of this world, the thing-in-itself against all phenomena."[36]

Music can complement "any scene, action, event, or setting" as "the most accurate and distinct commentary on it."[37] Schopenhauer explains why, for example, the real power behind the movie *Rocky* was its soundtrack. The plot and script were powerful, but the music reached into the psyches of underdogs everywhere and inspired action. The music was a communion of sorts between a viewer's reality and the image on the screen. In an alchemical sense, it was the Philosopher's Stone working the union of the viewer with the Rocky archetype.

Typical of the Gnostic, Schopenhauer possessed a despairing attitude regarding any sort of redemption for this world. He's known as a pessimistic philosopher. For him the world is by and large a selfish, unhappy place. Men are bloodthirsty, and even animals screaming in agony will be torn to pieces alive. The world is truly a vale of tears, and salvation can only occur through escape from want of material things.[38] Enter the saturnine personality type again, the troubadour, the melancholic soul pining away for transcendent love and finding peace only in music.

An atheist, Schopenhauer demonstrated another Gnostic trait. He identified with the mystical traditions in most religions,[39] particularly those decrying the flesh and seeking freedom from its allurements. He is another example of that mystical atheism which shows us the wizard behind the curtain in the "God is dead" theology. The adherent of a "God is dead" theology believes the God of tradition, the God of this world, the subject of traditional theology, is dead. A truer God is the God within us, a God to whom we have access through such things as music rather than through the Church or the investigation of nature.

Richard Wagner's Operas

Richard Wagner (1813-1883) is among the most significant composers to date both for the excellence of his music, but also for his opinionated philosophical essays undergirding his music. Mainly a composer of operas, his life's mission was to live out Schopenhauer's philosophy. He believed philosophy was perfected with Schopenhauer and read his *The World as Will and Representation* (1818) four times. True to Schopenhauer's philosophy, he had a statue of Buddha in his house named "Wahnfried," meaning "free from illusion."[40]

Wagner is a good case study of the conspiracy between music, romance, and Gnosticism as reflected in the Romantic era. Rougemont comments, "[Wagner, among others in the Romantic era, bore] witness to a profoundly renewed awareness of the relations between human love, the life of the soul, and the spiritual quest."[41]

Opera itself was birthed in the middle to late sixteenth century by a group of humanist thinkers known as the Florentine Camerata. Considering the polyphonic music of the day to be corrupt, they believed a restoration of the ancient Greek drama – with its balance of music, poetry, and drama – would not only bring music back to its firmer classical grounding, but improve society itself.

One of the first operas, Monteverdi's *Orfeo* (1609), worked out the ideas of the Florentine Camerata. It drew its theme from the ancient Greek myth of Orpheus. We saw how Orpheus lost his wife on his wedding night and manipulated the god of Hades with his lyre into releasing her, only to lose her again. He spent the remainder of his days longing for her, suffering, lugubriously playing his lyre. Orpheus embodied the idea that music is an unspoken language of love with the power, like magic, to manipulate the cosmos itself. His wife, Eurydice, is the Sophia figure of ancient Gnosticism. In the opera, Orpheus calls her the "light of the world" at their wedding. By the end of the opera, the god Apollo grants Orpheus an escape from his earthly vale of tears, so that he can gaze at Eurydice's image in the stars forever. Death is escape, a release into the realm of lights from which we came. A classic Gnostic attitude.[42]

Wagner took the operatic tradition and peppered it with strong philosophical overtones rooted especially in his reading of Schopenhauer. His famous *Ring* cycle (first performed in 1876), a cycle of four operas based in German myth, demonstrably shows the influences of Schopenhauer, whom he read during his long composition of the cycle. Wagner originally wrote the cycle as an ode to the power of love to triumph over power and greed. Its ending was to be an aria showcasing love's victory, but after reading Schopenhauer, Wagner absorbed his pessimistic view that evil is endemic in this world. His new ending, the so-called "Schopenhauer ending," ends not with a wordy aria but with wordless music. Language can't do the ending justice; only music could be "the most accurate and distinct commentary on it."[43]

His opera *Tristan und Isold* (first performed in 1865) invokes another legend with strong Gnostic undertones. The Tristan and Iseult legend is about adultery. Cornish King Mark, after defeating the Irish, brokers a political marriage with the Irish princess Iseult as part of the peace agreement. He sends his nephew Tristan to Ireland to retrieve the princess Iseult for marriage. On the voyage home, the two take a potion making them fall in love. Tristan and Iseult continue their affair at the king's court while the kindly King Mark struggles with the cold truth suspected by his advisers, that the two are committing adultery under his nose. Finally, evidence of adultery convinces Mark of Tristan's disloyalty, and he kills him. Meanwhile Iseult dies grieving over Tristan. The story is typical of the love-death theme found in other tales such as *Romeo and Juliet*, but the deeper meanings implied by the story are wherein the Gnostic elements are found. Wagner worked these meanings into his telling of the story.

He begins with what some call the most famous first chord in musical history (at least before *A Hard Day's Night* took the title). The chord invokes the craving for unattainable love, a chord begging for resolution. Spanning two measures, its two dissonant chords in the first measure segue into the next measure. One of the chords is resolved; the other remains dissonant. As one author put it, "in every moment the musical ear is being partially satisfied yet at the same time frustrated. And this carries on throughout the whole evening."[44] The same author claims that this moment was the beginning of modern music. The opera as a whole broke all existing rules. Opera singers couldn't sing it at first. Many thought it unperformable; they called Wagner a musical anarchist.

The dual telling of the story – mundane and spiritual – set off by the initial chord is accented through Wagner's dramatic devices. The sounds of the material world – the chorus of sailors, for example – are often offstage. On the stage is the real action of the inner world of spirit. The love of Tristan and Isold is in this inner world, represented by darkness and the night when their trysts occur. Meantime the rules of the day, of this world, do not allow their love, which is why it can only be consummated in death. But the inner world and thus the night are more real, more divine, because through the love of lovers the "deity of the world's eternal becoming" flows, as Wagner said. And night, as put by one Wagner scholar, "becomes the primal, motherly realm prior to all individuation and its inherent delusions."[45]

Constant craving, constant longing, longing to leave this world of illusion, individuation, and falsehood – with all its conventions and institutions like marriage (Wagner composed the opera amidst an adulterous affair) – and be reborn, such is the mark of the Gnostics. From Wagner: "The world, power, fame, glory, honour, chivalry, loyalty, friendship are all swept away like chaff, an empty dream. Only one thing is left alive: yearning, yearning, insatiable desire, ever reborn – languishing and thirsting; the sole release – death, dying, extinction, never more to awaken."[46]

Did Wagner's and Schopenhauer's views on the power of music have merit? Are their thoughts true? We look at the evidence: Marie Wilt, the soprano who sang the part of Brunhilde in *Die Walkure* (first performed in 1870), committed suicide after learning her part; Ludwig Schnorr von Carolsfield, the tenor who first sang the *Tristan* role died in a delirium of Wagner worship. Alois Ander went mad studying for the role of *Tristan*. Emil Scaria died insane after performing the lead role in *Parsifal* (first performed in 1882). We shouldn't forget that Wagner's most famous devotee, Frederick Nietzsche, died insane and in his latter writings exhibited frequent conniptions over Wagner. *Die Meistersinger* caused a riot in Time's Square in 1919. Wagner took such reactions in stride: "Completely good [performances of *Tristan*] are bound to drive people mad, – I cannot imagine what else could happen."[47]

What else could happen? A van-full of inner city children could be lulled to sleep while listening to Wagner.

That's quite a change in the course of seventy plus years. What happened?

The Rise of the Postmodern Creed and Music

Wagner lived until 1883, and if we consider the 1950s the starting point of the modern rock/pop era, we have about seventy years of intervening time during which a host of modernizing change fertilized the cultural soil. During this period the postmodern creed settled into the Western psyche via existential philosophy and pop psychology. Add the element of music to this historical development, and we see a new religion with a new sacrament replacing the old.

Existentialist religiosity – or mystical atheism, or Gnosticism – has its own history paralleling a now-familiar pattern we saw among modern scientists and the Romantic philosophers. Proto-existentialist Søren Kierkegaard (1813-1855) retained his Christian faith in, tellingly, the Pietist tradition. Schopenhauer had Buddhist tendencies. Albert Camus, famous French existential novelist, died prematurely, but rumors were he intended to go to India to study Buddhist philosophy. Nietzsche and Jean Paul Sartre held to their atheism, yet the former called for new gods and the latter joined progressive causes.

This is where psychology enters. Jung marinaded psychology in Gnostic terms, resulting in his Collective Unconscious. All humanity shares the Collective Unconscious. We reacquaint ourselves with our Collective Unconscious as we follow certain archetypes in our myths, dreams, and other arts. These call forth from Monad and draw us upward.

A review of Nietzsche shows how strongly Jung's doctrine of the Collective Unconscious parallels the exact effect he says music has on the soul. Jung himself developed his theory of the Collective Unconscious while on a trip to Africa, where he witnessed a tribal festival accompanied with dancers and music. Jung experienced for himself the effect of losing himself in the unconscious, fearing that he might "fall under the spell of the primitive."[48] Peter Gabriel's song *Rhythm of the Heat* (1982) – originally titled *Jung in Africa* – gave tribute to that event.

Nietzsche and Music

Frederick Nietzsche is the most profound precursor to existential philosophy. His views on music, and especially on Wagner's music, help us understand how music came to be such a potent ingredient in the postmodern creed.

Nietzsche idolized Wagner, reverentially speaking of him: "With him I feel in the presence of the divine." He was Wagner's frequent guest, visiting him frequently, and his letters hint he was in love with Wagner's wife Cosimo. He lauds Wagner's ability to create through music "the fifty worlds of strange ecstacies to which no one else had wings to soar."[49]

Among the topics uniting the two – Nietzsche was about thirty years Wagner's junior – was Schopenhauer. Nietzsche believed Wagner embodied the life and work of Schopenhauer. His first philosophical work, *The Birth of Tragedy* (1872), is largely a reflection of Wagnerian ideas.

In *The Birth of Tragedy*, Nietzsche sets as opposing types Apollo, Greek god of reason, with Dionysus, god of wine, drama, and sexual frenzy. Apollo represents the rational in life, the realm of Logos, whatever can be ordered, classified, or named. Apollo rules the external world, where the distinctions of separate beings allows for the appreciation of form and its beauty. So long as I, the viewer, remain distinct from what I'm viewing, I can replicate what I see through language, and also in the plastic arts. This is Kant's phenomenal world.

Dionysus by contrast is chaotic and unordered. In the Dionysian type, floods of human spirituality transgress the boundaries of the physical body, allowing for unity of spirit among individuals. Where Apollo's perspective emphasizes balance of form and moderation in habit, Dionysus prefers the use of extremes – tension and release – to educe a spiritual intoxication.

Identifying the art of music with Dionysian ecstasy, Nietzsche compares music to wine intoxicating the soul. Through it we unite with something outside ourselves: "Oneness as the soul of the race and of nature itself."[50]

Linking Nietzsche's views on music with Woodstock, Kathleen Higgins writes: "In the Dionysian experience, self-control is abandoned, and with it the boundaries between individuals. The result is the characteristic feeling that one is intimately connected with one's fellow human beings, even with all of nature. [Woodstock was] a more recent example of the kind of experience that Nietzsche associates with the

Greeks in their worship of Dionysus."[51]

Where Apollo's world of form and rationality allows the individual to be a detached observer, Dionysus' world erases boundaries between form, and music allows no one to sit as a detached observer. It affects everyone in its hearing. No one escapes or remains detached from its emotive impact; it's a shared experience. Music is formless, trans-rational: how can one put in words the sort of tension (*passion*) and release (*gnosis*), the catharsis, it induces? It's an emotional, spiritual experience uniting all who participate in it.

Nietzsche writes, "this is the most immediate effect of the Dionysian tragedy, that the state and society and, quite generally, the gulfs between man and man give way to an overwhelming feeling of unity leading back to the very heart of nature."[52]

The chorus of a Greek tragedy best exemplifies this oneness, as their song draws in all who hear it, and "[they] have a surrender of individuality and a way of entering another character."[53] This boundary-transcending effect of music is precisely what Schopenhauer identified with the Will, that single Will defining the noumenal world.

This fissure between Apollo and Dionysus serves a deeper purpose for Nietzsche. As the title of his book, *The Birth of Tragedy*, suggests, his aim in the book is to confront life's deep questions about human suffering, tragedy, and fate.

In many ways the traditional Christian approach to life's deep questions is Apollonian. It's rational according to its own inner logic. As foolish as St. Paul claims it to be, the cross – the fact that through the greatest injustice ever (the death of God) the greatest good resulted – puts human suffering and tragedy into a rational focus. If the Son of God himself descended into the pits of hell and ended up at God's right hand, surely the same triumph-through-tragedy is promised those who follow him.

Nietzsche regrets this historically Christian position. In his eyes, it's a lie, forever seeing real-life events as a perversion of some original perfection, and therefore never accepting life *as it is*. The Christian may rationalize tragedy in Apollonian fashion, but what if it cannot be rationalized? What if it just *is*?

For Nietzsche the Dionysian type provides a surer answer than the Apollonian. Music's tension-release dynamic, the nuts and bolts of catharsis, expresses a truer reflection of life's good/evil duality. Music allows us to transcend not only boundaries, but even moral boundaries like the boundary between good and evil. Music is life-affirming, not just life as understood by a Christian faith – which essentially is past-life (Eden) and future-life (Paradise) oriented – but life as it is totally experienced in *this* world today, with warts, suffering, tragedies, and all.

The musical-dramatic elements of Greek tragedy then act as a sort of communion. The hero in a Greek tragedy lives out a tragic and fateful life, and while in accordance with the Apollonian type we see this hero as detached observers in the audience, the music introduces the Dionysian element, and we are moved to share the hero's tragic experience and even recognize a variation of that experience in our own lives. Through sharing the tragic with both the hero and other audience members – united through the musical chorus – we deal with our own suffering vicariously through the hero's suffering. We find comfort in this cathartic event. Such is the brilliance, argued Nietzsche, of the Greek tragedy.

Yet, an inconsistency remains which might explain why Nietzsche went insane at the age of forty-four and died twelve years later. That is, life's coda is death. If music gives meaning to the span of life we have – embracing the fullness of tragedy and suffering like some ongoing blues song – then in a sense all it does is hide us from the dreadful reality of death, the cessation of our existence. One can embrace life as it is and imagine each moment as an "eternal present," as Nietzsche did, but still those eternal presents become fewer and fewer as we age. We *will* die. If anything, then, music serves as a flimsy substitute for dealing with the reality of death. It is, in a way, the perfect sacrament for a godless world, keeping us happy as we dance toward death. For all of Nietzsche's affirmations of life, still, the single reality marking life in this world is its end. To affirm life, then, is to affirm its ultimate negation. Nietzsche's philosophy is a high-brow way of saying, "Let us eat, drink, and be merry – peppered with a good dose of music – for tomorrow we will die."

In any event, Nietzsche shows us why we need music when the philosophical foundation is "God is dead." And as we evaluate the existential postmodern creed in light of this "God is dead" premise, we see why music plays the role it does in today's culture. It is essential, almost sacramental, to the development of the healthy Self. Atheist and humanist Kurt Vonnegut rejected every sort of organized religion, but yet allowed, "If I should ever die, God forbid, let this be my epitaph: *The only proof he needed for the existence of God was music.*"

In light of Ficino and Schopenhauer, this only makes sense. Music is the new sacrament to a new, Gnostic understanding of God, whose "new dawn," Heidegger told us, can only arrive once the old gods are swiped away.

Existentialism and the Beats

Existentialists Heidegger, Sartre, and Camus carried on Nietzsche's teachings. From Heidegger came the notion of the "authentic Self," a Self wrapped in external falsities born again through the vehicle of choice. As I choose my own Self – however I choose to define it against "the They"[54] – I become authentic.

Heidegger also spruced up an old mystical term and re-gifted it to us, *Gelassenheit*, further exhibiting existentialism's religiosity. In medieval mystical circles the term meant to let loose of one's self and depend solely on God. The modern expression *Let go and let God* is a direct descendant, as is the current *surrender* piety inspiring both religious and secular elements. For Heidegger, it meant a sort of *releasement* or *let it be.* (Paul McCartney's song was a hymn saluting the same idea.) The idea is, *Just go with the flow and let it go!*

How this attitude relates to being an authentic Self might be confusing. How can we at one time create our own authentic Selves and then go *with the flow*? Heidegger himself developed in his thinking on authenticity. In his early years authenticity was related to a resolute decision to be what one chooses to be. In his later years, it was related more to this idea of releasement, of *going with the flow*, kind of like how he *went with the flow* and became a Nazi.

His development has parallels to how our own culture has evolved. Being one's own person has somehow developed into an almost conformist *going with the flow*. Given the existential and iconoclastic bases of the postmodern creed – it's essential rebelliousness – this only makes sense according to the Gnostic and mystical view that true spirituality means breaking from convention while affirming the Self, *but the Self is collectively connected to other freed Selves* at the pleromic level.

Jean Paul Sartre, like Heidegger, embraced the "authentic life" over against oppressive conformity, which he called "the Other in us." He shared with Heidegger the idea that man is "thrown" into the world, "condemned to be free."[55] Sartre's popular novel *Nausea* (1938) excoriates the mechanized conformity of the modern world, telling the story of Antoine Roquentin, who settles in a French town only to become oppressed to the point of nausea by the conformity of the town. Only after facing the nothingness of his existence, the existential angst, can he be truly free, to carve out his own existence by his own freely-made choices.

Albert Camus, author of such works as *The Stranger* (1942), *The Plague* (1947), and *The Fall* (1956), also penned a nonfiction work titled *The Rebel* (1951). The true rebel, he explains, is not a political rebel, one who attempts to inaugurate a utopian state in the place of the established order – such a system invariably ends up being more oppressive – rather the true rebel is the one who rebels individually against the cosmos itself, its tragic indifference to human plight. He calls this rebellion a "metaphysical rebellion."[56]

Film director Nicholas Ray (1911-1979) voraciously read Camus and applied his ideas to his works, ripping the title from Camus' essay for his iconic masterpiece, *Rebel without a Cause* (1955). Ray is a classic example of the existential archetype, an artist who didn't quite fit in. He was an alcoholic, depressed, bisexual, and generally a misfit: he believed the rectangular shape of the screen was too oppressive. His perspective on the world lives out through the plagued lovers peppering his films. Unhappy, in love with the forbidden, the troubadour's plaintive song echoes, or the Sufi's romantic poem: the lonely misfitted lover seeks his way home, finding redemption through his Sophia, the beloved Woman.

Ray's era, the 1950s, also saw the rise of beat poets Jack Kerouac, Allen Ginsberg, and William Burroughs, the first two of which were introduced to Gnosticism by Professor Raymond Weaver at Columbia University in the 1940s.[57] The Beats represent a critical link in the chain from Nietzsche through the existentialists to modern music. They also laid the groundwork for what is most Gnostic about the use of music in today's world.

Recalling existential *angst*, when the soul peers into the abyss of nothingness, Kerouac commented on the word *beat*: "it implies the feeling of having been used, of being raw. It involves a sort of nakedness of mind, and, ultimately, of soul; a feeling of being reduced to the bedrock of consciousness. In short, it means being undramatically pushed up against the wall of oneself . . . [beat by] all the conventions of the world."[58]

Following the declaration of God's death, two separate philosophies had come to vie for meaning in the human soul. The first was Marxism, the second was existentialism. In popular culture, Marxism marked the period of bohemianism in the 1920s, the age of the so-called "Lost Generation." Existentialism defined the Beat Generation. Both were similar in their diagnosis of the perceived ills: the mass, conformist culture produced by democratic capitalism. Both were essentially faiths. The light of spirituality flickers at the end of the dark tunnel burrowed by existentialism just as it did with Marxism. Kerouac, for example, was into Zen Buddhism, writing the 1958 novel *The Dharma Bums* about Ray Smith, an American who rebels against conformist mass culture, escapes society, begins to meditate, and then reenters society with a new consciousness.

Describing the inherent spirituality of the Beats, John Clellon Holmes, author of the first beat novel *Go* (1952), compared the Beats to the Lost Generation: "unlike the Lost Generation, which was occupied with the loss of faith, the Beat Generation is becoming more and more occupied with the need for it. As such, it is a disturbing illustration of Voltaire's reliable old joke: 'If there were no God, it would be necessary to invent Him.' [The Beat] knows that disbelief is fatal, and when he has failed in every way to overcome it, he commits suicide because he does not have what he calls 'greatness of soul'"[59]

Continuing a familiar theme, the Beats embraced trans-rational means such as poetry and music in their effort to "invent God" and connect with ultimate Truth. Mildred Edie Brady in a 1947 *Harper's Magazine* article described Beat poetry, first quoting one of its young poets describing how their writing is "transcending logic, invad[ing] the realm where unreason reigns and where the relations between ideas are sympathetic and mysterious – affective – rather than causal."[60]

She continues, all but mouthing the postmodern creed with its Gnostic archetypes (even referring to the spark): "Only in art, today, can the fettered, mechanically burdened soul of man speak out his revolt against the dead hand of rationalism. Only through art is it any longer possible to reach that all but burdened spark of natural life dying under the intolerable weight of modern man's sadistic super-ego. And only through art will man find a path back to his spontaneous, natural creativeness."[61]

She then quotes beat hero Herbert Read: "Poetry in its intensest and most creative moments penetrates to the same level as mysticism."[62]

Working with another element of the postmodern creed, the Beats saw the institutions of family, state, and Church as things to be transcended on the way to authentic spirituality. Brady defined the beat mentality as "a combination of anarchism and certain concepts related to psychoanalysis which together yield a philosophy – holding on the one hand that you must abandon the Church, the state, and the family . . . and on the other offering sex as the source of individual salvation in a collective world that's going to hell."[63]

Poetry, sex . . . and also music. Holmes wrote: "I've been listening to bebop. It's the new insane music of this world. It's like the configurations of a wild mind. It pounds on and on, mechanical, disharmonic, the abstraction of an abstraction."[64] It was, in the words of another commentator, "a way of demonstrating solidarity with the primitive vitality and spontaneity they find in jazz."[65]

We've seen before how Gnosticism's beyond-the-Logos emphasis creates a new kind of tongues-speaking, in the purposely grammar-less prose of our college students, in the moaning and groaning of the modern Christian songstress, and in the more high-brow deconstructionist movement. Podhoretz observed something similar among the Beats and noted how they express "contempt for coherent, rational discourse which, being a product of the mind, is in their view a form of death. To be articulate is to admit that you have no feelings (for how can real feelings be expressed in syntactical language?), that you can't respond to anything (Kerouac responds to everything by saying 'Wow!'), and that you are probably impotent."[66]

Kerouac's iconic *On the Road* (1957) symbolized the beat generation, offering his rambling anthem to existentialism through self-referential characters who paint their lives on the canvass of mid-century American hip culture. Unbound by the conventional rules and expectations we generally think of when we think of the 1950s – going to college, marrying, getting a job – *On the Road*'s heros, Sal Paradise (Kerouac) and Dean Moriarty (Neal Cassady) bop around pointlessly from situation to situation, engaging in petty crime, damaging property, and hooking up with short-term love interests. Antinomianism somehow proves their authenticity. Throughout the novel, existential themes prevail. The point of the novel is life itself, embracing it to the full. Drinking bouts and "tea" smoking (marijuana), combined with jazzy bebop music are meant to convey a new approach toward life completely at odds with convention.

One particular episode in the novel involves a meeting that Sal (Jack) has with a country girl while *en route* from Chicago to Detroit on a bus. The conversation typifies the existentialist perspective:

"I took up a conversation with a gorgeous country girl wearing a low-cut cotton blouse that displayed the beautiful sun-tan on her breast tops. She was dull. She spoke of evenings in the country making popcorn on the porch. Once this would have gladdened my heart but because her heart was not glad when she said it I knew there was nothing in it but the idea of what one should do. 'And what else do you do for fun?' I tried to bring up boy friends and sex. Her great dark eyes surveyed me with emptiness and a kind of chagrin that reached back generations and generations in her blood from not having done what was crying to be done – whatever it was, and everybody knows what it was. 'What do you want out of life?' I wanted to take her and wring it out of her. She didn't have the slightest idea what she wanted. She mumbled of jobs, movies, going to her grandmother's for the summer, wishing she could go to New York and visit the Roxy, what kind of outfit she would wear – something like the one she wore last Easter, white bonnet, roses, rose pumps, and lavender gabardine coat. 'What do you do on Sunday afternoons?' I asked. She sat on her porch. The boys went by on bicycles and stopped to chat. She read the funny papers, she reclined on the hammock. 'What do you do on a warm summer's night?' She sat on the porch, she watched the cars in the road. She and her mother made popcorn. 'What does your father do on a summer's night?' He works, he has an all-night shift at the boiler factory, he's spent his whole life supporting a woman and her outpoppings and no credit or adoration. 'What does your brother do on a summer's night?' He rides around on his bicycle, he hangs out in front of the soda fountain. 'What is he aching to do? What are we all aching to do? What do we want?' She didn't know. She yawned. She was sleepy. It was too much. Nobody could tell. Nobody would ever tell. It was all over. She was eighteen and most lovely, and lost."[67]

Or maybe she was creeped out by a greasy Beatnik asking her about sex, and she just wanted to sleep. But again, her role was not to be human, a flesh and blood human governed by the regular dictates of happy and contented living, but rather to be a possible pretext for Sal's Sophia-lust, an object for the troubadour's worship. She didn't play along. In any event, Jack Kerouac the writer died young, penniless and an alcoholic. One imagines that this country girl grew up and, well, may be sharing popcorn with her grandchildren yet today. Or perhaps she grew into a character similar to Sal's aunt, who underwrote his existentialist wanderings through advanced money orders both from herself and from Sal's own veteran benefits. It's lovely to be able to pursue the heroic, ached journey of Self-actualization on the dime of family and state, all the while denigrating those very institutions as illusions.

The Beats did in literature and poetry what their existential predecessors did in philosophy. They also made artistically and philosophically acceptable the raw music of jazz and bebop. The pieces were all in place for the arrival of rock n' roll, and popular music in general.

Pop Music

According to the magical terms set up at the beginning of our section, the magician's role with phantasmic images has a parallel in music. Marketing and movie-making speak a language of archetypical shorthand, working phantasms in the subjects' psyches the way a manipulator works his marionettes.

Marketing itself is a unique term, one of those odd words turning a noun into a verb, the opposite of a gerund or infinitive, like the annoying new word *partnering* that hides the compulsory intent of the subject. If the more benign term, *advertising*, denotes a simple passing on of information about a product, *marketing* involves the creation of a market around a particular product through the manipulation of scenarios and images – *this can be your beautiful life, your beautiful wife, and your beautiful world . . . a world possible if centered on this product.*

Sale of music underwent a similar transformation. For a few years after pop music became accessible through radio and records, disc jockeys, like the older advertisers, saw their job as simply playing the music that reflected taste. Pass on the information, and let things be. Disc jockey Bill Randle (1923-2004) changed all that. He saw himself less a reflector of tastes and more a creator of tastes. He recognized the opportunity the new media gave him to be the master magician, a marketer. He even referred to himself not as a DJ but as a "performer."[68]

Randle's revolutionary stamp on the industry was his recognition of the power of marketing to sell records.[69] Recollecting the alchemical process, he believed it his duty to "rarefy new trends in teen culture at their onset, so that he could sell these trends back to the teens."[70] He consequently immersed himself in teen culture, test-marketed records, talked to the right people, headed sock hops, and allowed teens into his studio to observe him "perform." He tapped into an American teen culture made up of its various groups: the leaders, the rough crowd, beatniks, radicals, the middle majority, the hoodlums, and so on.

Whatever categories he used, Philip Ennis' gloss of the 1950s teen market is fascinating: "Teen industries, which included fashion, movies, and music, courted all groups but wooed especially the rough kids and the other subterranean minorities in the hope of controlling the middle majority. This strategy worked not only because of the irrelevance of adult culture in the schools but because of the leading crowd's infinite capacity to give in to the rough crowd and the rough crowd's infinite capacity for excess. It was this social dynamic that led the high school population into rocknroll."[71]

Why would marketing especially woo "rough kids and the other subterranean minorities?" Why not showcase the music of the honor students? It was because of the "rough crowd's infinite capacity for excess."

In other words, it's music straight from Freud's Id, from Schopenhauer's Will, from the troubadour's unsatisfied longing, from the Sufi's pained poesy, and ultimately from Jung's Collective Unconscious, explaining why it became *Pop*, that is, universally accepted. Though it tapped into ultimately destructive habits of behavior, it could be justified not only on existential terms – because it tapped into more authentic vibes – but on Marxist grounds – because it was said to be related to the same alienation the rough types felt with the conventions and institutions through which a happy life was said to happen. Honor students were far too willing to live out the "false Selves" accepted contentedly from their parents and other archons. The rough crowds found their voice in pop music, and soon the rest followed. Now we're all part of the rough crowd. It's proof of our authenticity.

And now, Bob Dylan's music is used to sell cars to yuppies. Who'd have thunk?

Pop Music and Iconoclasm

Bob Dylan forecast the new age his music was bringing in his classic, *The Times They Are a-Changin'* (1964). The song spells out the *evolve-or-die* message we see over and over again with new age ideas. Standing in the way of change, writes Dylan, are those Gnostic archontic culprits: cultural elites, state, and family. These must either join the movement or be swept away by it.

As he writes to the parents:

> "Your sons and your daughters
> Are beyond your command
> Your old road is rapidly agin'
> Please get out of the new one
> if you can't lend your hand
> For the times they are a-changin'"

This is not developmental history, building off of what precedes. This is revolutionary change, a complete structural change in the created order. Society, state, and family can either evolve with the change, or die. Only the Church is spared in Dylan's masterpiece.

Jimi Hendrix picks up the slack: "The establishment has set up the Ten Commandments for us saying don't, don't, don't . . . then all of a sudden kids come along with a different set of brain cells and the establishment doesn't know what to do. The walls are crumbling and the establishment doesn't want to let go. We're trying to save the kids, to create a buffer between young and old. Our music is shock therapy to help them realize a little more of what their goals should be. . . . We're making our music into electrical church music – a new kind of Bible, [a Bible] you carry in your hearts, one that will give you a physical feeling."[72]

This is a remarkable statement. The magician is granting us a peak behind the curtain. There's the fundamental Gnostic philosophy in the words "the walls are crumbling." Natural delineations historically believed to be natural, cosmic, or divine – the forms of the created order – are the walls that must come down. Walls between the government and the governed, parents and children, male and female, my property and my neighbor's, these are walls determined by nature and physicality. Gnosticism sees these walls as a prison cell, something to be transcended. As a political program this Gnostic view becomes revolutionary, a radical upending of social order, exactly what the prophets and poets of the coming age wanted.

Hendrix speaks of a "different set of brain cells." That's a terrifying comment: he sees a new race emerging, an evolved humanity superior to what preceded it. The further implication is that those of us from the old order are no different than animals. Here again we see Gnostic elitism.

Hendrix perfectly articulates the role of music in this Gnostic program. It's "shock therapy" that helps youth "realize a little more of what their goals should be."

What their goals *should* be? Hendrix rebels against the Ten Commandments with its "don't, don't, don't" while promising to help us realize what our goals *should* be. He has no problem replacing "don't, don't, don't" with "should, should, should." Of course there's no difference. *Should* and *don't* are both the vocabulary of a morality. The difference is whether this morality is given to us from Sinai – from the outside – or something we discover internally, through Hendrix's "realization" (an adequate translation of the word "gnosis").

Yet, the wizard-magician opens the curtain on himself and shows us exactly what's going on. In truth, it's his music guiding us to our proper goals!

Did we not fully appreciate the full mystery and power of music, this statement would frighten us with its tyrannical implications. *Guide us to our proper goals?* Extract that phrase from the musical context and put it on the lips of a political leader from, say, the Religious Right, and watch the fireworks! But place it on the lips of a cool legend, in the context of music, and somehow it seems right. Why is this so?

It speaks to the nature of music. Music melds our valuing and contemplative faculties with that of the musician – who himself is purported to be something of a shaman, a medium between the divine and human realms – who by the plies of his trade massages us to believe our feelings come from within, not from the music. The Hermeticist Ficino had no doubts about this nature of music, holding the Orphic belief that "the artist, who looks within himself to discover the harmony of the cosmos, by artistry leads others to an understanding and beyond. Indeed the artist not only reflects, he creates."[73]

But this is the new religion, according to Hendrix. It's an electronic Bible, carried in the heart. It gives us a physical feeling, and the music becomes a sacrament by which the divine communicates to us.

The Beatle's song *Revolution* (1968), written by John Lennon, conveys Hendrix' paradoxical sentiments as well. In the song Lennon acknowledges the revolutionary spirit of the 1960s: "We all want to change the world." But it's not political revolutions he's talking about. Of those he says, "you can count me out." He suggests a better way to change the world: "Well, you know [w]e all want to change your head." Lest we miss his point, he adds, "You better free your mind instead."

What Lennon is articulating is perfectly Gnostic. Revolution in our day doesn't happen through political force. It happens through changed minds. As the "brain cells" change, more and more people come on board the change express.

But the paradox persists. On one hand "you better free your mind." Evidently *we* initiate the journey of Gnostic discovery. Or does the musician change us? "We all want to change your head." Therein is the paradox.

We're back to the magician, whose craft was to manipulate a subject's decisions while convincing him he is making the decision on his own. Music is the magician's charm this time. Just as Nietzsche said, music spills the spirit over the borders: we feel we are part of a communal spirit though the music. The music is a communion through which we have union. We lose consciousness of ego (shaped as it is by provincial and mundane forces), finding our true Self (which connects us to the eternal, collective, subconscious Self), and this in turn is acted out politically, mind you not in a revolutionary fashion, but more in a slow, evolutionary manner. *Is it me? Is it John Lennon? It doesn't really matter. These are just labels. It's all of us as one collective. Lennon is just the mouthpiece.*

Lennon's song *Imagine* (1971) develops the theme. Harkening back to the Romantic preoccupation with the imagination,[74] the song bids us to use our minds to reach for *what could be*, to imagine a world where there are no borders, no religion, or no property. All such delineations are realties in a physical world, where real flesh and blood people tarnished by original sin try to coexist with limited resources. But for the Gnostic, imagination can become reality through the power of the mind. And maybe one day we can join Lennon and his enlightened compatriots, for history is flowing in a single direction, toward a communal world where fleshly delineations are erased, and we all live in single-minded agreement. Either we get on board or are left behind.

Discussion of iconic artists would not be complete without the inclusion of Michael Jackson. His song, *Off the Wall* (1979), from the album of the same name lacks the social implications of the other artists, but this only demonstrates the trajectory pop music took from the 1960s to the 1970s. What began as socially conscious and politically charged music gave way to disco. But what really changed? Both Dylan and disco at their heart call for rebellion. 1960s music was perhaps more intelligent in its rebellion, and 1970s music more primitive; but on Gnostic grounds, the further we are from *intelligent* (stuck in its categories and forms) and the closer we get to that primitive eros point, the better.

Jackson's lyrics in *Off the Wall* are essentially an anthem to everything we've been discussing on music to this point.

The song begins with "the world . . . on your shoulder." That is, the song is specifically for those for whom the realities of life have become cumbersome. In perfect Gnosticese, the implication is *there is an escape from the suffering and I'm going to tell you about it*. And what is that escape? "Livin' crazy, that's the only way." What exactly does this entail? Leave the nine-to-five job "upon the shelf" and "just enjoy yourself." Then "Groove [and] Let the madness in the music get to you." In addition to living crazy and letting the madness of the music get to you, the other suggestion is to shout. After all, shouting is no sin, Jackson informs us, and the "party people," tolerant fellows all, aren't going to "put you down."

Jackson then provides us a philosophy of life that, while wonderfully Gnostic in its antinomianism, in the end may not have suited him: "Do what you want to do / There ain't no rules / It's up to you." Unfortunately for Jackson there are some rules, like, don't lie naked in bed with underage boys, but we digress.

He goes on with words that would have made Heidegger proud, giving a disco spin on his *Gelassenheit*: "It's time to come alive / And party on right through the night, all right / Gotta hide your inhibitions / Gotta let that fool loose, deep inside your soul / Better do it now before you get too old."

In that nine-to-five job providing for my family I'm not alive, but I can come alive if I become a certifiable nutball and, like Jackson, "come alive" by becoming crazy, mad, foolish, and by shouting. Unfortunately, Jackson's life also demonstrated the pound of flesh owed, and in the end, he never found out what it's like to "get too old." He practiced what he preached, and following untold scores of other musicians, died ever in pursuit of that ecstatic rush of what he falsely believed was "coming alive."

Once again we see the Gnostic interplay between death and release. The Gnostic hero's death is the climax of a life of complete self-absorption, a glorious moment of transfer from a life here and now that cannot ever do justice to the possibilities of ecstatic living.

Four artists, five songs. These artists unarguably reign at the very apex of the pantheon of pop music. The reader may wonder about more contemporary artists in other genres, such as hip hop, which has replaced rock as the default music of youth. Really, there isn't much to say, because it's the same song over and over again. It's about iconoclasm, rebellion, and sexuality, banner attitudes in the great existential journey of the Self. But what seemed revolutionary and edgy is now mainstreamed. Donald Fagen of Steely Dan, commenting on his (and collaborator Walter Becker's) fascination with avant garde (i.e. Beat) music and literature in the 1960s, commented: "Now the whole world sees everything the way we did back then, but at the time, coming out of the conformist '50s and so on, it was sort of unusual, I guess. But it's not anymore."[75]

No, it isn't unusual anymore. The hallmarks of the existential/Romantic/Gnostic religion, as far as art is concerned, have become part of the American cultural DNA.

So much so, in fact, that for art even to be considered art, it has to pass the canonical test of the postmodern creed, focusing on the Self's struggle against the archons through erotic, ecstatic ascent. Morris Berman gives a good summary of the five traits modern art must have if it is to be considered true art in our age. These all now make sense now given what we've reviewed. First, art must derive from an internal conflict (like between Self and ego). Some sort of alienation is being worked out through the artistic creations. Second, "you create yourself out of your work." Third, the creative breakthrough is more authentic the more manically it ecstatically erupts from the unconscious, that is, some sort of palingenesia must occur. Fourth, successive works must always outdo what came before, generating compulsive habits in the artist (the melancholic disposition). Finally, it always involves the "eroticization of the activity."[76] The artist has a love relationship with his creations; his art is a sublimated love affair with Sophia.

We've gotten accustomed to seeing an artist ejaculating his Self through his art, and then in more reflexive moments – say, on a talk show – explaining the demons that drive him, the pain he's been through, and so on. One by one the above five traits can be checked off – over and over and over again – but America knows the drill and embraces the ritual with the well-rehearsed proficiency of an Anglican congregation. Never do we contemplate that our culture has become one big worn-out cliche.

The point being, once you get the shtick of what rock n' roll or pop is about, it turns out to be pretty conventional in its own right, embracing its own formal rules. But where did these rules come from?

Charles Mudede, demonstrating that hip hop is merely a continuation of the same old song, knows the answer to that question. He writes: "The metaphysical side of Heidegger, the side that is preoccupied with 'being-in-the-world,' is where I find the links to hiphop. The position of the rapper, the star of hiphop, is always 'within-the-world.' The rapper never sings in the third person, or looks at the world from a distance, objectively, but is always inside looking out. This is why it is so hard, if not impossible, to cover rap songs: They are written from the rapper's point of view, or 'self-point.' With a profound sense of their presence or occurrence 'within-the-world,' rappers then analyze their immediate surroundings. . . . Indeed, at their best, rappers stand in the world of the hiphop song and say to us, 'This is my philosophy,' as KRS-One famously put it."[77]

The author goes on to relate how even Heidegger's philosophical vocabulary makes its way into hip hop lyrics. For example the phrase "in the house" in hip hop, which Mudede writes "is to celebrate your arrival at what Heidegger called 'authentic self'," has affinities to Heidegger's "house of being," which he called language. The idea is that language can only take the contours of one person's experience; there is no true third person perspective.

What Mudede recognizes reiterates what Allan Bloom also said about Heidegger (and Nietzsche): "Our stars are singing a song they do not understand, translated from a German original and having a huge popular success with unknown but wide-ranging consequences, as something of the original message touches something in American souls. But behind it all, the master lyricists are Nietzsche and Heidegger."[78]

Case Study: Jim Morrison and the Doors

Missing in our analysis of pop music so far has been Sophia, the goddess inspiring the Gnostic quest. She's certainly present, but she doesn't have to be named. She's experienced in the longing. She's the grace conveyed to us by the new prophets of the "God is dead" God.

Typically she appears as the gender-neutral companion, the abstract Guide calling out to me through life's difficulties. She may be the Lady calling me to a higher vision, as in Jimi Hendrix's song *Angel* (1971): "Today is the day for you to rise / Take my hand, you're gonna be my man, You're gonna rise." She may be a friend or anyone who is there for us in tough times, as in the *Personal Jesus* (1989) confessed by Depeche Mode, who will "hear your prayers . . . who's there [when] Feeling's unknown and you're all alone." Olivia Newton John speaks on her behalf in the song *Magic* (1980). Sophia appears and invites us to "take [her] hand." From where does she come? "You should know me / I've always been in your mind." Of course she has! Magicians, marketers, and musicians all just help us unleash what's already inside. Where is she guiding us? Well, "There's no other road to take" but the one that leads to where we are "home free."

A good place to bring these strands together and unmask the Gnostic connection is with a discussion of the rock n' roll group, *The Doors*, particularly their number one hit single, *Hello, I Love You* (1968).

The song would work as a troubadour classic. A woman walks down the street ignoring "every eye she meets." She's unattainable. Love will never be consummated. The theme is overwhelming *longing*. Of course longing is exactly what is going on with the introductory words, "Hello, I love you." Those are powerful words for someone whose name the singer doesn't even know yet.

But that's the point. It's the nameless lover, a longing for a nameless abstraction. Learning the woman's name would be a buzz kill. *Names* mean *persons*, and *persons* mean *personalities*, and *personalities* mean personality *flaws*, and personality *flaws* mean *conflict*, and conflict demands – if one wishes a relationship with her – habits and traits such as patience, forgiveness, and endurance, and such things are institutionalized in something called marriage, and this song – and all songs of the eros type – cannot be about marriage.

Yet it claims to be about love. What sort of love? Exactly the sort of love touted in the pop/rock genre – both secular and Christian – the kind centered on wispy abstractions, emotions, and constant longing: eros as opposed to agape.

Further proof of the Gnostic role of woman is given in her description, "the queen of the angels." She's a divine abstraction. She's "Like a statue in the sky," an idol, a goddess of love, which we find out really has nothing at all to do with love as the song devolves into blatant lust, with Morrison growling out from the pits of his libido: "Her arms are wicked, and her legs are long / When she moves my brain screams out this song." Meanwhile the singer of the song, "fool" that he is, continues his self-debasement before this goddess, drifting off into constant longing as the song fades out: "I want you / Hello / I need my baby."

Intended or not, the song is the perfect anthem for a group named *The Doors*. They derived the name from Aldous Huxley's book *The Doors of Perception* (1954). Huxley in turn plucked the title for his book from William Blake's poem, *The Marriage of Heaven and Hell* (1793), particularly from this line: "If the doors of perception were cleansed every thing would appear to man as it is, infinite."

Blake (1757-1827) was a Gnostic. Hermetic scholar Wouter Hanegraaff's comprehensive book *Gnosis and Hermeticism from Antiquity to Modern Times* (1998) devotes an entire chapter by Jos van Meurs to William Blake's "Gnostic Myths." The above quoted line is a fine example of Blake's Gnosticism. What we see with our eyes is deceptive, unreal, and only through the "doors of perception" can we see infinite things.

Huxley ran with the thought and believed drugs, especially LSD, would open those doors. His experimentation with the thesis laid the ideological foundation for 1960s drug usage. *The Doors of Perception* was the result. The work lays down classic Gnostic (and Jungian) tropes, namely, that our physicality imprisons a universal mind – or "Mind at Large"[79] – into particular bodies, and this reduces our awareness. Language itself conspires in the subjugation, "confirm[ing us] in the belief that reduced awareness is the only awareness."[80] Drug use, however, will free the mind, allowing us to see what medieval mystic Meister Eckhart called *Istigkeit*, or "Is-ness,"[81] that is, the pure essence of something devoid of those linguistic parameters imposed by our minds.

At one point in his experiments with LSD, Huxley took a pill and, about an hour and a half later, was looking at a nosegay. Before taking the pill he was struck by the "lively dissonance of its colors." [82] At this point his mind still imposed judgment on the sight in the form of value-laden words. After taking the pill, all judging ceased: "I was not looking now at an unusual flower arrangement. I was seeing . . . the miracle, moment by moment, of naked existence."

When someone asked whether it was an agreeable sight, he said, "[It is] neither agreeable nor disagreeable . . . it just is."[83] He went on to use the language of late medieval mystics to describe the experience, something akin to grace.

One would have to be completely tone deaf not to see the religious component not simply in Blake and Huxley – given their powerful respect for medieval mystics – but in their heirs in the 1960s rock scene. Again, we refer to Hendrix's statement referenced above that "We're making our music into electrical church music – a new kind of Bible . . . a Bible you carry in your hearts, one that will give you a physical feeling." Simply put, the rock scene with its music and drugs is deliberately meant to be a replacement for traditional religion, a new formless sacrament.

Huxley says as much: "Countless persons desire self-transcendence and would be glad to find it in the church. But, alas, 'the hungry sheep look up and are not fed.' They take part in rites, they listen to sermons, they repeat prayers; but their thirst remains unassuaged. . . . Church may still be attended . . . God may still be acknowledged; but He is God only on the verbal level."[84]

The Doors' song, *Hello, I Love You*, nicely illustrates the end point of Huxley and Blake's spiritual trajectory. Not love with a name, but love that "just is in its glorious Is-ness," as Huxley might say, an abstraction devoid of linguistic and physical delineations, that ultimately devolves to primitive feeling.

But the harsh lustfulness of the Doors' song unmasks the nameless Beloved, and we find out she does have a name: Eros, the "statue in the sky," the one that romantically inspires eternal longing but more realistically inspires nothing more than lust.

What's the end game? We know what it was for the bard of *Hello, I Love You* – Jim Morrison. He died by drug overdose. Again, only death pacifies the constant longing for eros; only death releases the romantic and tortured soul. As the inscription on Morrison's grave reads: "according to his own daemon." He lived by his own rules. He lived by his own spirit. He lived by his own demon. It's his final confession of heroic, narcissistic self-absorption.

He's the perfect emblem for the postmodern creed, who along with Janis Joplin, Jimi Hendrix, Kurt Cobain, Michael Jackson, and others has been canonized in the Church of Rock. These were divines, shamans who bridged heaven and earth with their poetry, but the world wasn't fit for them. As Don McLean sang of Vincent Van Gogh in *Vincent* (1971): "This world was never meant for one / As beautiful as you. / Now I think I know what you tried to say to me, / How you suffered for your sanity, / How you tried to set them free. / They would not listen, they're not listening still. / Perhaps they never will."

Yes (*sigh*), the world is just too evil and harsh for the innocent artists, who themselves sacrifice their lives for our sakes, giving us a glimpse of the freedom we can have – Christlike figures, really, for whom death is their eventual glorious release from a world that won't hear them, or who end up like the madman from Plato's *Allegory of the Cave*. Just as McLean sings of Van Gogh, again conflating death and love: "On that starry, starry night, / You took your life, as lovers often do."

In the Gnostic myth, the archons were the doorkeepers. Yaltabaoth set them up over each planetary and starry sphere. Their role is cosmic, but also psychological. As the divine spark in us, the Self, awakens to its true source and home – the pleroma beyond the stars – it must first ascend through these cosmic spheres. As it arrives at each sphere, it finds a locked door. Certain code phrases, however, will open these doors. One such phrase is "Zozeze."[85] As the soul ascends and opens one door after another, it slowly becomes freed from the shackles of this world's existence. The last door, one might say, is death, the final separation of the soul from the body.

Here is the source of Blake's door imagery, when he applied it to our perception. Huxley applied it as the perfect metaphor for what drugs can do: open the doors locking us to an illusory perception and granting access to the Mind at Large. Then we come to its terminus in the name of an iconic 1960s rock group: *The Doors*, doors that are open, opened by the artist, the liberator, who himself shows us the way, living as he does by his own daemon, for whom death in the name of love is the final and glorious release.

For Jim Morrison, the door was opened, nameless love beckoned, and he stepped in, breaking on through to the other side, into his grave.

The Magical Technique of Music

How does music produce the experience it does, this sacramental quality giving a feeling of oneness with a divine current? Above we laid down some historical precedents for the ancient, medieval, and Romantic periods putting things in context on an intellectual level.

But what's actually going on at the somatic level? To hear accounts of how different philosophers and practitioners understand music is one thing. To get into the nuts and bolts of the physical effects of music is quite another. Of course, the very nature of music eludes some of what we are attempting to pinpoint. How do you describe that odd blend of authenticity, wholeness, confidence, catharsis, or whatnot you feel when you're listening to your favorite song? And how do you describe that sense of unity or shared common purpose you get when you're sharing your favorite song with others?

Still, there are a few things we can lay down.

First, even if it's indescribable, music can be labeled. Aristotle labeled the effects of different modes. Clement labeled certain melodies effeminate. Commercials know it, movies know it, and TV shows know it. Certain contexts call for perfectly-fitted music. It's essential to the sort of magic they're working. Who knows what makes a musical style fit a specific situation? Whatever it is, we know its various forms can't be switched around without a change in effects. The Church always knew this until recently: sacred words demanded sacred music, and sacred music had an objective quality to it. Plato understood it as well: changing musical forms changes the laws. Changing *Take Me out to the Ballpark* to Nine Inch Nails' song *Hurt* (1996) at the seventh inning stretch will effect the reception of that event.

More difficult is the next step, that is, being willing to identify a particular form of music as "enthusiastic" and recognize its use, on a popular level, as a conduit for God, taking on the role that sacraments used to. If a particular musical style is believed to connect us to God, certainly it would undermine the teaching that God communicates with us through external, objective, mediate, formal means rather than through internal, somatic, subjective, immediate, and informal means.

Aristotle had no problem doing taking this step. He knew certain music fit a certain spiritual orientation, in particularly the enthusiastic one, the one believed to infuse divine currents into the soul.

Johannes Quasten describes Aristotle's review of the enthusiastic music of the mystery cult: "Aristotle tells us that it is the task of the initiate to suffer and to let himself be brought to a certain frame of mind [Gr. pathein]. He is not to seek to acquire knowledge and increased understanding [Gr. mathein]. The significance of ecstacy in the mysteries is strikingly characterized by this statement. The precise aim of orgies in the mysteries was to induce such a heightening of consciousness in a man that he would be receptive to the god who came to be united with him. Such a person was then an *entheos*, an enthusiast. Music was the most important element used to include this condition."[86]

Aristotle was describing the Phrygian mode, the best contemporary examples of which are *Greensleeves, Scarborough Fair*, and Gordon Lightfoot's *The Wreck of the Edmund Fitzgerald* (1975). As hauntingly mystical as these songs sound, it's difficult to imagine being whipped up into ecstatic frenzy by a fast-paced, flute version of them. In the ancient world, nevertheless, something like that happened. The cultural context obviously mattered, leading us to wonder, *What is the American cultural context today affecting enthusiastic impulses from certain musical forms?* Aristotle opens the door into that discussion, bidding us to walk in and join that conversation.

Schopenhauer, Wagner, and Nietzsche, as well as the later Beats took part in that conversation, taking the position that certain music had the sacramental capacity to connect us to divine currents. A free-thinking populace retains the right to join that discussion as well.

I'm thinking specifically of the reaction defenders of sacred music get when they insist pop music isn't appropriate for the Church, as if they've introduced tyrannical thought forms upon authentic spirituality. No, they haven't. They've only done what the greatest thinkers of the past have done, labeling music that, precisely because of its enthusiastic nature, has the power to undermine the theological and sacramental foundations of the Church.

The same should apply whenever someone becomes so brazen as

to distinguish the content of a message from its musical delivery, as for example in John Lennon's song *Imagine*. Everyone may be having his wide-eyed mystical experience while imagining a new world without borders, religions, and possessions, but don't look at me as some heartless jerk if I peer through the affectations of the music and notice he simply put the *Communist Manifesto* to verse, a book responsible for millions dead. Sorry for that, but perhaps if more people made it their personal practice to re-frame every musically-formed message with carnival music in the background, we could avoid a lot of misguided enthusiasm.

A second trait of music is its tension-release dynamic, the sort of cathartic-inducing feeling Nietzsche referenced in his presentation of Dionysus. In Western music, tension is created by leaving the dominant interval. In "Oh, Christmas Tree," we leave the first note and ascend to the fourth interval and then beyond. Our souls feel like something is unresolved in the world until the song *comes back home* to its base note. Some songs can deepen the unresolved tension for extended lengths of time, causing us to beg – even to ache – for resolution, to such a point that the release moment is downright ecstatic. Bach was a master of the tension-release dynamic. Ravel's *Bolero* (premiered 1928) as well competes with rock n' roll's epitome of the formula, Lynyrd Skynyrd's *Free Bird* (1973).

The tension-release dynamic introduces a new grammar different from the grammar of the written sentence. Written prose centers on a subject and its status or movement within an objective or hypothetical environment at a given moment in time. Nouns denominate each item from the perspective of the subject; adjectives and prepositional phrases describe the accidental qualities particularizing the scene; verbs and adverbs describe movement and time. To live in the realm of prose is to live in some scene reflecting reality.

Music's tension-release dynamic gives us a whole new grammar, lifting us out of our experience with reality. How do you explain dissonance, the sense of something amuck in the cosmos? How do you explain the rush of release proclaiming that everything's OK, that you've "come home," or even that everything is better than it was before. You can't, which is why music is the perfect grammar for the Gnostic experience, fine in limited doses but something altogether revolutionary when it dominates our minds. It's one thing if as a seventeenth century person I'm exposed to this tension-release dynamic once a week at Bach's church. But what happens when we are plugged into it, when it's my daily fare?

A third trait, getting us more to that quality of modern pop distinguishing it from classical, is the importance of beat, repetitive motion, swaying, chanting, or hypnotic dancing. In the ancient mystery cults Aristotle described, such hypnotizing techniques were important. Margaret Thaler Singer in her book *Cults in Our Midst: The Hidden Menace in Our Everyday Lives* (1996) catalogs the physiological persuasion techniques used by cults to engineer the enthusiastic moment:

"Constant swaying motions, clapping added to chanting, or almost any repeated motion helps to alter a person's general state of awareness. Often the repetitive movements are combined with forms of chanting to blend the effects of hyperventilation and dizziness. Dizziness can be produced by simple spinning or spin dancing (in which the person also whirls around and around), prolonged swaying, and trance dancing (often done kneeling and rocking from side to side and backward and forward, with rhythmic repetitive drumming and background music). Again, the effects of these motions are relabeled by group leaders as ecstacy or new levels of awareness. . . .

"[One] group offering psychological expansion has taken aspects of North African desert tribes' traditional trance dances, applied them in classroom settings, and reframed the resultant giddiness and light-headedness as 'getting out of your head and into your heart.' [Another] cult offering a 'life forever' formula uses spin dancing to demonstrate members' newfound joy that no one need die. The group tells members giddy from spin dancing, 'you're coming into our world. Here we are. Spin, spin toward us . . . into your new self.'"[87]

Spinning into your "new self" recalls those Whirling Dervishes of the Sufis, who also used dance as a means of ascending to their higher selves. As Sufi Idries Shah writes: "The body-mind movements of the Whirling Dervishes, coupled with the reed-pipe music . . . is the product of a special method designed to bring the Seeker into affinity with the mystical current, in order to be transformed by it."[88]

Likewise do the Sufis have what is called the dhikr, described as "The repetition of a sacred word or phrase: The dhikr can be repeated vocally or silently. In some Sufi orders the dhikr is chanted at group meetings, producing a dynamically powerful and intoxicating effect."[89]

The effects of different modes, the tension-release dynamic, and the prevalence of beat each conspire in a way that makes modern pop music powerful. In a simple three minute song the force of any entire

Wagner opera is reduced to a most potent elixir and then multiplied to the nth degree as we bathe our lives in music. Wagner's operas led to riots. What happens when that revolutionary power is made pocket-sized, mass-produced, and given to everyone 24/7?

What happens is exactly what *has* happened: revolution of culture, religion, and politics. What happens is a society struggling under the despair and depression of tension, ever seeking the release through any number of means. What happens is revolution in language marked by the desire to magically manipulate through repetitive hypnotic techniques rather than through basic reality-reflecting grammar. What happens is a "spiritual but not religious" atmosphere that frames the religious experience in musical, no longer sacramental or verbal, terms.

What happens is a *spilling-over-the-boundaries* of the spirit, from the individual to the collective, a mainstreaming of the cult dynamic.

And to that collective we now turn.

Part III

Utopian Pursuits:
Gnosticism and Politics

✦ Chapter 8 ✦

Progressivism's Early Roots

The Religion That Is Modern Liberalism

Conservative pundit Jonah Goldberg angered a lot of liberals in 2007 when his book *Liberal Fascism* probed the connection between contemporary liberalism and the totalitarian impulses of the early progressive movement. Liberalism evolved from the same primordial sludge as both communism and fascism, he argued, a sludge which dominated political thought in the late nineteenth century. By his reckoning, totalitarianism of both the Left (i.e. communism) and the Right (i.e. fascism) share the same progressive orientation.

Goldberg ventures into terrain surveyed in this chapter, calling progressivism the "religion of government."[1] He shows how the fathers of totalitarianism appealed to religious language while establishing their ideologies. He even goes so far as to call early progressivism "Christian fascism."[2]

Compelling this label are several Gnostic orientations we've seen so far: (1) the belief in the government's role (as universal a government as possible) as the organic manifestation of humanity's essential, pleromic collectiveness; (2) the reoccurring inability of Gnostics to keep their salvation program a private thing, but turn it into a political movement; (3) the belief that history progresses as individuals become conscious of their transcendent collectiveness and cooperate with this divine force.

Several disparate pieces of our story – the millenarian movement of the Middle Ages, the early Neo-evangelical movement (Pietism and

Puritanism), and Hermeticism – will come together in this section and explore Goldberg's thesis at a deeper level.

In short, progressives believed a divine force was steering history into a dawning new age, the Christian millennium, an age in which the old problems of economic scarcity, hunger, and disease would fade away. Those in tune with this divine force – co-working with the divine – glimpsed the future and surveyed its complex terrain. They presumed to help the rest of humanity by becoming the elite engineers of the coming new order, crafting a new society governed according to the clean and efficient dictates of science. This intelligensia would manage the *totality* of human interactions; hence, *totalitarian*. (Progressives once liked the term before Nazis ruined the buzz.) Much in the way the brain dictates the movements of the body, the elite would manage the citizenry as the parts of an evolving, organic, collective whole.

The American Founders, if not intentionally, reflected Christian ideas of original sin in the US Constitution. If original sin truly stains human nature from birth until death, human perfectibility is impossible, and government needs checks on human nature in all its branches. Freedom needs restraint or it will naturally lead to *un*-freedom. Likewise does government need its restraints or it too will fail.

The fathers of progressivism rejected this model because – and this is key! – they embraced a different theological understanding of human nature *that is not new, but has a theological heritage*. For them, human nature was – to use the trendy thought of the day – *evolutionary*, able to progress, able to be changed for the better, even perfected. Each of the totalitarian movements believed human nature itself would change prior to the glorious new age laying ahead. They embraced some variation of the *New Man*, an evolved human specimen populating the *New Age*.

Of course, here enters one of the sad byproducts of progressive history: elements which refuse to change must be killed off (Lenin's old saw about breaking eggs to make an omelet) or allowed to die off (the old *evolve or die* mantra). The *breaking-eggs* program marked the French, Russian, and Nazi revolutions; the *evolve-or-die* mantra is where we are today. Just as John Lennon predicted: *You say you want revolution, but you'd better prepare to have your head changed*.

That's how the old totalitarian program continues. No one really imagines violent revolution will achieve anything. But minds can change, and this through a variety of means: education, media, political persuasion, or marketing. Around the same time Lennon penned his insights on revolution, contemporary liberalism calculated it could gain political victory through the "long march through the institutions," to use the Marxist phrase.   Not overthrowing, but *coopting*, traditional institutions, progressivism began insinuating itself into our cultural DNA. And now we are where we are. Government management of human existence from cradle to grave is all but accepted. Our reflexive response to any crisis is, *what will the government do?* Government has replaced the role God previously had in the human psyche.

Old theological conundrums like theodicy – the attempt to explain God's omnipotence and goodness in the face of chaos and evil – are replaced by a new political calculus: if evil happens, it's because government hasn't been given enough power and money to solve the problem. The government in turn hasn't been given enough power and money because the rich haven't given up enough of their money and power. Money and power exist because that's the way things worked in the institutions which shall soon pass away: capitalism, individualism, the rule of law, and whatever preserved the status quo.

The political framework is set up in Gnostic terms. On one side are those whose minds have not properly evolved, who are stuck in the past, who embrace the structures supporting individualism and traditional morality. They want to *turn back the clock*, which is meant to convey something uncannily, chillingly evil. These are the archons, the servants of Yaltabaoth standing guard at the prison gates, keeping us all trapped in their institutions, their systems, their constructs of reality.

On the other side are the enlightened forward-looking progressives who realize society is a collective, who, even if utopia is a word that means "doesn't exist," nevertheless believe history is evolving to a point where their envisioned project for a better society is imminent, just around the corner, if only those reactionaries would get out of the way.

Of course, the project *always* fails. As Hannah Arendt said, "The most radical revolutionary will become a conservative the day after the revolution." The only problem is, what they conserve (far more viciously than any "conservative") is an idealistic construct imposed on naturally-occurring societal arrangements, something that can only be implemented through a byzantine army of micro-managing bureaucrats whose implementations consist of a loveless checking off of boxes, forms, and other perfunctory exercises performed only to prove to one's superiors that standards are being kept.

But on the way to failure, there's a lot to be gained in the way of power, prestige, and wealth for those pied pipers who play the tune outlined by the above alchemy. As Milton Friedman answered Phil Donahue in 1979, when the latter asked him whether he had doubts about capitalism given how it "runs on greed," Friedman asked him, "Is there some society you know that doesn't run on greed? You think Russia doesn't run on greed? You think China doesn't run on greed? What is greed? Of course none of us is greedy – it's only the other side that's greedy. The world runs on individuals pursuing their separate interests."[3]

His common sense answer reflected an understanding of human nature rooted in the Founders as well as Biblical theology. The only thing the revolution brings is a new system through which the new man works out his inherently greedy condition. Only now the checks have been removed because the revolution's vanguards didn't think their *new man* needed any checks in the first place! What checks does a perfected individual need?

We don't notice the greed of the totalitarian if (a) we ourselves benefit from it and (b) their greed doesn't hurt anyone because they're underwriting their greed on tomorrow's dime. But eventually, as Margaret Thatcher said, the money runs out, and far worse, the engine of wealth expansion is stalled. We at this point in the early twenty-first century have the great joy of seeing the final chapter of this story unfold before our very eyes.

But the first chapter opens in the nineteenth century, particularly the mid-nineteenth century, and it begins in the theology of non-liturgical, enthusiastic churches. And this is not mere coincidence. It's part and parcel of what a non-liturgical church implies for theology, and ultimately for society.

American Politics: 1850-1900

In a massive study, *The Cross of Culture: A Social Analysis of Midwestern Politics 1850-1900* (1970), historian Paul Kleppner analyzed the voting patterns of certain demographic groups in the mid-nineteenth century Midwest. He concludes, "the data shake old shibboleths,"[4] like the assumption that ethnicity, immigrant status, education, or income usually determined voting patterns.

Not so. The most consistent factor determining how a demographic group voted, he discovered, was whether the group belonged to a liturgical or a non-liturgical church body.

In a chapter titled "Pietists versus Ritualists," he flatly concludes, "The more ritualistic the religious orientation of the group, the more likely it was to support the Democra[tic Party]; conversely, the more pietistic the group's outlook the more intensely Republican its partisan affiliation."[5]

He emphasizes the word "outlook," describing contrasting liturgical and pietistic "perspectives."[6] On these terms, he correctly states, "Religion involves more than an associational dimension; it is more than an organized body of doctrine relating to the supernatural. It is a perspective, a frame of reference for the organization of experiences. It is a *particular kind* of perspective, one that informs men broadly about the nature of reality."[7]

This point lays down the contours of my argument: *the same theological perspective demanding non-liturgical forms of worship will tend toward a certain political outlook.* Which outlook? The same political outlook that gave birth to progressivism and modern liberalism.

This is counterintuitive today because non-liturgical Neo-evangelicals are on the opposite side of liberals in the culture wars. But this divide is more like estranged bedfellows battling over what quilt to use. Both believe in the perfectibility of human nature. Both believe Christ's teachings are prescriptive for secular society. Both are easily wooed by charismatic rulers embodying their vision. Both pretend to be on the "right side of History." When Barack Obama asked Rick Warren to do the invocation for his inauguration in 2009, a critical reading of the event helps us understand the deeper meaning: the bedfellows were taking a step toward reconciliation.

We return to the nineteenth century, when the bedfellows were still one. Kleppner frames the "Pietist versus Ritualist" perspectives as follows:

The *ritualistic perspective*, more passive in nature, stresses intellectual assent to formal doctrine and traditional confessions. It is ritualistic and "eschews emotionalism." Its central theme is right belief. As far as its politics is concerned: "It views the world as a sinful one, *but one that has to be accepted as such, rather than as one to be molded into God's kingdom on earth*." (Italics mine.) He adds, "[the holder of a ritualistic perspective] does not seek to reach out and change that world, for there is nothing that man may change." Rather, he distinguishes between his religious and secular affairs.[8]

The *pietistic perspective*, by contrast, "emphasizes a personal, vital, and fervent faith in a transcendental God." Its central theme is right behavior. By nature more action-oriented, it emphasizes conversion, change of heart, personal piety, and informality in worship. While believing the world is sinful, the pietistic perspective "does not accept that condition but concerns itself with converting people, with helping them to make the change from a life of sin to one of 'being saved.'" Furthermore, "[for the Pietististic perspective, life is] a series of exciting *opportunities to re–create the world* for the greater glory of a personal knowable God."[9] (Italics mine.)

Finally, this latter perspective "encourages its adherents to think in terms of the 'Oneness of life,' to disregard distinctions between the religious and the secular, and to view everything as a means to the final goal of bringing a converted world to Christ."[10]

Now, what's remarkable about Kleppner's conclusions isn't his assessment of how differing theological positions on Christian sanctification correlate to a church's liturgical and sacramental theology – this is nothing new. What's remarkable is how these views determined the *political* persuasion of their adherents. The non-liturgical pietists who had a perfectionist view of sanctification tended to be Republican; the liturgical ritualists – Kleppner singles out specifically Irish Catholics and German Lutherans, who didn't have a perfectionist theology – tended to be Democratic.

By way of historical gloss, the two parties as we know them today have undergone a complete realignment.[11] In the 1800s the Republicans were far more the party of strong, central government, while the Democrats tended to be more libertarian. Through sheer historical happenstance the parties switched their ideological contours, Republicans now tending toward libertarianism. The two personages standing as signposts for this switch are William McKinley and William Jennings Bryant. The former was a politically savvy Republican who sought a broad coalition of Ohioans comprised of immigrant Catholic and Lutheran groups (the liturgicals). The latter was a zealous pietist who happened to be a Democrat almost by birth alone. Through a variety of other historical circumstances and personages – the rise of unions, industrialism, urbanization, Woodrow Wilson, Calvin Coolidge, etc. – we now have the political parties in their current manifestation.

According to Kleppner, a particular theological perspective fueled the Republican preference for powerful central government, one thinking in terms recalling progressivism, namely, that the political was everything, that there was a "Oneness [totality] of life," that the religious should be brought together with the secular; in short, where government is fused with the religious, a "Christian fascism."

The early Republicans – radical Pietists – had all the marks of proto-progressives, which might explain why the first progressives were, indeed, Republicans. Using words a conservative today might use to complain about modern liberals, Kleppner writes, "[the radical Pietists] sought to use the power of government, local, state, and even national, to enforce their value system and its social norms. . . . As they pursued their particular political goals, the pietists entered into an alliance with the party espousing positive government action, the party of 'great moral ideas,' the Republicans. In defense of their values, ritualists turned to the major opposition party, the party which opposed an expansion of the coercive power of the state, the Democracy."[12]

The Pietism of mid-nineteenth century Republicanism was revivalistic and millenarian, theology we associate with the Second Great Awakening. They believed the kingdom of God would manifest itself through American society, embodied in collective government action. The "Battle Hymn of the Republic," so favored as a national song, is – just as its title says – a *hymn*, a religious song. It's the perfect detritus from a bygone cultural milieu. The "coming of the glory of the Lord" would be instituted through government action.

How many people consider the theological significance of this song? The "coming of the glory of the Lord" is an end times event. Only according to a unique theological perspective was this coming seen as imminent, something inaugurated *through* this world. Accordingly, America was the New Israel, and its laws reflected the glorious kingdom of the Lord. Her laws would be moral in nature, reflecting their emphasis on personal sanctification: laws about the Sabbath Day, about drinking, and against slavery. The early woman suffrage movement was not about feminists demanding equal rights. It was about Pietists mustering upstanding, moral, home-minded women to the cause of moral advancement. Buttressing this view was the enthusiastic view that God speaks immediately to individuals – male *and female* – without the traditional intervention of a male-dominated Church.

The liturgicals with their ritualistic Roman Catholicism and formalistic German Lutheranism did not hold this theological perspective. They disliked American Pietists imposing their vision of the kingdom of God on them. They'd rather sit back on Sunday in their beer gardens and pubs, and not be told they were sinning. These liturgicals tended toward patriarchalism: the man went off to the pub and discussed politics – of course they had just come back from a church service centered on the ministrations of a God-ordained male – while the woman stayed back at home; she was less likely to get involved in politics, something the other side exploited.[13]

Ground Zero for this ideological divide was the schools. In another roll reversal with modern politics, Republicans favored public schools for reasons first laid down by proto-progressive John Stuart Mill (1806-1873), who called for "a system of education, beginning with infancy and continued through life, geared toward training the human being in the habit, and thence power, of subordinating his personal impulses and aims, to what were considered the ends of society."[14]

For the Republicans, their expressed purpose in pushing for public schools was to gain control of the education of the liturgical immigrant groups from Ireland and Germany, to indoctrinate them in the "ends of society," their vision of Americanism. The liturgicals, both the Irish Catholics and the German Lutherans, set up parochial schools to defend against the Pietists, the Lutherans fearing the "Godless" public schools would produce only "rationalists and Pharisees."[15]

The Republican ethos naturally evolved into early progressivism. The Republicans, in turn, had evolved from the Whigs, the party most dominant in Puritan New England. Puritanism means something quite specific as far as a theological posture goes, which we'll soon get into, and understanding this posture helps explain the posture of today's liberals.

History demands we remember something rather counterintuitive: early liberalism (progressivism) was profoundly influenced by a specific theology. Which theology? The very theology which has evolved into liberalism's archenemy: modern, non-liturgical Neo-evangelicalism.

And that theology is essentially Gnostic.

American Progressivism and Its Gnostic Roots

American progressivism derives its Gnosticism through two sources actually: the Pietism birthing the Social Gospel, and the "Religion of Humanity" ideas coming from progressive European thinkers like Auguste Comte. The latter sprung from Romantic philosophies current in the nineteenth century, which we've seen are essentially Gnostic. Pietism tapped into the millenarian stream going back to the early Middle Ages. Both share the same Gnostic taproot.

Pietism and the Social Gospel

Pietist ideas sprouted in America for historical, political, philosophical and theological reasons. *Historically*, America's first major immigrants, the Puritans, were the English branch of the Pietistic movement; they seeded the American gene pool with Pietistic ideas that have yet to be bred out of us, namely – in religion historian Sydney E. Ahlstrom's words – "that the world could be constrained and re-formed in accordance with God's revealed will."[16] *Politically*, as Tocqueville first observed, American Democracy was most suited to anti-institutional and individualistic spirituality. *Philosophically*, early American history coincided with the rise of two famous Pietists, Immanuel Kant and G. W. F. Hegel, whose transcendental philosophies – and their essential Gnosticism – should not be disconnected from their own Pietistic upbringings. *Theologically*, revivalism prevailed in the early nineteenth century, evidenced by the Second Great Awakening in New England and the tent-meeting revivals on the frontier.

Hand in hand with Pietism came the "communitarian impulse."[17] Ahlstrom writes about the spirit of the age, first quoting Emerson, "We are all a little wild here with numberless projects of social reform. Not a reading man but has a draft of a new community in his waistcoast pocket." Ahlstrom goes on, "The United States was the Promised Land for both American and European communitarian planters, and the antebellum half-century was their great seedtime."[18]

He tells the stories of the Shakers, the Society of the Public Universal Friend, Ephrata Community, Harmony, the Community of True Inspiration, New Harmony, the Oneida Community, Hopedale, and Brook Farm. These were all utopian projects. They all failed.

Progressivism mainstreamed these radical Pietist-communitarian ideas. In fact, most American Evangelicals embraced the general outlook to a greater or lesser extent. Timothy Smith summarizes the era: "Men in all walks of life believed that the sovereign Holy Spirit was endowing the nation with resources sufficient to convert and civilize the globe, to purge human society of all its evils, and to usher in Christ's reign on earth." And so the "evangelical foundations for the social gospel of a later day were laid."[19]

When industrialization and urbanization hit the scene, the social gospel movement was afoot. The movement had all the expected tropes arising from the intersection of Gnosticism and millenarian utopianism. Of course Social Gospel mouthpiece Rev. Josiah Strong (1847–1916) proclaimed the coming of a "new era" in which an ideal society would be based on the teachings of Jesus.[20]

Baptist minister Rev. Walter Rauschenbusch (1861-1918), a towering figure in the movement, looked back to the Anabaptists as the forerunners to his ideas.[21] Significantly he also recognized kindred elements in then-current philosophical trends: "The social gospel joins with all modern thought in the feeling that the old theology does not give us a Christ who is truly personal."[22] In this quote are Hegel's pietistic fingerprints, which come out more clearly in Rauschenbusch's idea that the "flow of history" reveals "the progress of the kingdom of God."[23] something begun when "the Reformation began to free the mind and to direct the force of religion toward morality."[24]

Social Gospel preachers gained traction because they rallied earlier communitarian revivalism in opposition to voguish Social Darwinism, popularized by Herbert Spencer (1820-1903) and minister (turned sociology professor) William Graham Sumner (1840-1910) as a justification for Guilded Age capitalism. Their argument wasn't against the Theory of Evolution per se. Rather, they said, through the prism of revivalist Evangelicalism (i.e. Anabaptist, Pietistic, Puritan dogma), the facts of evolution could be manipulated to suggest "a new concept of world unity, in which God's overall purpose was gradually unfolded in the progressive achievement of his kingdom here on earth."[25] They in essence were saying, "Evolution is on *our* side."

It was a sly move, because as we've been contemplating, evolution really doesn't lay down anything in terms of prescriptive social policy other than simply, *whatever is, is*. If *what is* happens to be unchecked competition for resources, which seems far truer to reality, an alternative view of evolution would need to be anchored in something other than the cold facts of nature. The Social Gospel theorists provided that anchor by putting the course of evolution in God's hands.

On this basis, then, the first era of progressivism was bound up with the Divine. If socialists like Benjamin Kidd (1858-1916) or Lester F. Ward (1841-1913) proposed the marriage between government and evolution to justify socialism's inevitability, Benjamin O. Flower (1858-1918) believed the big error of a rising secular socialism was that it wasn't tied to Christianity. By this he didn't mean the Christian Church, but Christ. (This was Oliphant's *Christianity-not-Churchianity* era, after all.) Rauschenbusch too hoped the advent of God's kingdom would be a revolutionary, but non-violent, socialist movement: "Christians . . . must unite to form the kingdom of God on earth."[26]

The stage is set for government to be a replacement Church. On these terms Rauschenbusch said baptism should no longer be about individual salvation, but a "really rational and Christian form of exorcization to break the infection of the sinful and illusive world-order and to explain the nature of a distinctly Christian order of life."[27]

Here we see how education became the catechesis program of the Social Gospel and progressivism, the counterpart to a perfectly progressive baptism, which is the moment of gnosis when one wakes up to the "illusive world order" and realizes his role in bringing about God's kingdom.

Of course progressivism was every bit a religion as Christianity is. It assumed the Church's work and social morality and folded it into American political mores, all the while removing not only the forms of the Church, but also the form of Christ himself. True, this was the very thing Flower feared. But as we'll see, Flower didn't properly understand his Hegel, who would have showed him how History is fated to get precisely to that point, where Christ's ethical and social teachings are so personally absorbed into our DNA that we no longer need him as a formal voice formally conveyed through formal, churchly means. It's the final Pietistic triumph over formalism, eradicating eventually the form of Christ himself. It's like the Sermon on the Mount minus Jesus, the message alchemically rarefied from the leaden cradle of a clunky scripture, an arcane God-man dogma, or an outdated Church, and then reconstituted through the golden promises of right governance.

Now no one thinks twice how it's the government's assumed chore to do all the things the Church used to do: catechesis (education), hospitals (health care), care of widows (Social Security), and charity (welfare). Today's secularists celebrate these governmental activities as the flowering of the progressive movement. In reality, they are the terminus of a project by nineteenth century Pietists, revivalists, and enthusiasts to bring about the kingdom of God. Obama himself said it while campaigning for president: "I am confident that we can create a Kingdom right here on Earth."[28] By electing him.

When progressive hero Theodore Roosevelt accepted the nomination of the Progressive Party, it was an apotheosis of sorts. His speech, titled "Confession of Faith" was interrupted with shouts of "amen!" The delegates sang Christian hymns like "Onward Christian Soldier" and "The Battle Hymn of the Republic," or the revivalist hymn

"Follow, Follow, We Will Follow Jesus." Only, instead of singing the word "Jesus," the delegates sang the word "Roosevelt."[29]

The Religion of Humanity

Rauschenbusch mentioned how his own Social-Gospel aspirations found an ally in "modern thought." He was referring to the "Religion of Humanity" ideas coming from the likes of Auguste Comte (1798-1857) and John Stuart Mill (1806-1873).

First a little background analysis.

When evolutionary progress is understood in religious terms – *as something prescriptive, not descriptive* – and applied to society, we have progressivism. True science should simply report what happens, but with a sleight of hand it can be manipulated to tell us what *should* happen. This is how Tim Radford's claim that "altruism becomes not just desirable but inevitable" is just another spin on the above quote that "God's overall purpose was gradually unfolded in the progressive achievement of his kingdom here on earth." In both cases, progress becomes God-directed, or at least directed by transcendent notions like altruism. Whatever it is, it's certainly not random. Also lingering without premise is the unchallenged assumption that *where evolution is taking us* is better than *where we are*, which amounts to another implicit divinization of the process. Of course, giving agency to the process – *where evolution is taking us* – divinizes it in the first place.

This legerdemain by which the evolutionary process is divinized interests us. It recalls Hermetical magic, by which the practitioner submits his mind to nature in order to master it for his own ends. In a sense, the social magicians do the same thing. They claim mastery – a secret knowledge or gnosis – about the evolutionary process regarding society, and then manipulate society to their own ends. They tell us it's inevitable science, when in fact it's nothing more than an ideological interpretation of the facts of evolution.

In our study, Ioan Couliano admitted as much when he said Hermetical magic could bring about "[a] homogeneous society, ideologically healthy and governable," whose leaders are "instructed to produce the necessary ideological instruments with the view of obtaining a uniform society."[30]

Now, it's one thing to assume the magical posture with nature to produce a better wheel, more efficient fire, or more expansive uses of the alphabet – humans have been tinkering with matter since forever – but the holy grail of magic, in both Hermeticism and alchemy, is the manipulation of *human* nature, especially at the societal level.   If Edison, like a Hermetical magician, can submit his thoughts to *physical* nature to produce the light bulb, another sort of inventor might submit his thoughts to *metaphysical* nature to produce an advanced *social* invention.   Edisons of the social material might even become inventors of new worlds. In fact this is exactly what the French revolutionaries, the socialists, the communists, and the fascists fancied themselves to be.   In America, progressivism carried the torch. It was, in the words of Fred Siegel, "the experimental method applied to politics."[31]

Beyond the oft-abused categorical error of assuming metaphysical nature can be reduced to simple laws in the same way physical nature can, the American Founding Fathers were not tinkerers. No scientist would have come up with the Electoral College.   This is what made the Constitutional Convention such a brilliant event in the history of democracy. It demanded the application of natural-rights principles to real-life situations. It didn't attempt to engineer human interaction and conform it to an ideology; rather vice versa: the American Constitution was crafted from the real-life stresses and demands of thirteen colonies trying to go about their business, yielding the bizarre, yet somehow workable, result.   In a sense it was like the English System of measurement, a system coming from *who-knows-where* and only later codified.

The progressives believed this foundation entirely too wobbly and too easily commandeered by "the system," to use the seminal phrase from progressive Lincoln Steffen's 1931 autobiography. Rather, as ardent progressive Edmund Wilson wrote in *The New Republic* in 1932, progressive goals could not be realized until its proponents "openly confess[ed] that the Declaration of Independence and the Constitution are due to be supplanted by some new manifesto and some new bill of rights."[32]

The America of the progressives is like the Metric System, a system crafted by scientists and imposed upon a population by their betters. After the success of the War Industries Board during World War I, the progressives seemed to have the proof they needed. Government, in the hands of wise planners, could be the instrument of humanity's betterment.

Around the time of the health care debate, President Obama articulated perfectly the progressive perspective when he explained in an interview with Katie Couric (CBS News, February 7, 2010): "Look, I would have loved nothing better than to simply come up with some very elegant you know, academically approved approach to health care. And didn't have any kinds of legislative fingerprints on it. And just go ahead and have that passed. But that's not how it works in our democracy. Unfortunately what we end up having to do is to do a lot of negotiations with a lot of different people."[33]

Perhaps the Framers didn't expect negotiations to happen about certain things which shouldn't be negotiated about in the first place, precisely because they had a healthy understanding of human nature and knew how negotiations would go given this human nature. Reality blindsided Obama, as it always does progressives, because of their ideological blinkers. There is their ideological vision, and then there is *what actually happens*, and the history of progressive-millenarian movement is over and over again cast in that dualistic interpretation.

In the history of American progressivism, the name Herbert Croly (1869-1930) looms large. Croly, a puritanical evangelical in the Pietist tradition, was described mockingly as "Crolier than thou." He penned the first classic of modern liberalism, *The Promise of American Life* (1909). In this pioneering work, Croly, reflecting his Pietism, believed in the perfectibility of humans, a project the government was uniquely suited to manage: "Democracy must stand or fall on a platform of possible human perfectibility. . . . What a democratic nation must do is not to accept human nature as it is, but to move it in the direction of improvement." To fulfill these aims, he proposed a fusion of religion and politics, a "religion of humanity . . . a religion based not on conjecture but fact."[34]

In theological terms, this fusion of religion and politics could fulfill the traditional role given to grace, which has always been the Christian answer to the problem of original sin. But different Christian traditions have different views on the effects of that grace. The Pietists and Puritans, among others, were more prone to "holiness" theology, believing that sanctification is a process of becoming better and better, even perfect. Throw this theology into the matrix of Hegelian philosophy – where social evolution distills Christian ethical teaching from formal, doctrinal, and ecclesiastical forms and works it out politically – and the state now has the capacity to work perfection in the human soul. So, Croly accepted the problem of original sin, that "most rebellious material," but his solution to the problem of original sin, his grace, was education.

"The real vehicle of improvement is education. [The] work of education leaves the actual social substance."[35]

Education would do the work of sanctification, once reserved to the Holy Spirit, by organically changing the "actual social substance." But the program doesn't work if only a fraction of society gets the appropriate education. Americans must accept their "collective purpose,"[36] and realize their subsidy was needed to construct a good and beautiful society. We're all in it together: some must pay for the others to attain proper Self-development. Until such happened, "the American individual will never obtain a sufficiently complete chance of self-expression."[37]

Croly believed this topdown imposition of a collectivist vision was scientific and rational. In this he was an intellectual disciple of Auguste Comte and his disciple, John Stuart Mill.

Auguste Comte (1798 - 1857) was the first progressive. He invented the term *sociology* to justify his application of science to society. Echoing a longstanding (millenarian) tradition in the West, Comte divided history into three eras: the age of theological thinking, the age of metaphysical thinking, and the age of scientific (or positivist) thinking. Each age *progressed* from the previous one. Those who embraced the new age were forward thinking, while those that did not were "retrograde" and stuck in old patterns of thought.[38]

Here again, by a sleight of hand, Comte justified a shift from *science-as-descriptive* to *science-as-prescriptive*. If society's progress into its new age is as natural as a rock falling to the ground, is he not merely *describing* the movement of history? Furthermore, if someone says to someone under a falling rock, "Move or die!" is this not the same as telling society, "evolve into the next age or die"? (We would answer that the "move or die!" injunction to the poor sap under the rock takes us beyond mere scientific observation of gravity into the realm of ethics. According to one reading of evolutionary theory his death could mean more berries for me and my kin. So again we're at the conundrum: *Whence the moral transcendence?*)

What are the elements of the last age, the positivist one?

Comte believed scientific experts should run society, or as his mentor Saint-Simon said, "Councils of Newton."[39] John Stuart Mill envisioned "a 'body of moral authority' which would rest with those possessing the greatest knowledge."[40] Foreshadowing the initial giddiness intellectuals had for propaganda (anticipating liberalism's obsession with the magical qualities of *messaging*, *optics*, and *narratives*), Mill also believed,

"The opinions and feelings of the people are, with their voluntary acquiescence, formed for them by the most cultivated minds which the intelligence and morality of the times calls into existence."[41]

British Marxist Harold Laski gives us a taste of what Mill meant when once he sat in on a meeting of such "cultivated minds," those being Herbert Croly and other progressive movement personalities.   He exuberantly reported, "They give us sage advice with the air of people who have private information about the constitution of the universe."[42] This is classic Gnosticism in the raw: *private information about the constitution of the universe known by an elite group of academics!*

These "cultivated minds" could claim what amounts to a *gnosis* about the true nature of the world, a nature unencumbered by convention and tradition.   Hegel for instance claimed such a status, so bold as to proclaim in his preface to *The Phenomenology of Spirit* (1807), "To help bring philosophy closer to the form of Science, to the goal where it can lay aside the title of 'love of knowing' and be actual knowledge [i.e. *gnosis*] — that is what I have set before me"[43]

All those other thinkers just *loved* wisdom. They were like the proverbial blind men describing different parts of the elephant. But not Hegel and his progressive allies. Their eyes were open, and they could see the whole elephant, giving actual *knowledge . . . or gnosis.*

Meanwhile, those without gnosis remained in darkness, thinking the world is just the way it is. Oliver Wendell Holmes (1841-1935) represented this blindness when he described how progressives are always "shrieking because the world is not the world they want – a trouble most of us feel in some way."[44] Kenneth Minogue comments in a similar vein, "It is the essence of the ideological critic [i.e. progressive] that he discovers oppression where the generality of mankind finds only an accepted condition of things."[45]

When Phil Robertson, the Duck Dynasty patriarch, said impolitic things about blacks in the Jim Crow era, it was heresy. "They're singing and happy," he said. "I never heard one of them, one black person, say, 'I tell you what: These doggone white people' – not a word!" He went on to suggest their faith helped them remain happy. His heresy was, like Holmes, observing that humans have the capacity to retain their humanity even in harsh circumstances. This was heresy because the only acceptable opinion, according to progressive dogma, is that blacks experienced nothing but sadness, the essential bondage of their human spirits in hellish misery, that their entire plight was one of longing, longing to be free of their oppression. This opinion, again, is not based on human experience – which tells us every day millions of people, even non-black people, find joy in adverse circumstances – but it's based in this Gnostic reading of human events, where the human soul can be nothing but trapped and longing to be free of systemic bondage.

Most people fold into their outlook a generally cynical attitude toward the world – whether that cynicism stems from a doctrine of original sin or from mere observation of things – and they seek to find happiness in the face of that reality. According to the Gnostic-progressive understanding, such people are not properly awakened to the true causes of their misery, which are all the systems and structures founded by powers alien to their Self-advancement, the archons.

With proper progressive enlightenment, such regressives will awaken to this truth. Of course, given how stuck in old paradigms they are, enlightening the masses to this supposed truth is not an easy task. Feminist Kate Millet remarks, "It is interesting that many women do not recognize themselves as discriminated against; no better proof could be found of the totality of their conditioning."[46]

If only the ignoramuses would think right.

Minogue rightly notes how this is a classic *petitio principii*, the logical fallacy of begging the question, where the conclusion of one's thinking is buried in his premise: *women think the way they do because society conditions them to think that way.* How Millet is spared this conditioning, again, is the paradox we constantly run into, but which makes sense according to Gnosticism, which grants enlightenment to the elite.

As Minogue rightly notes, the *petitio principii* fallacy is "commonly committed in the service of a dogmatism." He goes on, "Dogmatism is necessary because ideological criticism presupposes that there is only one correct way of construing a human situation."[47] Indeed, it is dogmatism, Gnostic dogmatism.

John Stuart Mill also recognized the inherently religious nature of the program he was proposing. According to his vision, humanity itself would replace God, and experts would be the new priesthood. Their task was to engineer society toward the ultimate good of humanity. How would the engineers steer a humanity with diverse ideas of what is good? Mill argued for a *Something* that would be the lodestar; a *Something* that was settled, permanent, and stable; a *Something* that would engender a feeling of common purpose. What was this *Something*? "This feeling may attach itself . . . to a common God or gods . . . . Or it may attach itself to certain persons."[48]

God, gods, or certain persons! Thus were the parameters set for a new secular religion, a religion of government, or the "Christian fascism" Goldberg referenced.

Traditional Christianity has always had some sort of "two kingdom" theology instructing its practitioners to neatly divide their obligations to God and Caesar. Ancient Christians confessed Christ as king while at the same time praying for Caesar and paying their taxes. They were content – much to the chagrin of nineteenth century abolitionists – to live lives of faith and hope even amidst such institutions as slavery. They were not radicals or revolutionaries. Martin Luther – in specific reaction to the millennial, enthusiastic, and communistic impulses of Thomas Müntzer – fell back upon the *two kingdom* theology of the ancients. Christians were not to be radicals, expecting to supplant the kingdoms of this world with a utopian government patterned after Christ's kingdom. His kingdom, if *thy kingdom come* truly be a petition of prayer, is known by faith, not sight, and thus anticipated in another world, something hoped for, the world to come after Christ's return.

The American Founders recognized the practical implications of the *two kingdom* theology and embedded it in the First Amendment to the United States Constitution. America is not a religious state, whether that religion is progressivism or Evangelicalism.

But we need to take things to the next step. If the American Founding and progressivism represent two divergent strains of Christian theology – and if it is true that these strains reflect the ancient divide between Gnostic and orthodox Christianity – then in order to understand fully what is going on, we need to go back to the doctrine of Christ's Person and what his redemption means for man and society.

The "two kingdom" position reflects an orthodox theology of Christ's incarnation. Christ is God in human flesh. Christ both redeems what was lost with Adam – by becoming in his person a "new Adam" – but also shows what awaits the believer *in the world to come*. Even as the redeemed creation "groans and labors with birth pangs"[49] while at the same time looking forward to the "world to come,"[50] the sinner likewise groans under the burdens of a fallen flesh, while at the same time looking forward to his redemption. This dual vision of human experience – seeing with eyes a fallen world while seeing with faith a redeemed world – sets the contours of an orthodox view of government: *it is a fallen reflection of the good order that shall be redeemed in the world to come.*

A Christian can see God's goodness even in a corrupt government. St. Paul was able to write "the authorities that exist are appointed by God"[51] in the face of a Roman government headed by the likes of Nero, who dipped the heads of Christians in pitch and set them ablaze to light his gardens.

From the beginning there has existed in the Christian imagination the temptation to fuse the two kingdoms together, to replace Nero with Christ *in this world.* Such a fusion is related to Gnosticism's radical dichotomy between spirit and flesh, precisely the dichotomy promoting a Christ who only appeared to be human, but in reality had nothing to do with corrupt flesh or its redemption. The flesh cannot be redeemed, nor can any earthly institution like the government. The only possible political hope for the Gnostic Christian is to have a government peopled completely by those who have received radical gnosis.

An orthodox Christian can fathom a government peopled not only with Christians but also by others who strive for universal principles available to all through the natural law (basically the Ten Commandments with its respect for life, property, and marriage). One ultimately doesn't have to be a Christian to embrace these principles; the anti-abortion argument can be made just as easily by an atheist as by a Christian, Jew, or polytheist. So also the pro-traditional-marriage case.

It's an entirely different thing to see the government as good only when it is the radical revelation of Christ's kingdom in this world. The former attitude jibes nicely with a view that the world and its governments, while fallen, still reflect God's good order: His Commandments remain in the hearts of all people.[52] The latter attitude aligns with a more Gnostic view of the world: everything of this world order is illusive, corrupt, and is only fit to be totally uprooted and totally replaced by those who have attained gnosis or palingenesia.

Of course, the very notion of a Gnostic politics belies their other-worldly claims, so to gain insight into this Gnostic attitude, we need to review ancient Judeo-Christian millenarianism. We've come across this word above when discussing revivalistic Pietism and its millenarian impulses.   But what is millenarianism and how does it relate to Gnosticism?

✧ Chapter 9 ✧

Ancient and Medieval Millenarianism

Judeo-Christian Millenarianism

The Gnostic sees nothing good in the created order. He cannot work with the material of this world order. He rejects it utterly, and for this reason Gnosticism was a-historical. History is just the acting out of a usurper deity's power trip. A Gnostic's salvation lifted him up and out of this world and its history. He seeks to escape history.

This is why we don't hear of Gnostic factions spearheading revolutionary movements in the Roman Empire. A true Gnostic suffers despairingly under the oppressions of the present world order. Only death is his final and permanent release. One Gnostic sect, the Carpocratians, practiced communal sharing of property and wives, but their social iconoclasm didn't translate into a political movement.

Yet there were other groups in the ancient world who, while sharing the same Gnostic attitude, assumed a more activist posture. These were the millenarians.

Millenarianism was an unfortunate by-product of the genre of literature known as *apocalyptic*, popular from roughly the fourth century before Christ through the New Testament era, of which the canonical books Daniel and Revelation are examples. Jews embraced apocalyptic literature because it explained events which didn't fit the divine plan as they understood it. In their mind, God should have protected Israel and made her great among the nations, but all the evidence contradicted what they believed. Large, imperial, oppressive systems were either squashing or absorbing Jewish identity.

Where was God amidst Israel's loss of national status? Where was God's kingdom when the only kingdom in town was that of the Roman or Greek?

The apocalyptic authors wrestled with these questions and provided an answer, for God unveiled to them the cosmic truths lurking behind the events of the day (*apocalypse* means "something revealed"). Far from things spinning out of control, God was powerfully working through history and in the institutions of the world, using the prevailing governments as tools for the sake of his people. His kingdom was hidden, yes, but also "at hand," a present yet future reality fully realized when the Messiah would come and replace the existing kingdoms with his thousand year reign – here is where the "millenarianism" comes in[1] – of peace and prosperity. To the faithful the apocalypses were a comfort, a bulwark for their patient hope in the world to come. But the key point is, hope was deferred to another world.

As far as Gnosticism is concerned, apocalypticism introduces an attitude exactly like that of the Gnostic, an attitude of despair for this present world order. They too shared the experience of living under similar historic circumstances, in which their individual identity was lost amidst oppressive world systems like the Roman Empire. But where the true Gnostic gives up any hope for this world's redemption, the apocalyptic believes the world will be redeemed: he merely needs to wait patiently for the coming kingdom in the world to come, the advent.

Both the Gnostic and the apocalyptic had dualistic visions. The dualism of the apocalyptic is horizontal, the age now and the age to come. His connection to that later world is by faith and hope. For the Christian apocalyptic, the Church's liturgy connects him to that eternal world even now; it's a mysterious pointer to what will one day be: Christ's reign in a redeemed world. But only at his bodily resurrection will he fully experience the things he believes and hopes in, this world to come. Death is the dark interlude between the two worlds. The future opened grave is the doorway into bliss.

Gnostic dualism by contrast is vertical, of overlapping worlds, the world of matter and the pleromic world. A Gnostic's connection to the pleroma is not through faith, but through gnosis, through ecstatic insight and ascent into the other world. It's immediately accessible, without any need for sacraments or mediation, or any mysterious pointers calling for disciplines of faith and hope. It's available in this world. Death is not the interlude between this world and the next world. Death is the final removal of a body whose only significance was to drag the spirit down from the world of spirit back into the world of matter. Death is the final release, the doorway into bliss.

For the apocalyptic, faith is the deposit of a glory to be revealed. For the Gnostic, gnosis *is* the real thing itself. For the apocalyptic, the present time is always unfulfilled; he "hungers and thirsts"[2] for his redemption until the day he dies. For the Gnostic, he gets the fullness (pleroma) now.

The role of the body is central in this comparison. For the apocalyptic, even while his faith is filled with hope of good things, he sees his body wilting away, struggling under the lusts of the flesh.[3] This is the tension of the Christian life under the cross. The restoration of his flesh is the ultimate goal and occupies his hopes. Meantime he takes up the struggles of the flesh against temptation. Here forgiveness enters. It "fills in the gap" between the reality of the now (sinful flesh) and the promise of what is to come (holiness). The Christian embraces that event where forgiveness was accomplished, the crucifixion of Jesus Christ, which itself is a cosmic statement of the reality of the world: God's broken-ness marks the world's broken-ness and, precisely because it's God on that cross, we know that redemptive triumph awaits, even if through temporary suffering.[4] The testament to that event, Holy Communion, anchors that faith, even as the resurrection of Jesus (participated in through Holy Baptism), provides a daily source for the renewal of faith and hope.

To the Gnostic, the body is a wet blanket; the sooner it's gone the better. Death is the final separation of body and spirit, and never the two shall meet again. I once had a discussion with a funeral director who observed that more people were asking for cremation. I asked him why he thought this was the case, and he said, "Low self esteem. People will say, 'Just throw my body out at the dump.'"

Interesting, but I would suggest it's this Gnostic spirituality going on. It's a rejection of the flesh as the locus of Self. "I am not my body," is the attitude, even as the "genderqueer" in our introduction claimed not to be "comfortable in my body."

But once the body is taken out of the equation, this has interesting implications for how one understands salvation. No longer is the doctrine of the resurrection needed. The Gnostic, *precisely because the body is taken out of the equation*, believes a true salvation can happen now, in the present, not just a foretaste – a mysterious, sacramental participation – but the real thing right now. The Christian needs the body to experience his full salvation; thus the waiting game for the resurrection and the Christian virtue of patient endurance. The Gnostic can skip the waiting because he just needs his inner Self for an immediate salvation.

When applied to politics, things get messy.

Again, classic Gnosticism eschewed any political programs,[5] but the sort of Gnosticism I am applying to modern politics is a fusion of Gnosticism and apocalypticism, an overlapping of the horizontal and vertical dualisms combining elements of Gnosticism and apocalypticism. Not to let pure Gnosticism off the hook. It's claims to otherworldliness are often pretension, something hinted at by philosopher A. O. Lovejoy (see *supra*, 31) when he remarked how Gnostics and mystics always "find something very solid and engrossing in the world," and therefore apply their gnosis to, among other worldly things, politics.

Political philosopher Eric Voegelin coined the phrase "immanentizing the eschaton" to describe this fusion of Gnosticism and apocalypticism. This is a fancy way of saying we can access now what was meant to be deferred to the next world. What only faith grasps (i.e. life in the world to come; the kingdom of God) can be realized through gnosis. The body's redemption need not await the world to come. It can be restored now.

This fusion is termed *millenarianism*. Throughout history millenarian sects have arisen, each of them constituting similar traits: (1) they are led by a God-filled visionary or prophet who claims divine insight into the future; (2) they are convinced by this divine insight that a new age will completely replace the old; (3) this world-historical change, they believe, will be anticipated by an organic change in the makeup of, even perfectibility of, human beings; (4) believing they are applying Christ's principles to social life, they practice communitarianism; (5) they expect the violent overthrow of the old order, *particularly its theological undergirding* (see Voegelin's "Murder of God" analysis[6]) in order to inaugurate the millenarian vision.

A millenarian is a Gnostic insofar as he despairs of the present world's redemption, believing something better is accessible through a gnosis granted only to the elite. But he is an apocalyptic insofar as he believes in the political implications of his gnosis, that it reveals the millennial reign of Christ or his teachings, a radical uprooting and replacement of the current world order. He trades away Gnostic hatred of the flesh for the apocalyptic resurrection of the flesh; meanwhile he keeps Gnostic *imminence-through-gnosis* while dispensing with apocalyptic *faith-in-a-world-to-come.*

In other words, the doctrine of the resurrection of the flesh is realized immediately through communitarian-political programs promising something akin to everlasting life for the body. "Health Care Now!" says the crusader for government-run health care. The statement betrays the millenarian amalgam. The *health care* (or *peace* or whatever) draws from the apocalyptic promise of a restored body and world; the *now* draws from Gnostic immediacy: fulfillment is available *now* and need not be deferred.

And those who struggle with the logic of the program – for whom mundane conundrums like the law of scarcity give pause as to the possibility of providing full care (defined how?) for every single human on earth – are missing the point. The case needs no rational explanation. It just is, and if we don't see how, it's because we haven't attained gnosis. Gnosis is supra-rational; no human logic can explain it: *Give up your phallo-centric logic you un-evolved lout!* Once evolved, we can imagine a world with enough doctors to provide full health care for six billion people, who will voluntarily train for ten years at eighteen hours a day, all to get paid a mechanic's wage. In such a world I will have a right to secure a biochemist's knowledge for my medicine because he donates his time to invent the new medicines granting restoration of my flesh. No, he didn't choose a different career after realizing his contributions wouldn't be compensated in accord with his value, under the forced calculus that others have a right to what he has to offer. Both the doctor and biochemist will choose to be the incarnated realizations of my right to health care. Why? Because in the new age, human nature itself will organically change; selfish impulse will be gone; all will realize they are part of the collective. The moment someone realizes he has the intellectual gifts to contribute to my health care, not the slightest twinge of selfish urging will lead him to choose a career in, say, plastics, where he's paid more. No, his mind is different in the new age. His first thought is my care. Notice the volunteerism of the Millennials! That's what fifty years of proper education, media manipulation, and political will-to-power can do. And it's a taste of the glorious things to come!

Or not. Because sometimes *actual* human nature causes those messy unintended consequences so frequently accompanying progressive-millenarian programs. (The next few decades will be a catechesis in unintended consequences as our nation deals with the fallout from the Affordable Care Act.)

I got into an argument with a Mennonite about this very subject around the time of the 2010 health care debate. I asked him how health care could be a right if it depends upon another individual (a doctor) choosing to provide his service. Don't rights exist independent of someone else's provision of it? I don't need anyone else to provide me the means for free speech, for example. Likewise the right to bear arms is not the right to the arms themselves. But health care requires a trained practitioner to make it available to me. But what if the doctors go on strike? His answer: "We'll *make* them provide care."

Ah yes, we'll *make* them. Always the end result of the progressive program: make people do things that their betters see must be done, violently if need be. This from someone in a religious group supposedly committed to non-violence!

Irony? Not at all once we understand how millenarianism works: *Peace Now and Exterminate Anyone Who Disagrees!* Someone who eats a hamburger isn't a cannibal; and neither is the evolved, peaceful New Man who exterminates the species that refused to evolve.

But let's explore his Mennonitism a bit further.

Joachim of Fiore and the Early Radicals

Founded by Menno Simmons, Mennonitism arose from the same medieval millenarian soup birthing the Radical Reformation. Simmons, a Roman Catholic priest, reconsidered his beliefs in transubstantiation and infant baptism after government officials killed his brother, an Anabaptist.

At first blush, his life introduces the typical narrative attached to the left wing of the Reformation: their sects were simple, peaceful folk who just wanted to be left alone. Meanwhile the powers that be sought to kill them. Why? Because, so the narrative goes, they were different, non-conformists, *the Other*. And that's what those archontic powers representing the institutions do, right? They go around murdering *the Other*.

Governmental overreach in defense of its animating principles is a topic worthy of discussion, but there's some sort of weird tautology going on in the charge that a governing body arbitrarily exterminates people simply for being *Other*. "They kill others because they're *Other*" is like saying, "He eats food because it's food."

This highly ideologically-driven line of argumentation is too easy a way out. It allows the Gnostic to sit comfortably in his cosmic myth without grappling with real theological issues at stake, like a woman telling herself, "Men don't like me because they fear me," when in fact they might not like her because she's a shrew. Of course, given the powerful stakes for one's self-perception, we get a clue as to the real psychological mechanisms going on: if I can frame reality according to my own myth-based constructs, I can ignore real issues, especially those I can't change. Gnostics face this dynamic all the time. We could say it's their driving psychological dynamic.

It's similar to our above-referenced feminist expressing how she needs to tell other women how to think right about the oppression they never knew they were experiencing. I likewise need to realize why I have a problem with certain theological or political positions that undermine the foundations of my faith or freedoms, and why I believe my Church or government should do everything possible to guard against these positions. *No*, says the Gnostic, *you really have these feelings out of fear for Other*. But what if I've explained the exact reasons for my position? *No. You haven't fully awakened to the psychic mechanisms at work in your soul. You're just using the old paradigm regime of analysis and rationality and "facts" to support your hate and fear of Other.*

How do you debate that? You don't, which is the point. As long as they can frame issues through the archetypical shorthand of "powers [archons] vs. the *Other*" rather than two competing theologies subject to debate, (a) they can ignore the potentially superior rationality of the ruling theology or philosophy, and (b) they can by their dualistic cosmic myth understand themselves as the agents of light against the dark powers.

The governments at the time of the Reformation, whether in cahoots with the Lutherans or the Roman Catholics, sought out Anabaptists because they recognized something inherently subversive in their theology and practice that could unravel the very fabric of civil life itself. If they took a position of "it's either us or them," it's because the thought lingered first in Anabaptist theology and was occasionally acted upon. If the Churches or state had reformed their institutions, the Anabaptists still wouldn't have been happy.

What was that theology? It was the expectation of lots of blood, the blood of anyone who was not Anabaptist. Most Anabaptists gathered quietly alone with their Bibles and love, but filling their minds was expectation of a millennial kingdom which Christ would set up in this world, destroying all who opposed it.

So far so good as far as the political implications are concerned. All Christians anticipate a final judgment that won't be so nice for those who oppose Christ, and these Christians can live next door to rabid atheists with no effect on the body politic. But one step takes us into terrain that's not so good: *if Christ is in me, and I have direct communication and connection with the Divine, Christ may be inaugurating his kingdom through me right now, and I am cooperating with Christ in his judgment.* This step is the millenarian step, the enthusiastic step, the exact step embedded in Anabaptist doctrine. All it took was a prophet here or there to fan this doctrine into a hot flame.

What's more, Catholic and Lutheran authorities had access to the greatest guide of political wisdom: experience. They had three hundred years of it going back to Joachim of Fiore (1135-1202), the father of medieval millenarianism.

As we've seen, Joachim divided history into three eras corresponding to the three Persons of the Holy Trinity. He believed he was ushering in the age of the Holy Spirit, believing himself the *dux e Babylone* (the "leader out of Babylon"). Church would be unnecessary in the age of the Holy Spirit, as each new man in this new age would have direct contact with God.

Here are the battle lines of the two theologies going back to the orthodox vs. Gnostic doctrines of Christ and reaching forward into the Pietist vs. Liturgical perspectives. It's the basic issue of whether the Church, as the incarnate, post-ascension continuation of Christ's Body, will mediate man's relation with God through liturgical acts (preached word and sacrament), or whether all this is just part of a Church Age surpassed by a new Age of the Spirit where no mediation point is needed, but each Christian subjectively connects to God.

In any event, based on calculations derived from the genealogy in the New Testament's opening chapter, Joachim believed human history would be transformed between the years 1200-1260. With the previous two ages, a "period of incubation"[7] prepared the way. Abraham prepared the way for the Age of the Father, as John the Baptist did for the Age of the Son.

Who would usher in the Age of the Spirit? The monks.

A new order of monks would catechize the world in the new gospel of the Spirit, and from the monks would arise the *novus dux*, a new leader who would convert the Jews and lead the world to set their minds on the things of the spirit. Three and a half years prior to the fulfilment of this glorious new age, the Antichrist – "a secular king who would chastise the corrupt and worldly Church until in its present form it was utterly destroyed"[8] – would set up shop.

Some members of the Franciscan Order naturally adapted Joachim's theology. As happens in all utopian, communalistic groups (evidenced by the periodic reform movements that might as well be scheduled for the monastic communities every hundred years) the Franciscans had become worldly, having to adjust to the "demands of every-day reality"[9] – always the damned reality – but a remnant recalled the strict poverty of its early days and took to the visions of Joachim; they were the *Spiritual Franciscans*. These new visionaries assumed Joachim's mantle and added to his writings, believing they were the new order of monks replacing the Church.

To be a millenarian is to wrestle with the question, "To what extent do we cooperate or co-work with God in the inauguration of the new age?"

On one hand, that age will be a time of peace and prosperity. Property will be shared. War will cease. The elite pioneers who have glimpsed this age and have tasted its glories are themselves peaceful and benevolent personages. *Really, they are!* On the other hand, this new age radically upends the age preceding it, so unfortunately there must be a political component. A few eggs must be broken to make that omelet. This reality invites radical political involvement, *particularly if the actors involved believe God commissioned them as agents of change.*

The Spiritual Fransiscans believed Frederick II of Germany (1194-1250) was the "chastiser of the Church in the Last Days."[10] His profile – blasphemer, excommunicated by the Church, abuser of the clergy – fit that of an Antichrist, and the Italian contingent of the new monks in their sidelined outpost reserved this role for him.

But in Germany, where Frederick's behavior against the Church was the stuff of legend among a people abused by Rome, his role merged with that of the *novus dux*, the messianic new leader. The pope by contrast was the true Antichrist. A certain Brother Arnold of Swabia adopted this perspective.

Promulgating a Joaichite manifesto, Brother Arnold believed God, through Arnold and his monks, would bring about the new age under Frederick's anointed regime, replacing the hierarchy of Rome (with Arnold's!) and redistributing the wealth of the Church among the poor.

Obviously such a revolutionary program, nixed when Frederick died, had the potential for bloody disaster.

The fantasy of a resurrected Frederick– the "leader" (*novus dux*) inaugurating a new age – haunted German thinking throughout the Middle Ages. In 1348 the monk John of Winterthur wrote, "As soon as [Frederick] has risen from the dead . . . , he will see to it that everything that has been stolen from minors and orphans and widows is returned to them . . . he will persecute the clergy so fiercely that if they have no other means of hiding their tonsures they will cover them with cow-dung."[11]

In the early fifteenth century a pamphlet called *Gamaleon* proclaimed a future German Emperor who would arise and suppress not only the Church, killing all its clergy, but also the neighboring countries of France and Hungary, and the Jews. (Medieval pogroms against the Jews were more often inspired by millennial fervor than by the established Church; often the clergy tempered popular hatred of the Jews. In the minds of millenarians, it was all a matter of the power elites – Jew and Church – sticking together.) A 1439 work known as the *Reformation of Sigismund* foretold a day when a "priest-king," the arisen Emperor Frederick, would rule a millennial kingdom without corruption and avarice, in which the needs of all people would be provided for.[12]

Finally there is the *Book of a Hundred Chapters*, authored by a fanatic who believed the Archangel Michael appointed him to gather other pious laymen – christened the Brethren of the Yellow Cross – who under the auspices of a resurrected Frederick would bring about an age of peace and prosperity. Their specific God-ordained commission was to eradicate all sinners who got in the way, to "smash Babylon in the name of God [and] bring the whole world under [Frederick's] rule, so that there shall be one shepherd, one sheepfold and one faith throughout the whole world." He adds, "Whoever strikes a wicked man for his evildoing, for instance for blasphemy – if he beats him to death he shall be called a servant of God."[13]

The clergy especially were due the wrath of the messiah. The author dreamt of a day when over the course of four and half years, 2300 clerics would be killed every day: "from the Pope right down to the little students! Kill every one of them!" For those counting, that amounts to 3.7 million ordained clergy.

Beyond the millenarian movements inspired by the Frederick myth, there's the heresy of the Free Spirit, arguably the first hippy movement. Cohn writes of them that "they did not find their followers amongst the turbulent masses of the urban poor. They were in fact gnostics intent upon their own individual salvation; but," he adds, reminding us of Lovejoy's observation that Gnosticism can't help but become political, "the gnosis at which they arrived was a quasi-mystical anarchism – an affirmation of freedom so reckless and unqualified that it amounted to a total denial of every kind of restraint and limitation. These people could be regarded as remote precursors of Bakunin and of Nietzsche."

Cohn adds, "Nietzsche's Superman . . . obsessed the imagination of many of the 'armed bohemians' who made the National-Socialist revolution."[14] In other words, again we encounter the paradox: an ostensibly peaceful, free-thinking movement always has lurking in its social iconoclasm the violent upending of society.

The heresy of the Free Spirit was widespread, influential through vast swaths of Europe. In its practice we see all the Gnostic traits identified in Chapter Two. They were anti-authority, rejecting the intermediary role of the Church. They were antinomian, believing the individual soul had achieved a state of perfection in union with God – even becoming God. Thus anything done through the body was permitted. Promiscuity was their rebellion of choice, a sign that they had become truly free.[15]

Making Woodstock look a gathering of Sunday School teachers, the medieval Free Spirits dived headlong into the then-flourishing cult of eros invading Europe. To the sexual act they gave a "transcendental, quasi-mystical value." Adultery was their *gnosis*, their moment of true freedom from all constraint: "Till acted that so-calle sin, thou art not delivered from the power of sin." Ritual nakedness, seen as the sign of a restored Eden, was practiced, as well as communal orgies. One self-proclaimed prophet of the new age claimed to "have a special way of performing the sexual act"[16] he would introduce once the new age was inaugurated.

What does all this have to do with a political program? If we see sexual license as the transgressing of marital boundaries – the rejection of marriage as a false institution – the same applies to property.

John Calvin identified a group of Free Spirits who applied their transgressive principles to property and thereby justified theft. Their motto was "Give, give, give, give up your houses, horses, good, lands, give up, account nothing your own, have all things common." Or again "All things which God created are common!"[17]

Whatever violence was done to the institution of marriage was justifiably done in society as well. Common sharing of women –

something Plato already introduced in *The Republic* – paralleled the common sharing of property. We saw how a Gnostic sect, the Carpocratians, likewise believed in the communal sharing of property.

The biblical book of Acts, chapter two, seems to lay down an ideal of apostolic communalism. The question is whether this ideal is acted out individually through charitable giving or the political blueprint for a restored Eden where there is no "mine or thine." The answer to this question is related to the question of sanctification: to what extent can the believer live out the Christian ideal? To what extent is perfection possible? The Bible itself gives a clear answer to these questions in that there is no evidence of communalism given in Scripture after Acts 2. But the ideal persisted after the apostolic era.

The monastic communities siphoned the energies of those who believed they could live up to the ideal. They became little sub-societies of elite spiritual warriors who kept the totality of Christ's call to self-denial . . . at least for a few years prior to their scheduled reformations. The Church fitted this spiritual yearning into its theology by proposing a two-tiered system of salvation, one for the monks and one for the rest. The former could live out Gospel precepts such as communitarianism on behalf of the latter.

Other mystically-minded Christians, Gnostics, and millenarians were a bit more holistic. Communalism was the primal ideal, something practiced in Eden, something restored in the new age. And it's something *all* true Christians should enter if indeed they have become "new creations."[18] New creations have no room for Luther's sinner/saint division of the redeemed believer or Roman Catholicism's life of penance. The sinner is gone. He needs no penance.

And gone also is the Law, which only sinners need.[19] The Ten Commandments, which assume and sanction private property (as well as marriage), they said, were God's accommodation of the post-primal reality of sin. There's God's primary intent and God's accommodation, a dualistic understanding of God close enough to the ancient divide between Monad and Yaltabaoth. Whatever the case, Gnostics and millenarians took St. Paul's "freedom from the Law" to a level the more orthodox were unwilling to go, rejecting the Law altogether as a residual effect of God's accommodations in the previous age. These laws only codified and sanctioned everything they saw as corrupt. Redemption demanded rejection of the law and all it codified.

Did this anarchic vision of property translate into a program for the violent overthrow of the status quo? Cohn notes, "All that was required in order to turn such a prophecy [of the communal ideal in the world to come] into revolutionary propaganda of the most explosive kind was to bring the Day of Judgment nearer – to show it not as happening in some remote and indefinite future but as already at hand."[20]

We're back at Voegelin's "immanentizing of the eschaton," the very millenarian spirit animating all totalitarian movements. On these terms, certain medieval revolutions serve as precursors to the totalitarian movements of later periods.

The Bohemians

Fifteenth century Bohemia, home to John Hus and the Waldensians, saw the rise of the Taborites, named after the Bohemian town Tabor. Going beyond Hus' benign reform aspirations and the pacifism of the Waldensians, the Taborites took the view of the *Pikarti* – wandering adepts of a cult convinced they were vessels of the Holy Spirit – to its logical conclusion and sought a complete break from Rome, believing it the abode of Antichrist. When Bohemian authorities rejected Taborite radicalism, they reacted violently, their preachers calling for the abolition of evil and destruction of towns and villages as a predicate to the coming new age. The poor responded and sold their belongings, giving the proceeds to these ministers, who in turn commissioned the poor to carry out the "necessary purification" of society. A certain John Capek added, "Accursed be the man who withholds his sword from shedding the blood of the enemies of Christ."[21]

From Bohemia the warriors of the millennial age would move on to the whole world. What sort of society awaited those who completed this task? A realm where "no sacraments would be needed to ensure salvation; the book-learning of the clergy would be revealed as vanity; the Church itself would disappear."[22]

What actually happened? Cohn drily notes, "the plan to establish world-wide anarcho-communistic order met with very limited success."[23]

Some of the poor sold their property and joined the Taborite army; others set up communalistic communities where there was no *mine or thine*. To them, glorious Eden had been restored, and they would be exempt from work, each living communally off the land. They ran into a big problem, however: "[they] were so preoccupied with common ownership that they altogether ignored the need to produce."[24]

Exhausting the proceeds from the sale of properties, they resorted to theft. But they were justified, of course. Who were they robbing but the enemies of the new order, the enemies of God himself? First this meant the clergy and nobility, then it meant anyone not a Taborite, in particular the local peasantry. A synod of moderate Taborites noted how their radical brethren "harass the common people of the neighbourhood in quite inhuman fashion, oppress them like tyrants and pagans and extort rent pitilessly even from the truest believers."[25]

Eventually Taborite fervor died down as the exigencies of the day called for the restoration of productive craft guilds and the election of their own bishops to administer funds. Against certain laws there can be no rebellion, like the law of scarcity. And again we see another law at work: the revolutionaries become the conservatives, far more dictatorial than what they thought they were replacing.

Some Taborites hung on to the old vision. Called the Bohemian Adamites, they "held that God dwelt in the Saints of the Last Days . . . and that that made them superior to Christ. . . . They accordingly dispensed with the Bible, the Creed and all book learning." Free love was the norm in this sect. "The sect was much given to naked ritual dances held around a fire and accompanied by hymn-singing." They too believed it their mission to inaugurate the new age by slaying the wicked of the land – cutting down or burning alive "every man, woman and child whom they could find" – and likewise they resorted to theft as a replacement for actually producing something.[26]

Taborite extremism eventually came to an end. Vestiges of their movement remain only in their modern heirs, the Moravian Brethren.

Some other examples of the Bohemian millenarian spirit persists in the mid-fifteenth century. There arose a self-proclaimed "Anointed Savior," a former Franciscan who coaxed two brothers into heralding his advent. He too believed in the Joachite fantasy of a third age marked by a "spiritual church without an external cult."[27]

A second interesting example is that of the "Drummer of Niklashausen," one Hans Böhm, a shepherd boy turned prophet who proclaimed the bloody inauguration of the millennium, an age where "All would live together as brothers."[28] Fearing his influence, authorities arrested him and placed him in prison. Böhm's immense following, spurred on by their divine mission, surrounded the castle where he was imprisoned thinking that like Jericho before Joshua, the walls would come a-tumblin' down. The only thing that came was cannon ordnance a-thunderin' over their heads first as a warning, then a second time for real.

Forty of his followers died while the others scattered.

Thomas Müntzer

Come the sixteenth century, the Reformation might seem to typify the anti-Rome, anti-institutional, anti-clerical, and anti-sacramental sentiment leading up to it. Far from it. The Lutheran Reformation was highly conservative. In particular the clash between Martin Luther and millenarian Thomas Müntzer (1489-1525) highlights that, in the historic contest between "incarnational, ritualistic, sacramental, ecclesiastical, cleric-ministered" orthodoxy and "spiritual, antinomian, anti-sacramental, inner-focused, lay-directed" Gnosticism, the Lutherans sided with the former.

Müntzer, an academic who first joined the Lutheran cause, eventually rejected Luther, trading Luther's more tame evangelicalism for "militant and bloodthirsty millenarianism."[29] Like the Taborites, he believed Joachim's third age was dawning, a millennial period in which "God was communicating directly with his Elect."[30] This Elect, in whom the "living Christ" (as opposed to the historical Christ) was indwelling, had perfect knowledge of God's will, and thus had full appreciation of their divine eschatological mission, to eradicate all evil with the sword and prepare the way for the millennial kingdom. Adopting that sort of anti-intellectualism we've been seeing repeatedly, Müntzer abandoned book-learning, rejected his academic titles, and christened himself "Christ's messenger."[31] What use are books when one has direct knowledge from God? Eventually he gathered about himself a sizeable peasant following, generating some concern among the nobility. Luther took a stand for law and order against Müntzer's budding revolt; Müntzer responded in a similar vein seen above: *God's laws were only used by the power structure to defend their hold on private property.*[32]

Müntzer tried to win the German princes to his side. Duke John of Saxony out of curiosity invited him to preach a sermon. Müntzer expounded on the apocalyptic book of Daniel, teaching typical millenarianism, about the end of the age of the "devil's empire" and the eradication of priests and monks who reigned in that empire. Electors like Duke John or his brother Frederick the Wise must choose sides, he preached, so that the "slaughter without mercy" of clergy would be done "honestly and properly."[33] They would be God's instruments of judgment and wrath. Of course, he continued, they couldn't possibly understand God's will and intent. Therefore just as God sent the prophet Daniel to guide Nebuchadnezzar, so must the political vanguards of the millennial age "have at their court a priest." *Who, oh who, would this be?* Müntzer of course, who hoped he might replace Luther in the hearts of the electors.[34]

He didn't. Luther wrote his *Letter to the Princes of Saxony* (1524), warning them of Müntzer's dangerous teachings, and the electors asked him to refrain from agitating the people. Müntzer incited revolution in response, claiming the princes "hinder the holy, genuine Christian faith in themselves and in the whole world, when it is trying to emerge in all its true, original force."[35] What to do when the forces of reaction stand in the way of the *emerging* new world order? They are slated for elimination. Wandering around from town to town, Müntzer sought followers whom he armed and led through the streets, fomenting revolution.

When the German Peasants' War broke out in the 1520s, Müntzer took common cause with them, although they were not entirely sympathetic to his millenarian leanings. In 1525 he established a church in Mühlhausen and began raising a small army. Their expedition consisted in destroying monasteries and convents, but to Müntzer this was only the beginning. "Start and fight the Lord's fight! It's high time. Keep all your brethren to it, so that they don't mock the divine testimony. . . . The Master wants to have sport, so the scoundrels must go through it. . . . Now go at them, and at them, and at them! It is time. . . . At them, at them, while the fire is hot! Don't let your sword get cold!"[36]

As the Peasants' War became hot in the area of Mühlhausen, Müntzer joined three hundred of his forces with eight thousand peasants. A standoff between the peasants and Philip of Hesse, leader of the nobles, resulted first in terms offered by the latter, until Müntzer intervened with an apocalyptic message: *God had promised them victory; they would literally catch the cannonballs in their sleeves.* When a rainbow appeared during his speech, the fervor intensified. Surely this was a sign of God's favor! The nobles fired their artillery as the peasants sang the hymn "Come, Holy Spirit." Confused, the peasants broke rank and dispersed, eventually slaughtered by the thousands. Müntzer was found, tortured, and beheaded.

Müntzer's legacy was immediate and long term. Immediately his memory was cherished by the Anabaptist movement. Long term he was embraced by Marxist historians as a hero in history's struggle to bring about the communist new age.

But, we might ask, shouldn't Müntzer's millenarian mysticism disqualify him in a movement calling religion the "opiate of the masses"?

Not necessarily. Not if the movement becomes "spiritual but not religious." *Spirituality* is not the opiate: *religion* is! As we'll see, Hegel clarifies the issue for us: the "Spirit" of history is precisely what brings about the new world order. If Müntzer mis-diagnosed that Spirit as a Christian fulfillment of Scriptural prophecy, this was merely a matter of misnaming, of applying labels to an unnameable spiritual force. Nevertheless, the Marxist invocation of Müntzer is revealing. Their totalitarianism is completely spiritual, as it was for the progressives and as we'll see is true for fascism as well. And again, that spiritualism has a very specific, theological, millenarian orientation.

Anabaptism and the "New Jerusalem" in Münster

In broad terms, the Reformation spawned three postures in Western Christendom. Doubling down on those medieval traditions offending the Reformers, the Roman Catholic Church codified these doctrines which distinguish her yet today. The Reformation Church established a posture of *confessionalism*, abiding by teachings as outlined in the creeds and confessions of the Church, particularly the confessions of the Reformation period.

A third posture arose, one continuing the millenarian spirit of the Middle Ages. This is the Anabaptist posture.

Anabaptists rejected popes and confessions. The Bible alone was their authority. This led to the multiplying of sects gathered around charismatic individuals, each claiming divine enlightenment regarding the correct interpretation of Scripture. Theology they rejected as so much book learning. Far better to focus more on the ethical precepts of Scripture. They were the first proponents of the *Deeds not Creeds* motto. Instead of going to church, where learned ministers taught theology and retained the sole authority to distribute the sacrament, they gathered in homes for mutual encouragement in Christ's ethical ideals.

Anabaptists were communitarian and excluded themselves from society.[37] Their defining characteristic, the practice after which they were named, was the second baptism which was said to be the true baptism of the Holy Spirit, as opposed to the ritualistic baptisms of the established churches. This practice fit their enthusiastic theology: God's grace acts directly upon the believer and is unmediated through any ecclesiastical forms. Once elected and baptized in God's spirit, the Anabaptist separated himself from society. Of course, the entire program is schismatic to the core, as history shows us, for always there are new *anointed ones*, more holy than the last, who supercede yesterday's leaders and gather about themselves their own followers. At the time of the Reformation there were some forty Anabaptist sects.

Most Anabaptist groups, while millenarian, were pacifist, but there was a strain of militant Anabaptism represented by one Hans Hunt, a follower of Müntzer. In 1528 he believed God had anointed him a prophet to proclaim the coming of Christ, at which time the sword of justice would be placed in Anabaptist hands. "The Saints would hold judgement on the priest and pastors for their false teachings,"[38] and Christ would establish a millennial kingdom marked by free love and communal sharing of property.

More impacting as an Anabaptist movement was the community known as the New Jerusalem in the city of Münster. The city was a Lutheran enclave, but soon under the influence of Anabaptist prophet Melchior Hoffman, the local Lutheran pastor converted to Anabaptism, and thus began a social revolution ensuing from 1532-34 and climaxing in a bloody reign of terror.

Prompted by Hoffman's communalistic message, middle class merchants canceled debts and shared their property. News of such beneficence drew the area's poor and alienated, who already tended toward millenarian militancy, "having run through the fortunes of their parents, [and] earning nothing by their own industry."[39] The remaining Lutherans and Catholics on the town council could only hold onto power for so long before the rising Anabaptist tide eventually forced them, literally, out of town.

Eventually Hoffman was arrested in another town where he believed the millennium was to begin. He was replaced by John Matthys, a man convinced God commissioned him to cleanse the earth with the sword. Matthys sent out "apostles" two by two to area cities, and when a pair arrived in Münster, fourteen hundred people ended up being re-baptized. The "apostles" moved on but were replaced by two "witnesses," one of whom was John Bockelson.

More Lutherans left town with their possessions. Münster was christened *New Jerusalem*, and Anabaptists in the neighboring countryside flocked there. Eventually the Anabaptists outnumbered the Lutherans, and like a critical mass being reached, social tension broke out in an iconoclastic fervor resulting in the destruction of religious art and books in the cathedral.

Soon Matthys himself arrived in Münster. He wanted to execute all remaining Lutherans and Catholics but was stymied by more practical advisors. Hardly more humane was his expulsion of the heretical townspeople at the hands of his armed bands in the midst of a snowstorm while "Anabaptists . . . rained blows upon them and laughed at their afflictions."[40] Those Lutherans and Catholics who remained were re-baptized, and thereafter the practice was enforced on penalty of execution.

Soon all of Münster, now Anabaptist – "a community bound together by love alone" – took to calling one another *brother* and *sister*.[41] The rule was: "everything which offends against love – all such things are abolished amongst us by the power of love and community."[42]

Love or else!

On the *love* side of the formula, Matthys began to fully communalize property. New laws cancelled debts and destroyed account books. Seven appointed deacons centrally managed food and goods for communal distribution.

On the *else* side, if anyone complained about the program, well, in the case of one blacksmith who tested the *else*, Matthys convoked a gathering of the community before which he summarily stabbed and shot the man.

Handing over one's property was a sign of faith. Meanwhile lack of faith was a capital offense. The reign of terror began.

Any thoughtful criticism of this regime merely demonstrated the dangers of book learning. After all, "the unlearned had been chosen by God to redeem the world."[43] So to the flames went all books but the Bible. Concerning that book only the divinely inspired leaders could interpret it for the people.

Matthys' work of inauguration laid a foundation for greater zaniness. The real fun lay ahead! After Matthys died at the hands of a troop of mercenary soldiers hired by the area bishop – who at the time lay siege to Münster – the attractive and dramatic character, John Bockelson, replaced him.

Bockelson, given over to bouts of "quasi-mystical enthusiasm," began his tenure by running naked through the streets, calling people to repent, and then falling into a trance. Women especially responded to his call, seeing visions "of such intensity that they would throw themselves on the ground, screaming, writhing and foaming at the mouth." After three days he emerged from his trance to inform the populace that "God had revealed to him that the old constitution of the town, being the work of men, must be replaced by a new one which would be the work of God."[44]

This new constitution put all power in Bockelson's hands and twelve elders under him.   In addition to furthering Matthys' communalistic fantasies, the new constitution imposed a regime of strict puritanical morality.   It permitted marriage, but only those of the Anabaptists, invalidating the marriages of Anabaptists to the godless. It also established and enforced polygamy. If a woman did not follow the directive to give up her "godless" husband to join the harem of an Anabaptist, she could be executed.[45]

The upending of social order took things to a new level. Bockelson renamed streets, abolished Sundays and feast days, and soon took on the trappings of royalty. Was not Christ a king? And even if the rest of the populace lived under a regime of "rigorous austerity,"[46] he assured them they too would enjoy the same regal treatment one day.

While all these shenanigans transpired, the bishop continued his siege, starving Münster.   To keep a hungry people transfixed on the imminent triumph of his vision, Bockelson mesmerized them with various dramatic displays, revealing, for example, that God had told him deliverance would arrive by Easter. When it didn't, he said it was only to be a spiritual salvation. Or again he revealed that God had set aside three days for games and dance, during which he desecrated the mass in parodies. Meanwhile the bodies of the starved piled up.

All along, the besiegers promised safe conduct to any Anabaptist who agreed to hand over Bockelson, his harem, and his twelve elders. Through sheer terror Bockelson kept his subjects loyal. Using a tactic later employed by Hitler, he set up twelve dukes over twelve separate sections of the city, each answerable only to him. They exerted control over the populations under them. Forbidden from meeting with other dukes, they reported to Bockelson alone about any meetings or gatherings of the people. The smallest trace of disloyalty he rewarded with swift punishment, usually at his own hands.

The headless and quartered bodies continued to mount.

By June of 1535, the siege ended when two men snuck out at night and informed the besieging army of entry points in the city's walls. The army soon invaded the city and began a massacre lasting several days. The Anabaptist leaders were all killed. Bockelson, after chained and displayed like a performing bear, was publicly tortured to death with a hot iron. To this day in Münster hang three human-sized cages from the bell tower of its cathedral. Here Bockelson and two others were suspended after their deaths as a reminder of the dangers of the Anabaptist spirt.

What is that exact danger, especially of a movement purportedly so benign, peaceful, and quiet? It's exactly that attitude taken by my Mennonite interlocutor: *We'll make them!* Anabaptism was targeted because it was potentially subversive and radical not just to the existing power structures, but to the very principles embedded in the Ten Commandments, that property, marriage, and the dignity of individual human life are protected.

"We in these parts are living in wretched anxiety," wrote a scholar to Erasmus during the Münster siege, "[because there] is scarcely a village or town where the torch is not glowing in secret."[47]

Wretched anxiety will indeed ensue when reports emerge of a movement believing private property and marriage are institutions entrenched under the dispensation of the Law, to be superceded by a coming new, antinomian age when all former laws will be overturned. People recognized that in the heart of an Anabaptist lurked millenarian radicalism, merely awaiting the right *leader* to fan that radicalism into a hot flame. If I know that my neighbor believes himself to be cooperating with the Coming Judge of humanity, yeah, I might have wretched anxiety as well.

The Millenarian Spirit in England and America: Puritanism

H. L. Mencken defined Puritanism as "The haunting fear that someone, somewhere, may be happy," which in any age seems an apt description of the do-gooder, morally-preening element of the population. Be that as it may, everything we need to know about Puritanism and its role in politics we can read from its name: *puritan*. The "movement of the Book"[48] began as a national movement intent on purifying the English Church of all vestiges of Romanism and corruption. It was a purification begun first in the individual soul, and much in the way the name *Cathari* (which means "the pure ones") was bestowed upon the perfectionist Gnostics of southern France, the name *Puritan* was pejoratively bestowed upon the English perfectionists.

Doctrinally Calvinist, the Puritans more closely embodied the enthusiastic spirit of the Radical Reformation, with all its accompanying mysticism and, in Ahlstrom's words, "those Platonic ideas which so often offered the Renaissance humanist a way of rejecting scholastic theology."[49] They believed in the superiority of individual illumination over the externals of church order, hence their mistrust of rite and worship. This rejection of external forms prompted Puritan dictator Oliver Cromwell to spearhead a frothy iconoclasm across England when he came to power in the mid-seventeenth century. The resultant attack on images and statuary wrought scars seen in her cathedrals yet today. This purge of traditional Christian churches suggests not only the enthusiastic impulses of Puritanism – the rejection of external form for immediate, internal spiritual operations – but also its potential for political action.[50]

Like the Anabaptists, the Puritans were separatist, separating themselves from the mainstream of society. Why this tendency always with the millenarian element? Because it works out geopolitically what occurs in the mind. It's a separation not simply of one's own thoughts from the mainstream of society – something anyone with a view on something will possess – but *the very paradigms of one's ways of thinking from that of the mainstream*. There is no "I can see your way of thinking" for the Gnostic, no possibility of discussion based on mutually agreed upon universal premises. There is only the God-inspired elite and the rest of humanity in their darkness.

Complaining about this separatist habit of New England Puritans, the more moderate Puritan, Thomas Hooker, observed how they claim a "special illumination of the Holy Ghost, whereby they discern those things in the word, which others reading yet discern them not." This habit results in "high terms of separation between such and the rest of the world."[51] Those on the outside looking in scratch their heads in bafflement at the scriptural interpretations of those on the inside. Those on the inside look at those on the outside as hopelessly submerged in darkness.

Like the Gnostics, millenarians, Free Spirit adherents, and Anabaptists who likewise had no central authority, the Puritans were a mixed lot, with political programs ranging from the quietist to the militant. The above-quoted Hooker, for example, broke off from the more strict New England branch of Puritanism and founded the colony of Connecticut. But all of their factions, as with the others just mentioned, were alike in their essential enthusiasm and other Gnostic impulses.

Puritanism began with the Calvinist emphasis on God's glory, positing that history is the unfolding of God's predetermined Will for the purpose of manifesting his glory.[52] The Holy Scriptures reveal his Will, but with the proviso that only the "inward illumination of the Spirit of God" gives the Elect a "saving understanding" of the Word.[53] The Scriptures reveal God's Will for political and social realms, but most importantly for our purposes, they reveal such truths *only to the Elect*. The Bible becomes a "totally infallible and adequate compend of moral and political guidance, a textbook in which the statesman discovers how to rule." This took things far beyond Luther and Calvin, and had the potential to make "theocratic claims almost inevitable."[54]

Furthermore, Puritans embraced the classic Calvinist doctrine that from eternity one was elect either unto salvation or unto damnation by God's unfathomable Will.[55] This doctrine had psychological ramifications for society.

It all begins with the crucial question of how one gains assurance of election. The *Westminster Confession* (1646), a Puritan confession, answers this question with language directing the believer inwardly, to the inner evidence of his personal appropriation of God's covenant. Psychologically pregnant adverbs dominate the confession's language in such statements as, "[the Elect are] such as *truly* believe . . . and love him in *sincerity*." [italics mine] Or again, the "infallible assurance of faith" rests upon "the inward evidence of those graces unto which these promises are made, the testimony of the Spirit of adopting witnessing with our spirits." Most importantly, the "proper fruits of this assurance" consist of one's "cheerfulness in the duties of obedience." These "duties of obedience" set the course for the pure lives that was the goal of the Puritan, their perfectionist tendencies.[56]

These two theological positions – the role of direct illumination along with its concomitant psychological component, combined with the view that history is the working out of God's glory and will – set the stage for a certain dynamic with political implications: one's eternal status depended on a correspondence between his inner life and the Divine Spirit working to bring about God's Will in the world; the same Spirit is at work in both. The extent to which I am invested in the "duties of obedience" is the extent to which I am a player in the plan of God in the world. The very assurance of my faith is tied to my success at bringing about God's kingdom. I as a "new man" am part of the plan to bring about a "new world," the inauguration of which is evidence that I am truly saved.

Ahlstrom puts it perfectly: "The Puritan preachers sought nothing less than a new kind of Englishman. Their aims, to use a modern expression, were countercultural . . . 'a revolution of the saints.'"[57] The new Englishman, in other words, would bring about "New England."

Using source material from Thomas Hooker, William Voegelin gives insight into the psychology of New England Puritanism, or as he calls it: "the psychological mechanism by which gnostic mass movements operate." [58]

First he describes how the Puritan preaches a standard of personal purity in stark contrast with those of the prevailing culture or economic conditions. The institutions of this world are corrupt, proclaims the preacher, not because of the inherent fallenness of all human institutions, but because they are led by impure and corrupt Christians. This theological premise is necessary because, if institutions were corrupt because of boring old original sin reasons, the Puritans would fall under that same curse, their proposals would fail under that same burden of the fall, and the hearer would be left without hope. Rather, the preacher sets up a light/dark contrast in the tradition of Gnosticism. He first fans into flames the latent worldly despair – the "dislike and discontentment at things present" in Hooker's terms – in which the Gnostic mind is ever marinaded, and then he provides his own "sovereign remedy of all evils," the new form of government.[59]

We're getting a bit ahead of ourselves, for we need to look at the Puritans first in their original English context. Their reason for emigrating to America, after all, was because they failed in their attempt to alter English government to their visions. From an American perspective the Puritans were pilgrims expelled from England due to their steady reliance on conscience, their refusal to conform to the state Church. This perspective holds in the American fantasy. In reality, the Puritans would have been perfectly happy to have all of British society conform to their millenarian vision, something the Irish Catholics learned from Cromwell after he established a Puritan regime in the years of the First English Civil War of the mid-seventeenth century.

Voegelin puts these English Puritans under the microscope in his essay, "Gnostic Revolution: The Puritan Case," examining a pamphlet written in 1641 entitled *A Glimpse of Sion's Glory*. He points out the Gnostic "glimpse" language. For the Puritan, the glimpsed gnosis revealed the imminent destruction of Babylon, the English political arrangements of the day, and its replacement with a New Jerusalem. Of course, as with all millenarians, the Puritan common folk would take part in this destruction by "dashing the brats of Babylon against the stones." Christ came, after all, for the poor, and his new kingdom would lay down a new social order, where kings would "bow down to thee, and lick up the dust of thy feet." The Saints, by contrast, "shall be clothed in white linen." Abundance and prosperity would negate the need for law.[60]

Voegelin writes, "All this has nothing to do with Christianity. The scriptural camouflage cannot veil the drawing of God into man. The Saint is a gnostic who will not leave the transfiguration of the world to the grace of God beyond history but will do the work of God himself, right here and now, in history."[61]

This is the heart of the millenarian spirit embraced by Puritanism and handed on both to progressivism and to other Evangelical traditions, that God is working through history to establish his kingdom, and that a body of *Saints* or *Elect* or *Elites* have connected to his will, knowing it internally, and have chosen to work with it.

Again we come to the *what-actually-happened* point with the Puritan movement in England. Once the Puritans won control over the English parliament, the natural question was, *what now?*

They believed the Holy Spirit would gather the Puritan Saints in various church societies and assemblies. As these multiplied, representatives from each congregational assembly would "rule the world," because God will have given them "authority and rule over the nations and kingdoms of the world." In the meantime they had to deal with the non-Puritan question, what to do with those Christians in name only and the unbeliever. Eventually, the pamphlet says, they would "suppress . . . the enemies of godliness for ever."[62]

Voegelin emphasizes the Gnostic light/dark contrast in the Puritan program. "Social evils cannot be reformed by legislation; defects of governmental machinery cannot be repaired by changes in the constitution; differences of opinion cannot be settled by compromise. 'This world' is darkness that must give way to the new light. Hence, coalition governments are impossible."[63]

The program is universal, or what would later be called totalitarian. Anticipating the Jacobins, the progressives, the communists, and the fascists, what is offered is nothing less than a world-historical change from old ways that cannot be reformed to new ways but require the machinations of the pure. New constitutions are needed. Federalism or provincialism is ruled out, even as the Gnostic mind is formatted in separatist, light/dark contrasts with room neither for an appreciation of another's way of thinking, nor for the thinking that has preceded it.

The Puritan regime ended in 1660 with the Restoration (i.e. of English monarchy) and the Act of Uniformity, reestablishing the *Book of Common Prayer*, the sacraments, and canonical ordination. All who didn't conform to this statute were ejected from the Church of England.

Naturally the Puritans did not conform; hence the *nonconformism* marking their history.

While Puritans in England were trying to pour the new wine of Zion in the old wineskins of the English parliamentary system, Puritans at Plymouth, Massachusetts found an easier path to the reign of Christ's Law in virgin territory. The Puritan band under the leadership of John Winthrop especially intended to abolish private property and set up a communalistic society patterned after the apostolic Church.

In his famous *City upon a Hill* speech Winthrop said, "[W]e must be knit together in this work as one man . . . always having before our eyes our . . . [c]ommunity as members of the same body . . . we must [c]onsider that we shall be as a City upon a Hill."

That city, of course, is Jerusalem, and that hill is Zion. The project ended when after three years starvation beset the struggling colony. Massachusett's governor William Bradford reinstated private property, referring to the "vanity of that conceit of Plato's . . . that the taking away of property and bringing community into a commonwealth would make them happy and flourishing; as if they were wiser than God." He went on to make a nature-based Aristotelian case that society arises from the male/female bond and the family: one will be productive on one's private property when caring for his own; by contrast, "when working for others he deems himself more a slave and his productivity wanes."[64]

The Puritans didn't abandon their experiment in manifesting God's Will through sanctified collective action. Coming full circle to an issue we began with, they stand as the first proponents of public education, imposing community taxation in order to set up publicly-funded schools in 1635. In 1686 they set up "the School of the Prophets," a divinity school commissioned for the production of an elite body of rulers to administer care for the body politic.

That school became Harvard.

As with the Pietists who set themselves against Lutheran and Catholic immigrants, the stated purpose of these schools was to train the citizenry to be pliant subjects of the Puritan way of life in an atmosphere far removed from the control of neglectful parents. The Massachusetts Education Law of 1642 reads, "This court, taking into consideration the great neglect of many parents in training up their children in learning, and labor, and other implyments which may be proffitable to the common wealth, do hereupon order and decree, that in euery town the chosen men appointed for managing the prudentially affajres of the same shall henceforth stand charged with the care of the redress of this evill."[65]

Need we go on? Parents can't be trusted; children must be trained according to the prudential wisdom of "chosen men appointed for managing." The rest of the law runs exactly as we'd expect from that ilk: "impose fines upon such as shall refuse," "they shall have power," "oversight of certain families" . . . every year the bureaucrats must give an account. In 1647, the Puritans added the "Old Deluder Satan Act" to protect children from neglectful parents. The law demanded that schoolmasters be set up wherever enough families warranted it. Their stated task was to prepare children for Harvard College.

The Massachusett's public school model spread. Soon Connecticut established the Connecticut Code of 1650, whose prologue lays down the collectivist vision: "Forasmuch as the good education of children is of singular behoof and benefit to any commonwealth."[66] Whatever behoofs the commonwealth! In this state Yale assumed the role that Harvard did in Massachusetts.

In the next hundred and fifty years, the influences of other American political leaders – who didn't share the utopian dream – tempered Church-sponsored governmental activity. Ironically, colonies south of New England became bastions of safety for those fleeing the oppressive Puritan regimes either in England (they went to Virginia and Maryland) or New England (they went to Rhode Island).

In this discussion Roger Williams looms large. Also a Puritan in the Pietist, enthusiast (Anabaptist) tradition, he became the type of a *reductio ad nihilum* tendency so suitable to Anabaptism due to its psychic machinations.

What does this mean? It speaks to that Anabaptist cycle occurring as separatist factions become the establishment, like the Puritans becoming the establishment in New England.

Once established, a new separatist element arises against the establishment. The new separatists also believe God immediately inspires them, so they're compelled to separate from the original separatists. Meanwhile the first separatist establishment, because God is still immediately inspiring them, add the new separatists to the list of those who must be expelled. But now the new separatists become a new establishment to separate from. The process goes on and on until only one remains, hence the *reductio ad nihilum*.

Williams was ordained a clergy in the Church of England, but saw it as too corrupt. He became a Puritan, but didn't like the conformity of the Puritan churches. Soon he found himself waiting for the coming of a new apostle who would reestablish the church of the original apostles. He himself was a divine "witness" of the Church. The colony he founded, Rhode Island (a veritable *nihilum* itself) became a fitting metaphor for his *reductio ad nihilum*. The Rhode Island colony welcomed Puritan refugees like Anne Hutchinson, a female minister whose belief in the immediate working of the Holy Spirit came in conflict with the established clergy. She eventually was accused of antinomianism, not witchcraft, but her trial and expulsion fit nicely the witch-hunting ethos of a half-century later.

Jefferson's "wall of separation" – a phrase first attributed to Williams – became embedded in the Bill of Rights. This wall was useful in the case of a Puritan doctrine with a history of confusing church and state. It helps protect the American citizen against the established Church dogma of any given Church body.

But what happens if Puritan social engineering animates a generally non-doctrinal belief system, like Unitarianism? What if Puritan impulses are abstracted from Puritan doctrine, the doctrinal forms left behind but its impulses kept? What happens to the separation of Church and state if *Church* becomes distilled from its religious trappings, if, again, "spiritual but not religious" replaces Church?

In fact, this was the exact trajectory New England theology took, when in the seventeenth and eighteenth centuries it trended toward "reasonable" Christianity characterized by anti-dogmaticism, mistrust of tradition, the denial of original sin, focus on the individual's inner life, and an optimistic appraisal of human improvement and progress.[67] This theology paralleled developments in Europe, gurgling up from an underground stream going back to late medieval mysticism, through Paracelsianism, Anabaptism, Pietism, Puritanism, and a host of others, all united in similar themes, all echoing the Hermetical theme of co-creating with God, or being God's instruments of political movement. (Telling is the title of an orthodox Lutheran book combating the tide of this rising popular form of Christian fanatical millenarianism in Germany: *Platonish-Hermetisches Christentum* (1690).[68])

What happens when this tide reaches its zenith and logical conclusion in a sort of anti-traditional, dogma-less, form-defying theocracy?

We find out exactly what happens, because it happened in 1805, when Harvard came under the control of Unitarians and socialists who shared the Puritan vision of state-controlled child-rearing but rejected its doctrinal forms. In this way did the Puritan impulse insinuate itself back into the legal code.

In 1837 Unitarian Horace Mann became the first Massachusetts Secretary of Education and promoted tax-supported education and a standardized curriculum. He visited Europe where he learned the Prussian model of education, based on compulsory education, standardized testing, and a uniform curriculum. The Prussian model itself was rooted in German Pietism and such lovely notions as that of philosopher Johann Gottlieb Fichte (1762-1814), that "If you want to influence [the student] at all, you must do more than merely talk to him; you must fashion him, and fashion him in such a way that he simply cannot will otherwise than what you wish him to will."[69] Mann brought these ideas back to New England.

Though he broke from his Puritan upbringing, Mann's outlook is all too similar if we simply abstract his thought from the forms of Puritanism. Enthralled with a trendy psychology (some things never change) known as phrenology (oddly referred to now as pseudo-science, as if psychological trends have ever been anything but), he believed the source of certain personality traits could be physically located at certain points on the brain. Through knowledge of one's brain, one could overcome negative personality traits. Some were better endowed than others, "whom," he said, "heaven had imparted the clear-sightedness of intellect and the vehement urgency of moral power," and were thus obligated to lift up the weak by "so arranging the institutions of society as to . . . supply the incentives to virtue to the second class."[70]

This moral obligation, this "vehement urgency of moral power," fueled his desire for compulsory education. Just as it was for the first Puritans, so it was for him. It was heaven's call to him on behalf of the less-endowed.

By 1852 the Know-Nothings, fearing Catholic immigrant groups, passed compulsory education requiring all children to attend government schools. Soon the "Massachusetts Model" spread, first to the South and then to the West, embraced by Pietists, Puritans, and Revivalists in the Evangelical tradition who believed it to be the best means of mustering the American people to the nation's collective purpose.[71] And so we come full circle, to the battle lines drawn between the Ritualists and the Pietists.

✧ Chapter 10 ✧

Modern Millenarianism

Modern Totalitarianism: Millenarianism Comes of Age

    The two totalitarian movements of the twentieth century –
communism and fascism – were wholly religious affairs, both rooted in the
notion that their movements constituted the advent of the kingdom of
God. Critical to an understanding of these movements is the thought of
G. F. W. Hegel.

The Age of the Spirit: Hegel's View of History

    Professor Glenn Magee of Long Island University, whose
scholarly interest lies "where the line between philosophy and mysticism
– and myth and poetry – becomes blurred," suggests most people
insufficiently understand Hegel because they ignore the Pietistic traditions
feeding his thinking as well as the Hermeticism fueling Pietism. Through
Pietism – with its focus on the inner spirit over against external form –
Hegel tapped into the mystical currents of the Renaissance such as
Hermeticism. Magee enlightens us on a nineteenth century study of Hegel
by one Ferdinand Christian Bauer, who first saw the intellectual chain
connecting Hegel to Renaissance mystic and proto-Pietist Jakob Boehme.
Voegelin too saw the connection when he penned the curtly titled "On
Hegel: A Study in Sorcery," which describes Hegel's thought as a "work
of magic."[1]

    What is the Hermetic, magical element? Klaus Vondung describes
it thus: "The Hermeticist . . . wants to gain knowledge of the world in

order to expand his own self, and utilize this knowledge to penetrate into the self of God. Hermeticism is a positive Gnosis, as it were, devoted to the world. To know everything is to in some sense have control over everything."[2]

Enter the Tinkerer, the Tinkerer of the material of history through whom God himself is working to bring about his kingdom. As Magee writes, "man is daimonic: a more-than-merely-human participant in the divine life."[3]

The Hegel 101 summary of his teaching always begins with his view of History (note the capitalized, therefore divinized spelling). For him, History progresses, spiraling upward through a gradual process of thesis, antithesis, and synthesis. "A" happens; "B" reacts against "A"; and then History resolves the conflict through a synthesized "C," which is always higher than the original state of things. Through this process, said Hegel, History reveals a "progressive revelation of freedom."

As with the millenarians of all ages, this revelation goes hand in hand with some sort of gnosis or palingenesia, or what Hegel calls a "gaining of consciousness."[4] That is, the ever-emerging, ever-progressing state manifests what is going on in the ever-awakening, collective consciousness of the people.

Once again echoing Joachim's threefold division of history, he identified three stages, or "three degrees of consciousness,"[5] of historical progress based on the extent to which any culture understands the essential freedom of the individual. Ancient oriental cultures were at the first stage; they recognized the freedom of one, the despot. The ancient Greeks advanced to the second stage; they acknowledged the freedom of a few, while many still remained in slavery. Finally in the last stage, said Hegel, "Only the Germanic nations have in Christianity come to the consciousness that man as man is free, that spiritual freedom truly constitutes his nature. This consciousness appeared first in religion, in the most inward region of the mind; but to inform the world with this principle was a new task whose solution and execution exact a long and painful effort or education."[6]

Christianity, says Hegel, proposes a dualistic opposition. As it works its central message – which to Hegel was the freedom of the individual – the individual comes to a consciousness of his own freedom. Soon this freedom of consciousness butts up against the reality of his external world. On the inside he sees his awakened conscience, his piety regarding chastity, poverty, and obedience. This realization needs no outside clergy or church structure to monitor or instill it. Meanwhile, on the outside he sees the world with its ordering institutions of Church, marriage, duties of work, and so on. Such was the state of affairs for the first 1500 years of Church history.

Only the Lutheran Reformation, says Hegel, brought about a "reconciliation [leading] to the consciousness of the temporal world's capacity to contain the truth within itself."[7] That is, the Reformation taught that truth can be contained within an individual without the necessity of outside ordering agents. This dawning enlightenment came through the Reformation's teaching on the *universal priesthood.* Hegel understood this doctrine to express the access of all Christians to unmediated truth. Emerging through this doctrine, he said, was the individual's essential freedom to judge truth fully without need for outside structuring entities. It's like a child internalizing good manners and no longer needing a trainer. Soon the outer forms can disappear altogether. This is the synthesis, the resolution of the conflict. At the same time religious trappings are fulfilled, they become unnecessary.

Hegel's Lutheranism is of a decidedly Pietistic bent. He praised Pietism because it acknowledged "no objective truth and opposes itself to dogmas and the content of religion, while preserving an element of mediation, a connection with Christ, but this is a connection that is supposed to remain one of mere feeling and sensibility."[8]

This Pietistic principle in turn animated his foundational political tenet: "the essential content of the Reformation [is that] man decides by himself to be free." Pietism – like Puritanism, Catharism, and the other Gnostic movements – placed the focus on the inward machinations of faith. It centered on the heart, the "feeling and sensibility." Hegel writes, "It is rather the heart, the sensitive spirituality of man, which can and ought to take possession of the truth, and this subjectivity is that of all men. Each must accomplish the work of reconciliation within himself."[9]

This may sound like subjectivism – each person working "within himself" – but the problem is done away with if each heart comes upon the same objective truth. What is this objective truth? For Hegel, whatever it is, it emerges through the historical process and thus ends up being quite objective. Again we're at Jung's emergence of the Self through the Collective Unconscious.

Because the Christian religion – Pietistically understood – plays an important role in the emergence of the modern state, Hegel opens up the door to the notion of a secular religion, or a Christianized state. Again, for Hegel, true Christianity was the emergence of a universal principle, the principle of freedom, the freedom of one's inner spirit. This universal principle is realized not through the Church as an institution, which would monopolize access to this freedom through external forms and rituals, but ultimately through the state. The offense of a "state Church" is removed if the trappings of "Church" – dogma, creed, ritual, sacraments – are removed because authentic (i.e., for him, Pietistic) Christianity obviates the need for such things, being an inner, not outward, process.

Thus for Hegel the progressive state is in a very real sense a state church, but because it constitutes authentic Christianity, not the ecclesiastical Christianity imposing that duality between Self and Church, it constituted a more *naturally, organically, authentically, internally-established* state church. Put another way, people don't need a *doctrine* of resurrection or charity managed by a catechizing minister in order to embrace universal health care or welfare. Such values have emerged in their own consciousness, and they no longer need a church to catechize them. Rather, the state's education program will lead them to this knowledge.

What's the difference between the Church's catechesis and state education? The difference is, the Church constitutes an *external-to-internal* process of a minister imposing doctrines, worship forms, and monopolizing access to God through the sacraments and his teaching authority. The state on the other hand oversees a more *realized-internal* process in which one comes to awareness of truths residing in his Self, and this through the guidance of various guru-type characters, like state-certified teachers armed with a universal curriculum.

These were the ideas on education fluttering around at the intersection of both Horace Mann's ideas and those of the Transcendentalists. Hegel fed at the same trough that Horace Mann and others fed at, the Prussian system of rational government, with its body of state workers who managed the affairs of state with scientific efficiency.

This Prussian state imposed the "Prussian Union" uniting the Reformed and Lutheran Churches, something cheered by Pietist and universalist alike. For Hegel, such a union was precisely the sort of state activity justified by the emergence of consciousness. External Church forms and dogma work divisions in the emerging universal state, but if Christianity is understood in its true, inner sense, such forms are unneeded. All can be one.

For the "Old Lutherans," those who in the millenarian sense were still stuck in the "Church Age" with its forms, sacraments, and rituals, the Prussian Union was an offense to their consciences. They left for America and settled in Missouri, becoming eventually the Lutheran Church Missouri Synod.

Meantime, while their boats sailed for American shores, Horace Mann and his new bride were fresh off their honeymoon-pilgrimage in Prussia, armed with Hegelian ideas on education, namely, that the state embodied the collective spirit of its individual members and inculcated all its citizenry in its universal aims through education, finding obvious kinship with his own Puritan upbringing. The intellectual table was set for the battles between the ritualistic immigrant groups of Lutherans and Catholics against the more nativist Pietists regarding public education.

Communism

Marx took over Hegel's rejection of a *telos*,[10] embracing the view of ever-emerging, progressive change, an unfolding of what he called dialectical materialism.

What exactly is dialectical materialism? It's Hegel's historical process of thesis-antithesis-synthesis applied to economics. For Marx, the thesis/antithesis contrast explained, at his time, the distinctions between upper and lower classes. He fit the system of classes according to economic terms: who's doing the producing; who owns the means of production; etc. As new means of production would arise – i.e. with the advent of communism – new social relations would arise and this *paradigm shift* in societal relations, the so-called synthesis, would negate the thesis/antithesis contrast it replaced.

This historical process is the cause of "all collisions in history."[11] Marx's use of the word "collision" is deliberate, for as Joseph Cropsey tells us, "the conflict cannot be resolved through compromises or mutual accommodations but only . . . by revolutionary changes in which the existing classes are annihilated and replaced by a synthesis 'on a higher level.'"[12] In other words, the historical process necessitates a series of revolutions, as the conflicts between thesis and antithesis work themselves out.

Thus does Marx carry over Hegel's understanding of a "spirit of History" at work in history. This embrace of the *spiritual* might seem paradoxical given his dialectical *materialism*. Yet, on what basis can he claim a synthesis on a "higher level" in the historical process unless he does so by divinizing the historical process? If he were positing a truly materialistic process, he couldn't proclaim one phase "higher" than another any more than someone could proclaim the movement of a body from rest to motion, or vice versa, as a change from worse to better. "Worse to better" is a moral judgment avoided by true scientists. Yet Marx applies the moral judgment and does so in a way justifying revolution. In other words, those of the higher *synthesis* side of the historical equation are on the side of angels, doing the work of angels as instruments of History.

Through Hegel, Marx harbors the millenarian understanding of history, but he takes it to the point where God is cut out of the equation. On these terms we might propose our own three phases of totalitarianism: (1) The millenarians believed that God was working through history to bring about his kingdom and that they in turn helped inaugurate it; (2) Hegel took over the idea that God works out his will through people, to bring about the historical process; they in turn are directly worked by God to such a degree that the duality between Self and God – which had been formalized through the existence of the Church – disappears; (3) Marx cuts out God altogether, leaving only the Self as a participant in the historical process, which itself nonetheless is drawn magnetically to ideals which in previous progressions would be called divine.

In his own words Marx explains the evolution of religion and its necessity in history, writing in *Das Kapital* (1867), "it is necessary at first to give man's spiritual forces a religious form by erecting them into autonomous power over against him."[13]

That is, humans have yearnings and fantasies about a primitive state of utopian, communalistic bliss: Eden. With the rise of power structures – state, Church, cultural institutions (the archons!) – these fantasies and the possibility of realizing them in reality are suppressed. Hope of their realization becomes channeled into religious dogma and faith. Doctrines like the resurrection of the body or the future glory in a sinless existence become the content of faith formed by the Church's creed. Because they keep the poor masses happy and content while slaving away under oppressive systems, the Church and its creed become an opiate for the masses. As long as the masses keep their faith and hope on future bliss, they won't notice how they're being exploited in the present by capitalists.

For Marx, the religious stage of psychic development was necessary, part of the historical process. It kept alive the hope for a utopian world. The ultimate aim of the historical process, however, was for this psychological need for the Church to be rendered obsolete because the utopian world would be realized. When the communistic, utopian state arrives, what need would there be for hope in a future resurrection and sinless state if that state exists today?

Thus even according to Marx's own terms, communism represents the fulfillment of religion. It is religion without the external forms, creeds, and clergy, so internalized as to obviate the need for its external forms. Philosopher Martin Buber (1878 - 1965) rightly called Marx's thinking a "socialist secularisation of eschatology," which is another way of saying "imminentizing the eschaton" (as Voegelin said) or simply: millenarianism without God. Karl Popper (1902 - 1994) too recognized the advent of communistic revolution as a "great religious movement" because it was characterized by faith (in the ultimate aims of the historical process) and hope (in the possibility of a utopian state). Joseph Schumpeter (1883 - 1950), the economist who christened the phrase "creative destruction" to describe how the free market works, bluntly said, "Marxism is a religion."[14]

Arthur Koestler contributed an essay in the aptly-titled, anti-communist book *The God that Failed* (1949) in which he described his dealings with communism in religious strokes, involving conversion, initiation, dogma, the unyielding priesthood of leaders. His conversion story described his gnosis: "Every page of Marx, and even more of Engels, brought a new revelation. . . . [T]he demonstration of the historical relativity of institutions and ideals – of family, class, patriotism, bourgeois morality, sexual taboos – had the intoxicating effect of a sudden liberation from the rusty chains with which a pre-1914 middle-class childhood cluttered one's mind. . . . [I]t is difficult to recapture that mood of emotional fervor and intellectual bliss."[15]

Later he was able to see the religious dimension of the faith he embraced: "From the psychologist's point of view, there is little difference between a revolutionary and a traditionalist faith. . . . [T]he revolutionary's Utopia, which in appearance represents a complete break with the past, is always modeled on some image of the lost Paradise, of a legendary Golden Age."[16]

How *traditional* a faith his conversion paralleled is arguable – Gnosticism is hardly a traditional faith – but as far as we are concerned, he opens the door into the millenarian orientation when he writes, "Devotion to pure Utopia, and revolt against a polluted society, are thus the two poles which provide the tension of all militant creeds."[17] Again we see the millenarian vision, this absolutist dualism between the past and the possible future. The past is not built on, developed, or reformed. It can only be wholly rejected, revolted against.

The Russian Revolution certainly began as a religious movement. Early Russian Marxists like A. V. Lunacharsky and Maxim Gorky called themselves the *bogostroiteli*, or "god-builders." This self-understanding reflected the Nietzschean thought revolutionizing Europe at the time. Nietzsche articulated how traditional religious forms weren't satisfying the spiritual urges of his day. This God had died. In place of the dead God, man himself would arise as the übermensch, the superman satisfying spiritual striving through cultural creativity, developing new forms to replace the old. Where Nietzsche spoke more concerning specific enlightened individuals and their ability to become gods – the rest of us classified as herd animals – these Marxists spoke more collectively. *The people* would replace God.

Lunacharsky, who calls Marxism "the most religious of all religions and Marx the most deeply religious of men," in his *Essays on a Realist World View*, describes this deification of the people: "The faith of the active human being is a faith in future mankind; his religion is an aggregate of those feelings and thoughts which make him a co-participate in the life of mankind, a link in the chain which stretches toward the overman [the übermensch], towards a beautiful and powerful creature, a perfect being." He added, "In Russia and in the West a new religion is being elaborated," a religion that unlike the old one was able to inaugurate a final victory over the "presence of evil in the world."[18]

Clearly no doctrine of original sin animates such thoughts, and no checks would be needed on any government based on these ideas! Again, a perfected man or nation needs no checks.

Gorky believed that even the problem of death – the desperate reality driving religion – would be solved as *the people* saw themselves not as individuals but as a whole: the collective would enjoy resurrection through perpetual existence.

A poet, he penned words not exactly exemplifying Marxist materialism: "We . . . children of the sun, born of the sun, the shining source of life, will conquer the dark fear of death . . . the sun burns in our blood . . . it is an ocean of energy, of beauty, and of soul-intoxicating joy."[19]

Or as Lunacharsky put it in his words, the Marxist "religion of mankind" would "fill men with a sense of joyous union with the triumphant feature of our species."[20]

Vladimir Lenin was more prosaic, unwilling to yield to any hint of the opiate religion offers the people. To him, the idea of God is used by man to subjugate the masses into sleep. With the revolution would come the elimination of God, replaced by a "new man" who would awaken from this slumber, lose all sense of "I" – the "no mine or thine" of the millenarians – lose all emotions concerning himself, and submit to the greater whole. As Marxist philosopher Abram Deborin (1881 - 1963) put it, "socialist ideas . . . can transform the whole human being and his psyche in all their complexity."[21] Through this transformation the problems of individualism (fear of death, confusion as to one's place in the world, coexisting with others) would be eliminated, as one loses his individuality in the collective.

Of course, if this isn't a faith, a faith in where History is taking humanity, a faith in the organic changing of the human person, one wonders what is. Regardless, this faith bred a sense of optimism among the early communist leaders. They were, after all, avatars of divine History leading the world to its next stage of existence. But because its dogmas hid behind the facade of being scientific, few people understood it as a religious movement.

When reality set in, and communism was shown to be the ineffective, inefficient, brutal, soul-smashing failure it was, Marxism, to put it politely, officially left the realm of science. If you predict a rock upon release will fly up to the heavens, and another law at work pulls it to the ground like a lead balloon, your original theory has left the realm of science. Such was the case with communism. At first the Marxists believed God was working through the laws of the historical process, and thereby they could eliminate the psychic need for God, just as the law of gravity eliminates the need to say that God pulls the rock down. But when history and science showed Marxism to be a failure, their God, as understood originally, seemed to be against them. That forced a new understanding of their movement and thus of God: *they now needed myths to support their vision.* What they originally thought *will happen* by scientific laws evolved into something that *could happen* if only X, Y, or Z can happen first, and such could happen only after people's minds have marinaded in new collectivist myths.

Enter Jung.

Certainly not a communist, Jung's ideas could nevertheless be readily applied to the broken pieces of communist philosophy. He provides the much needed spiritual component lost in later communism.

In his *Introduction to the Science of Mythology* (1951), he argued that myths draw off of subconscious "psychic forces that demand to be taken seriously."[22]   In other words, our Collective Unconscious, while suppressed by our individuality, nags us through certain archetypes in our dreams and in our myths. The communists' error was to cut themselves off from this voice. The medieval Christians heard it, but they channeled it through, in the words of postmodernist thinker Jeremy Carrette (echoing Hegel), their "Religious beliefs, ceremonies and ritual," which established "relations of power" and "a system of control through the mechanism of pastoral authority."[23]   Far better, as a basis for the future revelation of the collective, would be the more "authentic" spirituality of the Anabaptists.   The communists mistakenly threw the baby of Anabaptism out with the bath water of general Christian theology, so married were they to their materialistic determinism.

Today, if we can at least resurrect Jung's "mental life of the primitive tribe"[24] (the pre-Yaltabaothian pleroma), perhaps the foundations for a new collectivism might spring forth.

Who would spearhead this propagation of myths? Sociologist Peter Berger ironically proposes the categories of traditional religion, yielding a sort of civic religion that can become the source of meaning and purpose and defend against social disintegration. In his essay *The Heretical Imperative* (1979), he noted how religions of the world were meeting as never before, and their intermixing could usher in the next important phase of human development. Wilfred Cantwell Smith (of *The Meaning and End of Religion* (1991) fame) and John Hick suggest a "global theology" that could do justice to all the religions of the world. What would be the aim of such a global theology? Environmentalist Edward Goldsmith proposes a "new myth of earth" that could replace the collapsed socialist model.[25]

This sets up a theme in a later section and brings us back to where we began, the reintroduction of religion into the collectivist project by the likes of Jung, Berger, Smith, Goldsmith, and others. Now that the project taps into primordial myths – of which Eden sets the archetypical pattern – it lays the groundwork for Christian Church leaders to jump at the opportunity to participate once again in the conversation regarding history's divine course.

What is the current state of affairs as far as the millenarian spirit and political Gnosticism goes? Clearly the environmental movement currently commandeers the spirit of political Gnosticism. It too is a religion rooted in a despairing attitude toward the present state of affairs and the possibility of a new earth free of the toxins not simply of industrialism, but the toxins of the entire system of individualism (and its concomitant evils like nations, borders, classes, races, genders, etc.) breeding industrialism. The solution is collectivist, but this time around, the movement will fight not with guns, but myths and magic.

We've all seen the commercials where a single voice begins mouthing some slogan, "I want to change the world, but alone I can't do it," and then one by one new people join in, chanting the mantra as one voice, "But together, we can make a difference." Soon the camera pans backwards and we see a host of glaze-eyed zombies joined arm in arm. Individual characteristics blur into a great collective blob, *and you too can join if only you'll awaken.* This is nothing less than the millenarian impulse of today. And just as we suspect, it's rooted in utter myth. Really, how often do masses of people gather together in large fields arm in arm?

Or again, we see Goldsmith's "new myth of earth" dredging up Jung's "mental life of the primitive tribe" through the manipulations of Hollywood. It's impossible to ignore the glut of movies and television shows, especially of the animated variety, painting the picture (a) of an ideal, primitive world where, say, a dinosaur undergoes the modern journey of Self-actualization, behaving more like a twenty-first century angst-ridden, Emo teen than a carnivorous reptile, or (b) of a world where – against all evolutionary theory – animals live in blissful harmony and (c) where the culprit is almost always some archontic power, like industry.

For the love of God, the spokesman for squishy love in the last several decades has been a purple Tyrannosaurus Rex. If that isn't the magical conjuring up of myth, what is?

Animation is wonderful. Based on the Latin *animus* meaning "soul," the creator, the magician, literally creates a world of his own making, putting a soul into creatures manufactured not on the basis of reality – something a regular movie has to do (because it's hard to find animals that talk) – but based on his own creative yearnings. What does it portend for America that these animated myths have been painted into their fantasy lives for the better part of half a century? At a minimum it sets a lot of people up for disappointment when they learn that reptiles are, well, reptiles, or for that matter, that grouchy monsters in garbage cans are actually kind of a scary (nay, demonic) concept.

I can't think of a better metaphor to end our discussion of

Marxism. Aesop tells the fable of the scorpion and the frog. The scorpion asks the frog if he could give him a ride on his back across the river. The frog replies that if he does so, the scorpion will sting him, to which the scorpion says, "If I sting you, you will sink and so will I." The frog agrees to the logic and agrees to carry the scorpion over the river. Half way across, the scorpion stings the frog. As they both begin to sink, the frog says, "Why did you sting me?" The scorpion says, "Because this is my nature, to sting."

It was human nature that brought about the demise of communism. It was the scorpions of the human soul that – unchecked because the communists believed their ideology had triumphed over the effects of original sin – ended up massacring millions. Now we're told we can achieve the collectivist vision again without these side effects, because we'll be better prepared through a couple generations of magical and mythological manipulation.

Yes, human nature will have changed! Goodness, if a Tyrannosaurus Rex can change, certainly we can as well, especially with such "evolutionary flashpoints" as those brought about by the Magical One, Barack Obama.

Yet, no amount of myth-making can eradicate human nature, and no amount of normalizing the monstrous can make the monstrous go away. Yet for some reason, that doesn't stop millenarians of all ages from trying.

Adolf Hitler: Homo Gnosticus

Leo Strauss coined the logical fallacy known as *Reductio ad Hitlerum*, a variation of the *guilt-by-association* logical fallacy. The idea is that any argument ends when it's concluded, *But that's what Hitler did!* And that in itself is meant to debunk the original premise, something akin to, *Tom Selleck has a mustache, and so does Hitler; that tells you something about Tom Selleck, doesn't it!*

Logical fallacies are fun. Finding them is a good parlor game for the armchair lawyer in all of us, but they also can keep us from seeing the forest from the trees. With every little logical point whittled away, we think the broader argument has no merit, when perhaps logic is missing something more grand in scope. Gnosticism loves offending logic, rationality, and cogent thought in the first place. Lawyerly sympathizers of Gnostic spirituality deny they're Gnostics by honing in on specific details of whatever doctrine they're espousing, diverting our attention away from the larger scope. They're like someone saying, *the world doesn't move, look how still that stone is over there!* To which we answer with Galileo's famous words, based on the bigger picture: "And yet it moves."

The answer to the *guilt-by-association* fallacy is the "if it walks like a duck and talks like a duck" cliche. As Supreme Court Justice Potter Stewart put it, commenting on when art crosses the line into pornography, "I know it when I see it." With a narrow perspective, every step toward profane art seems justified: at which point is the neckline too low? It's like Greek philosopher Zeno's paradox: logically no one ever gets to his destination because as he walks half way he halves his distance, and as he goes on he only keeps on halving the distance *ad infinitum*. The logic at a narrow level seems to work, but from a broader perspective, we all know when art has crossed the line, when the neckline has gone too low, and when someone has arrived at his destination. As far as the logical fallacies go, sometimes the slope is slippery, the straw man has breath, and the paradox resides only in the mind of the logician.

And sometimes the association denotes real guilt.

The bottom line is, the connections between the Gnostic traits identified in Chapter Two and Adolf Hitler are there. The man was a new ager, a millenarian, and a mystic, but if I might offer one defense against the *Reductio ad Hitlerum* fallacy, it's that my purpose here isn't to propose Hitler as the climax to my argument, but rather to place him as one part of the greater progressive project, or political Gnosticism. He's a small part of an ongoing, bigger story.

Certain aspects of Hitler reveal intensely mystical, Gnostic characteristics: his belief in the new man, his claim to a new age with new gods, his elitism, his romanticism, his shamanistic understanding of leadership, his embrace of magic, and his personal history of ecstatic insights. To do this I go to the source, to a series of interviews with Der Führer conducted by former Fascist Party member Hermann Rauschning.

Rauschning lays down a description of Hitler's personality so typical of modern man we should coin a term for it: *Homo Gnosticus*. He is "the typical person with no firm foundation, with all the short comings of the superficial, of the man without reverence, quick to judge and quick to condemn. He is one of those with no spiritual tradition, who, being caught by the first substitute for it that they meet, hold tenaciously to that, lest they fall back into nothingness. He belongs also to the type of German who is 'starving for the unattainable.'"[26] In short, he's perfect fodder for that modern dilemma: *where is the light at the end of the nihilistic tunnel?*

As we've seen, nihilism creates a climate most conducive to Gnostic ideas, where someone regularly leaves his spiritual tradition and finds himself drifting about aimlessly seeking whatever suits his fancy. Having rejected traditional thought structures and traditional religions – dealing with such things ironically and irreverently – he finds himself at the abyss of nothingness. He embodies that romantic longing, that "starving for the unattainable." In enters the Gnostic demon, offering a salvation program promising to counterbalance the feeling of nothingness.

Hitler's personality fit this romantic mood perfectly. Rejecting the modern rationalism, the very rationalism founding democracy and capitalism, he was far more comfortable with modes of thought we've seen in the Romantic era. "Propaganda is a matter of the emotions," he said.[27] Reflecting the feminine element of the Romantic movement, he loved gathering about himself gullible women who fed his mystical self-understanding.[28]

Hitler was "self taught" but his ideas "seemed to him to be mysterious inspirations" which in fact were nothing more than "the general intellectual outlook of today, of which he was constantly absorbing the germs."[29]

In particular he imbibed the teachings of Nietzsche, particularly Nietzsche's understanding that new types of man – the god-man, the superman – would signal the advent of an advanced world after the death of God. To Hitler these ideas were all his own.[30] He's that small man on the shoulders of a giant, thinking he walks on the clouds because of some mysterious inner enlightenment. Again, the parallels to today are undeniable.

Homo Gnosticus always has a despairing attitude about the current *systems*, or those *paradigms of the past*. For Hitler that paradigm was the cosmic architecture set in place by the Judeo-Christian tradition.

Hitler blamed Christianity for Western individualism. "To the Christian doctrine of the infinite significance of the individual soul and of personal responsibility, I oppose with icy clarity the saving doctrine of the nothingness and insignificance of the individual human being." Rather, like the communists, Hitler saw the notion of the collective replacing this "significance of the individual soul." He says, "[T]he dogma of vicarious suffering and death through a divine savior gives place to that of the representative living and acting of the new Leader-legislator, which liberates the mass of the faithful from the burden of free will."[31]

Far more offensive to Hitler was that *Judeo* part of Judeo-Christian. His rejection of the "Jewish God" marks the first intersection with the Gnostics, for whom the evil usurping god Yaltabaoth was the Old Testament deity.[32] As it was for the Gnostics, so it was for Hitler. By rejecting the Old Testament God they participated in a grand cosmic drama. All the Jewish God represented stood against Hitler's changing spiritual paradigms.   Rauschning notes how Hitler's "own esoteric doctrine implies an almost metaphysical antagonism to the Jew . . . one god excludes the other." He adds, "At the back of Hilter's anti-Semitism there is revealed an actual war of the gods."[33] It's classic Gnostic dualism, the cosmic battle of two opposing deities, Monad the Light God vs. Yaltabaoth, the Jewish God of darkness.

The rejection of the Judeo-Christian God is no mere switch from one God to another.   It's a complete deconstruction of the cosmic architecture implied by the Jewish God, to be replaced by a new, reconstructed one.   A host of elements derive from this cosmic architecture: the centrality of God's name, the importance and essential goodness of creation, the separation and naming of the created order, the importance of ritual to sacralize the redeemed elements of creation, the role of sacrifice or sacrament, the sanctity of the individual and his most immediate means of socialization – the family, the importance of the Word, of grammar, of logic.

It's not simply Yahweh or Jesus that Hitler rejected. He aimed to dismantle the entire orientation derived from the Judeo-Christian tradition.

As Rauschning put it, rephrasing Hitler's thought: "Was not this degenerate race the protagonist of the independence of the spirit, and thus the mortal enemy of the coming age? Were not its members among the most eminent in science, that insubordinate outsider which in Hitler's view, destroys life instead of promoting it? And was not the whole hated doctrine of Christianity, with its faith in redemption, its moral code, its conscience, its conception of original sin, the outcome of Judaism? Was not the Jew in political life always on the side of analysis and criticism?"[34]

That "analysis and criticism" – which Hitler believed typified the Judeo-Christian intellectual heritage – is precisely the sort of cosmic architecture he hoped to deconstruct in preparation for his coming age. It's the universalistic New Age of Aquarius replacing the rationalistic Age of Pisces; it's a new feminist age replacing the patriarchal age with its linear, phallic thinking; it's the New Reformation or New Pentecostal Age or Emergent Age of the Neo-evangelicals replacing the old paradigms of ritualism and dogmatism; it's the communistic age replacing the capitalistic age.

It's all the same ethos at work, reapplied, in Hitler's case, to race. The dark, swarthy Jew represents the old age, the Yaltabaothian Age, in juxtaposition to the coming age with its own representative new man, the light-filled Aryan. Hitler tells Rauschning, "Our revolution is not merely a political and social revolution; we are at the outset of a tremendous revolution in moral ideas and in men's spiritual orientation. Our movement has at last brought the Middle Ages, medieval times, to a close."[35]

Here explains Hitler's relationship with science and capitalism, which he considered "bourgeois."[36] He rejected "Liberal-Jewish science," which "could only occur in the age of Liberalism." He anticipated the multiculturalists and recognized only "the science of a particular type of humanity and of a particular age." It is "a social phenomenon." Far more useful to him was a "Nordic science," the sort of science evaluated according to the "benefit or injury it confers on the community."

And so, for example, when it came to the science of learning Germany's primitive beginnings, Hitler had no use for the prevailing historical hypotheses "that change every year or two." The fascist myth of Germany's prehistory, for him, was just as good. What role does truth or falsehood have for Hitler? Just as Nietzsche proposed, in the coming age humanity will move beyond such *good and evil* categories: "there is no such thing as truth, either in the moral or in the scientific sense."[37]

What would replace science? Hilter channels Bruno: "A new age of magic interpretation of the world is coming, of interpretation in terms of the will and not of the intelligence."[38] In magic, the willful master-magician interprets the world for his subjects through well-crafted phantasms and archetypical shorthand. The enemy of magic, always, is a reality discovered through rational analysis, through science, or through philosophies and dogmas whose quest is objective truth. But magic always has a ready-made defense against these challenges by grouping them as their own phantasm – a two-dimensional representation of pure, systemic evil – or by dismissing them through some archetypical shorthand: it's them Jews, or those white men, or the Church, or the capitalists, or Western Civilization, or whatever.

As far as capitalism goes, liberals love to point out Hitler's connections to German industrialists to prove he led a right wing movement. Beyond the simple point that his industrial connections only prove fascist corporatism – a marriage of government and business hardly reminiscent of any conservative love for the free market – they miss the point. Hitler firmly rejected capitalism as an invention of the Jews, telling Rauschning, "It was the Jews, of course, who invented the economic system of constant fluctuation and expansion that we call Capitalism. Let us make no mistake about it – it is the invention of genius, of the Devil's own ingenuity." Yet, Hitler boasted he had commandeered the capitalistic impulse, answering it by first using it to his ends, and then by challenging it with his own "system of unending revolution."[39]

In other words, capitalism (like science) can be workable if *unjewified*, to coin a new term. What exactly is Jewish about science or capitalism calling for unjewification? It's their placement in that Jewish cosmic architecture referenced above, it's focus on individualism, criticism, analysis, the dignity of the individual, and so on.

Far from seeing this cosmic architecture as built on the basis of the laws of nature or human nature, Hitler preferred to see it in Gnostic terms, as unseen powers, archons, working through a dark "superstate planted by them above all the states of the world in all their glory." On these terms Rauschning refers to his "inflation of the Jew into a mythical prototype of humanity."[40] The Jew with his laws set up the systems of the world like capitalism and democracy – Hitler believed that the Jew ultimately was behind the Allied nations – and freedom could not happen until Hitler liberated a new race of people set against the Jew. Or put in Gnostic terms, until the cosmic guru (or avatar) awakened the spark in the divine race and freed them from the archontic prison house of the current world system.

Here enters the danger of Gnostic politics. The Gnostic myth lays the foundation for two levels of humanity, one possessing the spark of a superior divinity and one slavishly submitting to the cosmic architecture constructed by Yaltabaoth and his archons. When fused with the millenarian myth, these two forms of humanity take on a historical dimension. As superior humans awaken to their role in history, the elimination of the inferior elements becomes a fact of cosmic history. The likes of Hitler are simply doing what *History* is demanding. Groups of people are abstracted from their flesh and blood humanity. They become symbols of Yaltabaoth's system, prototypes of something uncannily evil. We saw this before among the first millenarians, how they looked at the clergy. Or how the Jacobins saw the aristocracy, or how the communists saw the industrialists. People become abstracted through archetypical shorthand.

Hitler too justified his genocide by dehumanizing his enemies according to this Gnostic myth of the "new man." As he said, "The two types [of man] will rapidly diverge from one another. One will sink to a sub-human race and the other rise far above the man of today." Hitler then channels Nietzsche, adding, "I might call the two varieties the god-man and the mass-animal."[41]

Rauschning reports an animated exchange he had with Hitler – *is there any other kind?* – when he was attempting to understand what exactly Hitler meant by calling the Jew the "ruler of the economic world empire" and his own movement the cosmic opponent of the Jew. Did he mean this symbolically?

"No!" said Hitler. "It's sheer simple undiluted truth. Two worlds face one another – the men of God and the men of Satan! The Jew is the anti-man, the creature of another god. He must have come from another root of the human race. I set the Aryan and the Jew over against each other; and if I call one of them a human being I must call the other something else. The two are as wildly separated as man and beast. Not that I would call the Jew a beast. He is much further from the beasts than we Aryans. He is a creature outside nature and alien to nature."[42]

A clearer indication of Gnostic dualism and its implications for the tiering of humanity could not be given!

What exactly, then, did Hitler advocate to replace the old world and its old species?

Hegel and Marx had already carried the millenarian flame in their own new age views on History. Always and ever "vast world change"[43] (Hitler's expression) is imminent. Always and ever Western History is at a "turning point"[44] (also his expression). History is not developmental; it thrusts forward in revolutionary spurts.

Hitler's program, like that of the millenarians, was future-oriented with a look to a prehistorical past: "Prehistory is the doctrine of the eminence of the Germans at the dawn of civilization."[45] His version of the millenarian new kingdom (the third reich) would be based on race, a "new order" conceived "in terms of race that transcend [national] boundaries."[46]

But what of the entrenchment of historical national boundaries? Hitler was steadfast: "I as a politician need a conception which enables the order which has hitherto existed on historic bases to be abolished and an entirely new and anti-historical order enforced and given an intellectual basis . . . I have to liberate the world from dependence on its historic past. Nations are the outward and visible forms of our history. So I have to fuse these nations into a higher order if I want to get rid of the chaos of an historic past that has become an absurdity. And for this purpose the conception of race serves me well."[47]

It's the millenarian equation all over again: N will be the basis by which we will transcend the current state of things and exist in a new world. So far the unknown quantity has been any number of things. For the Puritans it was the pure life, worked out politically; for the communists it was labor; For Hitler it was race. The one thing it cannot be is people *as people* struggling within the confines of a fallen human nature needing government only as a check on negative behaviors affecting others. Government goes from being a negative check on fallen nature to a positive means of redemption itself: the organic embodiment of the new human, something collectively understood, or in Hegel's term, the "God-state."

Hitler sided with this latter view. The new age he led would bring in a new order of humanity. Says Rauschning, "The coming age was revealing itself in the first great human figures of a new type. Just as . . . the world has continually to renew itself, the old order perishing with its gods, just as the Nordic peoples took the sun's passing of the solstices as a figure of the rhythm of life, which proceeds not in a straight line of eternal progress but in a spiral, so must man now, apparently, turn back in order to attain a higher stage."[48]

This *spiraling up* of history, in addition to recalling millenarian impulses as well as Hegelianism, has exact parallels with Hinduism. Savitri Devi, a Hindu and Nazi sympathizer (and Nazi spy in India), believed Hitler was the avatar foretold in Hindu sacred story, the one ordained by the spiritual forces of History to bring about a new age. She combined the "Hindu cyclic theory of time with more Manichaean and dualistic notions of Judaeo-Christian apocalyptic prophecy."

The concept of an *avatar*, a periodic descent of a god into a man, finds its roots in ancient Zoroastrianism, a mystery cult similar to Gnosticism in ancient Persia.[49] Like the millenarians, the avatar not only heralds the next age; he also manages the destruction of the previous age. In her book *Pilgrimage* (1958), Devi wrote on behalf of the avatar, "When justice is crushed, when evil is triumphant, then I come back. For the protection of the good, for the destruction of evil-doers, for the establishment of the Reign of Righteousness, I am born again and again, age after age."[50]

These ideas find their source in the Hindu text *Puranas*, which speaks of the cycle of ages and the coming of the avatar: "When the close of the Kali age shall be nigh, a portion of that divine being who exists of his own spiritual nature in the character of Brahma, and who is the beginning and the end, and who comprehends all things, shall descend upon earth. . . . [H]e will destroy all whose minds are devoted to iniquity. He will then reestablish righteousness upon earth; and the minds of those who live at the end of the Kali age shall be awakened, and shall be a pellucid as crystal. The men who are thus changed by virtue of that peculiar time shall be as the seeds of human beings, and shall give birth to a race who shall follow the laws of the Krita age, or the age of purity."[51]

The Cathars (meaning "the pure"), the Puritans, and now the race following the laws of Krita in the "age of purity" – we should be noticing a theme repeating here: the intersection of immediate contact with the Divine, purity of being, and the perfecting of a new world. Hitler took Gnostic ideas of the purity of light to the level of race; the white Aryans were literally filled with pure Light.

Like all Gnostics, millenarians, communists, and progressives – that whole crew – Hitler believed an elite body of adepts would emerge to inaugurate the new reich. He looked to the Freemasons and the Catholic Church for guidance, for they "form a sort of priestly nobility." He pleadingly added, "Don't you see that our party must be of this character. . . . An Order, that is what it has to be – an Order, the hierarchical Order of a secular priesthood."[52]

Federalism, compromise, a developmental view of history, respect for tradition, these were all *verboten*: "This spiritual landslide will be brought about by us and by us alone."[53]

Of course Hitler himself was the foremost new man, the avatar, the "prophet of the rebirth of man in a new form."[54] Fascinated with magic, he believed human progress would culminate in the outpouring of the gift of "magic insight," a gift he believed he possessed. He evidently had a mystical experience while temporary blinded from a wound during World War I. Even as a boy, after attending a performance of Wagner's *Rienzi*, a friend reported how the future dictator was "pale and sinister. [He] began to speak, his words bursting forth with hoarse passion . . . It was as if another Self spoke through him in a state of ecstasy or complete trance." The friend continued, "In sublime, irresistible images, he unfolded before me his own future and that of our people . . . He now spoke of a mandate that he was one day to receive from our people, in order to lead them out of slavery, to the heights of freedom."[55]

Like the millenarians he had no use for book learning. He envisioned a new humanity that would "have no intellectual training" as he himself did not have, for "Knowledge is the ruin to my young men."

Continuing his thoughts, speaking in almost homoerotic terms – doing a sort of Sophia job on the blonde, male youth – Hitler described the new man: "In my *Ordensburgen* a youth will grow up before which the world will shrink back. A violently active, dominating, intrepid brutal youth – that is what I am after. Youth must be all those things. It must be indifferent to pain. There must be no weakness or tenderness in it. I want to see once more in its eyes the gleam of pride and independence of the beast of prey. Strong and handsome must my young men be. . . . In my *Ordensburgen* there will stand as a statue for worship the figure of the magnificent, self-ordaining god-man; it will prepare the young men for their coming period of ripe manhood."[56]

Rauschning develops the erotic overtones of Hitler in a section on Hitler and women. The man had a pornography habit, and he was greatly boosted in his delusions of grandeur by the "gushing adulation" of women "carried to the pitch of pseudo-religious ecstasy." At meetings where Hitler spoke, widows always filled the front rows, and "Anyone looking down from the platform on those front seat women and watching their expressions or rapturous self-surrender, their moist and glistening eyes, could not doubt the character of their enthusiasm." Evidently the SS referred to these women as the "varicose vein squad." Rauschning concluded with words recalling the magical machinations of Bruno: "Eroticism is an important political factor in modern mass propaganda, the erotic effect of a speaker's voice, of tonality and speaking melody."[57]

Later Hitler graduated to pretty young blondes whom he surrounded around himself at meals. "He stroked their hands. He permitted himself little intimacies. The whole thing was play-acting." Rauschning describes the erotic atmosphere of Hitler's circle: "Most loathsome of all is the reeking miasma of furtive, unnatural sexuality that fills and fouls the whole atmosphere round him, like an evil emanation. Nothing in this environment is straightforward. Surreptitious relationships, substitutes and symbols, false sentiments and secret lusts—nothing in this man's surroundings is natural and genuine, nothing has the openness of a natural instinct."[58]

Of course nature and natural instinct become foreign: Gnosticism is a rejection of nature, claiming nature is a construct of some imagined archon, the Jewish God, something to be revolted against and replaced. At least that is the case with modern political Gnosticism, where Gnostic rejection of nature is taken to the realm of politics.

The Neo-Evangelical Movement and Millenarianism

It may not seem appropriate to go from Hitler to current Neo-evangelicalism, but our discussion which began with Puritans and Pietists needs to be brought to conclusion. If nothing else, it proves I'm not falling for the *argumentum ad Hilterum* fallacy. Rather, both Neo-evangelicalism and fascism draw from a larger millenarian, progressive stream. To progressives who cast judgment on Neo-evangelicals by comparing them to fascists, Jesus' words "Physician, heal thyself" seem appropriate, as they do for Neo-evangelicals who frightfully identify the fascist-like deification of government done by progressives. Both groups entertain similar vibes such as: the centrality of charismatic leadership, the divinization of mass gatherings, the role of music as a shamanistic tool to connect followers to the Spirit, the belief in a new age, the quest for mysticism, miracles, and magic.

Neo-evangelicalism's latest trend – at least at time of writing (always a necessary caveat when writing about ephemeral Neo-evangelical movements) – is the Emergent Church movement. Emergent Christians believe God is leading a new Church to emerge out of the old one. This evolution is said to constitute a complete reorientation of paradigms. It's yet another claim to deconstruct the cosmic architecture. Traditional Christianity's cosmic architecture is marked by external form, ritual, dogmaticism, objectivism, rationality, confessionalism (and unfortunately, but necessarily, its concomitant denominationalism), hierarchicalism, institutionalism, and an external understanding of the sacrament. Emergent Christianity upends these paradigmatic structures, yielding a Christianity marked by spontaneity, mysticism, poetry, art, conversation, intuition, flirting with different traditions, universalism, and a relational understanding of the sacrament.

Politically, Emergents tend toward progressive politics. One Emergent debuted his column at an online magazine (titled "Evangelical, Republican, Progressive, Me") writing, "Being progressive . . . shouldn't be controversial for a Republican, even if contemporary public opinion suggests otherwise. The Progressive Era was, after all, highly supported by Republicans at the turn of the century."

He then asks, "Is it possible to be Evangelical, Republican and Progressive? Are there many more people like myself who just aren't represented in politics, religious leadership and the media?"[59]

Yes, in fact, there are. It's where Neo-evangelicalism was destined to head because of latent genetic traits in its DNA: its belief in the ever-dawning new age of the Church, its belief that God is moving in history no differently than he did at the first Pentecost, its belief that its leaders are a "guild of prophets" charged by God to lead the Church into its new incarnation,[60] its cult of youth, its belief that the lines between Self, Church, and society are, to say the least, fuzzy. We've followed the stream going back to Joachim of Fiore, through the Fransciscans, the Taborites, the Anabaptists, the Puritans, the Revivalists, and now the Emergents. These movements (like the later communists and fascists) in some way claimed to be God's operation in history. God was using an elite body of saints who, cooperating with him, were inaugurating his kingdom. Communism and fascism ended up with the same program but cut out the God part: it's actually a quite logical move once you posit that the Self is God. As we'll see in our next section, Emergents even verge on this radical leap.

Already in Neo-evangelicalism's Baby Boomer permutation – the seeker-service crowd centered on Self-directed themes (the very "consumeristic Christianity" of the mega-churches which Emergents claim to be emerging out of) – the millenarian spirit was alive. Evangelical guru Robert Schuller claimed the mantle in his "Self Esteem Reformation" and believed the vanguards of this reformation "will be caught up in a vision of a cause, a crusade, a divine calling ... [they] will accept God's invitation to play our important part in the kingdom he is busy creating NOW in this world."[61]

The newer Emergents too are creating something NOW. They must, because the millennium cannot be anything but imminent – NOW – and if I am not a cooperator in its inauguration, I am not truly Christian. There can be no coasting or maintenance of existing structures or paradigms. Just as the New Age/business mantra goes, *if you're not moving forward you're moving backwards*. Neo-evangelicals internalize this motto as a reality of personal sanctification.

Emergents claim the millenarian mantle. Rooted in the same Anabaptist and millenarian Christology promulgating a "living Christ" (as opposed to the historical or sacramental Christ) indwelling the saints, Emergents say Christ embodies everything. Orthodox doctrine delineates between Christ's presence on earth and in the Church: Christ fills all things but has a unique, salvific presence in the Church. Emergents reject these delineations as attempts to control God. If I say "Christ is here in the sacrament" and "not there in that John Lennon song," then I own a certain power as I administer the sacrament: true Christians must gather around me for the sake of their salvation. The very notion is anathema to the Anabaptist as well as to the Emergent. For the Anabaptist, Christ embodies everything, from John Lennon's song to the sacrament, and this embodiment sort of "emerges" from the different stories of the people who claim it. "The practices of the church are, then, gifts of the Holy Spirit and as such participation in God's embodied story."[62] Each person has his story, through which Christ is embodying his presence.

That story in turn is framed in terms we've seen in Gnosticism as well as in the existential postmodern creed. The Self awakens to the prison he is in, governed by archons and systems preventing his liberation. He begins his journey out of the prison led by gurus, "Christs," and Sophia figures.

Sherry Paul describes liberal Neo-evangelical Jim Wallis' meaning of Christ for the individual: "Christ's life, death, and resurrection have brought victory over 'the powers.' He shattered the myth of their absolute authority by demonstrating his freedom in relation to them. He challenged their rule and would not submit to them. Indeed, the fallen powers were so exposed and threatened by Christ's actions that they acted in collusion to kill him. The cross symbolizes that freedom in which death is swallowed up in victory. Christ's resurrection vindicates his manner of life and death, seats his victory, and allows others to live freely and humanly in the midst of 'the powers' by their 'being in Christ.' This must be the proclamation and witness of the church of Jesus Christ."[63]

This personal theology in turn fuels political action. Wallis, aging hippy and vanguard of the progressive wing of Neo-evangelicalism, has penned such books as *The Soul of Politics: A practical and prophetic vision of change* (1982); *Who Speaks for God? A New Politics of Compassion, Community and Civility* (1996); *The Great Awakening: Reviving Faith and Politics in a Post-Religious Right America* (2008); *Rediscovering Values: On Main Street, Wall Street, and Your Street* (2010). All the millenarian tropes come screaming out here: the cooperation of the Christian community with God, the dawn of a new age, and the politicizing of Christian ethical teaching regarding the poor.

After reviewing Wallis, Ms. Paul glosses his teaching: "The church is a new force in history which is a sign to 'the powers' that their dominion has been broken. The very presence of a body of people who exercise their moral independence is an essential element for Wallis because 'without a visible and concrete demonstration of independence, all the church's outward attacks upon the institutions of the world will be doomed to failure.'"[64]

Does any self-reflection permit the Emergents to see how they are simply the latest version of the millenarian spirit? Do they see the obvious parallels they have with previous millenarian movements? Aren't they at least curious with some modicum of self-awareness? At a minimum, wouldn't they become somewhat concerned about becoming a historical cliche, something akin to death for such folk?

No. First off, to look at history is to apply intellectual tools – like logic, facts, data, and such – that are the very paradigms we're evolving out of. So there's no worry about the facts of history intruding in on self-perception. George Barna and Frank Viola's book *Pagan Christianity* (2002) is nothing less than a complete rejection of ALL Christian history and tradition, a magical interpretation of history if ever there was one. They claim a clear understanding of a more pristine time, that is, first-century Christian history. Though this obscure era of Christian history has eluded far better historians than they for several centuries, they alone have, just now, discovered that, *abracadabra*, it supports everything they believe!

What chance do logic and data and facts have against an Emergent Tim Keel who claims, quoting the beginning of *The Fellowship of the Ring*, "The world is changed. I feel it in the water. I feel it in the earth. I smell it in the air." We saw how Hitler basically invented a prehistory of fascism and rejected true history as part of the cosmic architecture of Judaism and Christianity. That's the sort of stuff you do when you believe God has – and you can just feel it in the air – liberated you from natural laws.

Second, there's always the possibility that this time, yes this time, we're coming upon a dawning new age of reoriented spiritual paradigms. We saw in a previous chapter the amusing example of a scholar dispassionately writing about millenarianism, but then concluding, "I believe with great conviction that our own age is in fact different from previous ages. . . . Such predictions are now based on a scientific observation rather than on religious inspiration." Along similar lines, one Emergent asks: "why should we expect God not to do such a thing [i.e.

give a new Pentecost] in our time?"[65]

It's this millenarian presumption separating Emergents from Orthodox and Catholic monasticism, which they idealize as authentic expressions of Christianity. Traditional monks – like the ones Joachim separated himself from – don't go far enough. Ironically the Emergents part ways with the monks precisely where they are attracted to them in the first place: prayer. Traditional monks are content simply to pray for peace, political justice, and whatnot. But prayer cannot be the posture taken by those who "cooperate" with God. Prayer says "God's doing it all; I'm laying everything on God. I'm not doing it." In prayer, the Christian prays "Thy kingdom come." Petitioner and petitioned remain separate. God completely works his kingdom, now by faith, but soon in the world to come. Meantime, I pray. And this I do until I die and receive faith's reward.

Emergent Tim Keel favorably reports the prayerful attitude of Orthodox monks he met, quoting one of the monks: "The monk flees far from the world, not because he detests the world, but because he loves the world, and in this way he is better able to help the world through his prayer, in things that don't happen humanly but only through divine intervention. In this way God saves the world."[66]

But then Keel ironically concludes his essay with words belying his esteem of these monks. "I see a disconnect between the world where people live and the world were people worship. It is my hope that these two worlds can be reconciled in Christ for the sake of the Gospel – God's work in the world. . . . We need mystics. We need poets. We need prophets. We need apostles. We need artists. . . . We need a different kind of leader – one who can create environments to nurture and release the imagination of God's people."[67]

The disconnect between Church and world, which Keel sees as emblematic of a deficient age, is a substantially important component of traditional Christian doctrine. It explains why Christians have always seen themselves as pilgrims in the world. It explains why prayer must be the final posture in a world always set antagonistically against them. God and man must ever remain separate, save in the Person of Jesus Christ, and prayer codifies this distinction like few other practices.

A millenarian cannot bear to leave it at prayer, because he believes *he is causing the kingdom to come.* He is part of God's work in bringing about the kingdom. He answers his own prayer!

Emergent Clara Barnhill says as much, describing the *petition*

"Thy kingdom come" as an "artistic tool" along with such *commands* as "love your neighbor" and "seek first the kingdom." But clearly the latter two "tools" are commands, whereas the first is petitionary. The Christian may imperfectly follow Christ's command to love his neighbor or seek first the kingdom, but he most certainly does not bring about that which only comes by petition, God's kingdom, else he wouldn't need to petition it in the first place. God does that! The grammar is clear, but again, if such linear thinking with all its Westernized grammar, forms, and categories is replaced by Keel's mysticism, poetry, and art, damn the grammar! His underlying theology undermines the grammar, and that is the millenarian pretense that we, as Barnhill concludes, "participate . . . in God's embodied story."[68] Of course we answer our own prayers if we embody God's action.

Thanks to Nietzsche and the existentialists, transcendental status has been given to the human will. Their elimination of God left the human will as the sole determiner of transcendent truth. Jung added the spiritual dimension: authentic human choice is tapped into a Collective Unconscious at some transcendent level. Human art, poetry, intuition, prophesying, music – all such non-rational endeavors – become means by which the authentic human expresses universal archetypes. The liberated person literally creates his Self on a blank canvas, but because he's in communion with the Collective Unconscious, archetypes emerge connecting him to all truly liberated people.

The Emergents have adopted this existential lexicon, inserting Christian meaning into existential terms. Thus they embrace, not the elimination of God, but the elimination of old paradigms of theology. The human will tapping into the Collective Unconscious becomes nothing less than the action of the Holy Spirit. The emerging archetypes are the different stories, the sacred stories of each Emergent, through which the new Church emerges. And just as Jung's more blatant and secular Gnosticism will bring about a new age of new politics, so will that of the Emergent: "By the grace of God, we are artists freed like the romantics, gifted to sketch in participation with God, inspired by the breath of God to recognize and join the future of the story as it comes to us."[69]

It's the same Hermetical posture which fueled Pietism and Anabaptism. We co-create with God. Staid pieties so resolutely laying everything on God would just be *passe*, and if our culture is anything, it can't be *passe*. To be *passe* is not just to be off a note or two in terms of style. It's to be on the wrong side of History and of the angels.

Perhaps this speaks to the American cult of youth. "Cult of youth" is an interesting phraseology. It means the adoration, sacralization, and even deification not simply of youthful persons, but of youthful ways of thinking: idealism, emotionalism, spontaneity, eroticism. Hollywood and Madison Avenue have promulgated the numinous *youth* for years: he's authentic, his own person, cool, socially conscious, idealistic, moody, artistic, musical, sexual, and he always speaks wisdom. He's not unlike the *Magical Negro* character, or the Sophia character, the attractive female who will liberate a stuffy male from his neurotic ruts. As in the case of President Obama and Justice Sotomeyer, sometimes people believe the myths, believe their divine status as avatars of the phantasm. The same holds true for youth. They arrive on the scene and because of the phantasm spun by the cultural myth-makers, they believe they embody divine forces at work. Because youth doesn't last except in ever new people, movements by their very nature must become ever new.

Obviously this explanation doesn't account for the previous millenarian movements. The age of the Taborites didn't include myth-making by Hollywood and Madison Avenue. There's was more of a raw, biblical millenarianism. It was able to be dealt with as a small movement. But our age does include those cultural myth-makers, and thus portends a larger, societal dynamic at work. When an Emergent claims the Anabaptist mantle to be the vanguard of a great change in spiritual orientation, he'll find he's on terrain already landscaped by those cultural myth makers, equipt with ready-made vessels crafted over the years, vessels like the numinous *youth*.

What does this mean? It means the potential exists for the flaring up of society-wide movements, for Münster events at a grand scale. Liberals reveled in President Obama's huge margins of victory among the *youth vote*. His embrace by hotties – the so-called "Obama girl" – and by authentic hipsters seemed to legitimize him. He incarnated their idealism, their sense of *cool*, their eroticism, their belief that cosmic forces working together through them could literally change the world. It was numinous youth following the Magical Negro. Perhaps he was Keel's "different kind of leader."

Or perhaps another *dux*, another *Führer*, another *leader* – another *prostatēs* – is awaiting that mantle.

Part IV

Gnosticism and Religion: Neo-evangelicalism

✧ Chapter 11 ✧

The Worship Wars

The Rise of Contemporary Worship

On March 8, 2009, a man walked into First Baptist Church in Maryville, Illinois, pulled out a gun, and shot four rounds at the pastor, Rev. Fred Winters. The first of the four rounds hit the pastor's Bible, blasting a spray of confetti into the air. The next three bullets ended the pastor's life. Eventually three members subdued the gunman, ending the horrific scene. Police said that worshipers initially thought the episode was a skit.

A skit?

Medieval morality plays could introduce some pretty horrific scenes of the sufferings in hell, but everyone knew these were plays, not worship – Thomas Becket's murder in the cathedral stands as the textbook example of transgressing sacrilege. Meanwhile, here in a typical Neo-evangelical church, murder happens and members get comfy in their padded chairs, rub their hands, and think, "Oooo, what thrills does the ministry team have for us today!"

And this odd worship expectation is just the tip of the iceberg.

In the Detroit area, a pastor dresses up as Chewbacca and stands at a street corner inviting people to worship. "Come to the real battle between good and evil!"

Another church in Ohio offers "Pajama Pants Sunday." As the pastor justified it, "as long as it doesn't compromise our integrity or morals, or go against the Bible."[1]

No limits, says another mega-church in its literature: "We agree to do anything short of sin to reach people who don't know Christ." It's quick to point out, "This includes music styles and outreach methods. Remember, anything short of sin; nothing sinful."[2]

OK, got it. So if that means sitting around round tables sipping "Red Bull and sodas" at Erwin McManus' hip church of "young, primarily single, and very attractive" members where "more than a few audience members were checking each other out," so be it. In the church – or is it Tiki bar? – "the lights in the theater are kept low, and the walls are adorned with Mayan motifs and fake lanterns with flapping orange cellophane mimicking flames."[3]

Sports nuts might like this litany for one of America's new liturgical holidays, Superbowl Sunday, where minister and congregation go back and forth:

"Minister: This is Superbowl Sunday, Lord. Millions will watch as the winner in each league battles for the championship and for a prized trophy.

"Congregation: We thrill to the skill, the ability and the performance of many who will play today.

"Minister: We thank you for the outstanding players in the life of your church – superstars like St. Paul, Peter, John, Stephen and Mary.

"Congregation: Most of us will never be Superbowl material, our Father."[4]

A prayer explaining to the Creator how Superbowl teams are selected – "the winner in each league," in case you or the Lord were wondering (I wasn't, but if I were I'd know it's the winner in each *conference*) – is a far cry from the plaints of the ancient Psalmist hanging his harp on willows and weeping for Zion.

But that is where we are at. And it's not just a few churches. It's what's happening with Contemporary Worship. Contemporary Worship, for our purposes, covers all non-historical, non-liturgical worship. It includes everything from Superbowl Sunday litanies to other purportedly contemplative services using the music of U2 for their "U2-charist."[5] It has swept the Christian landscape as congregations seek to avoid the slow exodus from the Church by "giving people what they want," pretending this blatant consumeristic strategy is really the Holy Spirit using charismatic church marketing experts to move his Church into the next great paradigmatic shift. Because sometime around 1980, God decided to scrap his everlasting history of intractability regarding worldly things and hire the Baby Boom generation as his image consultant. They're special that way. Just ask them.

Many are unaware how pervasive, radical, and upsetting the new worship forms have been in certain Christian circles, a revolution just as radical – if not more radical – than anything we've seen in other traditional institutions during that same post-1960s period. When the mega-church off the highway boasts in its ad, "We're not your grandmother's church," they ain't a-kiddin'!

The roots of Contemporary Worship harbor the same Gnostic traits driving our course of study: the antinomian rejection of form, the deprecation of sacramental piety, the anti-intellectual disavowal of bookish knowledge, the relativistic erasing of distinctions (between, for example, man and woman, pastor and lay, or noble and base music), the personality cult centered on one person's charisma, and the enthusiastic understanding of music. Echoes of Gnostic namelessness reverberate through the Contemporary Worship wasteland, where the first things to go are always the Trinitarian elements of the Church's liturgy (the *Gloria in Excelsis* and *Sanctus*, for example or the historic Christian Creed). Hearing the name of the Triune God or even the name of Jesus is the exception rather than the rule in all too many contemporary services. As we saw, God's namelessness is foundational in Gnostic circles. From there they abstract a generic new spirituality for which music is far better suited for reasons we've surveyed. Then, the gurus of the worship revolution proceed to remove, like the iconoclasts of old, every vestige of sacred place and sacred time: crucifixes, altars, pulpits, pictures, anything reminding someone he's in a place of worship.

This is deliberate. Driven by a misunderstanding of St. Paul's "I have become all things to all people," (I Corinthians 9: 22) Church leaders believe the proper way to do evangelism is to make people as comfortable as possible when they come into the church. You have to *speak their language*, and that means adapting to their psychic habits. Their psychic habits, in turn, are Gnostic, so to an uncanny degree the Church begins displaying a lot of the Gnostic traits we've seen. In short, Contemporary Worship has become Church for the "spiritual but not religious" crowd.

It's too generous, however, to say this is merely a flawed understanding of evangelism made by overzealous Christians who just want to save the lost. If that were the case, the bloody trail of divided congregations and hurt souls – all refugees from the worship wars – would have scared off any Church leader with a modicum of care for Christian unity and peace.

Instead, like ecclesiastical Jacobins, modern Church leaders accept the carnage as collateral damage in their revolution. After all, we are at the dawn of a "New Reformation." A new Pentecostal spirit is afloat. If the Spirit of God himself is at work in this epic change in historical course, and if the vanguards of the worship revolution are the avatars of this new age, then we're at the "evolve or die" point all over again, or Lenin's "broken eggs to make omelets" applied to the Church. If a few Grandma Schmidts and stodgy old deacons harumphing in the back pew with folded arms haven't caught the new wave of Pentecostal fervor, oh well, they just don't understand; they're not "in the know" about how the future dictates the present course for the Church. They are of a lesser *spiritual* species.

Yet, despite all their efforts, the Church still is declining in membership and attendance. If America is a sick patient, sick on the effects of Gnosticism – breakdown of order, addiction to ecstacy, depression, misguided do-gooderism – the contemporary Church has only been offering its own version of the same medicinal cocktail, and doing so over and over again with increased doses, thinking a little more will do the trick.

Whatever trendy movements there are in the Church today – the Church Growth movement, the Mega-Church movement, the Emergent Church movement, the post-this and post-that movements, "New Paradigm" and what have you – they're all animated by the same Gnostic spirit. They all begin with an elite body of *in-the-know* specialists who cast their futurist vision, enlighten us on culture's new great paradigm shift, and then inform us on what the Church must change in order to survive. The movement catches on for a few years, becomes designated "real" and "authentic," simmers down, and then becomes the stale old paradigm of yesterday, to be transcended by yet another new paradigm, embodied by a new class of cool, authentic hipsters.

Oh, but no, my movement is different. It's more authentic. In fact it's "post-movement" itself!

Right, and President Obama's political platform was "post-politics," the U.N. will lay down a "post-national" world, and humanity will evolve into post-humans. We've seen this movie before.

We await with anticipation the debut of the "post-post" movement, presented in some edgy fashion, like a simple, mysterious P^2 in some test-marketed font sure to conjure up gothic and authentic sensibilities. (I'm partial to the Papyrus font myself with it ephemeral, dissipating borders suggesting the jagged no-man's land at the fringes of language, although the Maiandra one carries the same effect minus some of the mystical pretensions, if that's not your thing.)

ᑭ² *It's the rave of the future!*

Until next week . . .

Gnosticism has infiltrated American Christianity through two specific channels. The first channel is the theology of America's dominant religious tradition, Evangelicalism, which falls directly in the Radical Reformation (Anabaptist) camp and which we saw was the flowering of medieval millenarianism. We've covered that.

The second channel is where we focus our attention in this section. Neo-evangelicalism owes its very name to a *neo* movement of old Evangelicals who believed the Church must engage culture to remain relevant. It began as a movement after World War II, under the likes of Billy Graham and associate Carl F. Henry. Henry's book *The Uneasy Conscience of Modern Fundamentalism* (1947) was a "bombshell on the evangelical community." The book argued for a tempering of the "rigidity and anti-intellectual leanings of the fundamentalist body."[6] By "intellectual," he wasn't thinking about the old academic disciplines of medieval or Reformation theologians. He was thinking of science, the social sciences in particular, and also marketing and other modernist developments. Evangelicals should become more culturally savvy, he argued, more culturally engaged, and appeal at a more popular level. With that change in tone, and with the example of Billy Graham's exploitation of new media, the Neo-evangelical movement came of age, and it has never shaken off these early characteristics.

Its motto might be: *Whatever it takes to win souls for Jesus!* Or *Wherever people are at, go there and get 'em.* If getting "em" means dressing the Gospel in the garb of modern culture, so be it

The problem is, the culture is Gnostic, which means Neo-evangelicalism must cloak itself in the forms of a theology which fundamentally undermines Christian teaching, particularly the incarnation. It must, for instance, tip its hat to the notion that music is a communication with the divine truer than any externally-formed means like sacraments. Though this is a completely Romantic, almost pagan notion, it shouldn't surprise us that this has steadily become a de facto Neo-evangelical position, if not in the teaching of her leaders, at least in the minds of its adherents. And this is exactly the criticism of Neo-evangelicalism today, that it has severed itself from the Church's proclamation in an effort to be relevant to today's Gnostic culture.

In three areas we offer our critique: the rise of Contemporary Christian Music, the cult of the Self, and the dominance of business and marketing philosophies.

✧ Chapter 12 ✧

The New Communion:
Music

Contemporary Christian Music

In the 1960s, when rock music swept the cultural scene, Christian rock was born, which in turn spearheaded the Contemporary Worship movement. Music has always been the vanguard of the worship revolution, just as it's been in our culture. Jimi Hendrix was right: music can change heads and eventually society itself. So was Plato: change the music forms and you change the laws. The Italian humanists knew the same truth when they invented opera. The leaders of the worship revolution understood the same thing.

The first Christian rockers laid down their premise with the rhetorical question, "Why does the devil get all the good music?"[1] If a retort might be made: the devil makes his choices based on what he is, which last we checked was pure unbridled evil, suggesting we should perhaps reconsider what we think is "good music."

Needless to say, the 1960s Jesus Freak movement proposed "Jesus Music" as an answer to the negative aspects of rock music (never, of course, asking why the rock style seemed so naturally to draw negative aspects in the first place). Christian rock pioneers such as street hippy Larry Norman were millenarians, revivalists, enthusiasts, and musicians, as if embodying every medieval incarnation of Gnosticism, from the street-wandering Cathars to the lute-bearing troubadours, from the militant millenarians to the enthusiastic mystics, all cloaked in the garb of a Free Spirit antinomian.

With names like the *Jesus Army*, *Campus Crusade*, and *Christian World Liberation Front*, it's hard to ignore the millenarian tone of these movements. Of course, their moment in history constituted the inauguration of great societal change. They were soldiers from God come to bring about the Kingdom of God on earth. The early progressive movement, when it was still tied to the Social Gospel, also boasted its *armies* and *crusades*. The Salvation Army is one such residual organization.

Clearly these groups felt themselves to be the Christian answer to the dawning Age of Aquarius. Richard Quebedeaux writes in his *New Charismatics* (1983) that the 1960s were especially conducive toward a new charismatic movement, when young people once again began to "relate emotionally with nature again."[2] Harold Bloom goes so far as to invert the order, seeing the hippy movement as a late-bloom flowering of American revivalism. On these terms Cane Ridge, the birthplace of Pentecostalism, and Woodstock were the same events, in which participants "underwent the singular experience of blending into an Orphic unison . . . rapt by ecstacy."[3]   The role of music in both movements cannot be overemphasized. Just as it was for the mystery religions, music becomes sacramental, the means by which the worshiper becomes one with God.

Contemporary Christian Music most interestingly intersects with Gnosticism at the eros point. We previously saw how the cult of eros helps us understand certain tropes in modern pop music, such as the nameless lover, or the romantic longing for the unattainable. Contemporary Christian Music easily adapts to these erotic impulses.

Translating the Jesus of orthodoxy – the supreme Judge on his throne around which angels and saints eternally worship – into a Gnostic Jesus – the Sophia-Redeemer character who guides me home on my journey – comes easy, especially in a Neo-evangelical tradition established on Anabaptism's highly individualistic premises, namely, that God communicates personally with me outside any greater community context. Gnosticism's Sophia-Redeemer figure is the *Jesus* of Contemporary Christian Music. Abstracted and then dislocated from any doctrinal, ecclesiastical, or sacramental grounding – these things being way too establishmentarian – *Jesus* must become a mental projection, an internally-created invisible Guide, a phantasm. Phantasms, as we know now, are worked by magicians, which is what the good Neo-evangelical preacher, or musician, really is.

I remember growing up, convinced Anne Murray's song *You Needed Me* (1978) was a Christian song. It made my eight-year-old heart cry when I applied its words to Christ: "I cried a tear / You wiped it dry / I was confused / You cleared my mind / I sold my soul / You bought it back for me." The eponymous refrain got the tears jerking: *Jesus needed me? Little old me?*

It's a classic Nameless-Lover song in the tradition of eros. Yet, were it truly a Christian song, the entire premise of it would be rank heresy undermining the self-sufficiency of God. God doesn't need me or any part of his creation. Only in a context where my Self is seen as one with God would I be lifted up to such a status. The only way this song could be Christian is on millenarian terms.

Regardless, this number one hit shows how readily the Christian Gospel can be delivered in the music and language of romance. The Nameless-Lover archetype fuses with my own mental projection of Christ and delivers its own sort of physical comfort, resulting in tears. And not a single minister, sacrament, or church was needed! The residual heresy can be ignored. Weren't those chilling medieval Inquisitors all about heresy? And wasn't it that established, institutional, post-Constantinian Church driving those more authentic "heretics" into the hills?

It's striking how many secular songs with the Nameless-Lover or Beloved-Guide archetype have parallels to Contemporary Christian Music. Many of them could be plopped into a contemporary Christian setting and pass for a Christian song, even as many contemporary Christian songs could be plopped into the play list at the adult contemporary radio station and pass for love songs. We recall Clement's warning – "let love songs be banished far away" – and saw why he, like Aristotle and Plato, was so alert to their sensual, enthusiastic, erotic dangers.

Sonicflood's *Rushing in* (2003) is illustrative: "I feel like I've gone astray just like a runaway from the grip of Your love," but then "Your love comes rushing in pouring over me I know when I come running / You're there for me there's no way that I could ever lose my way / I know I'm a captive in Your arms."

Is this about the Son of God who sits at God's right hand or about my high school sweetheart? We don't know because there's no mention of the one we're singing about! Of course, the song's purpose is erotic, not confessional, and eros always needs its nameless lover.

Nichole Nordman's *Holy* (2002) provides an odd take on the divine name of God, working with one of the classic Trinitarian canticles confessing God's name: *Holy, Holy, Holy*. The song begins with the typical ached longings of our lost lover – "How many roads did I travel / Before I walked down one that led me to You?" – but when the chorus comes, we find out where resolution is to be found: "Only me on my knees Singing holy, holy / And somehow All that matters now is You are holy, holy."

Holy, holy? Where's the third holy? Which Person of the Holy Trinity is cut out? I can't imagine this is deliberate, but it's a good metaphor for Neo-evangelicalism's tendency to cut out the history-bound, incarnate Son – his Gospel, sacraments, and Church – and invent a more culturally-friendly religion about the Father's got-the-whole-world-in-His-hands providence or the Spirit's be-quiet-and-listen-for-his-voice daily inspiration. To the extent that the Christian message has become nothing more than feel-good, Christ-less banalities, we can thank the music.

Why is the name of Christ or Jesus like kryptonite in so much Contemporary Christian Music?

One answer is mercenary. Frankly, Jesus doesn't sell. Amy Grant, around the time she gained a more secular following, explained the noticeable shift in her lyrics away from Christian language: "What we're trying to do is take Christian principles and make them understandable. Even if it doesn't say Jesus, it doesn't matter."[4] Her brother-in-law explains, "We never played many churches with Amy. That was the way everyone else had done it, and nobody had ever made it."[5]

The nineties ska band Ghoti Hook avoided mentioning even the word *God*, defending themselves thus: "Sometimes people give us a hard time because we don't mention God onstage. . . . I know that a lot of other bands and people are called to talk about God onstage a lot more than we do, and that's great, but we just feel that our calling is to get people interested in our MUSIC, interested in US."[6]

Christian hair band Stryper adds its own thoughts to the theme: "You won't pick up this record *[Against the Law]* and hear anything that says 'God' or 'Christ.' That was intentionally done. We were tired of people coming back with excuses, saying, 'Sorry we can't play this.' MTV's got to play this and the radio's got to play it or it doesn't serve the purpose"[7]

A second answer delves into this cult of eros and points to that yearning for the nameless One grounding Gnostic spirituality. Contemporary Christian Music assumes the posture of an individual on his personal spiritual journey of the soul, for whom Christ is the Spirit

Guide who holds him up.

Harold Bloom observes the trait even in early Evangelical music: "Each Southern Baptist is at last alone in the garden with Jesus, to cite one of the principal Baptist hymns."[8] Bloom, a self-described Gnostic, defends the Baptists: "If you reject the Catholic idea that the Church is the mystical body of Christ, then why cannot you be free of congregation, preacher, and text, and so be wholly alone with Jesus, walking and talking, spirit with spirit, spirit to spirit?"[9]

It's true the Psalms are full of *guide-me* type pleas, as in Psalms 31, 32, or 73. It's true the Psalms abound with references to the Lord as our companion though life, who guides us as we walk our journey through this world. But back to Bloom's distinction: does the Lord guide us through the mystical Body of Christ (the Church), or does the Lord walk and talk with me, spirit to spirit?

Contemporary pop adapts to the latter, Gnostic position, turning the Guide or Companion into a psychological abstraction, an archetype who exactly replicates, and has inherited, the role Sophia had in the Gnostic myth. Be it Hendrix's angel, Depeche Mode's personal Jesus, Olivia Newton John's guiding hand (see *supra*, 207ff), or whomever Anne Murray is talking about, they're all the same, arising from a spiritual force undelineated by any doctrinal, sacramental, or linguistic forms.

And then Contemporary *Christian* pop takes over the Guide archetype, essentially Sophia, but applies it to Christ, who so often – and so typically – remains unnamed. Consequently we fill in the blanks according to our default Gnostic yearnings. Jesus is the "guiding hand" that leads me to freedom, a Cosmic Christ abstracted from his flesh and blood. He becomes the "angel" who takes my hand. He becomes the one who "cleared my mind" and "needed me."

But how? Both Gnosticism and Neo-evangelicalism claim it happens through some sort of intuitive, non-rational, enthusiastic experience, the gnosis. But if that's the case, how exactly *do* we discern between Hendrix's angel and Jesus Christ? Many (as we will see in one stark example) might say, *You don't! And that's the beautiful point. Christ is not confined to the Church, but all people have access to him through their own means. Hendrix stumbled upon Christ in his poetry, as did Olivia Newton John in hers, as did Anne Murray in hers. He's an archetype to which we each have access.*

Many people indeed may hold to this way of thinking, but they need to appreciate how Gnostic, unprecedented, and unorthodox this way of understanding Christ truly is. At a minimum this thinking explains why Neo-evangelicals fall for Emergent Church universalism so readily.[10] Such universalism was implicit in their theology! It's the "living Christ" of the Anabaptists, the "uncreated Word" Luther warned about, the Christ abstracted from his humanity. Once dislocated from his flesh and blood, the boundaries at which point the suppliant might find him open to include whatever the suppliant now imagines. Their music set them on this universalistic course, precisely because, as Nietzsche said years ago, music has the effect of spilling us out of boundaries, like the boundaries between doctrines, or the boundaries of the very person of Jesus Christ.

Why, one can be forgiven for wondering, even continue the charade of going to church when one can have his *me-and-Jesus* journey at home in his heart with his favorite Christian song? Because the communal aspect of the contemporary church service is precisely what both Schopenhauer and Nietzsche identified, that *spilling-over-the-boundaries-of-form* aspect of music. This is the spirit that rockers feel at their concerts, the one leading mass groups to join together in a great collective flow, or the experience pianist Arthur Rubinstein described as "this thing in us, a metaphysical power that emanates from us."[11]

As in our introduction, in our citing of the Chris Tomlin song – the song climaxing in the "oooo ahhhh" like some orgasm capping off Chesterton's erotic understanding of God – the boundaries between music, erotic desire, and spirituality are let down, or as Tomlin puts it, "The walls are coming down." The walls come down between my individuality and that of another, and we join as a collective body. These are walls, after all, set up by Yaltabaoth and his legalisms. Music liberates us.

And then a new community of the liberated is created, not a community created by communion – sharing a body of doctrine or literally the Body of Christ – but by a bodily feeling that reaches me at my core . . . and also the guy next to me . . . or if I am lucky, the girl next to me . . . oh heck, why not the guy next to me, because as we'll see in a bit, *Jesus is not a homophobe*! The Agape Meal becomes an Eros Moment.

It's all about the feeling, a drug in the tradition of the ancient mystery cults. Heroin purportedly gives the user the feeling of a mother's love, Mother Sophia's embrace: total relaxation, security, a *whatever* feeling, the perfect remedy for the desperate, melancholic conditions of our reality.

So much of modern Christian song-writing presents God in these terms, as if God's grace were merely the Christian alternative in the great

American market for escapist highs.

Mark Schultz' song *Back in His Arms Again* (2001), in addition to being another example of a nameless confession, exhibits this trait: "I believe that He loves you where you are / I believe that you've seen the hands of God / I believe that you'll know it when You're back in His arms again." This is of a piece with FFH's *Watching Over Me* (2004): "But in Your comfort / I have found / A safe place to fall / And I'll be alright / Safe inside . . . " or Sonicflood's *Unconditional* (2003): "I feel your arms around me."

Emphasizing God's love is wonderful, but again, in what form does this love come? Invisible arms embracing me and giving me a *whatever* feeling? The above-mentioned *Watching Over Me* leaves us only with a groundless feeling, something replicated by any number of pharmaceutical programs. Whether it's a secular or Christian artist evoking the feeling of mother wrapping her arms around me, it doesn't matter. All Saints' Episcopal Church in Briarcliff Manor, N.Y. offers a U2-centered service "that uses U2's best-selling songs as hymns." A fifteen-year-old girl testified to what the bottom line truly is: "It makes you, like, warm inside."[12]

We shouldn't ignore the enthusiasm either. Kutless' song *Run* (2002) has Christ himself – the needy, scorned lover – calling out to us, "Why do you run / why do you hide / oh don't you know / I just, just want to be with you . . . Whatever happened to the love, the love you had for me / When you first came to me . . . Find a place of solitude, and I'll speak to you . . . I'm waiting here missing the time the times we shared / oh, please come to me."

If I come it will be with a restraining order.

Anyways, here is the classic "be quiet and listen for God's still, small voice," suiting our Gnostic times so well: "Find a place of solitude, and I'll speak to you." Suffice it to say, Mohammed once found a place of solitude and believed God spoke to him . . . so did Joseph Smith. But this is the Anabaptist impetus in modern spirituality and it deserves mentioning. (Beyond that, the whole episode with Elijah and the "still, small, voice" is one of the most misinterpreted passages ever. The point is that he heard the opposite of God's voice, or "sheer silence" as the New Revised Standard Version puts it. Cf. I Kings 19. How much false piety has arisen from people claiming to *live* by the still, small voice!)

Finding Contemporary Christian Music amplifying the eros theme is a bit like shooting fish in a barrel. The disinterest in naming the

God they claim to be worshiping is prominent, as is the weird, self-absorbed, mother's-love subjectivity. The focus on these squishy feelings of love, described in the fashion of eros, or romantic love, dominates the genre.

What gives?

What gives is best summarized by one particular listing of "100 Greatest Worship Songs of All Time" given at Brett McCracken's website called "The Search."[13] Brett McCracken penned a book entitled *Hipster Christianity* (2010) which is actually a good read and nicely describes Neo-evangelicalism's obsession with being accepted by pop culture. Unfortunately his list is peppered with hipster music. He should know better.

Among other Christian hymns he includes the following "Worship Songs" in his list: *Imagine* by John Lennon, *Every Breath You Take*, by the Police; *Round Midnight* by Miles Davis; *Das Rheingold* by Richard Wagner; *Danny Boy*; *I've been High*, by REM; and *Yesterday*, by the Beatles.

But what do all the songs in the list have in common (other than the real source of modern sacredness, that McCracken has *chosen* them)? McCracken admits: "This list is not limited to songs that make me think about God and Jesus (though obviously a lot of them do). No, these are simply the songs that pack the biggest holiness punch when I listen to them."

McCracken describes this "holiness punch." "They are the songs that you can't help but close your eyes to – the songs that are so beautiful, so alive, so longing, so emotional, that you feel the true transcendent power of art: what George Steiner calls 'the most "ingressive," transformative summons available to human experiencing.'"

McCracken goes on, bringing us to familiar territory: "After I compiled this list I looked over it to see what – if anything – these songs had in common. I found that a large number of them deal with topics of home – of 'homelands' or 'homelessness' – and also of memory/nostalgia/loss. A lot of them are sad and melancholy, reflecting upon the pain of unfound peace. These are the songs that make longing visceral – that point to the holy other and the heavens. To quote Steiner again, these are the songs 'which inform us of the visitor's visa in place and in time which defines our status as transients in a house of being whose foundations, whose future history, whose rationale – if any – lie wholly outside our will and comprehension.'"

Dealing with the feeling of homelessness, of nostalgia, the visceral longing, the melancholy, "transients in the house of being," these are all very specifically Gnostic themes. The doctrinal component – that which leads us to "think about God and Jesus" – takes backseat (or stuck bound and gagged in the trunk) to wispy feelings of "holiness punch" and "the true transcendent power of art." It's all straight out of the Romantic/Gnostic playbook. McCracken, so attuned to the constant draw of Neo-evangelicalism to hipsterism, should be alert to what it is in the Neo-evangelical DNA that so draws them to it. But were he to do so, he would cease to be a Neo-evangelical.

As it was for the secular rock n' roll scene, the eros theme is more than a philosophical postulate dominating Contemporary Christian Music. Anticipating the later string of sexual scandals peppering the Neo-evangelical movement, we see the same trend among early Jesus Freak pioneers. Tony Alamo, Jesus Freak founder of the Alamo Christian Foundation, is a convicted sex offender, and Lonnie Frisbee, associated with the Vineyard and Calvary Church movements, was an active homosexual and died of AIDS in 1993.

Is it mere coincidence that in a massive 2008 study, Neo-evangelical youths – despite having more conservative views on sex – were more sexually active than Mormons, mainline Protestants, Roman Catholics, and Jews? The study concluded, "Among major religious groups, only black Protestants begin having sex earlier."[14] The erotic element is strong in the Neo-evangelical tradition, as it has been throughout their history, because their theological posture is framed in erotic terms. Evangelical hero G. K. Chesterton admitted as much in his famous and oft-quoted sentiment, "Let your religion be less of a theory and more of a love affair."

We get a good example of the end game of untethered erotic religiosity in the story of Miriam Williams. In her book, *Heaven's Harlots* (1998), she describes her time as a "sacred prostitute" with the Children of God cult. The cult began as one of the many Christian hippy movements in general kinship with the wider Jesus Freak movement. They were "radical Christians who lived in a commune and spent most of the day witnessing about Jesus. . . . [They were] living true Christian communism."[15]

Echoing antinomian themes we saw in the medieval Free Spirit movement, part of their radicalism included "revolutionizing the world, and [replacing] the old morality."[16] Evidently the new morality included using sex as a way of bringing people to Jesus.

Williams' testimony should be highlighted if for no other reason than what it says about the role music had in her journey into the cult. As she tells it, music was her invisible Guide leading her from one hippy movement to the next, eventually into the bedroom: "I drifted toward the music [here, and then] .... Always looking for something new, I drifted toward the blues music [there] .... I danced solo to the music, oblivious to anything but the movements of my body .... I walked home with him to listen to music in the privacy of his bedroom ... [and after having sex for the first time] I was surprised by the pain .... This isn't free love, it's free sex."[17]

After that she entered the Children of God cult and began her work as a sacred prostitute. Cult leader David Berg revealed the secret to his magical charms that led such women into his grasp: "Music is the language of this generation, and we speak it. ... Our music is the miracle that attracts so many to our message about the Man. It's the magic that heals their souls and wounded spirits and proves our messiahship."[18]

Members of the Children of God cult, along with anybody who was anyone in the Jesus Freak movement, naturally ended up at Contemporary Music's coming of age moment, the Expo '72 event in Dallas. Called the "Christian Woodstock," this event established Contemporary Christian Music as *the* driving force in the churches which are the institutional heirs of the Jesus movement.

For Schopenhauer, Wagner, Nietzsche and others, music had something approaching sacramental qualities to it. In a Christian context, it offers the chance to transcend traditional Christian elements like doctrine, ritual, and ethics. It becomes a replacement sacrament. The analogy isn't even hidden. One baby boomer waxes theological: "Face it, for the first fifteen hundred years of Christianity the presence of God was experienced in the Eucharist. The Reformers moved the presence of God from the Eucharist to the Word. Today, the new revolution in worship is locating the presence of God in music."[19]

This relationship with music has other purposes as well. Megachurch Pastor Perry Noble, defending his church against criticisms that it's more a rock concert than a traditional church, resorts to rock's iconoclasm as the final justification: "I don't want to be normal when it comes to church in America because normal is dehydrated, normal is dead, normal is predictable, normal is boring, normal is lifeless."[20]

He throws *predictable* and *boring* so casually together with *dead* and *lifeless*, without considering how he's dancing to a tune from the Romantic playbook, which dreads the "dull round" and "lethargy of custom."[21] The Romantics offered their sacraments of deliverance – poetry and music – which tapped into another world, said to be where a more authentic reality is.

Enter Pat Boone offering his observation that "young people are searching for reality." He goes on to explain, "The church, as they see it today, doesn't have it . . . doctrine, no matter how pure or correct it may be, is not enough."[22] We're beyond rationality, book-learning, linear, analytical thinking again. Reality, it is assumed, cannot be contained by such things. Music is truer.

Nor does communion play near the role it once did.[23] If it's even offered, the focus is on "genuine religious experience rather than abstract doctrine . . . an emotional encounter with the divine." Far more important than weekly communion in mega-churches like Bill Hybel's Willow Creek are the "songs and dramas that relate to peoples' tastes and concerns."[24]

The justification for this revolution may seem benign, a simple matter of updating styles. Chuck Fromm from Contemporary Christian Music flagship, Marantha! Music, fears that "We better think about our sound and how we are reaching our community, or we will be the Amish of the twenty-first century."[25]

That's a worthy concern. But as we see over and over again in the above analysis and throughout justifications for Contemporary Christian Music, the music involves way more than the outer castings in how the Christian Gospel is presented. It involves the fundamentally subversive belief that music offers a more authentic connection to God than traditional forms. We've seen how this idea comes straight from the Romantic playbook. It also involves the too-often-overlooked belief that churches should cater to my personal music tastes, or else I'll shop for a new church. This is classic existentialism, that my authentic choices are essential to the healthy creation of my Self. In short, the popular acceptance of Contemporary Christian Music portends the final victory of two Gnostic movements – Romanticism and existentialism – over Christianity.

These, in turn, relate to the general movement of spirituality from the outside to the inside. This is no mere update in style. This is a complete inversion of the traditional Christian creed and embrace of Christianity's perennial enemy, Gnosticism.

✧ Chapter 13 ✧

The New God: The Self

How the Self Replaced God in American Christianity

Nietzsche proposed that in the vacuum created by God's death, we ourselves must rise up and become new gods. Our own Selves would be god. And this god, the existentialists said, would be crafted by our own choices, our own striving to be *authentic*, not bound by conventions imposed upon us by parents, Church, or society.

The Self is the new god. Meanwhile, as Jung showed us, the Self ultimately leads to a Collective Unconscious shared by everyone. This collective first reaches out to us from the pleroma through common archetypes found in our dreams, myths, and fantasy lives – the stuff of our popular media – and then it manifests through the collective action of people, either politically or culturally.

The New Age often speaks in terms of *emerging* paradigms or *emerging* consciousness. This fits well with the new god. The idea is, something from our Collective Unconscious is awakened in people one by one until a critical mass is reached, and mass change follows.

Then the process is divinized. God's Spirit is said to be working behind the emerging collective Self. Those who awaken to the paradigm shifts literally cooperate with God to change the world.

The connection to Gnosticism is in the affinities existentialism has with Gnosticism, particularly in their understanding of the Self. The *divine spark* of Gnostic myth is "the Self," and both existentialism and Gnosticism share similar ideas on the place the Self has in the cosmos.

Gnostic scholar Hans Jonas has delighted us with these connections.

In the 1950s, these ideas came of age. Pop psychology and Self-help arose from the Self-focused philosophies of the day, and true to its newly-christened mission, Neo-evangelicalism began to take on a Self-help flavor. Billy Graham and Norman Vincent Peale were friends because they drew from the same spiritual and philosophical stream. "To win over the world," said Peale, beginning with a premise that is not exactly the Gospel call, "a man must get hold of some power in his inward or spiritual life which will never let him down."[1] The inside-out religious program accords nicely with the Anabaptist tradition and greased the pathways between Neo-evangelicalism and Depth (Self-help) Psychology.

In the 1980s, Robert Schuller pronounced the marriage between Neo-evangelicalism and psychology in his *Self-Esteem Reformation* (1982). "What the church needs, more than anything else," He wrote, "is a new reformation – nothing else will do! Without a new theological reformation, the Christian church as the authentic body of Christ may not survive."[2]

His motivation for such a project is telling: "For the church to address the unchurched with a theocentric attitude is to invite failure in mission."[3] That's an astounding comment recalling the original Neo-evangelical mission: we must engage culture; if culture is Self-centered and not God-centered, then the Church must put more focus on the Self.

His goal is radical. "The church must be willing to die as a church and be born again as a mission."[4] What church does he want to die? Schuller cites a poll concluding that "ritualistic attendance at typical church services and the formal recitation of prayers do not in themselves contribute to a positive self-esteem."[5] That's the Church he wants dead – the one that does all that praying – all because they don't build peoples' Self-esteem. If traditional forms of Christian worship do not appeal to people's quest for Self-affirming authenticity, the problem is not culture, he says, but the Church.

Schuller claims his unique cocktail of psychological Self-help tips and orthodox Christian theology can heal people of their emotional wounds, leading to his goal, the "healthy human being." How is this defined? Here he lunges headlong into a term we've seen before: *enthusiasm*. "If we know we are being led into a vital and exciting life filled with new possibilities and dynamic potential, we can be enthusiastic about tomorrow – today! Enthusiasm is a positive emotion that deserves our attention. For the alternative too often is cynicism, despair, and depression."[6] What exactly constitutes this enthusiasm? "Divine dreams are the tap roots of enthusiasm."[7] An ancient mystery cultist couldn't have put it better! Nor could have Carl Jung, modernity's favorite dream-interpreting Gnostic.

The above quote references the despair we see periodically among the Gnostics, which they in turn contrasted with the gnosis they offered as its immediate remedy. The millenarians turned this immediate remedy – "we can be enthusiastic about tomorrow *today*!" – into a social movement. Curiously, Schuller's program does just this.

Ever embodying the fine Evangelical tradition of social involvement – always involved in some crusade – he writes, "The awareness of our divine roots will inspire the pursuits of divine fruits. We will be caught up in a vision of a cause, a crusade, a divine calling." He goes on, "[W]e will accept God's invitation to play our important part in the kingdom he is busy creating NOW in this world. God needs you and me to help create a society of self-esteeming people."[8]

We saw it with the millenarians; we saw it in Hegel. "God needs you" to help him bring about the new world order. And, no different than the radicals demanding whatever utopian dream NOW, he too appeals to the imminence of God's needy demands. Again, this is not entirely keeping with the doctrine of his self-sufficiency, but smacks of the Hegel-Pietistic-Hermetic-Millenarian-Gnostic belief that God immediately has contact with my Self and through me will inaugurate – indeed "needs" me to inaugurate – his kingdom on earth.

Maybe Anne Murray was on to something.

Schuller also echoes Jung's emerging collective as he lays the foundation for a Self-esteem-centered "Kingdom of God," which he says, "is a noninstitutionalized divine organism that positively infects the secular society."[9] The key words are "noninstitutionalized" and "divine organism." Where the historic Church is an institution and its entire program of salvation takes on institutional form – from its formed grace (eg. the ministry, the preached word, the sacraments) to its formed charity (eg. Catholic Charities, Lutheran Social Services, etc.) – not so the "New Reformation." It will be a "divine organism," working enthusiastically through the new "Self-Esteem" Gospel, which will liberate people to embark upon a "crusade" that will transform society.

In other words, Schuller's program simply updates the millenarian cause in the tradition of medieval communitarianism; nineteenth century abolitionism, temperance, and sabbatarianism; and now twentieth century

Self-esteem. It will be a political movement, but one proposed under the pretense that it's just a grassroots movement of organically-changed individuals having their new status reflected as a political, societal reality.

George Martin sees the blatant connection: "the Christian Right [will legitimate] change by integrating the psychology of self-assertion and self-esteem into a nineteenth century revivalism." Such a strategy has the potential to "construct a new social order . . . to institute their own vision of the cultural order."[10]

Far from being a movement of the "Right," such statements reveal Schuller as a Leftist, precisely because he cannot entertain the notion that his movement would be contained in an institutionalized form – we call that the Church – and be protected along with other institutions in a free society. In the American system, society is made up of various institutions each doing their thing, often at odds with one another, but all under the regime of political freedoms and rights to do so.

This at least should be the promise of life in America, that the "societal" can be different than the "political." Both the Amish community in Indiana and the gay community in San Francisco should be able to live under the same political regime, that is, of freedom. The point is, "societal" is one thing, and "political" is another.

Like the millenarians and all Leftists, Schuller doesn't see the distinction. For them, society is something to "construct," something to "order." And this ultimately occurs politically.

The traditional Right (as opposed to the misnamed "Christian Right") tends toward a politics much in the tradition of the American Forefathers, where different interests are cobbled together, where the federal government assumes lowest-common-denominator concerns, like defense of borders, and then state and local governments hone in on more detailed concerns. The Right emphasizes the constitutional right of free assembly to fill in gaps a universalist government cannot fill.

The Left, by contrast, holds the hope of changing society through politics. It's a one-size-fits-all program. First, change happens in the minds of a few (or so they think), then a few more, then a majority, and as soon as they can, they change the political environment to reflect their supposed organically-changed minds, the minority be damned. But then, so the hope goes, the minority will be bullied into following in line, through speech codes and perpetual media manipulation – with thought reduced to the archetypical shorthand reminiscent of Bruno's hermetical magic – and voilà, Christian self-esteem is the common currency of the land . . . or gay marriage.

Fine and great, but if the millenarian analogy holds, there will always be a "what happened?" moment, based on the truth – really an orthodox Christian truth rooted in original sin doctrines – that humans don't really *organically* change. Humans will fall back to their natural proclivities, their natural societal arrangements, and faced with the choice between their natural tendencies and whatever universalist, idealistic vision is being pushed by the latest prophet, they'll choose the former in the end. Then things break down. The communalist Pilgrims go back to private property. The Taborites realize the need to produce. The USSR breaks apart. The Eighteenth Amendment prohibiting alcohol is repealed.

So, *what happened* with Schuller's movement? Schuller's Self-esteem reformation, in fact, did not become the Christian movement he expected it to become. Rather, it's only helped de-Christainize society and usher in the "spiritual but not religious" Gnostic religiosity we've been surveying. All it's done is make it confusing where Christianity ends and where secular Self-esteem thinking begins. It's resulted in a sort of "Calendar Christianity" where self-affirming banalities coupled with syrupy pictures of angels, clouds, balloons, and children pass for Christianity. It's resulted in a Christian world that cannot discern the inherent unorthodoxy in the likes of Oprah Winfrey, Joel Olsteen, or Rick Warren.

What it's done, in effect, is make the mega-church the halfway house between traditional Christianity and New Age Gnosticism, a place where people can rest comfortably in the pretense that they're Christian while being processed in their spiritual core for the new "cultural order" of Self-obsessed Gnostic spirituality. Schuller's program is clearly the animating message of the mega-church movement and all the church bodies running after them like lost puppies (my own included).

If Robert Schuller is the brains of the mega-church movement, Church Growth guru George Barna is the brawn, strong-arming recalcitrant traditionalists into the inevitable future through his seminars and scientific approach to evangelism. He hosts seminars for church leaders that teach things like "the wisdom of worship strategies such as seeker services, blended services and self-directed worship."[11]

Self-directed worship! Such a concept would have been considered blasphemous only a half century ago, but here we are. A great swath of American Christianity has joined the great American Cult of the Self along with New Agers and existentialists. All of them feed at the trough of consumerism, where *what-fits-me* replaces *what-is-true* or *what-is-good* as the operating principle, yet where the ultimate decision of *what-fits-me* is manipulated by the magicians, those crafting the archetyipical shorthand by which we think, the marketers and culture-makers in media.

This Cult of the Self effects both content and packaging.

As far as content goes, Schuller's crusade has degenerated into the massage for the Self passing for so much of the contemporary church's message. Consider Joel Olsteen's *Your Best Life Now* (2007). The "now" in his title signals exactly the sort of immediacy the millenarians sought, while the "Best Life" describes the Self-focused goal. It departs a bit from historic Christianity's "New Life Later" message, but again, that's the "revolution" Schuller promised, a message devoted to the Self.

Church Growth pastor Doug Murren explicitly counsels pastors to "browse the self-help section of local bookstores in order to design messages based on the themes of the top ten sellers."[12] A brain formatted to ignore an idea because it's found in the eleventh best seller is not exactly in the tradition of Christian discernment.

A Lutheran Church Growth congregation (just to show that the disease is viral) advertises the grand opening of its new campus: "We're a church where you can be yourself and feel free to explore spiritual issues at your own pace." *Be yourself!* The old Gospel call was "Deny yourself," now it's "Be yourself." This is nothing less than a complete upending of the Church's central point that goes back to Schuller's replacement of God-centered theology with a more Self-centered focus, to say nothing of the lurking existentialism.

Another mega-church poses the issue: "Ever felt unloved? unlovable?" And then stretching a translation of Jesus' words beyond recognition it asks "Are you tired? Worn out? Burned out on religion? Come to me. Get away with me and you'll recover your life." Then it concludes "Join us this year as we focus exclusively on the teachings of Jesus. Escape religion . . . and focus on Jesus."[13]

We're back to the Renaissance problem of melancholia, now updated, and through Schuller fused with traditional terminology. Jesus, *specifically a Jesus devoid of traditional religious trappings*, is the new remedy for depression. He's spiritual Zoloft!

When we unravel what this exactly means, we discover that this is related, again, to music. At the above-mentioned church, the climax of one of its services was the Chris Tomlin song referenced in our introduction, *No Chains on Me*, which explains how "Now is the time for freedom / Abandoned by cold religion / my heart on fire / We hear the sound / the sound of revival coming."

That the placement of this song in the worship is exactly where traditional Christianity places the sacrament is no coincidence. If in traditional worship the "Service of the Word" leads up into the "Service of the Sacrament," the upgraded counterpart is a program beginning with the massage for the Self climaxing in rousing, inspiring song, the formation of the collective as the attendees get up, dance, and wave their arms to the beat of the song. It's all about engineering relationships, like a big group hug after a therapy session.

As far as packaging goes, Robert E. Webber remarks, "many new churches are being built with relational seating. This makes the community more aware of the presence of Christ, the head of the church, who assembles with his people, the body of Christ."[14]

This too is revolutionary on a par with the revolution in content. In the old model, Christ's Body radiated out from the *corpus verum*, the True Body of Christ at the altar in the sacrament. Faith was the needed spiritual faculty, certainly not some Gnostic "awareness" generated through the manipulation of how chairs were arranged.

The new model begins in the altar of the Self within. Individual Selves create the body of Christ by assembling with one another. As one mega-church advertises, "It's not a religion, it's a relationship." The move is from the presence of Christ located in the forms of bread and wine, to the presence of Christ located in relationships. The old model rested in the distinction between Self and Christ, both of whom are bound by flesh and blood, thus requiring the coming together of two distinct beings through some medium. Traditionally, the elements of the Sacrament – bread and wine – are the shared thing, the *koinonia* (communion) of two things sharing something as one, namely me with Christ's body and blood. Christ and the individual are in communion, yet they retain their distinctiveness. In the new model, "Christ" is some sort of principle of my spilling outside myself and becoming one with other people. The relationships are the manifestation of Christ himself.

But relationships on the basis of what? It could be whatever: musical styles, or edginess, or whatever code of hip-ness is dictating how the numinous "young people" think. In reality, whatever *Jesus* we become *aware of* through our *relating* has more to do with those choices I make in my eternal quest for the authentic Self. Jesus becomes nothing more than an abstracted projection of my Self re-cloaked in a Jesus deconstructed from the Gospels, and given back to me in a way that says, *Hey, you're OK just the way you are, because I am just like you . . . I AM you.* This in turn constitutes my inspiration. When I feel most *authentically me*, then I'm in touch with the Divine Spirit animating my words and feelings.

It's the supra-incarnate Logos, the living Christ, the uncreated Word, all over again: a Christ rarefied from the Church, its sacraments, and Scriptures. Schuller opens the door into this groundless, hazy realm when he wonders whether Protestantism has gotten to the point it has because it places all authority in the written Scriptures rather than in the "Eternal Word." "[T]he Eternal Word transcends the written Word," he writes, "Christ is the Word made flesh. Christ is the Lord over the Scriptures; the Scriptures are not Lord over Christ."[15]

And how do we access this Bible-transcending Christ?

Certainly not in such magisterial authorities as books, confessions, or councils. These are man's traditions. Rather, we access this transcendent Logos through our *minds*. "Then let Christ enter our minds as Lord over all," Schuller writes, "The answers will be found in Jesus Christ, our Savior and Lord. Before his feet we bow, and in His Spirit we prayerfully and humbly seek a resolution."

But he doesn't stop there, leaving this access to Christ up to each individual. No, he's quite willing to inform us what Christ has revealed in *his* mind. Of course, as with all millenarians, God speaks to all the chosen, but to some a bit more. Schuller was chosen to speak for the collective because, well, he's more tuned into what God is saying: "Deep down in our hearts I believe we know that Jesus would say something like this to us: '. . . Receive and enjoy the fruit of salvation: Self-esteem, self-worth. Hear God's call to you. He would save you for high and holy service – to be proud of who you are. Then, stop putting yourself down. Start enjoying the dignity that is your God-intended destiny.'"[16]

Again, that's what "Jesus would say," and that trumps what Scripture actually says Jesus says, and the access to this truth is what you know "deep down in [y]our hearts." And what is Jesus saying? Schuller's own Self-esteem theology!

He becomes yet another prophet claiming to ascend into the mind of the supra-incarnate Logos and then proclaim to us his own unprecedented, idiosyncratic, novel, pride-based theology, a theology, by the way, from which he made millions. And this, we are told, is the humble way to approach things.

✦ Chapter 14 ✦

The New Initiation Sacrament:
Consumer Choice

Neo-Evangelicalism Goes Corporate

There was once a day when Christian iconography was no different than the paraments or architecture of a cathedral. It was part of the overall liturgical atmosphere, *anonymously contributed*. The Renaissance came, and art began to be titled. Paradoxically, the age that reintroduced Neoplatonism – where individuality is seen as an aspect of our fallen condition, and the many will one day be absorbed back into the One – also abetted the great Western inflation of Self. Well, for reasons we've seen, this isn't too much of a paradox. In any event, since that time Christian music and art has been titled as well.

We've gone to the next level. Christian churches have now become retail outlets for the latest in Contemporary Christian Music. Warren Cole Smith describes in his *A Lover's Quarrel with the Evangelical Church* (2009) how "churches that use these songs must pay a licensing fee to an organization called Christian Copyright Licensing International (CCLI)). The size of the copyright fee depends on the size of the church, but a five-hundred member church would pay about $300 per year. Currently, approximately 140,000 churches are CCLI license holders.

"That means that about $50 million per year is collected and redistributed to copyright owners. . . . [Contemporary worship songs] are a revenue stream for copyright holders and music publishers. They are aggressively promoted and now make up a significant share of the 4.5 billion [dollar] Christian retail market. . . . [H]ere's the larger point: there was a time when theologians and the wisest minds of a church determined what was said and sung in a church. Today, who makes those decisions? Becky. What Becky likes gets played on Christian radio, and what gets played on Christian radio gets promoted to church musicians and church leaders, both intentionally as a part of the machinery of the Christian-industrialist complex, or unintentionally, just because these songs are on the air.

"The result: our churches are filled with songs not because they reflect our highest and best thinking and artistry or because they remind us and teach our children important truths, but because they are – as many Christian stations say about themselves – 'safe for the entire family.'"[1]

I would take issue with that final point. When the children are ushered off quickly to the nursery because the music and imagery of the main service are too edgy, it really isn't safe for the entire family. Christ may be conjured up through the magical cone of relationship power at these services, but somewhere in this charmed dance the part of Jesus that said "Let the little children come to me" doesn't get communicated.

Needless to say, Smith pretty much nails it as far as his "Becky" observation goes. "Becky," of course, is all of us. She represents the primacy of human choice – *what Becky likes*. If the Self is the new god and music is the new sacrament, *choice* is the initiation rite, the new baptism. Contemporary Christian Music becomes sacred not due to its content or timeless truths, but because more people with wide-eyed excitement choose to gather around its sound than around that older sound designated "sacred." And purely by virtue of this greater gathering, the proponents of this strategy point to the results and say, "See? The Holy Spirit at work!" Because of what Becky chooses.

Kimon Howland Sargeant describes it this way, "We are observing, to use sociological terms, the shift from religion as an ascriptive identity based on birth to an achieved identity based on choice. This shift is at the core of the emergence of consumerism as a primary characteristic of American religious practice."[2]

Choice is the initiation sacrament of the religion of the Self. It's the existentialist formula: *I can't be who I am authentically meant to be unless I have the freedom to make the choices that define who I am.* Choice becomes sacralized.

We proposed the postmodern creed, that existentialist creed

written into the DNA of every American, particularly embraced in the teen years. At that fresh age adolescents are most in tune with the existentialist vision of human striving.

Church Growth guru Lyle Schaller unquestionably accepts the assumptions of this vision in a *Parish Paper* (his monthly one-page church consulting publication) which poses the question, "Where Do Teenagers Want to Go to Church?"[3] He works with data showing that, while about a quarter of teens stick with the church of their parents, about a quarter of all teens leave the congregations of their families to find one "that they themselves choose." His entire article never once evaluates the object of teen choices or the processes by which their choices are made. To do so would be to undermine the existential creed, that *one's authentic choosing* is the determinant sacred act.

When, for example, he points out that "Music is one of the most heavily used and effective channels of communication in these churches, [an] important expression of self-identification," he leaves the question hanging whether an "expression of self-identification" is the proper purview of an institution rooted in Self-denial, to say nothing of the discernment needed to understand the inherently solipsist tendencies of music. Or, when he remarks that beyond Bible study and prayer, these kids are looking for "music, hand-clapping, dance, and movement," these Orphic characteristics – a Sufi would feel right at home in these churches – elude his discernment.[4] All that matters to Schaller is the *choice. Choice* is sacred. *What teens choose* should be revered and analyzed without any application of a standard. It's all about the *will-from-which* as opposed to the *standard-to-which*.

After presenting the data, Schaller asks, "Has the time come to redesign your congregation's ministry with today's teenagers in mind?"

Wait a minute! What about the equal percentage of youth who didn't leave? Why don't their choices matter? Why not develop their implicit respect for the traditions passed on by their parents? As far as a wise strategy for growth goes – so important to this crowd – even the NFL knows of a draft-and-develop philosophy working with what you've got rather than trying to win free agents over to your program. It's worked for the Green Bay Packers, New England Patriots, and Pittsburgh Steelers, who haven't done so bad in the Superbowl department (someone inform the Lord that this is the last NFL game). Not so the Church Growth crowd. For them, those teens leaving the church are more authentic because they haven't slavishly trudged in the footsteps "of their parent's choice." They've gone out and made their own choices. Heidegger is giving the thumbs up from the grave (even if in Purgatory for that Nazi slipup).

We've long known marketers strive to bend teenage choice in the direction of their product for several reasons. There's the effective *get-'em-young* strategy; also teenagers have vast stores of disposable income. That this age has been exploited by our default existentialism only helps the cause of marketers. *Buy our product and be yourself!* We've discussed the convergence of consumerism and existentialism above.

What's remarkable is how the sacredness of customer choice has effected contemporary church life. Contemporary Christianity has become an industry dominated by principles of marketing atomizing Christianity into demographic groups, all based on the principle that one's choices – along with all others who make those choices – should be given sanctity in the Church. It's also a sort of *youth cult* – if the young are choosing a specific service, it must be more authentic, real, and alive, and not simply a matter of cuter girls being there letting loose.

A pamphlet titled with this gem of a phrase, "Building a Church for New Generations"[5] promises a conference designed to teach us how to reach Boomers, X-ers, and that wily Millennial bunch ("Here come the Millennials!"). Throughout the conference attendees are promised "three unique worship experiences!" At the first, they will "Enjoy a Spirited-Traditional Worship Service." The next night they will experience a "Boomer-Oriented Outreach Service." Finally they'll participate in a "Gen X Service with Communion and Prayer." Something for everyone, even for those gothy Gen X types who want prayer and communion.

It's no longer the exception, but the rule, to find congregations offering several different worship styles. The early bird elderly get their traditional service at 8 AM. The happening young hipsters get their late Sunday *Fusion* service or whatever trendy word is out there – in any event you can be assured everyone will be authentic there, which generally means shabbily dressed, unshaven, and moody. The prime time morning slot is reserved for the moneyed Yuppies, the holy grail of all church marketing, who attend the Praise Service led by the motivational speaker on speed.

Jim Beilby, a theology professor at Bethel University, gives an account of a youth service at Wooddale Church in Eden Prairie, Minnesota, where "the guitar-driven rock accelerated and five mammoth video screens flashed with high-speed urban imagery [as] hundreds of young people swayed in a dark and crowded hall, ready to start the party."[6]

He explains its popularity, citing the "profound sense of frustration with church as usual." Such data from the likes of a fifteen-year-old attendee (Becky?) certainly prove his point: "I've gone to [church] forever, but I like this much better than the other services here. . . . The contemporary service, that is more like, for our parents. But a band with a bass guitar and drums? That is just the best."

The particular worship service that she, like, liked focused on the symbol of a curtain bisecting the stage, but which "Jesus strips away," the point being that Jesus strips away whatever divides us. One wonders if Jesus strips away the divisions imposed upon the congregation by the wizards of demographic marketing who recommended a church service menu where "On a recent Sunday, four generations attended. [The great-grandma and her son and daughter-in-law] worshiped at a traditional service. [A granddaughter] attended a contemporary service with her husband . . . . A second daughter . . . went to the Gathering with her husband . . . after putting [their baby] in the nursery. To [the granddaughter], the contemporary service, which attracts many young families, has the best music and pacing. [The other daughter] wanted something edgier, and found it in the Gathering."

Something for everyone but the baby.

The eight services offered by this church suggest something more profound than evangelistic overreach. A fourteen-year-old participant at one of the services remarked "I've been to a few Catholic services, but I feel closer to God here. . . . You can only hear your own thoughts, and send them toward God."

She frames her understanding in terms of stylistic preferences, but what she says betrays a clear theological contrast between a traditional liturgy centered on God's action as expressed through formal, Scripture-based rites, and a different service where she may "feel closer to God" through her own Self-generated thoughts.

Sargeant's assessment of consumeristic Christianity substantiates her taste: "According to seeker church proponents, genuine faith is best expressed through direct devotion to God. Formal rituals and liturgies can only obstruct this devotion because they all smack of 'dead' traditions."[7]

In his discussion on the worship revolution spearheaded by Willow Creek's Bill Hybels, Sargeant answers the question why we need such a paradigm change. He cites a study of American religious life that concludes, "The *most prosperous religious organizations* [italics mine: pause for a moment to reflect on that revealing phraseology] today are those that realize that this generation does not feel comfortable with traditional services full of rituals."[8]

What is the solution? What will help a church get back on the road to prosperity? He answers: "a pronounced emphasis on the subjective and internal aspects of faith and an accompanying de-emphasis on the objective and external elements of Christian tradition (e.g., sacraments)."[9]

The point is, something way beyond wise church planning is going on when Grandma Schmidt goes up to communion singing, "He has raised our human nature / On the clouds to God's right hand; / There we sit in heav'nly places, / There with Him in glory stand" while guitarist Keegan with his soul patch leads the hipsters in, "I'm in love with you Jesus / in your arms forever / I feel so much love / In your presence I don't wanna let you go" (repeat line 70 times . . . no, really, look it up).

Such is the typical behavior of the growing suburban parishes across the country, the consumeristic radio-dial approach offering something to everyone. Of course, there's always that element for which consumerism, precisely because it appeals to the masses, is the very definition of unhip.

To the rescue comes "Reality LA,"[10] a church offering something for the "overwhelmingly attractive twenty-somethings . . . clad in skinny jeans and Converses and adorned with artistic tattoos." They have become, according to *Details* magazine, "The Hottest Pickup Spot in Hollywood." The church boasts how it sets itself apart from the typical mega-church with its "cul-de-sac" Christianity. Recognizing that "beautiful people like to commune with their own," the church realized that "no one was really bringing the Word to this particular demographic: young, attractive hipsters."

A Jesus can be tailored for everyone, even for those who don't like hanging around ugly or uncool people. A quick websearch of the word *Jesus* combined with any number of different styles will eventually yield one tailored to everyone. There's body-builder Jesus, tattooed Jesus, hippy Jesus, woman Jesus, communist Jesus, homosexual Jesus, working man Jesus, and so on and so forth. Jesus can become the image justifying all your authentic choices, who you have created yourself to be, or who you aspire to be.

A couple years ago a gay high school student made news for

wearing a T-shirt advertising "Jesus is not a homophobe." I believe he was quoting St. Cyril of Jerusalem. No he wasn't. Nor has he studied the traditional canonical authorities by which we derive Jesus' actual teachings on the issue. Jesus is a stand-in for *everything about me that I want to be OK*. It's a remarkable sleight of hand. I infuse my Self in the image of Jesus, and then worship that image. I think I'm worshiping Jesus when in fact I'm worshiping my own Self. It's Self-worship masquerading as Christian worship. And when my Self-worship can be draped in the sweet sentiment of the piano's cascading chords or guitarist Keegan's teen-angst, pained-look, moody chic, how can this worship not be truly authentic?

The old Christian formula was: repent and be conformed to the life of Christ; you are crucified to this world. Easily following this formula is the principle of catholicity which is the quest of every traditional Christian creed. Each Christian leaves behind his Self and joins something greater and more universal (thus catholic) than himself.

The new formula is: mold Jesus to your own values. Repenting of your sins may cross the line into the sacred zone of the Self's authentic desires, so best to stay away from it. People no longer church shop with the intent of finding redemption through repentance and forgiveness – that was the old formula; rather, people do precisely what that obnoxious phrase mentioned above says: they *church shop*. They seek a church that "fits our needs" or "fits us." By such language people admit that the Self is god. They're not looking for a place to repent; they're looking for a place that repents for them.

I recently saw a church marquis – always a gold mine for the silliness of contemporary Christianity – with the phrase, "Jesus believes in you."

That's the very definition of upending the traditional Christian creed, the likes of which used to be recognized as the sacrilege it was. At a minimum Harold Bloom, who can hardly contain his glee as he welcomes back with open arms the Neo-evangelical tradition into his Gnostic camp, ought to be taken seriously. His verdict is curt. Precisely because of this focus on the Self, he writes,"[W]e think we are Christian, but we are not. . . . There are indeed millions of Christians in the United States, but most Americans who think that they are Christian truly are something else."[11]

Ouch.

✧ Chapter 15 ✧

The Emergent Church

The Latest *Really* Real Christians

In reaction to this commercialization of Church, the Emergent Church spawned, a Neo-evangelical assimilation of the inner-focusedness settling on the culture – essentially the Christian mainstreaming of the New Age – in which quiet meditation, mysticism, and ancient practices found new currency. Bloom, writing back in the Reagan era, predicted the rise of Emergent Christianity precisely because he saw the New Age connection, its expectation of a "great leap forward in paradigms" drawing parallels to Neo-evangelical's own self-understanding as always the embodiment of God's latest operation in history, with whom the Neo-evangelical cooperates just as the New Ager also cooperates to bring about the change.[1]

If he is correct, and the New Age is actually a "charming parody"[2] of the American Evangelical tradition, we're back at the Gnostic point through yet another channel: Emergent Christianity was simply the next step in Evangelicals discovering their Id, their true Gnostic roots.

The seeker-sensitive churches of consumeristic Christianity arrived at their Gnosticism by way of the Cult of the Self and its sacralization of choice. Still, typically its overt consumerism masks at least the pretense of a doctrinal tradition. Their purpose after all is to lure seekers in through music and entertainment and then give them that old-time religion. It's a classic bait-and-switch program. Throw out the Gnostic Self-orientation bait and switch in orthodoxy. After the smoke from the concert has cleared, while the janitor is sweeping up the balloons, caramel corn, and confetti, in some special enclave in the deep recesses of the church's campus, the real Christians sneak in by the dark of night and learn the old Calvinist doctrine, or Fundamentalism, or whatever, like the attendee at Community Church of Joy who admitted, "We probably came here for a year before we knew it was Lutheran."[3]

Emergent Christianity took the position of what the Romanticists led us to suspect, that perhaps the feeling induced by the bait is where it's at in the first place, so why bother with those rigid categories of doctrine? Maybe there's no reason to distinguish between that feeling you get listening to a Christian song versus the one you get listening to a secular "socially conscious" song. If that feeling is God's spirit at work, why impose boundaries through our rigid theology establishing what is of Christ and what is not? That was exactly the thinking process of above-quoted Emergent, Brett McCracken, with his "holiness punch" devoid of Christ or God.

Getting beyond the obvious recall of Hegelian philosophy (and its theological counterpart in Process Theology, in which theology "emerges" through the historical process), Emergent Church suits the current zeitgeist. It's the micro-brewery of churches. Rebelling against the mass-marketed appeal of, say, Budweiser, micro-breweries claimed to restore the taste and feel of an old-time brew. A tavern serving micro-brewed beers may build a structure to look old or feel like an old pub. They'll tear down a genuine old building to do so! We might call it *manufactured, mass-marketed authenticity.* So also is the Emergent Church. To wit: *we'll do Greek Orthodox in a cool, trendy way that makes us look edgy and outlier, but God forbid we actually have anything to do with those stale old Greek women praying their formulaic prayers!*

Of course, the whole event is all about staging an image, but it's an image today's suburbians are seeking to counteract their ennui; they seek some connection to something other than the boring conventions they come from, whether that be the mysterious past, or the raw realism of an industrial park. The alternatively gothic or industrial feel of Christian marketing – in websites and in its marketing literature – is an Emergent trend, a salute either to a medieval past when mysticism ruled, or to the Marxist view that the laborer represents rawer and more authentic personhood. Whatever it is, it bucks bourgeois, consumeristic convention, which is its real point. Still, it's able to sell itself not as the latest branding of Christianity – *look at our cool new label with dark, muted tones, not the obnoxious bright colors of the consumeristic decades of yore* – but as authentic Christianity.

Speaking to their medievalist fetish, we've seen how Tim Keel referenced Greek Orthodox monks at Mount Athos just after World War II, lauding their separatist piety, devotion, and simple wisdom. Or again, Jonathan Wilson-Hartgrove (his first last name is his wife's surname) leads the New Monasticism movement centered in North Carolina. Another Emergent regularly participates in Roman Catholic prayer services and has written a book *Flirting with Monasticism: Finding God on Ancient Paths* (2006).

I'm sure this is just what the monks need, representatives from the Church of the Beautiful and Hip coming over to flirt with them because monks are cool and stuff. Regardless, this embrace of monasticism, mysticism, sacraments, and other items which they handle like children playing in the attic of Christian tradition prompts us to ask, *Why don't they just become Roman Catholic or Greek Orthodox?*

Why? Because that would take away the millenarian, Gnostic buzz. They are the avatars God is using to bring about the new *emerging* age. One Emergent sees himself and his comrades as a "guild of prophets" within the Church commissioned to "readapt . . . prior symbols shared by postliberal and postevangelical Christians."[4]

Their movement began, another Emergent says, when "a bunch of us had experience after experience that did not fit our views of the world. Something wasn't right. [We noticed] disorientations occurring between the way things used to be and the way things are today, and how we hoped they would be."[5]

That nondescript feeling in the air, that disorientation, that despairing posture beginning every Gnostic journey – we recall how Keel could smell cosmic change in the air (perhaps the Sufi who figured out *Why is the sound of an onion?* will enlighten us what this smells like) – all this is believed to be God's spirit moving the futurist elite to become co-laborers with Christ bringing about the new, emerging Church.

Seeing their spiritual orientation mirrored in secular society, in the drift of young people from the Church, the Emergents don't double down on traditional Christian faith but actually endorse the drift: "so many young white people across Europe and North America and elsewhere are distancing themselves from Christianity . . . they do not want to be part of a white man's religion . . . that feels like a step backward or a malingering in a world that should be left behind."[6]

Authentic young hipsters can't go backwards! That's something akin to death! And neither can the Neo-evangelicals who framed their self-understanding as *wherever the culture is, either we join them or die.*

And so, paralleling exactly how modern Gnostics view the old age – the Age of Pisces, the Enlightenment Age, the Age of Rationalism, the Patriarchal Age, whatever – the Emergent Church views the traditional Church as stuck in the same old paradigm all of the West is stuck in, the paradigms where things like logic-based philosophy, grammar-based language, and form-based Christianity rule.

Echoing the Gnostic critique that science and rationalism represent a Yaltabaothian desire to control, Keel says, "[O]ur culture is undergoing a transformation. Unfortunately, most of our systems and structures are ill-prepared to deal with this new environment and the opportunities and challenges it presents. The modern age was ruled by science and structures of control."

He even brings up that same New Age bugaboo, "linear thinking," describing the old world as one of "mere facts, data, and cognition . . . dominated by modern, linear, cognitive, Western paths of knowledge."[7]

Keel continues, "In the postmodern milieu, the humanities are asserting themselves . . . with a language all their own – creative, artistic, intuitive, organic, prophetic, and poetic. New structures and systems are emerging."[8]

The parallels to the relationship the Romantic movement had with the Enlightenment are clear. Like the Romantics, Emergents prefer action, intuition, poetry, and "play" to the theological enterprise. Romanticism began the drift in the West away from its intellectual heritage, through existentialism, to current *postmodernism.* The Emergents don't mind the appellation. When Emergent leader Brian McClaren had to defend his positive appropriation of the word *postmodern* against old-guard doctrinaire Evangelicals wary of the nihilistic overtones, he piously tells us (he's so far beyond us, you see), "I don't want to argue with these good people about these matters. I'm too busy with other endeavors. . . . I'm more concerned whether the person is doing justice, loving mercy, and walking humbly with God."[9]

It's not about categories of right or wrong – that's the stale pretension of Western Christianity, precisely the thing they're emerging from – it's more about the conversation, the story that emerges in peoples' lives, or in their political action. And so, yes, at the table of this discussion should sit the deconstructionist position of eco-feminists Sallie McFague and Mary Grey, who have "explored the ways in which the Western approach to knowledge was also very much about Western males seizing and maintaining power."[10]   Also sitting at the table are universalists, environmentalists, multiculturalists, and every basic representative of contemporary progressive thinking.

The Emergent movement deceptively appeared to be a healthy step away from the consumeristic Neo-evangelicalism it's replacing. Yes, it embraces the liturgy and the sacraments (in an almost pantheistic way), but it leapfrogs over Reformation confessionalism – with its "Western" focus on objective confessional standards, doctrine, and worship – and embraces a sort of fusion between postmodernism and late medieval mysticism in a bizarre attempt to "deconstruct . . . the spiritual experience."[11]

Says Emergent proponent Robert Parham, "Protestants seem more about filling the hour and sanctuary with sound than filling the soul with God's presence." He goes on to trump the benefits of Taize spirituality, which is "about listening to God, not a sermon."[12] Or as put in reference to above-mentioned hipster pastor McManus, "[He] takes the emphasis off of the institutional and places it on God. The church is deeply mystical. . . . McManus urges people to look inside themselves for answers to their questions about God."[13]

This is classic enthusiasm, invoking the Gnostic tendency to transcend the *formed Logos*, which is what orthodoxy confesses Christ to be and what a good sermon has historically done. But to the Emergent, understanding the Gospel according to any sort of theological category, to say nothing of language itself, would box God in. And though the first Pentecost was precisely that – an event filled with lots of sounds that the Apostle Peter formed into words as he quoted Scriptures and proclaimed the Christian Creed, leading to baptisms, catechesis, and communion – the new goal is to wait "for the still small voice of God that comes to us . . . when the clamor of popular culture fades away."[14] In fact the possibility exists for a "wordless faith" in which one "serves Jesus in substance rather than in words."[15]

Once words and names – the stuff of dogma – enter the picture, says the Emergent, exclusiveness also enters. Words set boundaries on doctrines outside of which is "false doctrine," and names set boundaries on beings like *Christ*, outside of which is damnation. This is problematic, for the name *Christ* can become a stumbling block to Native Americans who "[m]oved by the Holy Spirit . . . reject the idea of allegiance to the name of Christ and, instead, want to be like him and thus accept him at a deeper level."[16]

Samir Selmanovic, the author of these lines, argues that believing in the supremacy of Christianity is a sin. Why? Because God is bigger than form and any attempt to claim exclusive reception of him through such forms. Forms like "the Christian faith" are an attempt to "manage God,"[17] making us the controlling gods of him, and not vice versa. And that's the very definition of idolatry.

The Emergent Church abstracts Christ into some sort of wispy action. What exact actions? We don't know: being a nice guy? sharing your property? hanging out with non-white people? cleaning up a park? some sort of action derived from a group consensus after a Bible Study? In any event, whoever shares in those actions are the *authentic* Christians or Jesus-followers. Those who, by contrast, simply have faith and believe in Christ are idolaters because they supposedly worship the forms and formal structures by which Christ has come rather than Christ himself. It's a Christ abstracted from his humanity and his Church once again, or alchemically understood, a Christ rarefied from his historicity and ecclesiastical grounding and reunited with the Self. Ultimately it's a rebellion against created forms, a rejection of them as idolatrous, the very position taken by the Gnostics.

Where does that leave us? When a leper sought salvation, he went to a human form named Christ and cried out a formal prayer – with grammar, words, logic and all! – "Christ have mercy." Spelling out the implications of this incarnated, formal presence of the Divine led to the Church's position that, outside of it there is no salvation. In both cases, in Christ's local (pre-ascension) presence and in his mystical (post-ascension) presence, there are forms framed by boundaries. Inside of these boundaries is salvation. Outside is not salvation.

But even here the Emergents tell us that this doctrine, the orthodox doctrine of the incarnation, may need some "emerging from." Already in the Gospel, we are told, Christ's form sort of blended into the background like the nameless cowboy riding off into the dust in *High Plains Drifter*, which (spoiler alert) we learn is a ghost, or at least some sort of supernatural being incarnated as Clint Eastwood.

And that's how Christ truly should be understood, not nailed down by our categorical declarations like "there he is" or "that's Jesus" but allowed to be accessed in freer ways, ultimately causing everything to have a sacramentality to it,[18] because Christ embodies everything. That's the meaning of *relational*, because Christ's presence emerges from your and my relationship. That also leads to the new meaning of *incarnational*, namely, *everything* has Christ in it.

Yet, the profundity of the incarnation is that, though God is everywhere, he has chosen to confine himself to an earthly form in order to be tangibly present for us on a human level. How will any theologian claiming to be Christian work this profound Christian teaching into his novel understanding of the incarnation?

The Emergents answer, *though culture*. The Son of God – the Logos – becomes the particularized presence of God through culture, or cultural forms. Richard John Neuhaus gave a good example of this thinking in his *Freedom for Ministry* (1979), in which he drew out the implications of Christ's incarnation for the Church and warned of the Platonic error when it, say, abstracts Western ideas of worship or mission and declares these to be "universal." Some jump at these words and use them to justify their view that "[t]he visible church is always particular and through many particulars changes the world." Thus, for example, it is not through imposing the Western liturgy or Western dogma on other cultures, but by "adopt[ing] and adapt[ing] certain forms under the direction of God's Word."[19]

It's this very thinking that, on one hand, leads to a U2-charist service using the music of U2 – you can't adapt to culture much more than that! On the other hand, this line of thinking is used to make Westerners feel guilty for "imposing" the historic liturgy on indigenous populations in Africa or Asia. They do things their own way, so the thinking goes, so let them glory in whatever they do.

The idea that anything in Christian theology or practice has universal currency is lost, and in effect the Christian world becomes fragmented into hundreds of mutually incommunicable cultures. Yet, obviously at some level Christianity shares common themes across the world. But what exactly can we retain as we translate Christianity to "the Other" in mission?

The answer ends up being whatever any particular Emergent Christian wants. For the more radical, it means eliminating missions altogether. One Emergent divines this conclusion from the fact that the dog from *Family Guy* talks like a human. "I wonder if [because the dog from *Family guy* talks like a human] we need Missions anymore? I wonder if what we now deem as Missions solely emerged out of a bloody history for dominance (for example: a la Constantine) and what we now have is an over-spiritualized simplified version of domination of that which is other?"[20]

That's the problem with this line of reasoning: to deconstruct the tradition leaves only the subject as the sole determiner of how he receives Christ, who Christ is, and how Christ translates to other Christians. The above-quoted Emergent references Jesus' conversation with the Samaritan woman to conclude "that we should worship God as ourselves,"[21] and for him, the dog from *Family Guy* factors into his theologizing.

The dog from *Family Guy*, U2 services, Pajama Pants Sunday, yeah, I can see where this reconstructed, highly-Americanized Christianity would be incommunicable to Asian Christianity struggling under a communist regime, or an African Church competing with radical Islam.

Whatever the case, this is the unintended consequence of a Christology centered on the "uncreated Word" Luther detected in Anabaptist theology: the supra-incarnate Logos, Christ abstracted from his flesh. Irenaeus' description of the Gnostic view of Christ perfectly fits: they "ascribe whatever they recognize themselves as experiencing the divine Logos!"

It's what St. John specifically designated antichristian, the abstracting of Christ from his flesh into some tickly feeling and then reconstructing him through utterly idiosyncratic forms. As we have been seeing, this vibe has a connection to something relating to the Cosmic Christ of New Age and Gnostic spirituality, the Divine Guide we only incidentally name *Christ* (but could be named *Great Spirit* or *Buddha* or *Sophia* or whatever) that leads us to the Monad. Such a Christ need not be bound or boxed by labels or doctrines or certainly not sacraments: "Most of us are Christians, or were Christians," says one Emergent, "or at least [we] dig Jesus – but not everyone would hang their hats on any of these etymological pegs and that's okay, too." After all, they "believe the thumbprint of the divine is present in all things and all people." Some claim the presence of Jesus within themselves, others claim it is an "internal divinity that exists in everyone."[22]

Jesus the Cosmic Hippy is perhaps not what the early Neo-evangelicals had in mind when they decided to make nice with the world, but unfortunately, when your entire program is to go "from the head to the heart," you don't exactly have the discernment skills to think critically about such things.

That this revolutionary theology emulates exactly what is going on in our *spiritual-but-not-religious* Gnostic culture doesn't seem to bother

Emergent music director Jay Greener. "Although it is a cliche to say it," he says, "this change is a major shift in paradigm. We have entered an era where propositional truth is not nearly so important as the experience of it." Greener knows his own self-parody but can't help himself: always the new era, the new paradigm! *No, this time, it's really REALLY real and authentic!* "If God found it good for his followers to break out of the confines of a religion two millennia ago," says one Emergent, "why should we expect God not to do such a thing in our time?"[23]

But wait, I thought the Self Esteem Reformation was the latest greatest paradigm shift inaugurating the great transformation of the Church. Here we see the wizard behind the curtain and notice Emergent Christianity is no different in its understanding of history than the Consumeristic Christianity it claims to replace. Predictably, it mirrors what's going on in culture, calling to mind the initial Neo-evangelical mission: wherever culture is at, absorb it, become it, live it, and gain members through it. Their bottom line is that of a business: *whatever has mass appeal.*

Mega-church guru Bill Hybels of Willow Creek, always on the cutting edge of the evolving Church industry *vis a vis* its mass appeal, recently completed a study concluding his consumeristic model of church fostered a membership with a mile-wide/inch-deep spirituality. Reacting to evidence suggesting the traditional mega-church paradigm had failed, he said, "We made a mistake. What we should have done when people crossed the line of faith and become Christians, we should have started telling people and teaching people that they have to take responsibility to become 'self feeders.' We should have gotten people, taught people, how to read their bible between service, how to do the spiritual practices much more aggressively on their own."[24]

Hybel's references to "self feeders" and "spiritual practices [done] aggressively on their own" correctly describes where Americans are at spiritually – ever quick to form their own idiosyncratic beliefs – but his conclusion that the Church must once again change its paradigms to appeal to this ethos only highlights the inherent nihilism of his entire project.

What after all is the difference between the "Self-directed" Boomer worshiper in his khakis and polo shirt who wants rousing but shallow music and the "Self-feeding" Millennial worshiper with his tattoos and piercings bringing his personal musings on last night's foray into Theresa of Avila or Emerson or Bob Dylan, whose services "have an arty, counterculteral tone"?[25] It might be Neo-evangelicalism's left side of their brain competing with the right side,[26] but it's still all about the Self. Emergent Church writer Tim Conder describes how he had to eat crow when he came back from an Emergent gathering armed with what he thought were revolutionary ideas, only to find out his beloved Emergent Church "had retained many of its radical, missional values from its genesis in the early 1970s."[27]

Neo-evangelical author Matt Mikalatos humorously describes the yin-yang tension between these flip sides of the Neo-evanglical coin. On one hand, there's the older, more traditional Evangelicalism where "Jesus waits for us outside the church door every Sunday morning – or, with a slightly disapproving frown, on Saturday night. *What, you can't make time on Sunday morning?* He smells our breath for cigarettes. He checks to make sure we're carrying our Bibles. (Partial credit for having it on your smartphone.) He returns our hip flasks to us after sniffing its contents. He takes out a tape measure to make sure the hems of women's dresses aren't too far removed from their knees. He makes sure the men wear collared shirts."

On the other hand, there is Neo-evangelicalism's newest incarnation, the Emergent Church. Mikalatos continues, "Not certain that's the church for us, we head downtown to another church – one that meets in a pub and where Jesus leans against a wall, his hair in dreads, wearing an old, beat-up army jacket for ironic effect. This Jesus has a checklist, too. He checks ID cards at the door to make sure everyone's the right age (old enough to get into a pub, young enough to fit in). He hands out pints and watches through narrowed eyes to make sure we're free enough in Christ to drink. He checks wrists and ankles to make sure there's some ink – a few Hebrew words or a tiny fish or the blue outline of a dove."[28]

So where does that leave us? What's the end game?

A greater exhibition of the endpoint of the Neo-evangelical ethos could not be mustered than the narrative arc of pastor Spencer Burke, "a longish-haired laid-back surfer type," in other words, one of them authentic, Emergent types.[29]

Burke stands in the forlorn frontiers of Neo-evangelicalism's futuristic vision, the Dude Lebowski of Neo-evangelicalism. He first worked at a Mariner's Church, a mega-church, but was unfulfilled. He moved on to a more Emergent-style ministry, where his flock met in parks and homes. But this model proved too institutional; perhaps they fought over which picnic table to sit at. Finally, he "abandoned house church in favor of home church." The punchline? "I think there is a major transition afoot in the church," he told an interviewer as they sat "in [his] cluttered garage."[30]

Evidently missing the last major paradigmatic transition which came a fortnight ago, Burke believes we are on the threshold of a spiritual resurgence which will occur "in people's lives outside of the structures of the church . . . [a] general spirituality where labels aren't important, where the idea that there is one right way to worship will be rejected." This movement will be a new Reformation, one not centered on confessions and doctrinal formulations. "Instead of finding what divides us we're moving together toward what unites us."[31] And what exactly is that? It's a focus on deeds.

Yes, he really did come up with that, having emerged out of the emerging church to be the emerging vanguard of Neo-evangelicalism's next incarnation, the home church. How is this one different than any of the other Anabaptist-millenarian sects shedding off yesterday's skin over the past 800 years (the snake was a symbol of Gnosticism for this reason; see the 2014 movie, *Noah*)? Those Emergents are tools, we suspect, caught up in their Emergent categories of thinking, all their terms and ways of talking, expecting the pack to speak in similar terms: *conversations, stories, narratives, followers of Jesus, authentic, sacramental, embodied, incarnational.* Just more idolatry of forms and categories by which we control God! But Burke's new paradigm will be really different . . . because it's just him . . . alone in his cluttered garage . . . no labels . . . alone with his deeds.

That Burke believes his way of thinking is (a) new and (b) genuine highlights both his abysmal knowledge of history as well as human nature. But again, if it's all heart and no head, what possible safeguards from the head would prevent such foolishness?

✧ Chapter 16 ✧

Neo-Evangelical Gnosis

Neo-Evangelicalism's Gnostic Roots

Harold Bloom writes, "Southern Baptists [*Neo-evangelicals* would be a more accurate label] call themselves Christians, but like most Americans they are closer to ancient Gnostics than to early Christians."[1]

To glean through the mountains of Neo-evangelical materials from pamphlets, papers, reports, television ministries, conferences, and whatnot is to bump over and over again into those Gnostic traits laid down in the second chapter. Examples from Neo-evangelicalism (and those that look up to them) have peppered our study.

Leland Jamison identifies four characteristics of nineteenth century revivalism that Neo-evangelicalism retains yet today: (1) millenarianism, (2) universalism, (3) individual illumination, and (4) perfectionism.[2] We've worked with millenarianism in the previous section and saw its relationship with Gnosticism. We've touched on universalism in Emergent syncretism and in the "spilling over the boundaries" effects of music.

The latter two traits deserve a bit more attention.

Individual Illumination

Neo-evangelicalism, even if it establishes the Bible as the sole authority, leaves the interpretation of it up to the individual, which means that the rules of interpretation – a hermeneutic – cannot be *imposed* from the outside (from a pope, a council, a creed, a confession, a tradition, or any such thing). *My Creed is the Bible!* the Neo-evangelical proudly says, and for such a one, his own internal resources will supply the governing rules of interpretation. Why? Because these internal resources come directly from the Holy Spirit.

In effect the Bible becomes incidental. Simple logic says, if Person A and Person B come upon two different truths from a single authoritative statement, and both truths are considered valid in themselves, then that single authority really is not an authority at all. One wonders in awe how a mega-church pastor can divine the most amazing things about finances or personal wellness based on his reading of, say, the book of Joshua. I once watched with bafflement a popular television preacher explain how Jesus' healing of the lame man at the pool of Siloam teaches us how to get out of our comfort zones and hug our children. After all, he added, "to stay in the comfort zone is to stay in the dead zone." My head was spinning trying to figure out what "comfort zone" is in the original Greek.

Such preachers make these leaps not based on what the Scriptures teach but on the basis of what he is, a shaman with a special connection to the divine. If two interpretations contradict, the problem is not the contradiction. The problem is whatever intellectual tool we apply to tease out that contradiction, like logic. Logic is a sinister tool insinuated into Western thinking, precisely what we're *emerging* out of.

The Bible, the Emergents taught us, doesn't use logic. It's a story, a story we're continuing yet today. Such verses as "This is my body" can mean anything anyone wants it to mean for one's personal story, save "This is my body." One Emergent tells us it means we should buy "organic, locally grown food."[3] The fact that for two millennia the verse meant something akin to "This is my body" baldly displays the untrustworthiness of man's traditions and the gross apostasy of the Church, the sort imposing Westernized modes of thinking onto God's Word, yielding exactly that crazy conspiracy of logic and grammar allowing phallo-centric male Church leaders to impose linear conclusions like, "This is my body" means "This is my body."

But my sarcasm misses the point. I recall getting into an argument with a young Neo-evangelical in which I was appealing to the perfect tense of a verb to prove the real presence of Christ's body and blood in the sacrament. He responded, "God is bigger than the perfect tense."

Indeed! And who better to know God's transcendent awesomeness than the subject, whose personal contact with the unformed Holy Spirit trumps grammar, logic, or traditional standards of hermeneutics? We saw how Robert Schuller did precisely this as he came up with his Self-esteem theology.

I also remember a popular and successful pastor in my church body informing us young seminarians that "when I hire a new minister at our congregation, I don't care how much he knows about Greek. All I want to know is if his heart pumps for Jesus." Sure, but what if Jesus spoke Greek? Wouldn't our heart-pounding Jesus-lover want to understand what his lover was saying? Or rather, to be more technical and open the door into a more involved and interesting theological question, what does it mean if the apostles had Jesus speaking Greek (for he most likely spoke Aramaic)? But again . . . let's not get caught up in all that gobbledygook, all that useless book learning . . . what matters is not Jesus or the language Jesus spoke. What matters is the pumping heart, the intensity of one's feelings, for that is where the Holy Spirit is really working.

The consequences of such a program are obvious, the first being anti-intellectualism and the second being relativism.

As to the former, anti-intellectualism certainly explains rising Neo-evangelical universalism. We would expect a mainstream Protestant or Roman Catholic to espouse universalism. It follows their theology, either the natural progression Protestantism has had toward Unitarianism, or the openness divined by liberal Catholics in Vatican II. But when a Pew Forum on Religion and Public Life survey finds that 57% of Neo-evangelicals "believed people who follow religions other than their own can enjoy eternal life" or that "half believed that everyone, atheists included, was going to end up in heaven"[4] – Pew was so surprised by the results they repeated the survey – something is going on.

Somewhere between the message of their leaders (Rick Warren's universalism notwithstanding) and the reception of it, something gets lost. That something is the intellectual component, the ability to defend one's faith intellectually, and it gets lost, literally, in the music. When church is nothing more than entertainment, what do we expect?

But even the leaders aren't excluded, as when ABC News reported that the wave of atheist apologetics from the latter part of the last decade, of the likes of Richard Dawkins, was enough to dismantle the faiths of two Baptist ministers. One of the minister's reflections is telling: "I realized that everything I'd been taught to believe was sort of sheltered, and never really looked at secular teaching or other philosophies."[5]

Understanding Christian teaching over against the popular

philosophies of the day used to be the bread and butter of seminary training, but if one's pastorate merely calls one to have a heart "committed to the Lord" and to feel called – that and a six week online seminary program – should we be surprised?

As to relativism, the evangelicals anticipated the deconstructionists, relativists, and multiculturalists by about a hundred years, when in a pamphlet in the middle of the Second Great Awakening a revivalist encouraged women to "think for themselves" and "with the aid of the Holy Spirit . . . not be governed by the views of any man, or set of men."[6]

But what if the Holy Spirit already established a set of men (we call them apostles) to lay down certain teachings (we call those apostolic)? No matter, for the author submits himself to his own creed: "I believe it to be the solemn duty of every individual to search the Scriptures for themselves."[7]

Evangelical Nancy Pearcey defends the inherent subjectivity of Evangelicalism by claiming, "Like the Pietists before them . . . [the Evangelical's] goal was to cultivate a *subjective* experience of *objective* biblical truths."[8] She regrets how when Evangelical revivalistic groups broke off from mainline denominations, they broke away from their objective confessional standards and took on an anti-intellectual character. Curiously she speaks as if the breakaway habits of Evangelical groups are the exception, not something written in the Evangelical DNA. But what do we expect will happen when you begin with the premise that the forms of objective standards are inferior to, if not deceptive substitutes for, subjective experience? It's one thing to speak of objective standards in the abstract, but quite another to put form to those objective standards. Confessions or creeds? Those are "man's traditions." Logic and grammar? Those are Western intellectual tools boxing God in. Popes or clergy? Ha! That's a bunch of men telling us what to think.

The focus on personal illumination presents a paradox, then. How do we maintain an objective, unifying doctrine when each person has personal access to God's illumination? The Anabaptists with their dozens of sects certainly provided no guidance. The Church Growth answer to the paradox was to water down doctrine, focus on the Self, and ignore the crazy results. Unity will be based on consumer choice and style – what Becky wants – rather than on objective doctrinal subscription: *we're the "beautiful people" church, we're the "pajama pants" church*, and so on. The Emergent Church solution is to emphasize the *conversation* going on among the variant intellectual traditions, through which the Church along with my personal growth will emerge. But where is the uniting element? We saw above that for some on the fringe, it's the Cosmic Christ that doesn't hang on "etymological" pegs. *You call him tomAYto; I call him tomAHto.* And for others, non-Western cultures can't join the conversation because of the incommunicableness of cultures. They have to keep to their own – the dog from *Family Guy* says so.

Such a situation is indeed a crisis, the sort that Mark Noll confronts in his *Scandal of the Evangelical Mind* (1995), in which he lays out for critique the anti-intellectualism of Neo-evangelicalism. He too cites the Pietists as ground zero for Evangelical subjectivism, recognizing how Pietism "played a part in developing the humanistic romanticism of the nineteenth and twentieth century." Once the subjective becomes determinative, it should be no surprise if one's personal ideas "spun off as meteorites with no fixed center."[9]

The millennialism going hand in hand with Evangelicalism doesn't help. If we're on the threshold of Christ's return, what need is there for book learning and intellectualism? Such is the thought process we saw repeatedly among the millenarians. But the habit continues today. Evangelical preacher Martyn Lloyd-Jones complained already in 1941, "the enduring influence of movements in the early nineteenth century . . . which emphasized the imminence of the Second Advent or the availability of gifts of prophecy in a manner . . . lessened the need for scholarship."[10]

Today the millenarian spirit translates into the *latest greatest paradigm* shifts some new trendy Evangelical author, some *futurist* reveals to us, and woe betide the pastor or theologian who invokes the wisdom of the past to address the new thinking. Like the millenarians, the immediate work of the Holy Spirit on the individual soul – at least as sanctioned by whatever "leader" is doing the job – trumps any objective standard save that of the leader. Ultimately things degenerate into pure enthusiasm. We recall the handsome and dramatic John Bockelson running naked through the streets claiming revelations from God for his Anabaptist flock, particularly the gullible women, that element the New Age tells us are better equipt in the intuitive department.

George Barna may not be running naked, but I don't mind saying this Emperor of Church Growth thinking, along with "organic church" guru Frank Viola, has no clothes. Their book, *Pagan Christianity* lays their cards down clearly: they believe that just about every doctrine and practice in the Christian Church is a bastardized compromise with pagan practice, a departure from pristine early church doctrine and practice. Even the Emergent Church falls victim to their critical knife.

They embrace the "apostate Church" thesis of Christian history referred to in Chapter Three. The Church began with the right footing for about three minutes before Satan took over and turned it into Churchianity, with creeds, infant baptism, the real presence in Holy Communion, and other *traditions of man*. Soon Satan instituted Sunday School and altar calls and Christmas and Easter, pulpits and pews and music teams and choirs and clergy and just about everything anyone would ever connect to the idea *Church*.

Evidently they've discovered the next paradigm of Church, the aforementioned "organic church," which falls in line with the Anabaptist tradition and amounts to a house church where people come together like the pieces of a puzzle and organically manifest the Body of Christ. At one point, to prove their point that most Christians are not truly Christ-centered, they challenge: *how can you say that Christ is the head of your congregation if, say, I were to come into your congregation and had a message from Christ to give you, and you didn't let me speak.*

Again, a remarkable statement, but what in other contexts would be called a delusion of grandeur – someone claiming to speak for God – is here accepted because the followers accept the premise: God speaks to individuals internally outside of the context of traditional canonical (to say nothing of intellectual or academic) authorities.

Of course, as with the Anabaptist sects, this leads to chaos and confusion. An Associated Press article reports on the house church movement, "Sometimes groups with diverse religious backgrounds break up over doctrinal issues or personality conflicts, moving on until they find or make a better fit."[11]

Barna and Viola acknowledge the fallacies of all these other modern church movements and all these errant, chaotic tendencies, which is why they spend a book or two delineating clearly and exactingly (*achtung!*) what a true, organic church really is. Toward the end of their *Pagan Christianity*, they ask, "Having read this book, you must make a decision: Will you act upon what you have read, or will you simply be informed?"[12]

Must? Who do these people think they are? The answer is they believe they are God's instrument and hand in modern history, God's modern prophets. And, though an "organic church" is supposed to develop naturally and freely and involves all the people, without clergy and laity (another pagan distinction, they say), still, the movement needs the likes of Barna and Viola to guide it, name it, plant it, midwife it, and define the fallacious versions of their model. But don't confuse this with authoritarianism or a cult of personality – two people rejecting all that preceded them in order to set up their own idiosyncratic system, and then telling everyone they must hear them – no, they're just the mouthpiece for what you "deep down in [y]our hearts really know to be true," as Schuller said when *he* was that mouthpiece.

They are a good example of the next natural step of the *God-speaks-to-me* habit we've seen in all Gnostic spiritualities. The progression goes like this: *God speaks to me. He also speaks to you. He's the collective Spirit uniting us all, and sometimes one person embodies that collective Spirit to help guide and lead you, and that person is, well, me.*

Heidegger, we recall, began as the granddaddy of existentialism and ended up a fascist. The idea is "Be yourself, feel the universal spirit in the depths of your Self, join the flow, and look over there, there's a leader embodying that spirit. Follow him."

Consequently Gnostic spirituality is obsessed with leadership. Barna with one hand slaps the notion of Christian clergy, but with the other hand he receives money for his seminars on "Developing Leaders for Ministry: Turning Pew Warmers Into Dynamic Leaders."[13]

Gnostic clergy as we saw were called *leaders*, (Gr. *prostatēs*), not *bishop* or *pastor* or *minister* or *priest*. These latter, orthodox terms suggest an office rooted in the duality you need when you administer a formal doctrine or sacramental gifts. It's really sort of an obvious point: a gift can't be a gift (grace) unless it begins as distinct and external to the one receiving it, hence the need for a giver of that gift. The Gnostic *leader* by contrast was the one endowed internally with the *gnosis*, the *charismata*, the spirit of Christ infusing him with his very person so he can lead others into the same internal apotheosis in an almost shamanistic sense. The string of personalities fitting this model take us from the ancient world to today, to pick just a few: Simon Magus, Nicolai, Carpo, Montanus, Cerenthis, John of Winterthur, John Capek, Thomas Müntzer, John Matthys, John Bockelson, John Wesley, Charles Finney, Rick Warren, Joel Olsteen. What these characters all have in common, aside from the name *John*, is their status as avatars of gnosis, people endowed immediately with the divinity, around which the enlightened gather.

Leadership is a huge business in American Christianity. Take out the *changing paradigm* talk, and the weekend retreat at the hotel might cease altogether were it not for *leadership* talk. At such conferences Christians will learn the art and techniques of leadership, however it is defined by the current sociological theories on leadership.

I once attended a leadership conference where we watched clips of movies after which our breakout groups were supposed to evaluate what sort of leadership was being used. After a few minutes of chatting, the leader of the conference raised his hand in a gesture akin to a salute, and we were all supposed to follow suit, raising our hands in a similar gesture as we hushed up. I know, I know, it's the Boy Scout salute, their method of shutting everyone up, but I couldn't let the unsavory image go. I asked my breakout buddies, "Is this appropriate? We're at a leadership conference, and the leader raises his arm in a gesture, and we all follow suit. Should we also click our heels and say 'heil' to *der Führer* as well? Something unsavory about this."

Gnostic leadership centers on the personality cult, the charismatic figure. Leadership training in the church is all about developing one's ability to be that charismatic salesman, that man with the gleaming smile, the bright eyes, the winsome demeanor, the engaging conversation. Neither Moses with his stuttering speech nor St. Paul with his weak bodily presence would pass for good leaders in today's atmosphere.

At this particular conference, we were told to go back to our congregations and *act genuine*. How does one *act genuine*? The very notion is an oxymoron. *Acting* by definition is manifestly to *not* be genuine. The Biblical word *hypocrite* means "one who plays a part on the stage, a player, actor."[14] Yet this is what we were told to do. But the leadership program came by its attitude honestly, because playing the part of being genuine is exactly what we are told to do in our culture: *Be the unique you by buying what we tell you to buy. Be a genuine leader by doing what I tell you to do.* It's all the same paradoxical message that goes back to the narrative arc of Heidegger's life: *be yourself, join the flow, follow the leader.* It's Bruno's magician again, manipulating his subjects to believe they are choosing on their own.

What naturally follows, as we saw in the numerous sects of Anabaptism, is schism. There is no central unifying doctrine or ecclesiastical authority; there are only multiplying leaders all claiming direct messaging from God. Of course schism will result. Phyllis Hodgson aptly describes mysticism as "a word which starts in 'mist' and ends in 'schism'."[15] *Schism* is the Greek word for *division*. Morris Berman bluntly observes: "Western religious experience [i.e. Gnostic experience] is essentially schismogenic in nature. There is no end to this game, and it is still with us today in the form of charismatic movement, 'born-again' Christians, cults and sects of various sorts, and even political splinter groups."[16]

The only explanation for this schismogenic nature of Neo-evangelicalism is Gnostic elitism. After all, as Barna and Viola asked us, *Now that I have told you the truth, and Jesus is speaking through me, what are you going to do with it?* I tremble to think what will happen if I think what they say is garbage.

No I don't.

The Perfectibility of the Soul: the Journey of the Self

Central to Neo-evangelicalism's salvation program is its belief in the perfectibility of the soul, defined in any number of ways. The Puritans claimed to be pure; the Pietists emphasized personal sanctification; the Holiness movement claimed immediate holiness for the converted. We recall John Bockelson's rigid moral code imposed in the city of Münster. Nineteenth century Sabbatarian and temperance movements invoked this vibe. Even twentieth century "positive thinking" is a form of moral, or at least personal, perfectionism. Contemporary obsession with Self-improvement is a close cousin to Neo-evangelicalism's perfectionism, and both are rooted in the hermetic (and alchemical) belief that the human soul can literally change its constitution to become better. Original sin and its stain on human nature can even be undone, completely, if one is fully dedicated to the program.

As we've seen, fantasies of human perfectionism fuel the myth that government is not a negative check on human behaviors – itself checked by its three branches – but a positive means of collective societal improvement. This understanding is rooted in nineteenth century Social Gospel teaching, which itself spawned from a fusion of Evangelical revivalism and social evolutionism.

Critical to the Evangelical is that moment of conversion entailing a deliberate act of *surrendering* to Christ's lordship and becoming a new creation, a moment that Carl Jung also commandeered for his own Gnostic psychology when he coined the term *metanoia*, the Greek word for *repentance*.

Like the existentialists, *choice* is the sacralized moment when one's new life begins, which explains why infant baptism is rejected: babies and children hardly fit as candidates for the existential experience; it's more a teen thing. But what this moment of choice means for Evangelical conversion has a different meaning for different Evangelicals.

For some the focus is on issues of personal morality: sexual purity and sobriety seem especially important to them. As I was told once in college by an acquaintance who left the Lutheran faith to become a Neo-evangelical: "Before I was born again, I used to masturbate; now I don't anymore." (I should have retorted that his self-obsessed onanism simply moved from the fleshly regions to the spiritual.)

For others the focus is on issues of societal morality: care for the poor and speaking against public greed exercises them. The flow from older, more Puritanical morality to updated, socially-conscious morality may simply be an issue of "No one can stop masturbating and sexing around [as evidenced by the studies on sexuality among Evangelicals] but I still have to be perfect. Now, what would Jesus *really* do? He'd feed the poor! Jesus said nothing, at least not a lot, about sex, but he did feed the 5,000!"

This moralism explains the popularity of gimmickry like the WWJD (*What Would Jesus Do*) bracelets. It also explains the latest trendy phrase Neo-evangelicals use for themselves, "followers of Jesus." This designation is meant to differentiate themselves from all those "churchianity" types who think they're saved just because they've been baptized, believe in Jesus, and go to Church. No, these Jesus-followers *really* follow Jesus because they go on mission trips, clean up parks, and help out at soup kitchens, or because they've kept themselves sexually pure (or at least to the idea of sexual purity). "Deeds, not Creeds," says Rick Warren.

This perfectionism strain would seem to be surprising if we regarded Neo-evangelicalism as Protestant, as a Reformation movement. Wasn't the Reformation all about being saved by faith, not by works?

The premise is wrong. First off, Neo-evangelicalism is not a Reformation movement any more than the previous millenarian movements were reform movements. Their roots go deeper than Luther's Reformation, reaching back and fanning into flames the dormant, radical-millenarian embers of Bohemia. Including but also going beyond millenarianism, Neo-evangelicalism comfortably finds kinship with the general preoccupation of the Cult of the Self that arguably has occupied Western imagination since the Middle Ages.

What does this mean?

In our studies the twelfth century has popped up occasionally as a watershed point in Western History. One commentator says that the West "rediscovered its Self" in this century. The Cathar, troubadour, as well as millenarian movements all came of age around this point. This was the high point of medieval scholasticism and several monastic movements. It was the beginning of medieval alchemy and other nascent semi-mystical psychological programs, to say nothing of church-sanctioned mysticism itself. The roots of Neo-evangelicalism, in terms of its focus on the Self, would better be located in this time frame in which questions of faith blur with questions of Self.

Ronald W. Dworkin in an essay on the modern obsession for therapy describes the twelfth century in terms of the cult of eros we've covered in connection to it: "Love ideology then infected organized religion. Previously, Christianity had viewed sensual love as a kind of sickness. In the 12th century, love ideology began to penetrate Christianity, causing sensual love to lose its sinful quality. Over time, many clergymen envisioned a new alliance between religious love and sensual love, one that would let people enjoy the happiness of a private passion while, at the same time, forever coaxing them to widen their circle of romantic love to include all mankind, thereby spreading romantic love ever wider and wider, thus moving them closer to God's perfection."[17]

During this period, mysticism began to embrace the concept of a *spiritual marriage*, that is, a marriage of the soul to the universal spirit they believed to be the supra-incarnate Christ (the Logos). Eros ideology became sublimated in a highly individualistic program of mystical ascent. *Church as meditation point* slowly became replaced by the *universal spirit to which each true mystic had access in his solitary Self.*

Christianity, in other words, was evolving into a Self-help program. Far from joining Luther in his highly personal confrontation and final rejection of this path, the early Neo-evangelicals embraced this tradition and forsook all pretenses of sacraments or ritual whatsoever.

Perry Miller, for example, brilliantly observed how the Puritans "liberated men from the treadmill of indulgences and penances, but cast them on the iron couch of introspection."[18] This couch takes on literal qualities in the "anxious benches" that revivalist Charles Finney (1792-1875) provided for the "almost saved."[19] This obsession with the Self obviously translates today into the mountains of Self-help devotional literature littering the Evangelical literary landscape. To be Evangelical is to have one's heart ever besotted over the murmurings of the interior life, not unlike, well, just about everyone else in modern life, who themselves have gotten to this point through other intellectual streams.

Was this the work of Luther, to reduce the Western world to pathological navel-gazing of the likes he himself underwent? Absolutely not. Luther's story is actually more about becoming free from the iron couch of introspection. What then? Ultimately it comes down to an understanding of what faith means.

If faith is seen objectively, as in *"the* faith," this would be more in line with Reformation thinking. "The faith" is something external and confessed. It forms the worship of its adherents, literally putting itself on their lips. It remains central in the Church as a lodestar, something into which the young grow and the sinner returns. It doesn't change. According to this understanding of faith, even a Reformation Church can continue the medieval formula "outside the Church is no salvation." "The faith" cares little for the psychological ups and downs of the soul. Nor when "the faith" is understood objectively do we have to play a theological game of Twister to explain the faith (or lack thereof) of infants or the mentally infirm. "The faith" is a form into which one may be put, and his personal appropriation of (as opposed to *experience of)* that faith, is a secondary focus.

If faith is seen primarily in psychological terms, then we're moving beyond Luther to the more Anabaptist traditions. Luther understood that when doubts and temptations attacked a suffering soul, the best advice is to reflect on the truth, "I am baptized!" In other words, even one's personal faith finally rests *extra nos*, outside of the person. Not so the Evangelicals.

Furthermore, appealing to John Calvin and his Reformed confessionalism doesn't make the problem go away. Describing Calvinism's Christological foundations, theologian David Scaer writes, "The Lutherans saw the old heresy of Nestorianism being revived in Reformed [i.e. Calvinist] Christology, in which the divine and human natures of Christ were understood as incapable of embracing each other. Platonism's principle that the transcendent ideal is incapable of full expression in the material things of this world was responsible for the aberrant Christology of Arianism as well as Nestorius and now was seen again in the Christology of Calvin and his followers."[20]

Nestorianism was an ancient heresy which believed Jesus was not God and man in one person (two natures; one person) but God and man in two persons (two natures; two persons). Nestorians made a distinction between Christ and God. Mary could be called the Christ-bearer, but not the God-bearer (Theotokos). The only way to arrive at this point is by denying that the Person named Jesus is wholly God in human flesh.

Whether or not John Calvin himself is justly attributed the quote, later Calvinism adopted the principle that "the finite cannot contain the infinite," leading them to deny that in the Eucharistic bread is a communion in the real, physical Body of Christ. It's the same theology driving my Neo-evangelical student's "God is bigger than the perfect tense" or the "God can't be boxed" ideas we see over and over again.

This fundamental disconnect between the physical properties of Jesus and his divinity poses a problem: no longer is salvation located in Christ's ecclesiastical, physical presences (the preached word and sacraments), because no longer can God's work be truly identified in these earthly forms, things for which the incarnation of Jesus sets the ultimate premise for God doing precisely that. Nor can man find solace in such external things as baptism or communion. These are signs, rather, to something higher, something to which the faith of one's heart ascends. But how does faith know when it has connected to this ascendant comfort? The answer boils down to some internal testament of the Holy Spirit, precisely the sort of psychologically-charged soteriology identified in Puritanism and later Evangelicalism.

This is the exact "iron couch of introspection" to which Calvinism ultimately directs the soul. One is forced to turn inside himself in his understanding of Christian faith, because all external things are seen as disconnected from what is ultimately true.

Hence also the preoccupation with Heideggar's "authenticity" and its overuse in Evangelical-speak today. Faith becomes blurred with the Self and the Self's journey and development.

Needless to say, there's gold in that there journey, gold in the form of motivational seminars for ever new perfectionistic, revivalistic movements, new books to be sold, or new models of ministry to peddle at the hotel conference.

This is what we see as Calvinism's history evolved. It was almost inevitable that it would eventually give way and prepare the way for more typically Anglo-American Evangelicalism of the Pietist and Puritan variety, offering a cocktail of theology centered not on the Church, but on one's own inner journey, development, and sanctification. For the Puritan and Pietist, one's election is made evident not by his allegiance to objective creedal standards, but rather by the purity and sincerity of his deeds. Of course this leads in turn to more self-doubt and despair, which in turn invites each Sunday Service, each retreat, each new best seller, to be a new revival of one's spirit: *this time it will really stick!*

The Puritans carried the perfectionist flame to American shores climaxing in the First Great Awakening of the mid-eighteenth century. Also in the Second Great Awakening preceding the Civil War a "great surge of perfectionism . . . swept almost every denomination."[21]

This perfectionism in turn *always* led to social movement: again, what happens in the individual soul can have implications for society at large; individual perfectibility translates to societal perfectibility, or utopianism. The Puritans in both England and America inaugurated an intense program of social engineering, and the perfection demanded of Charles Finney's revivals fueled the social movements of the early nineteenth century, most notably abolitionism, sabbatarianism, and temperance, but also several experiments in communalism like the Oneida Community. The Holiness movements of the latter nineteenth century equipt the Social Gospel with its imperative.

If we might ask our ongoing, deflating question again, "What happened?"

What happened is that these movements failed,[22] each one of them. They all gave way to new movements, each one believing itself to be the next great thing.

Greg Hawkins, an executive pastor at Willow Creek, was asked what his church was going to do now that evidence showed his seeker service paradigm had failed. "Our dream is that we fundamentally change the way we do church. That we take out a clean sheet of paper and we rethink all of our old assumptions. Replace it with new insights. Insights that are informed by research and rooted in Scripture. Our dream is really to discover what God is doing and how he's asking us to transform this planet."[23]

Something's getting transformed, but it ain't the planet.

✧ Postlude ✧

God Outside His Box

The Cover of this Book

Gnosticism punctures the contours of form. The puncture causes leakage and dramatically blurs the very borderline between Self and God. This foundational move leads to a leakage of everything else, the blurring of the contours of what words mean, the blurring of the borderline between Self and Other. Formal doctrine, formal practice, and formal ethics all leak beyond the contours of their forms into my heart. This is no problem, however, because my heart itself blurs with the divine. Whatever I feel is divine.

Jesus himself leaks into my heart; I derive personal authority not from traditionally formed structures, the extent to which I am in conformity with them, but from my own "personal relationship with Jesus." What need is there for Creed, for catechism, for formal worship, or for formal ethics? Forms steadily topple like dominoes before trending Neo-evangelicalism: first fall the worship forms (replaced by Contemporary Worship); then go the doctrinal forms (replaced by doctrinal minimalism: "as long as you have Jesus in your heart"); next go creedal forms (replaced by the "deeds, not creeds" mantra combined with a budding universalism); and finally as we are now seeing, ethical forms give way as well (young Neo-evangelicals increasingly accepting homosexuality).

One popular phrase housing this anti-formalistic Gnostic way of thinking is, as we've seen, "Letting God out of his box." As I designed the

354

cover for this book, I knew I wanted to incorporate several images. I wanted to select a New Age symbol. I found that easily enough. Behind this first image I wanted an American theme, given the title. And then I wanted the outline of a worshiper at a praise service that's hard to distinguish from any other rock concert. I thought the juxtaposition of those images would be unsubtle enough to make my point.

I found a great picture at a blog entitled "My Word His Message." Along with the picture was the following testimony. It is reproduced verbatim here:

"*I recently attended a leadership seminar and let me just say that it was amazing. I learned so much that weekend, but if I brought home anything it was, that there is great liberty in loving and worshipping my Father.*

"*The worship service was like attending a concert, it was loud and fun and anointed. Men, women and children were dancing wherever they had the most room, they were dancing and singing before the Lord.*

"*The energy was amazing, it was contagious. And yes they even ran around the church. I know some of you might be thinking "what?" But trust me when I say it was done in order in fun and all for Jesus. Some of you may be content standing up in a quiet church just clapping your hands and that's perfectly ok. God honors the heart regardless if you prefer quiet or loud.*

"*Personally I prefer loud, when it comes to worship anyway. I want to dance and be free I want to lift my hands and my voice without fear or condemnation. And I did.*

"*The praises of the people created such an amazing atmosphere. The worship leader, a true psalmist took us into heartfelt worship and a powerful anointing. People were weeping and falling on their faces. God filled that place like I had not felt in a very long time.*

"*And I believe it was because the people were hungry, they cried out to him, they just loved on Him with no regard to time. It brought tears to my eyes thinking about how this act of intimate worship must have brought great joy to God.*

"*I believe that is what most of us are missing in our personal lives and our church's. True Worship. The kind that says, "nothing else matters." The kind that says, "I'm not leaving here until I get what I came for, prayer, healing etc."*

"*A lot of you have asked why you can't feel God, well maybe God is using his humble servant today to let you know how God will be manifested in your life. Through Worship!! God says he inhabits the praises of his people, so if we praise him he will enter in.*

"I believe we need to stay in an attitude of praise. Praise Him when you don't feel like it, Praise Him even when you don't feel Him moving. God wants to know that you love Him for who He is, not for what He can give you.

"I believe if we are to truly see God in all His glory we need to take Him out of the box that we have so carefully placed Him in. Quit playing Church and start seeking His face, quit worrying about scaring off new believers. The Holy Spirit is a gentleman. If the Holy Spirit is allowed to move freely without restrictions then people are going to come to church but more importantly they will stay.

"Some people have this idea that they can minimize what the Holy Spirit wants to do in their services and still experience all that God has for them. While, we can certainly limit what God wants to do in our services, it will never be all that it was meant to be as long as man is running the church and not God.

"Regardless of what's going on in your church, you can Praise Him in your own way. Just continue Praising Him, loving Him and seeking Him and He will gladly enter in."[1]

This testimonial puts a face on the Gnostic spirit we've been hunting. Like most Americans, at least as the polls are telling us, the author wants something traditional Christian worship hasn't provided.

This worship service is the remedy. The service "let's God outside the box." The "box" restricts God with all the traditional dogma and language making up traditional Christian doctrine, worship, and practice. Like a bunch of whirling dervishes, or like the liberated characters in *The Matrix*, song and dance and running around the building demonstrate a new understanding of God. Tapped into God, the worshipers have "great liberty" from all restrictions, freed from formal worship. Here is Gnostic antinomianism, an iconoclastic liberation from form itself.

Curiously, while all this liberated fun is going on, the Holy Spirit himself is somehow the only gentleman there, politely awaiting an invitation, still in the grips of those uptight rules of formality. Perhaps he should hang loose, surrender to the party, let go and let, er, himself?

Feelings dominate her review. The worship was favorably described as "loud and fun . . . the energy was amazing . . . an amazing atmosphere . . . heartfelt worship . . . people were weeping and falling on their faces . . . I had not felt [that way] in a very long time . . . it brought tears to my eyes . . . this act of intimate worship." The writer proposes this sort of worship for those who complain they can't "feel God." Feelings are the sacrament, the true contact with God, evidenced by

America's current ironclad proof of authenticity: tears.

Of course her standard for authentic worship is the rock concert: "I believe that [the rock concert worship] is what most of us are missing in our personal lives and our church's. True Worship." Fine, but how does she distinguish her authentic feeling of wholeness and healing from the same feeling claimed by people at a rock concert, by people extracted from their comfort zones in the weekend retreat's breakout sessions, by people zoning out in front of the computer or TV, or by people on crack?

Yes, lots of people have that Gnostic sense of despair because something is missing. That's because the American soul is raised on perpetual dissatisfaction, from marketing, from utopian promises of "a better world," and from utopian promises about the Self's possibilities. Drugs assuage the dissatisfaction, which explains why we are a drug-seeking, addictive society, whatever those drugs are, legal or illegal, identified as such or not. Do a websearch on the phrase "Jesus is my drug" and see the almost 300,000 hits. You can get the T-shirt.

Her personal preferences are determinative: "Personally I prefer loud, when it comes to worship anyway. I want to dance and be free I want to lift my hands and my voice without fear or condemnation. And I did." *I prefer . . . I want . . . I want.* But that's OK because "it was done in order in fun and all for Jesus . . . God honors the heart regardless if you prefer quiet or loud."

We wonder what's really central if her *preferences* are meant to stay intact absent any repentance, any yielding to catholic forms uniting all ages and places, or any change in his heart from secular to sacred as she enters the Church. Worship is a time when "God honors" her heartfelt desires and accepts her just the way she is. It's the perfect testimony in a day when the Self and its preferences replace God. It's the default existentialism in the American soul.

Which is why it shouldn't surprise us when she writes, "maybe God is using his humble servant today to let you know how God will be manifested in your life."

Of course God is using her because God is using everyone, that is, anyone who recognizes a "God thing" whenever a sizzling frisson pulsates through his nerves. So long as we just let go and stop restricting that feeling, the Holy Spirit can do his thing. All that other worship is "man . . . running the church and not God," but not when this happens. No, this is something entirely different, something special, something divine.

The gnosis couldn't be more clear.

✧ Conclusion ✧

America at the Crossroads

Gnostic America is about a culture at the crossroads. It's not that there are two paths we can take theologically, ideologically, or politically. There are lots of those paths. Rather, it's a more fundamental, binary choice about the cosmic architecture by which we will decide those theological, ideological, and political questions in the first place.

Is truth derived from nature and nature's God, from something *extra nos*, outside of us? Or is it derived from the inner Self, *intra nos*? How we answer that question determines, among other things, how we raise our children. Do we draw them out of their little worlds to experience and observe the world in its objective reality? Or do we direct them to their inner spirits, getting them to view their world through an ideological lens because there is no such thing as objectivity?

Will societal rules be informed by tradition, the distillation of human experience (see *supra*, page 42)? Or will tradition be indiscriminately gutted as so much rotted wood from yesterday's cosmic architecture, to be replaced by new laws and codes and enforced societal pressure? How we answer that question determines the extent to which we want the government and its escalating legal regime to replace what used to be simple common sense. I mean, now that traditional marriage has been destroyed, and the "any two people" definition has all but run its course – to be replaced by polyamory, asexuality, and who knows what – now what? If ten random people want to live together and adopt children, but then four want a divorce, leaving the remaining six to care

359

for the children, who's going to sort out that custody mess? The answer is, a highly complex legal regime understood only by a few. Is that the world we want? With tradition forsaken, are we prepared to accept a court simply deciding the definition of marriage willy nilly, because in chaotic situations, people accept arbitrary dictates as a fact of life, anything to bring some order?

Will we live our lives in the real world, where our vision is filled with, you know, real live things? Or will our future be like the movie *Her* (2014), where urbanites engage the real world only incidentally as they stroll though the city plugged into their futuristic smart-devices, talking to the air, enjoying their inner world to their own personal music score, and where the possibility is actually entertained that a man could fall in love with his operating system? Talk about a bizarre commentary on current society. A man is walking around gushingly talking to a woman who is not real, and a majority of movie critics sees this, not as clinical insanity, but as smart and innovative. They've answered the above question, positively contemplating a future "peopled" by phantasms and archetypes, abstractions of humanity. Are we prepared to face on a mass scale what the Hermeticists understood, that melancholy follows the mind saturated in fantasy, drifting saturninely far from the real world?

What about those set in positions of authority? Do we want servants whose task is to administer objective, easily-understood traditions of higher principles, principles seen to be naturally and self-evidently good and true? This is what was once known as the "rule of law." It goes back to Moses himself. Once his father-in-law Jethro visited him in the wilderness while he was swamped with all sorts of judicial cases. Moses had learned in the school of Egypt that Pharaoh embodied both law and divinity, and he was stuck in that way of thinking, but was becoming overwhelmed. Jethro suggested a simple law code everyone could understand and which could be adjudicated by what were in effect lower courts. That became the Ten Commandments. Or was Moses a servant of Yaltabaoth, only putting into effect archontic systems of control – private property, parental authority, respect for individual lives – who would be far better replaced by a leader, a Pharaoh-like law-giver establishing his authority by the force of pure charisma alone? *But*, we are told, *Pharaoh is all of us. Just look at that pyramid. It's one, a collective of perfectly fitted stones all working together . . . but it does need its top.* According to the old cosmic architecture, this is not exactly the American way. But by the reckoning of others, the drones programmed to the wise guidance of the queen bee are more true to evolutionary fate. Is that really what we want? The Borg?

Finally, will the word have primacy over image, or will the image have primacy over the word? And if the latter is the case, as it obviously is, what does it portend when we have a society that doesn't read but gets most of its information through musically-framed messages, ideologically-edited programming, sloganeering sound-bites, phantasy-driven media, and archetype-based marketing? and when confronted with a basic syllogism the mind curls up into a fetal position, begging to get back to its electronically-thrilling pap? *If A = B, and B = C, then . . . aww, screw it!* What does it mean for our democracy that these people vote?

How will American Christianity answer these questions?

Will those who have rejected tradition as so much Pharisaical ritual be equipt to invoke the wisdom of a past they deem unredeemable and irrelevant? When every Christian trend is embraced as the latest outpouring of the Pentecostal spirit and every attempt to be discerning about these trends is dismissed as so much "legalism," how will such a Christianity possibly respond when a mass movement arises having all the marks of a divine movement, but which errs from anything resembling orthodox Christianity?

Will those who frame the Christian Gospel in terms of one's "personal relationship with Jesus" be able to counter those who also claim a special relationship with the divinity within? Perhaps it really is just a matter of names, those "etymological pegs" of the Emergents (see *supra*, page 336), or the "incarnation patterns" of the divine (see *supra*, page 17). I mean, really, who are we to judge another person's personal relationship with God?

Will those contemporary churches which have replaced catechism study and didactic preaching with media-crafted messaging – video montages, drama, everything made visual, everything draped in popular music – prepare the next generation of Christians to understand complex doctrines enough to defend the faith against a rabidly anti-Christian society? How will Christian children respond when they grow up and discover life requires a faith going deeper than the K-Love, amusement park Christianity they'd been fed?

What will happen to that vast body of Christians who were told Christianity is a matter of personal wellness, a competitor in the market for Self-therapy, when these shaky foundations no longer hold? Joel Olsteen says heaven has a warehouse full of blessings with my name on them. The only reason I don't have them is because I don't believe hard enough. What will happen when I finally determine I'm not cut out for this Christianity thing because my faith just doesn't pass muster?

If Ken Ham is to be believed, it's already too late. The next generation is "already gone" (see *supra*, page 114). These are the Millennials who have actuated in their twenties what was in their hearts when they were twelve, that is, Christianity was something best grown out of and left behind. They've made their choice, answered the questions. And of those who remain, one wonders what it portends that 44% of younger evangelicals support gay marriage. It shouldn't be too much of a stretch to observe this position has more to do with cultural trends than with serious Scriptural contemplation, or contemplation on any serious theological thought, but try telling them that. Not only would that require transcending the latest slogans, but it would require considering an authority above the dictates of one's Self, and that is heresy in the religion of Gnosticism.

But nature has a way of being what it is despite people's attempts to deny or reject it, to say nothing of nature's God. Nature, for example, will have the final vote on the gay marriage issue. No matter how hard two men try, they will never ever make a baby. Nature won't allow that. And eventually people will begin asking what the point of marriage was in the first place. Oh yeah, because two certain types of people – biology calls them male and female – make babies. Or again, human nature will have the final vote on the progressive experiment in collectivist action, say, in health care, and if history is a guide, that vote won't end well for progressives. We truly are individuals, not the Borg.

Finally, the law of economic gravity will soon kick in on our national debt as well, reminding us that what can't go on forever won't. Then the fun begins. History teaches that days of leisurely indulgence, the sort which has always begotten Gnosticism, are numbered. It's one thing to shake your fist at the world when living a comfortable existence. Boutique rebellion against Yaltabaoth's systems of control is always fun. It's another thing to be hungry and need a damn bite to eat, or to be cold, because "the system" was finally broken beyond repair. Right around then we hear a galloping sound in the distance. That's the four horsemen coming to do what they are appointed to do.

Marantha.

S. D. G.

✧ Notes ✧

INTRODUCTION: SURVEYING
THE CULTURAL LANDSCAPE

1. Personal experience at Cedar Creek Church, South Campus (2150 South Byrne Road, Toledo, OH 43614), April 7, 2012.
2. Chris Tomlin, "No Chains On Me," *And If Our God Is for Us . . .* , (Sparrow Records, 2010. CD).
3. Harold Bloom, *The American Religion* (New York: Touchstone, 1992), 52-53, 59.
4. The actual quote is, " . . . the young man who rings the bell at the brothel is unconsciously looking for God." Bruce Marshal, *The World, The Flesh, and Father Smith* (Boston: Mifflin Company, 1945), 108.
5. Nnedi Okorafor, "Stephen King's Super-Duper Magical Negroes" *Strange Horizons*, December 12, 2003.
6. Mark Steyn, "Obama in 2-D," *National Review Online*, November 1, 2008. Retrieved from http://www.nationalreview.com/articles/226183/obama-2-d/mark-steyn.
7. James W. Ceaser, "The Roots of Obama Worship: Auguste Comte's Religion of Humanity finds a 21st-century Savior," *The Weekly Standard*, January 25, 2010, Vol. 15, No. 18. Retrieved at http://www.weeklystandard.com/articles/roots-obama-worship.
8. Mark Morford, "Is Obama an enlightened being? / Spiritual wise ones say: This sure ain't no ordinary politician. You buying it?" *San Francisco Chronicle, Web*, June 6, 2008. Retrieved from http://www.sfgate.com/entertainment/morford/article/Is-Obama-an-enlightened-being-Spiritual-wise-2544395.php.
9. *Hardball with Chris Matthews*, MSNBC, June 5, 2009.
10. Former senator Ted Kennedy 's endorsement of Barack Obama for president on January 28, 2008 was typical: "I believe that a wave of change is moving across America. If we do not turn aside, if we dare to set our course for the shores of hope, we together will go beyond the divisions of the past and find our place to build the America of the future."

11. Posted by Nick25 on January 31, 2010. Reference no longer available.
12. CJ Kellman, "17-Year-Old to Facebook: I Exist, and Gender Identity Is Also a Civil Rights Issue," *Huffpost Gay Voices*, May 22, 2012. Retrieved from http://www.huffingtonpost.com/cj-kellman/facebook-gender-identity_b_15348 32.html.
13. Dietrich Bonhoeffer, *Creation and Fall: A Theological Interpretation of Genesis 1–3* (New York: Macmillan, 1966), 46.
14. Genesis 1: 2, 11-12, 24-25.
15. John 1: 1.
16. WIN-Gallup International, 2012, "The Global Index of Religiosity and Atheism," *The Washington Post*, Retrieved from http://articles.washingtonpost.com /2012-08-13/national/35491519_1_ new-atheism-atheist-groups-new-atheists.
17. H. P. Blavatsky, "The Secret Doctrine," *Light*, (London, Vol. VIII, No. 416, December 22, 1888, pp. 634.) Retrieved at http://www. katinkahesselink.net/ blavatsky/ articles/v10/y1888_099.htm.
18. Alexis de Tocqueville, *Democracy in America: Volume 2* (New York: Vintage Books, 1945), 26, 32.
19. Erich Fromm arrives at the term *orientation* through a similar thought process. He writes, "[A]ny satisfying system of orientation implies not only intellectual elements but elements of feeling and sense to be realized in action in all fields of human endeavor. Devotion to an aim, or an idea, or a power transcending man such as God, is an expression of this need for completeness in the process of living." He goes on to give examples of non-theistic religions, and then he concludes, "For lack of a better word I therefore call such systems 'frames of orientation and devotion.'" Erich Fromm, *Man for Himself* (1947; repr., New York: Henry Holt and Company, Inc., 1990), 47-48.
20. *24*, "Day 2: 5:00 p.m.-6:00 p.m.," episode 10, January 14, 2003.
21. Albert Cook, *Thresholds: Studies in Romantic Experience* (University of Wisconsin Press, 1985), 220.
22. Michael Gillespie, "Martin Heidegger," *History of Political Philosophy*, 3rd Ed., edited by Leo Strauss and Joseph Cropsey (Chicago, IL: The University of Chicago Press, 1987), 901.
23. Ibid., 903.
24. Ibid., 905.

CHAPTER I

GNOSTICISM: ANTICHRIST ARISING

1. I John 2: 18.
2. I John 2: 22 – "Who is a liar but he who denies that Jesus is the Christ? He is antichrist who denies the Father and the Son." I John 4: 3 – "every spirit that does not confess that Jesus Christhas come in the flesh is not of God. And this is the spirit of the Antichrist, which you have heard was coming, and is now already in the world." II John 1: 7 – "For many deceivers have gone out into the world who do not confess Jesus Christ as coming in the flesh. This is a deceiver and an

antichrist." (New King James Version)

3. Pope John Paul II, *Crossing the Threshold of Hope*, edited by Vittorio Messori, (New York: Alfred A. Knopf, 1994), 90.

4. Genesis 1: 2 – "The earth was without form, and void; and darkness was on the face of the deep." The Hebrew word תהו (tohu) translated "without form" conforms with the translation "formlessness" suggested by *The New Brown-Driver-Briggs-Gesenius Hebrew-English Lexicon*. (Peabody, MA: Hendrickson Publishers, 1979), 1062.

5. The Hebrew mîn has a debatable meaning, but in general it denotes the intelligible crafting of distinct beings through a process of separating one thing from another. "Ludwif Koehler would have it come from the noun temûnâ 'form' with some such meaning as 'to think out' or to invent." Skinner's International Critical Comentary on Genesis rejects this line of reasoning and selects rather an Arabic root meaning 'to split (the earth in plowing),' with the resulting idea of dividing." *Theological Wordbook of the Old Testament: Volume 1*, edited by R. Laird Harris, Gleason L. Archer, Jr., and Bruce K. Waltke (Chicago: Moody Press, 1980), 505.

6. Warren B. Smith gives a good summary of this tendency in certain New Age figures (Alice Bailey, N. D. Walsch, and B. M. Hubbard), where separation is "an illusion," "not believing you are a part of God," "self-centeredness," "not love," "fear," "hatred," "evil," "Satan," "sin," "sickness," "lawlessness," "crime," and "a 'lack' that must be corrected." Warren B. Smith, *False Christ Coming: Does Anybody Care?* (Magalia, CA: Mountain Stream Press, 2011), 112-113.

7. *Nag Hammadi Library*, "The Gospel of Philip," edited by James M. Robinson (New York: HarperCollins Publishers, 1988), 150.

8. Marilyn Ferguson, *The Aquarian Conspiracy: Personal and Social Transformation in the 1980s* (Los Angelos, CA: J. P. Tarcher, Inc., 1980), 382.

9. Ibid., 367.

10. Ibid., 368.

11. "In keeping with the Gnostics' negative evaluation of materiality, Gnostic saviors were purely spiritual beings who descended from heaven to earth in order to save humanity from further enslavement by the powers of ignorance. . . . Some texts went so far toward Christian incarnationism as to allow that the spiritual Christ entered the flesh of the man Jesus at his baptism. Gnostics did not concede, however, that Christ incarnated as Jesus from his conception onward." Daniel Merkur, *Gnosis: an esoteric tradition of mystical visions and unions* (Albany, NY: State University of New York Press, 1993), 125.

12. *Nag Hammadi Library*, "The Apocryphon of James," 35.

13. Quoted in Wouter J. Hanegraaff's *New Age Religions and Western Culture: Esotericism in the Mirror of Secular Thought* (New York: State University of New York Press, 1998), 193. Original quote, David Spangler & William Irwin Thompson, *Reimagination of the World: A Critique of the New Age, Science, and Popular Culture* (Santa Fe: Baear & Co., 1991), 138.

14. Bloom, *The American Religion*, 32.

15. A blog post from "Rediscovering the Faith . . . " titled "I believe in God but not the Church," retrieved from http://chrisclouse.wordpress.com/2009/01/26/i-believe-in-god-but-not-the-church-part-2/, is a good example of the sentiment:

"One person . . . asked me to develop my thoughts more fully regarding one of the statements I made in my post entitled I believe in God, but not the church. This post is dedicated to that purpose. The phrase I have been asked to develop is found in the following sentence: The more I think about the frustration and disappointment expressed by many toward the modern version of the church with all of its man-made baggage and theological pollution, the more I understand their cry and identify with their feelings. What do I consider man-made baggage and theological pollution? This is a great question, one with a rather surprisingly simple answer. Used as a contrast to the pure, unpolluted living water of Jesus; the phrases man-made baggage and theological pollution describe the rules, regulations and interpretational laws that man has added to, mixed with or used in place of the pure teachings of Christ and his apostles. The result of this man-made baggage and theological pollution is a tainted gospel and distorted image of the Savior. Shame on us!" The blogger goes on to define the true Church as that which can "comfort the broken-hearted, put its arm around the woman who chokes on her loneliness, give strength to the addict who struggles everyday with his addiction, . . . be a family to the widow, give hope to the single mom who feels overwhelmed." But is not his definition just as much an application of "manmade interpretational laws" as that which he rejects? The fact that he believes his understanding is "pure, unpolluted water" whereas all the theologians of the past were merely imposing their man-made ideas constitutes precisely the sort of narcissistic attitudes arising in a Self-absorbed, Gnostic culture.

16. Robert C. Fuller, *Spiritual But Not Religious: Understanding Unchurched America* (New York: Oxford University Press, 2001), 8.

17. Ibid., 5.

18. Amazon.com reviews a book of this title, *God Outside the Box: A Story of Breaking Free*: "Born of a Catholic mother and Moslem father, Patti is never sure what religion to follow, or any at all for that matter. In her youth and early twenties, she explores numerous religions, but none speak to her soul. She can't accept the idea that one group has the whole truth and everyone else is wrong, or confused, or infidels, or a cult, or going to burn in hell for all time. To limit her thinking for religious purposes is like living in a cubicle and not being allowed to look over the wall and see what is going on outside. She wants to think for herself, to study, to analyze and to practice without inhibitions. Why would God only accept the practices and prayers of one particular group and not others? An omniscient God can't be that petty, can he-or she? She finally concludes that she just doesn't know and flounders in a spiritual void for a time. But when she is diagnosed with a serious illness and haunted by inner demons of her past, she cracks and falls apart. Deep, buried emotions erupt to the surface, shaking her to her core. Propelled to seek answers and find inner peace, she cries out to the heavens for help. Consequently, she tumbles into a spiritual adventure that explodes her concepts of reality and opens her to a brave new world where souls talk, trees emit energy fields, rocks have life, and God is everywhere."   Retrieved from http://www.amazon.com/God-Outside-Box-Story-Breaking/ dp/1434367754./1434367754.

19. Kurt Rudolph, *Gnosis: The Nature and History of Gnosticism* (New York: HarperCollins Publishers, 1984), 55.

20. Everett Ferguson, *Backgrounds of Early Christianity, Second Edition* (Grand Rapids, MI: William B. Eerdman's Publishing Company, 2nd Edition, 1993), 362.
21. Fuller, *Spiritual, But Not Religious*, 2.
22. From the subtitle of his book, *A Generous Orthodoxy* (Grand Rapids, MI: Zondervan Publishing, 2006).
23. Provided, of course, that the conversation is "honest," which we presume to mean "according to his terms." Cf. *An Emergent Manifesto of Hope*, edited by Doug Pagitt and Tony Jones (Grand Rapids, MI: BakerBooks, 2007), 143, 151.
24. *The Allure of Gnosticism: The Gnostic Experience in Jungian Psychology and Contemporary Culture*, edited by Robert A. Segal, and June Singer and Murray Stein (Chicago: Open Court Publishing Company, 1995), 97.
25. *Nag Hammadi Library*, "The Thunder: Perfect Mind," 297-303
26. Rudolph, 53.
27. Wouter Hanegraff, *New Age Religion and Western Culture: Esotericism in the Mirror of Secular Thought* (New York: State University of New York, 1998), 518-519.
28. Ibid., 107.
29. Police, "Spirits in a Material World," *Ghost in the Machine*, A & M Records, 1981.
30. Hans Jonas, The Gnostic Religion (Boston: Beacon Press, 2001), 241-250.
31. *Nag Hammadi Library*, "The Gospel of Philip," 142.
32. Jonas, *The Gnostic Religion*, 250.
33. Rudolph, *Gnosis*, 61-65.
34. Ibid., 58.
35. *Nag Hammadi Library*, "On the Origin of the World," 173.
36. Rudolph, *Gnosis*, 78-80.
37. *Nag Hammadi Library*, "The Gospel of the Egyptians," 215.
38. Ibid., "On the Origin of the World," 175.
39. Cf. Rudolph, *Gnosis*, 59-67.
40. Rudolph, *Gnosis*, 88.
41. Ibid., 104.
42. Ibid., 148-171.
43. Ibid., 119-120.
44. *Nag Hammadi Library*, "The Gospel of Philip," 150.
45. Rudolph, *Gnosis*, 88.
46. Harold Bloom, 259,
47. Rudolph, *Gnosis*, 220.
48. Ibid., 241, 188.
49. Ibid., 225.
50. Ibid., 241.
51. Ibid., 157.
52. *A Dictionary of Early Christian Beliefs*, edited by David W. Bercot (Peabody, Massachusetts, Hedrickson Publishers, Inc., 1998), 252.
53. Rudolph, *Gnosis*, 245ff.
54. Segal, Singer, and Stein, *The Allure of Gnosticism*, 100.
55. *Nag Hammadi Library*, "The Gospel of Philip," 150.
56. Segal, Singer, and Stein, *The Allure of Gnosticism*, 110.

CHAPTER 2

GNOSTIC TRAITS

1.   *Gnosticism and Hermeticism: From Antiquity to Modern Times*, edited by Roelof van den Broek and Wouter J. Hanegraaff (New York: State University of New York Press, 1998), 4.
2.   *Nag Hammadi Library*, "The Teachings of Silvanus," 387.
3.   *Nag Hammadi Library*, "The Gospel of Truth," 49.
4.   Rudolph, *Gnosis*, 62.
5.   Eckhart Tolle, *A New Earth: Awakening to Your Life's Purpose* (New York: Penguin Books, 2005), 15.
6.   Pagitt and Jones, *An Emergent Manifesto*, 192-193.
7.   *Nag Hammadi Library*, "The Gospel of Philip," 142-143.
8.   Ferguson, *The Aquarian Conspiracy*, 369.
9.   *Nag Hammadi Library*, "The Gospel of Truth," 47.
10. Rudolph, *Gnosis*, 192.
11. Ibid., 193.
12. Hanegraaff, *New Age Religion and Western Culture*, 115.
13. Ibid., 114.
14. *Nag Hammadi Libraary*, "The Gospel of Philip," 155.
15. C. G. Jung, *Memories, Dreams, Reflections*, recorded and edited by Aniela Jaffe, translated from the German by Richard and Clara Winston (New York: Random House, Inc., 1963), 379.
16. Ibid., 138.
17. Hanegraaff, *New Age Religion an d Western Culture*, 124.
18. Emergent Christian Ryan Bolger, beginning with a Gnostic premise ("Many subcultures in the West today are holistic. They see connections between art, spirituality, economics, and politics. The construct their world in webs and networks – not simply in linear fashion [i.e. Western logic, dogma, confessionalism]. They create their way of life around images rather than the printed word.") concludes that "Those who follow God's reign embody Good News . . . . The church has the opportunity to participate with God in the world's redemption." (Pagitt and Jones, *An Emergent Manifesto*, 133-134.) The sentiment exists also in the Church Growth Movement.
19. Hanegraaff, *New Age Religion an d Western Culture*, 119-139.
20. Segal, Singer, and Stein, *The Allure of Gnosticism*, 49.
21. Ibid., 47-48.
22. Ibid., 41.
23. Ibid., 42.
24. Ibid., 43.
25. Llewellyn Vaughan-Lee, *Sufism: The Transformation of the Heart* (Inverness, California: The Golden Sufi Center, 1995), 59.
26. Rudolph, *Gnosis*, 213-215.
27. Ibid., 216.
28. Ibid., 213.

29. Ibid., 213.

30. Ibid., 213.

31. Donna Minkowitz, *Ferocious Romance: What My Encounters with the Right Taught Me about Sex, God, and Fury* (New York: The Free Press, 1998), 28.

32. Carol Lansing, *Power and Purity* (New York, Oxford University Press, 1998), 108.

33. Segal, Singer, and Stein, *The Allure of Gnosticism*, 109.

34. *Nag Hammadi Library*, "The Gospel of the Egyptians," 209.

35. Rudolph, *Gnosis*, 80. (See also 270-271.)

36. Lydia Parafianowicz, "Swedish parents keep 2-year-old's gender secret," *The Local: Swedish News in English*, June 23, 2009, http://www.thelocal.se/20232/20090623/, accessed June 23, 2009.

37. *The Yogyakarta Principles: Principles on the application of international human rights law in relation to sexual orientation and gender identity*, March, 2007, PDF document retrieved at http://www.yogyakartaprinciples.org/principles_en.pdf, 6.

38. Ibid., 11.

39. Transgender Law and Policy Institute, "Non-Discrimination Laws that include gender identity and expression:" retrieved from http://www.transgenderlaw.org/ndlaws/index.htm#jurisdictions)

40. Retrieved from http://www.christiannewswire.com/news/5002918668.html.

41. Cf. Jae Curtis, "Guys and Dolls: Reducing Gender Stereotypes in Your Home," *Education.Com*, March 11, 2012, retrieved at http://www.education.com/magazine/article/gender-stereotypes-kids/. See also Vaughan-Lee, *Sufism*, 43.

42. *Nag Hammadi Library*, "The Gospel of Truth," 43.

43. *Nag Hammadi Library*, "The Exegesis of the Soul," 196.

44. Hanegraaff, *New Age Religion and Western Culture*, 7.

45. Normon Cohn, *The Pursuit of the Millennium: Revolutionary Millenarians and Mystrical Anarchists of the Middle Ages* (New York: Oxford University Press, 1970), 151.

46. Idries Shah, *The Sufis* (New York: Doubleday, 1964), 372.

47. *Nag Hammadi Library*, "The Gospel of the Egyptians," 210.

48. Segal, Singer, and Stein, *The Allure of Gnosticism*, 75.

49. Ferguson, *The Aquarian Conspiracy*, 149.

50. Paul Davies, *Romanticism and Esoteric Tradition: Studies in Imagination* (New York: Lindisfarne Books, 1998), 42.

51. Segal, Singer, and Stein, *The Allure of Gnosticism*, 94.

52. David Mulroy, *The War Against Grammar* (Portsmouth, N.H.: Boynton/Cook Publishers, Inc., 2003), 7.

53. Ibid., 19.

54. Ibid., 19.

55. Edward Feser, "Hayek on Tradition," *Journal of Libertarian Studies*, Volume 17, no. 1 (Winter 2003), 18.

56. Minkowitz, *Ferocious Romance*, 35-36.

57. M DeYoung, "The World According to NAMBLA: Accounting for Deviance," *Journal of Sociology and Social Welfare 16* (March, 1989), 111–126.

58. Cf. Queers United: The activist blog uniting the Lesbian, Gay, Bisexual, Transgender, Queer, Intersexual, Asexual community & Allies in the fight for equality. Retrieved at http://queersunited.blogspot.com/2008/11/open-forum-

asexual-rights-movement.html on November 9, 2008.

59. *Nag Hammadi Library*, 218.

60. Richard Stivers, *Technology as Magic: The Triumph of the Irrational* (New York: Continuum, 2001), 10.

61. Rosemarie Tong, *Feminist Thought: A More Comprehensive Introduction* (New York: Westview Publishers, 2008), 276.

62. Ferguson, *The Aquarian Conspiracy*, 149.

63. Jeremy R. Carrette, *Foucault and Religion: Spiritual Corporality and Political Spirituality* (London and New York: Routledge, 2000), 85-108.

64. Segal, Singer, and Stein, *The Allure of Gnosticism*, 75.

65. Ibid., 73-74.

66. Ibid., 73.

67. Bercot, *A Dictionary of Early Christian Beliefs*, 306.

68. Cook, *Thresholds: Studies in Romantic Experience*, 234.

69. Ibid., 74.

70. Richard Smoley, *Forbidden Faith: The Gnostic Legacy from the Gospels to the Da Vinci Code* (New York: HarperCollins Publishers, 2006), 34.

71. Segal, Singer, and Stein, *The Allure of Gnosticism*, 94.

72. Smoley, *Forbidden Faith*, 33.

73. Rudolph, *Gnosis*, 214-215.

74. Johannes Quasten, *Music and Worship in Pagan and Christian Antiquity* (Washington D. C.: National Association of Pastoral Musicians, 1983), 33-36.

75. Cited in *Self and Self-Transformation in the History of Religions*, edited by David Shulman and Guy G. Stroumsa (New York: Oxford University Press, 2002), 93.

76. A. Ple et. al., *Mystery and Mysticism* (New York: The Philosophical Library, 1956), 12.

77. David Knowles, *The Evolution of Medieval Thought* (New York: Vintage Books, 1962), 57.

78. "Many people far away from the church, walking along the village street or pursuing their various avocations upon the lonely hillsides, felt for a moment a thrill of affection or devotion, as this great wave of spiritual peace and strength passed over the countryside." Charles Leadbeater, *The Science of the Sacraments*, Chapter Two "The Holy Eucharist" (retrieved at *The Global Library*, http://www.

79. Denis De Rougemont, *Love in the Western World*, translated by Montgomery Belgion (New York: Pantheon Books, 1956),153.

80. Ibid., 156.

81. Alister E. McGrath, *Luther's Theology of the Cross* (New York: Wiley -Blackwell, 1991), 154.

82. Ibid., 150.

83. Ibid., 10.

84. Quasten, *Music and Worship in Pagan an d Christian Antiquity*, 35-36.

85. Morris Berman, *Coming to Our Senses: Body and Spirit in the Hidden History of the West* (New York: Simon and Schuster, 1989), 139.

86. Ibid., 140.

87. Ferguson, *The Aquarian Conspiracy*, 374.

88. Ibid., 384.

89. Rudolph, *Gnosis*, 94ff.

90. "Sleep" and "Dreams," *The Hymns of Orpheus*, (Grand Rapids, MI: 1993), 155-156.

91. Cohn, *The Pursuit of the Millennium*, 185.

92. Ferguson, *The Aquarian Conspiracy*, 372.

93. Heidegger's appraisal of Nietzsche is a good example of this process. He gives Nietzsche's quote that all truth (but his own) is an illusion, and then explains: "There are things that demand stricter kind of thinking. If truth is to reign in all thinking, then its essence presumably cannot be conceived by ordinary thinking and its rules of the game." Martin Heidegger, *Nietzsche, Volumes III and IV: The Will to Power as Knowledge and as Metaphysics*, Edited by David Farrell Krell (San Francisco, CA: Harper & Row, 1991), 27-28.

94. Leo Strauss, *Natural Right and History* (Chicago: The University of Chicago Press, 1965), 26ff.

95. Hanegraaff, *New Age Religion and Western Culture*, 108.

96. David Yonke, "Ethicist: Transhumanism 'inevitable'," *Toledo Blade*, April 21, 2012.

97. Tolle, *A New Earth*, 15.

98. Rudolph, *Gnosis*, 256.

99. Jonas, *The Gnostic Religion*, 254ff.

100. Ibid., 260-262.

101. Daniel Merkur, *Gnosis: An Esoteric Tradition of Mystical Visions and Unions* (New York: State University of New York Press, 1993), 121.

102. Rudolph, *Gnosis*, 257.

103. Ibid., 255.

104. Merkur, *Gnosis*, 113.

105. Jonas, *The Gnostic Religion*, 46.

106. Ibid., 272.

107. Liddell and Scott's *An Intermediate Greek-English Lexicon, Seventh Edition* (Oxford: Clarendon Press, 1996), 535.

108. Rudolph, *Gnosis*, 268-270.

109. Robert E. Webber, *The Younger Evangelicals: Facing the Challenges of the New World* (Grand Rapids, MI: Baker Books, 2002), 179.

110. Ibid., 257.

111. Ibid., 257.

112. Rudolph, *Gnosis*, 256.

113. Richard Smoley and Jay Kinney, *Hidden Wisdom: A Guide to the Western Inner Traditions* (New York: The Penguin Group, 1999), 219.

114. Rudolph, *Gnosis*, 249.

115. Rev. Fr. Troy W. Pierce, *The Path of Gnosis* (Blog), comment posted July 12, 2007. Retrieved from http://gnoscast.blogspot.com/2007/07/questions-children-and-liberation.html.

116. Thomas S. Hibbs, "Little Children on *Revolutionary Road*," NationalReview.com, January 30, 2009, retrieved at http://www.nationalreview.com/articles/226789/little-children-thomas-s-hibbs on January 30, 2009.

117. Ferguson, *The Aquarian Conspiracy*, 397.

118. This is the idea connoted by the Greek word *splanchna*, meaning both "bodily innards" and "deep affection." The best English rendering of the word would be "gut-wrenching love."

119. Minkowitz, *Ferocious Romance*, 27-28.

120. Plotinus, *The Essential Plotinus: Representative Treatises from the Enneads*, edited and translated by Elmer O'Brien, S. J. (Indianapolis, IN: Hackett Publishing Company Inc., 1964), 38, 40-41.

121. M. H. Abrams, *Natural Supernaturalism: Tradition and Revolution in Romantic Literature* (New York: W. W. Norton and Company, Inc., 1971), 293-294.

122. Cf. Arthur C. Brooks, *Who Really Cares: The Surprising Truth About Compassion and Conservatism* (New York: Basic Books, 2007).

123. Segal, Singer, and Stein, *The Allure of Gnosticism*, 100.

124. Francis A. Yates, *Giordano Bruno and the Hermetic Tradition* (Chicago IL: The University of Chicago Press, 1191), 156.

125. Ibid., 144.

126. "An Infinity of Jimis," *Life*, October 3, 1969, 74.

127. Paul D. Zimmerman, "Rebirth of the Blues," *Newsweek*, May 26, 1969, 82.

128. Ioan P. Couliano, *Eros and Magic in the Renaissance*, translated by Margaret Cook (Chicago, IL: The University of Chicago Press, 1987), 91-92.

129. Jeff M. Sellers, "The Higher Self Gets Down To Business," *Christianity Today*, February 1, 2003, retrieved at http://www.christianity today.com/ct/2003/february /1.34.html?start=2.

130. Rudolph, *Gnosis*, 284.

131. Cited in Joseph Hamburger, *John Stuart Mill on Liberty and Control* (Princeton, N.J.: Princeton University Press, 2001), 111.

132. *The Apocalyptic Vision in America: Interdisciplinary Essays on Myth and Culture*, edited by Lois P. Zamora (Bowling Green, OH: Bowling Green State University Popular Press, 1982), 183.

133. Berman, *Coming to Our Senses*, 141.

134. Fuller, *Spiritual, But Not Religious*, 5.

135. Ferguson, *The Aquarian Conspiracy*, 371.

CHAPTER 3

THE UNDERGROUND STREAM

1. For a discussion on the idea of Christian orthodoxy, see Walter Bauer, *Orthodoxy and Heresy in Earliest Christianity*, translated by a team from the Philadelphia Seminar on Christian Origins (Mifflintown, PA: Sigler Press, 1971), 302ff.

2. Berman, *Coming to Our Senses*, 181.

3. *Sufi Thought and Action*, assembled by Idries Shah (London: The Octagon Press, 1990), 96-97.

4. This is the argument of Frank Viola and Geroge Barna in their book *Pagan Christianity: Exploring the Roots of Our Church Practices* (Tyndale House Publishers, 2002).

5. Hanegraaff, *New Age Religion and Western Culture*, 319.

6. Broek and Hanegraaff, *Gnosis and Hermeticism*, 98-99.

7. Ferguson, *Backgrounds of Early Christianity*, 288.

8. Merkur, *Gnosis*, 113.

9. Segal, Singer, and Stein, *The Allure of Gnosticism*, 103.

10. Knowles, *The Evolution of Medieval Thought*, 57.

11. Yates, *Giordano Bruno and the Hermetic Tradition*, 117.

12. Herbert B. Workman, *The Evolution of the Monastic Ideal: From the Earliest Times down to the Coming of the Friars* (Boston, MA: Beacon Press, 1962), 29.

13. Owen Chadwick, *John Cassian* (Cambridge: Cambridge University Press, 1968), 50ff.

14. David Knowles, *Christian Monasticism* (New York: McGraw-Hill Book Company, 1969), 17.

15. Workman, *The Evolution of the Monastic Ideal*, 98.

16. Ibid., 98.

17. Boethius, *The Consolation of Philosophy*, translated with an introduction by V. E. Watts (New York: Penquin Books, 1969), quote from Introduction, 7.

18. Ibid., 35-36.

19. Knowles, *The Evolution of Medieval Thought*, 194.

20. Vaughan-Lee, *Sufism*, 28.

21. Shah, *The Sufis*, 392.

22. Shah, *The Sufis*, 138.

23. Shah, *The Sufis*, 133.

24. Shah, *The Sufis*, 47.

25. Shah, *The Sufis*, 56.

26. Shah, *The Sufis*, 56-57.

27. Malcolm Lambert, *The Cathars* (Oxford: Blackwell Publishers, 1998), 135.

28. Michael Costen, *The Cathars and the Albigensian Crusade* (New York: Manchester University Press, 1997), 49.

29. Ibid., 50.

30. Broek and Hanegraaff, *Gnosis and Hermeticism*, 87-89.

31. Ibid., 94-95.

32. Ibid., 96-97.

33. Smoley, *Forbidden Faith*, 76.

34. Ibid., 76.

35. Maria Rosa Menocal, *The Arabic Role in Medieval Literary History: A Forgotten Heritage* (Philadelphia, PA: University of Pennsylvania Press, 1987), 121ff.

36. Vaughan-Lee, *Sufism*, 35.

37. Smoley, *Forbidden Faith*, 81.

38. Rougemont, *Love in the Western World*, 85.

39. Ibid., 110.

40. Eric Voegelin, *The Collective Works of Eric Voegelin, Volume 5: Modernity without Restraint: The Political Religions; The New Science of Politics; And Science, Politics, and Gnosticism*, edited by Manfred Henningsen(Columbia, MO: The University of Missouri Press, 2000), 178ff.

41. Ibid., 300ff.

42. Martin Luther, *Career of the Reformer*, vol. 31 of Luther's Works, edited by Jaroslav Pelikan and Walter A. Hansen (Minneapolis, MN: Fortress Press, 1957), 13.

43. C. S. Lewis, *The Joyful Christian: 127 Readings* (New York: Macmillan Publishing Company, 1977), 222.

44. *Lutheran Service Book* (St. Louis, Concordia Publishing House, 2006), 556.

45. *Tertullian, Part Fourth: Minucius Felix; Commodian; Origen, Parts First and Second,*

vol. 4 of Ante-Nicene Fathers, edited by Alexander Roberts, D. D. And James Donaldson, LL. D. (Peabody, MA: Hendrickson Publishers, 1994), 285.

46. Walther von Loewenich, *Luther's Theology of the Cross* (Minneapolis, MN: Augsburg Publishing House), 155.

47. Merkur, *Gnosis*, 128.

48. Martin Luther, *Lectures on Romans*, vol. 25 of Luther's Works, edited by Jaroslav Pelikan and Walter A. Hansen (St. Louis, MO: Concordia Publishing House, 1972), 287.

49. St. John of the Cross, *The Collected Works of Saint John of the Cross* (Washington D.C.: ICS Publications, 1991), 54.

50. Martin Brecht, *Martin Luther, His Road to Reformation* (Philadelphia, PA: Fortress Press, 1981), 143.

51. *The Book of Concord: The Confessions of the Evangelical Lutheran Church*, edited by Robert Kolb and Timothy J. Wengert, translated by Charles Arand et. al. (Minneapolis, MN: Fortress Press, 2000), 213.

52. Peter Erb in his "Introduction" to Johann Arndt's *True Christianity* (New York: Paulist Press, 1979), 16.

53. Couliano, *Eros and Magic in the Renaissance*, 192.

54. *The Pietist Theologians: An Introduction to Theology in the Seventeenth and Eighteenth Centuries, 1st ed.*, edited by Carter Lindberg (New York: Wiley -Blackwell, 2004), 7.

55. Shah, *The Sufis*, 230.

56. Lindberg, *The Pietist Theologians*, 7.

57. Ibid., 7.

58. "Hermes," *The Hymns of Orpheus*, 80.

59. Yates, *Giordano Bruno and the Hermetic Tradition*, 12.

60. Ibid., 12.

61. Ibid., 64.

62. Ibid., 432ff.

63. Ibid., 144.

64. Ibid., 146.

65. Francis Bacon, *The New Organon*, edited by Fulton H. Anderson (New York: Macmillan Publishing Company, 1960), 40.

66. Yates, *Giordano Bruno and the Hermetic Tradition*, 452.

67. Dan Burton and David Grandy, *Magic, Mystery, and Science: The Occult in Western Civilization* (Indianapolis, IN: Indiana University Press, 2004), 327-328.

68. Steve Martin, *Wild and Crazy Guy*, Warner Brothers, 1978.

69. Humphrey Carpenter, *Robert Runcie: The Reluctant Archbishop* (London: Hodder and Stoughton,1997), 88.

70. Strauss, *Natural Right and History*, 8.

71. *How Bad Can I Be?* written by John Powell, Cinco Paul, and Kool Kojak, performed by Ed Helms, Universal Pictures/Interscope Records, 2012.

72. Cited in Nancy Pearcey, *Total Truth: Liberating Christianity from Its Cultural Captivity, Study Guide Edition* (Wheaton, IL: Crossway, 2005), 172.

73. Cited in Nancy Pearcey, *Total Truth*, 208-209; Robert Wright, *The Moral Animal: Why We Are the Way We Are* (New York: Vintage, 1994), 336, 351, 324-325, 350, 355, 325, 376, 336.

74. Cf. Randy Thornhill and Craig Palmer, *The Natural History of Rape: Biological Bases of Sexual Coercion* (Cambridge, MA: MIT Press, 2000).

75. Cited in Pearcey, *Total Truth*, 213; Steven Pinker, "Why They Kill Their Newborns," *The New York Times*, November 2, 1997.

76. Cited in Pearcey, *Total Truth*, 217-218.

77. Tim Radford, "The Selfish Gene by Richard Dawkins – book review," *theguardian.com*, retrived at http://www.theguardian.com/science/2012/aug/31/the-selfish-gene-richard-dawkins-review.

78. Cited in Pearcey, *Total Truth*, 218; Richard Dawkins, The Selfish Gene, 20th Anniversary Edition (New York: Oxford University Press, 2006), 215.

79. Cited in Pearcey, *Total Truth*, 190; George Wald, quoted in Dietrick E. Thomsen, "A Knowing Universe Seeking to be Known," *Science News* (February 19, 1983), 124; Freeman Dyson, *Disturbing the Universe* (New York: Harper and Row, 1979), 250.

80. Cf. Ben Stein's interview with Richard Dawkins, *Expelled: No Intelligence Allowed*, by Kevin Miller and Ben Stein (Premise Media Corporation and Rampant Films, 2008); interview retrieved at http://www.youtube.com/watch?v= HEcVOucw7Cc.

81. Erik Davis, *TechGnosis: Myth, Magic, and Mysticism in the Age of Information* (New York: Random House, 1998), 229.

82. E. Michael Jones, *Monsters from the Id: The Rise of Horror in Fiction and Film* (Dallas, TX: Spense Publishing Company, 2000), 244ff.

83. Bacon, *The New Organon*, 39.

84. Straus, *Natural Right and History*, 247.

85. Jacques Barzun, *Classic, Romantic, and Modern* (Chicago, IL: University of Chicago Press, 1961), 20.

86. *Grease*, written by Barry Gibb (RSO Records,1978).

87. Ferguson, *The Aquarian Conspiracy*, 396.

88. Cited in Albert Cook, *Thresholds: Studies in the Romantic Experience* (Madison, WI: University of Wisconsin Press, 1985), 5.

89. John Keats, *Letter to George and Georgiana Keats*, April 21, 1810 (retrieved from "Keats on "The Vale of Soul-Making", http://www.mrbauld.com/keatsva.html)

90. Davies, *Romanticism and the Esoteric Tradition*, 109-110.

91. Davies, *Romanticism and the Esoteric Tradition*, 42.

92. De Rougemont, *Love in the Western World*, 63-64.

93. Cited in Davies, *Romanticism and the Esoteric Tradition*, 35.

94. Cited in Davies, *Romanticism and the Esoteric Tradition*, 38.

95. Ralph Waldo Emerson, "The American Scholar," from *Addresses*, published as part of *Nature; Addresses and Lectures, Ralph Waldo Emerson Texts*, retrieved from http://www.emersoncentral.com/amscholar.htm.

96. Ralph Waldo Emerson, *Nature: Addresses and Lectures, Essays: First and Second Series, Representative Men, English Traits, and The Conduct of Life* (Digireads.com, 2009), 30.

97. Cited by Natalie Wolchover, "Will Science Someday Rule Out the Possibility of God?" *Life's Little Mysteries*, September 17, 2012, retrieved at http://www.lifeslittlemysteries.com/2907-science-religion-god-physics.html].

98. David Cogswell, *Existentialism for Beginners* (Danbury, CT: For Beginners, 2008), 163.

CHAPTER 4

THE FULLNESS OF TIME

1. "Christianity Is No Longer Americans' Default Faith," *Barna Group*, January 12, 2009, retrieved at https://www.barna.org/barna-update/article/12-faithspirituality/15-christianity-is-no-longer-americans-default-faith?q=born#Ukmj55rD-Uk.
2. Alexis de Tocqueville, *Democracy in America, Volume 2* (New York: Vintage Books, 1945), 26.
3. Ibid., 4.
4. See Sigmund Freud, *The Ego and the Id*, edited by James Strachey and translated by Joan Riviere (New York: W. W. Norton & Company, 1960), 27.
5. Cited in Ferguson, *The Aquarian Conspiracy*, 375.
6. Davis, *TechGnosis*, 170.
7. See John Markoff, *What the Dormouse Said: How the 60s Counterculture Shaped the Personal Computer* (New York: Penguin Books, 2006).
8. Ibid., 170.
9. Cited in Yates, *Giordano Bruno and the Hermetic Tradition*, 148.
10. Tony Dokoupil, "Is the Web Driving Us Mad?" *The Daily Beast*, July 9, 2012, retrieved at http://www.thedailybeast.com/newsweek/2012/07/08/is-the-internet-making-us-crazy-what-the-new-research-says.html.
11. Joshua Cooper, "Finding God on the Web: Across the Internet, believers are re-examining their ideas of faith, religion and spirituality," *Time*, December 16, 1996, 67.
12. Cf. Rudolph, *Gnosis*, 34ff.

CHAPTER 5

THE POSTMODERN CREED

1. Jonas, *The Gnostic Religion*, 334.
2. Cf. Allan Bloom, *The Closing of the American Mind* (New York, Simon and Schuster, 1987), 200ff.
3. See Bloom's discussion on the effect of German philosophy on the American psyche in *The Closing of the American Mind*, 147ff.
4. Jonas, *The Gnostic Religion*, 320.
5. Ibid., 320.
6. Ibid., 322.
7. Ibid., 322.
8. Ibid., 323.
9. Ibid., 323.
10. Ibid., 323.

11. Ibid., 334.
12. Ibid., 323.
13. Ibid., 324.
14. Ibid., 324.
15. Ibid., 327-328.
16. Ibid., 328.
17. Ibid., 331.
18. Ibid., 332.
19. Jeremy R. Carrette makes a comparison between Dionysus' negative theology and Michel Foucault's understanding of the same. Dionysus is like a sculpture who must chip away at matter to get at the hidden image. By contrast, "In Foucault's work there are no 'hidden images' to be discovered, rather continually shifting sands which form different patterns." (Jeremy R. Carrette, *Foucault and Religion: Spiritual Corporality and Political Spirituality*, 2000), 100.
20. Ibid., 339.
21. Ibid., 340.
22. Ibid., 340.
23. Segal, Singer, and Stein, *The Allure of Gnosticism*, 15.
24. Ibid., 14.
25. Ibid., 16.
26. Ibid., 18ff.
27. Ibid., 3.
28. Ibid., 35.
29. Ibid., 19.
30. Ibid., 19.
31. Ibid., 19.
32. Ibid., 20.
33. Ibid., 21.
34. Ibid., 22.
35. Ibid., 26.
36. Broek and Hanegraaff, *Gnosis and Hermetism*, 157.
37. Segal, Singer, and Stein, *The Allure of Gnosticism*, 27.
38. Ibid., 27.
39. Ibid., 50.
40. Smoley and Kinney, *Hidden Wisdom*, 228.
41. Ibid., 231.
42. Hanegraaff, *Gnosis and Hermeticism*, 194.

CHAPTER 6

MASS MEDIA AND PHANTASMS

1. Couliano, *Eros and Magic in the Renaissance*, 22.
2. Ibid., 4.
3. Ibid., 5.
4. Ibid., 16.

5. Ibid., 16.
6. Ibid., 31.
7. Ibid., 32.
8. Ibid., 72.
9. Ibid., 67.
10. Ibid., 78.
11. Ibid., 76.
12. Ibid., 78.
13. Ibid., 78.
14. Ibid., 82.
15. Ibid., 89.
16. Ibid., 90.
17. Ibid., 96.
18. Ibid., 97.
19. Ibid., 97.
20. Ibid., 98.
21. Ibid., 104.
22. Ibid., 103.
23. Ibid., 105.
24. Ibid., 105.
25. Ibid., 106.
26. Ibid., 105.
27. Ibid., 80-83.
28. William Shakespeare, "The Tempest: Epilogue," *William Shakespeare: The Complete Works* (New York: Metrobooks, 1994), 1159.
29. Michael Brearley and Andrea Sabbadini, "The Truman Show?: How's it going to end?" *The International Journal of Psychoanalysis*, Volume 89, Issue 2, April, 2008, 433-40.
30. "Return to Normandy," Special Treats Production Company, 1998.
31. Ibid.
32. Translation retrieved at http://lyricstranslate.com/en/Tu-Es-Partout-Tu-Es-Partout.html.
33. The Nielsen Company, 2011, retrieved at http://www.nielsen.com/content/dam/corporate/us/en/newswire/uploads/2011/04/State-of-the-Media-2011-TV-Upfronts.pdf.
34. Jane Alexander Stewart, "The Feminine Trickster Hero in Contemporary Cinema," a presentation for the *Aphrodite and Hermes Colloquium at the University of Alabama*, retrieved at http://www.cinemashrink.com/femtrickster.html.
35. Julie Gunlock, "The Rise of Mommy Fearmongering: Be Afraid... Of Everything! How one mother learned to stop being afraid and enjoy modern conveniences" *thefederalist.com*, November 26, 2013, retrieved at http://thefederalist.com/2013/11/26/rise-mommy-fearmongering-afraid-everything/.
36. Ronald W. Dworkin, "The rise of the Caring Industry" (*Hoover Institution Stanford University*), June 1, 2010; retrieved from http://www.hoover.org/publications/policy-review/article/5339.
37. Davis, *TechGnosis*, 71.

38. Couliano, *Eros and Magic in the Renaissance*, 52.
39. Vaughan-Lee, *Sufism: The Transformation of the Heart*, 44.
40. Ibid., 49.
41. James Bowman, "Avatar and the Flight from Reality," *The New Atlantis*, Number 27, Spring 2010, 77-84.
42. Tony Dokoupil, "Is the Web Driving Us Mad?"
43. Ibid.
44. Retrieved at http://www.borrellassociates.com/component/content/article/45-general-reports/195-borrell-associates-2011-ad-forecast-memo.
45. Couliano, *Eros and Magic in the Renaissance*, 32.
46. Ibid., 35.
47. Ibid., 37.
48. Cited in Couliano, *Eros and Magic in the Renaissance*, 100.
49. Davis, *TechGnosis*, 177.
50. Cited in Jones, *Monsters From The Id: The Rise of Horror in Fiction and Film*, 179-180. Original quote from Edwards L. Bernays, *Propaganda* (New York: Horace Liverright, 1928), 9.
51. Cited in Couliano, *Eros and Magic in the Renaissance*, 76.
52. Ibid., 49.
53. Peter Drucker, *Landmarks of Tomorrow* (Piscataway, NJ: Transaction Publishers, 1996) 264-265.

CHAPTER 7

PHANTASMIC SOUND

1. Couliano, *Eros and Magic in the Renaissance*, 91.
2. Plato, *The Republic of Plato*, translated by Allan Bloom (New York: Basic Books Inc., 1968),101-102.
3. Cited in Johannes Quasten, *Music and Worship in Pagan and Christian Antiquity*, 126.
4. Bercot, *A Dictionary of Early Christian Beliefs*, 468.
5. Ibid., 467.
6. Ibid., 467.
7. Henry Chadwick, *The Early Church: The story of emergent Christianity from the apostolic age to the foundation of the Church of Rome* (London: Penguin Books, 1967), 275.
8. Rudolph, *Gnosis*, 286.
9. Mark P. O. Morford and Robert J. Lenardon, *Classical Mythology*, 3rd Ed. (New York: Longman, 1985), 282-287.
10. Guthrie, *Orpheus and Greek Religion*, 75.
11. "Orphic Fragment," *The Hymns of Orpheus*, 31.
12. "Soul Ladder," *The Hymns of Orpheus*, 32.
13. Rougemont, *Love in the Western world*, 61.
14. Ibid., 63-64.
15. John Warden, *"Orpheus and Ficino," Orpheus: The Metamorphoses of a Myth*, edited

by John Warden (Toronto: University of Toronto Press, 1982), 90.

16. Cited in Warden, Opheus: *The Metamorphoses of a Myth*, 96.

17. Ibid., 41.

18. Vaughan-Lee, *Sufism: The Transformation of the Heart*, 1.

19. Cited in Mojdeh Bay at and Mohammad Ali Jamnia, *Tales from the Land of the Sufis* (Boston, MA: Shambhala, 1994), 13.

20. Ibid., 81.

21. Abu Hamaid Huhammad al-Ghazzali, *The Alchemy of Happiness*, translated by Claud Field, revised and annotated by Elton L. Daniel (New York: M. E. Sharpe Inc., 1991), 59.

22. Shah, *The Sufis*, 379-380.

23. Rougemont, Love in the Western World, 81.

24. Ibid., 74.

25. Menocal, *The Arabic Role in Medieval Literary History*, 71.

26. Ibid., 74.

27. Ibid., 76.

28. David Gates, "Dylan Revisited," *Newsweek*, October 6, 1997.

29. Rebecca Leung, "Dylan Looks Back," *CBS News*, June 12, 2005.

30. Bryan Magee, *The Tristan Chord* (New York: Metropolitan Books, 2000), 158-159.

31. Cited in Magee, *Tristan Chord*, 155.

32. Ibid., 158-159.

33. Cited in Magee, *Tristan Chord*, 156-157.

34. Cited in Magee, *Tristan Chord*, 162.

35. Ibid., 170.

36. Ibid., 170.

37. Hartmut Reinhardt, "Wagner and Schopenhauer," *Wagner Handbook*, edited by Ulrich Muller and Peter Wapnewskim translated by John Deathridge (Cambridge, MA: Harvard University Press, 1992), 290.

38. Magee, *Tristan Chord*, 166.

39. Ibid., 166.

40. Ibid., 182.

41. Denis de Rougemont, *Love Declared: Essays on the Myths of Love* (Boston, MA: Beacon Press, 1963), 12.

42. Timothy J. McGee, "Orfeo and Euridice, the First Two Operas," *Orpheus: The Metamorphoses of a Myth*, edited by John Warden (Toronto, University of Toronto Press, 1982), 163ff.

43. Magee, *Tristan Chord*, 181-182.

44. Ibid., 208-209.

45. Muller and Wapnewski, *Wagner Handbook*, 292.

46. Cited in Charles Osborne, *The Complete Operas of Richard Wagner* (North Pomfret, VT: Trafalgar Square Publishing, 1990), 141.

47. Bryan Magee, *Aspects of Wagner* (Oxford: Oxford University Press, 1988), 42.

48. Jung, *Memories, Dreams, Reflections*, 242.

49. Magee, *Tristan Chord*, 294.

50. Kathleen Marie Higgins, *Nietzsche's Zarathustra* (Philadelphia, PA: Temple University Press, 1987), 25.

51. Ibid., 26.

52. Cited in Higgins, *Nietzsche's Zarathustra*, 34-35.

53. Higgins, *Nietzsche's Zarathustra*, 35.

54. Cf. Gillespie, "Martin Heidegger," *History of Political Philosophy*, 893.

55. Cogswell, *Existentialism for Beginners*, 116. See also Jean-Paul Sartre, *Existentialism and Human Emotions* (New York: Philosophical Library, 1985), 23, 68ff.

56. Cited in Cogswell, *Existentialism for Beginners*, 126.

57. Robinson, *Nag Hammadi Library*, 545.

58. Jack Kerouac cited in John Clellon Holmes, "This is the Beat Generation," *The New York Times Magazine*, November 16, 1952, 10-22; from *The Beats: A Literary Reference* (New York: Caroll & Graf Publishers, 2001), 43ff.

59. *The Beats: A Literary Reference*, 45.

60. Cited in Mildred Edie Brady, "The New Cult of Sex and Anarchy," *Harper's Magazine*, April 1947, 312-322; from *The Beats: A Literary Reference* (New York: Caroll & Graf Publishers, 2001), 40ff.

61. *The Beats: A Literary Reference*, 41

62. Ibid., 41

63. Ibid., 41.

64. John Clellon Holmes, *The Beat Vision* (New York: Paragon House Publishers, 1986), 73ff.; from *The Beats: A Literary Reference* (New York: Caroll & Graf Publishers, 2001), 42.

65. Normon Podhoretz, "The Know-Nothing Bohemians," *Partisan Review*, spring 1958, 305-318; from *The Beats: A Literary Reference* (New York: Caroll & Graf Publishers, 66. Ibid. 2001), 76-77.

67. Jack Kerouac, *On the Road* (New York: Penguin Books, 1999), 231-232.

68. Philip H. Ennis, *The Seventh Stream: The Emergence of Rocknroll in American Popular Music*, (Hanover, NH: University Press of New England, 1992), 154.

69. Ibid., 153.

70. Ibid., 154.

71. Ibid., 250.

72. Cited in Tobias Churton, *Gnostic Philosophy, From Ancient Persia to Modern Times* (Rochester, VT: Inner Traditions, 2005), 399-400.

73. Warden, *Orpheus*, 90.

74. See Paul Davies, *Romanticism and the Esoteric Tradition: Studies in Imagination*, 67ff.

75. John Del Signore, "Donald Fagen, Steely Dan," *Arts & Entertainment*, June 13, 2008, retrieved at http://gothamist.com/2008/06/13/donald_fagen_steely_dan.php.

76. Berman, *Coming to Our Senses*, 323-325.

77. Charles Mudede, "In the World with Hiphop and Heidegger: A Philosophical Investigation into 'I'm Feeling You'," *theStranger*, retrieved from http://www.thestranger.com/seattle/in-the-world-with-hiphop-and-heidegger/Content?oid=5164.=5164.

78. Allan Bloom, *The Closing of the American Mind*, 152.

79. Aldous Huxley, *The Doors of Perception* (New York: Harper and Row, 1954), 23.

80. Ibid., 23.

81. Ibid., 17.

82. Ibid., 17.

83. Ibid., 17.
84. Ibid., 69.
85. Rudolph, *Gnosis*, 173.
86. Quasten, *Music and Worship in Pagan and Christian Antiquity*, 35-36.
87. Margaret Thaler Singer, *Cults in Our Midst: The Hidden Menace in Our Everyday Lives* (San Francisco, CA: Jossey -Bass Publishers, 1996), 131.
88. Shah, *The Sufis*, 133.
89. Vaughan-Lee, *Sufism: the Transformation of the Heart*, 54.

CHAPTER 8

PROGRESSIVISM'S EARLY ROOTS

1. Jonah Goldberg, *Liberal Fascism: The Secret History of the American Left from Mussolini to the Politics of Meaning* (New York: Doubleday, 2007), 202.
2. Ibid., 15.
3. Retrieved at http://www.youtube.com/watch?v=RWsx1X8PV_A.
4. Paul Kleppner, *The Cross of Culture: A Social Analysis of Midwestern Politics 1850-1900* (New York: The Free Press, 1970), 70.
5. Ibid., 71.
6. Ibid., 71.
7. Ibid., 72.
8. Ibid., 72-73.
9. Ibid., 73-74.
10. Ibid., 74.
11. Ibid., 338ff.
12. Ibid., 75.
13. Ibid., 80ff.
14. Joseph Hamburger, *John Stuart Mill on Liberty and Control* (Princeton, NJ: Princeton University Press, 2001), 115.
15. Kleppner, *The Cross of Culture*, 80.
16. Sydney F. Ahlstrom, *A Religious History of the American People* (New Haven, CT: Yale University Press, 1972), 637.
17. Cf. Ch. 30, Ahlstrom, *A Religious History of the American People*, 491ff.
18. Cited in Ahlstrom, *A Religious History of the American People*, 491.
19. Cited in Ahlstrom, *A Religious History of the American People*, 638.
20. Arthur Alphonse Ekirch, *Progressivism in America: A Study of the Era from Theodore Roosevelt to Woodrow Wilson* (New York: New Viewpoints, 1974), 54
21. Ibid., 205.
22. Walter Rauschenbusch, *A Theology for the Social Gospel* (New York: The Macmillan Company, 1922), 148-149.
23. Rauschenbusch, *A Theology for the Social Gospel*, 146.
24. From Rauschenbusch's *Christianity and Social Crisis*, cited in Ahlstrom, *A Religious History of the American People*, 785.
25. Ekirch, *Progressivism in America*, 52-58.
26. Ibid., 54-58.

27. Ibid., 200.
28. Quoted by Nick Gillespie, "Obama's Kingdom of Heaven on Earth," reason.com, October 8, 2007, retrieved from http://reason.com/blog/2007/10/08/obamaskingdom-of-heaven-on-ea.
29. Murray N. Rothbard, "The Progressive Era and the Family," *Ludwig von Mises Institute: Advancing Austrian Economics, Liberty, and Peace*, June 30, 2003, retrieved at http://mises.org/daily/1259; originally from *The American Family and the State*, edited by Joseph R. Peden and Fred R. Glahe (San Francisco: Pacific Research Institute, 1986).
30. Couliano, *Eros and Magic in the Renaissance*, 105.
31. Fred Siegel, "Taking Communism away from the Communists: The Origins of Modern American Liberalism," *Telescope: Critical Theory of the Contemporary*, April 4, 2009, retrieved from http://www.telospress.com/taking-communism-away-from-the-communiststhe-origins-of-modern-american-liberalism/.
32. Ibid.
33. Retrieved from ChicagoSun-Times, http://blogs.suntimes.com/sweet/2010/02/katie_couric_super_bowl_obama.html.
34. Herbert Croly, *The Promise of American Life*, edited by Arthur M. Schlesinger, Jr. (Cambridge, MA: Harvard University, 1965), 399.
35. Ibid., 399.
36. Ibid., 409.
37. Ibid., 409.
38. Ceaser, "The Roots of Obama Worship: Auguste Comte's Religion of Humanity finds a 21st-century Savior."
39. Ibid.
40. Cited in Hamburger, *John Stuart Mill on Liberty and Control*, 109.
41. Ibid., 109.
42. Charles Forcey, *The Crossroads of Liberalism: Croly, Weyl, Lippman and the Progressive Era, 1900-1925* (New York: Oxford University Press, 1967), 7.
43. G. W. F. Hegel, *Phenomenology of Spirit*, translated by A. V. Miller (New York: Oxford University Press, 1976), 3.
44. Cited in Siegel, "Taking Communism away from Communists." The quote is in the context of the trial of anarchists Ferdinando Nicola Sacco and Bartolomeo Vanzetti.
45. Kenneth Minogue, *Alien Powers: The Pure Theory of Ideology*, 2nd ed. (Wilmington, DE: ISI Books, 2008), 52.
46. Cited in Minogue, *Alien Powers*, 52.
47. Ibid., 52.
48. Cited in Hamburger, *John Stuart Mill on Liberty and Control*, 116.
49. Romans 8: 22.
50. Hebrews 2: 5.
51. Romans 13ff.
52. Romans 2: 14.

CHAPTER 9

ANCENT AND MEDIEVAL MILLENARIANISM

1. Cf. Revelation 20.
2. Matthew 5: 6. The beatitudes nicely lay out the apocalyptic understanding of faith.
3. Romans 7: 24-25.
4. Cf. Romans 8.
5. Rudolph, *Gnosis*, 264-265.
6. Voegelin, *Modernity without Restraint*, 278.
7. Cohn, *The Pursuit of the Millennium*, 109.
8. Ibid., 110.
9. Ibid., 110.
10. Ibid., 111.
11. Cited in Cohn, *The Pursuit of the Millennium*, 117.
12. Cohn, *The Pursuit of the Millennium*, 119.
13. Ibid., 121.
14. Ibid., 148ff.
15. Ibid., 177.
16. Ibid., 180.
17. Ibid., 183.
18. II Corinthians 5: 17.
19. I Timothy 1: 9.
20. Cohn, *The Pursuit of the Millennium*, 202.
21. Ibid., 212.
22. Ibid., 214.
23. Ibid., 216.
24. Ibid., 217.
25. Ibid., 218.
26. Ibid., 219-221.
27. Ibid., 224.
28. Ibid., 228.
29. Ibid., 235.
30. Ibid., 236.
31. Ibid., 238.
32. Ibid., 244.
33. Ibid., 238-239.
34. Ibid., 239.
35. Cited in Cohn, *The Pursuit of the Millennium*, 241-242.
36. Cited in Cohn, *The Pursuit of the Millennium*, 247-248.
37. Cohn, *The Pursuit of the Millennium*, 253-254.
38. Ibid., 255.
39. Cited in Cohn, *The Pursuit of the Millennium*, 259.
40. Ibid., 263.
41. Ibid., 263.
42. Cited in Cohn, *The Pursuit of the Millennium*, 266.

43. Cohn, *The Pursuit of the Millennium*, 267.
44. Ibid., 268.
45. Ibid., 270.
46. Ibid., 273.
47. Ibid., 266.
48. Ahlstrom, *The Religious History of the American People*, 92.
49. Ibid., 127.
50. Ibid., 128.
51. Voegelin, *Modernity without Restraint*, 199.
52. *Creeds of the Churches: A Reader in Christian doctrine from the Bible to the Present*, 3rd Edition, edited by John H. Leith (Atlanta, GA: John Knox Press, 1982), 195, 198, 199, 201, et. al.
53. Ibid., 195.
54. Duncan B. Forrester, "Richard Hooker," *History of Political Philosophy*, 357.
55. *Creeds of the Churches*, 198.
56. Ibid., 212-213.
57. Ahlstrom, *The Religious History of the American People*, 129
58. Voegelin, *Modernity without Restraint*, 199.
59. Ibid., 198.
60. Ibid., 206.
61. Ibid., 207.
62. Ibid., 208-209.
63. Ibid., 210.
64. William Bradford, *Of Plymouth Plantation, 1620-1647*, edited by Samuel Eliot Morison (New York: Modern Library, 1967), retrieved at *The Founders' Constitution*, Volume 1, Chapter 16, Document 1, The University of Chicago Press, http://press-pubs.uchicago.edu/founders/documents/v1ch16s1.html.
65. Cited in "Massachusetts Bay Colony," *Quaqua Society Inc.*, retrieved at http://www.quaqua.org/pilgrim.htm.
66. Ibid.
67. Ahlstrom, *The Religious History of the American People*, 357.
68. W. R. Ward, *The Protestant Evangelical Awakening* (Cambridge: Cambridge University Press), 49.
69. *Addresses to the German Nation*, 1807. Second Address: "The General Nature of the New Education" (Chicago and London, The Open Court Publishing Company, 1922), 21.
70. Jonathan Messerli, *Horace Mann: A Biography*, New York: Knopf, 1972), 351.
71. "Massachusetts Bay Colony," Quaqua Society Inc.

CHAPTER 10

MODERN MILLENARIANISM

1. Cited in Saman Mohammadi, "Glenn Alexander Magee – Goeth the Alchemist" *The Excavator*, retrieved at http://disquietreservations.blogspot.com/2013/04/glenn-alexander-magee-goethe-alchemist.html. Original quote from the website for Long

Island University, no longer available.

2. Ibid.

3. Ibid.

4. Pierre Hassner, "Georg W. F. Hegel," translated by Allan Bloom, *History of Political Philosophy*, 739.

5. Ibid., 740.

6. Hegel cited in *History of Political Philosophy*, 740.

7. Ibid., 740.

8. Philip M. Merklinger, *Philosophy, Theology, and Hegel's Berlin Philosophy of Religion, 1821-1827* (New York: SUNY Press, 1993), 183.

9. Hegel cited in *History of Political Philosophy*, 741.

10. Joseph Cropsey, "Karl Marx," *History of Political Philosophy*, 810.

11. Marx cited in *History of Political Philosophy*, 812.

12. *History of Political Philosophy*, 812.

13. James Thrower, "Marxism and Leninism as the Civil Religion of Soviet Society," *Studies in Religion and Society*, Volume 30 (Lewiston, NY: The Edwin Mellen Press, 1992), cf. 28ff.

14. Ibid., 28.

15. Arthur Koestler in *The God that Failed*, edited by Richard Crossman (New York: Bantam Books, 1959), 16.

16. Ibid., 12.

17. Ibid., 12.

18. Thrower, *Marxism and Leninism as the Civil Religion of Soviet Society*, 33-34.

19. Cited in Thrower, *Marxism and Leninism as the Civil Religion of Soviet Society*, 38.

20. Cited in Thrower, *Marxism and Leninism as the Civil Religion of Soviet Society*, 38.

21. Cited in Thrower, *Marxism and Leninism as the Civil Religion of Soviet Society*, 102-103.

22. Cited in Thrower, *Marxism and Leninism as the Civil Religion of Soviet Society*, 124.

23. Jeremy R. Carrette writes on Michel Foucault's view on spirituality: "The 'spiritual', as Foucault elaborated in his 1982 lecture series at the College de France, involves a transformation of the subject. It is, as he tentatively stated in a later interview, "a subject acceding to a certain mode of being." The 'spiritual', in this sense, refers to the construction of the subject through a series of power relations which shape life, the body and the self. Religious beliefs, ceremonies and rituals enact those relations of power and maintain a system of control through the mechanism of pastoral authority. Religion is constituted as a political force which brings people under a certain system of control." (Jeremy R. Carrette, *Foucault and Religion: Spiritual Corporality and Political Spirituality*, 136.)

24. Ibid., 124.

25. Ibid., 127-128.

26. Hermann Rauschning, *The Voice of Destruction* (New York: G. P. Putnam's Sons, 1940), 221.

27. *Secret Conversations with Hitler*, edited by Edouard Calic, translated by Richard Barry (New York: The John Day Company, 1971), 31.

28. Rauschning, *The Voice of Destruction*, 245, 264.

29. Ibid., 225.

30. Ibid., 222.

31. Ibid., 225.
32. Ibid., 233.
33. Ibid., 235.
34. Ibid., 235.
35. Ibid., 222.
36. Ibid., 224.
37. Ibid., 223.
38. Ibid., 223.
39. Ibid., 238.
40. Ibid., 235.
41. Ibid., 246.
42. Ibid., 241-242.
43. Ibid., 226.
44. Ibid., 244.
45. Ibid., 228.
46. Ibid., 232.
47. Ibid., 232.
48. Ibid., 245.
49. Nicholas Goodrick-Clarke, *Hitler's Priestess: Savitri Devi, the Hindu-Aryan Myth, and Neo-Nazism* (New York: New York University Press, 1998), 118.
50. Cited in Goodrick-Clark, *Hitler's Priestess*, 119.
51. Cited in Goodrick-Clark, *Hitler's Priestess*, 124.
52. Hermann Rauschning, *The Voice of Destruction*, 245.
53. Quoted in *Secret Conversation s with Hitler*, 25.
54. Hermann Rauschning, *The Voice of Destruction*, 244.
55. Goodrick-Clark, *Hitler's Priestess*, 119-120.
56. Hermann Rauschning, *The Voice of Destruction*, 252.
57. Ibid., 265.
58. Ibid., 262.
59. Frank Fredericks, "Evangelical, Republican, Progressive, Me," *Relevant: The Magazine on Faith, Culture and Intentional Living*, July 3, 2012, retrieved at http://www.relevantmagazine.com/current/politics/evangelical-republican-progressive-me.
60. Pagitt and Jones, *An Emergent Manifesto of Hope*, 69.
61. Robert H. Schuller, *Self Esteem: The New Reformation* (Waco, TX: Word Books, 1982), 79.
62. Pagitt and Jones, *An Emergent Manifesto of Hope*, 63.
63. Paul Sherry, "Book review, Agenda for Biblical People," *Theology Today* 34, July 1977, 2.
64. Ibid., 2.
65. Pagitt and Jones, *An Emergent Manifesto of Hope*, 199.
66. Ibid., 227.
67. Ibid., 233.
68. Ibid., 63.
69. Ibid., 67.

CHAPTER 11
THE WORSHIP WARS

1. David Yonke, "Comfy with idea, Findlay church to hold 2nd Pajama Pants Sunday," *The Toledo Blade*, January 14, 2012.
2. "Why We Do What We Do: Our Five Agreements," CedarCreek.TV, borrowed from Lifechurch.TV.
3. Monique El-Faizy, *God and Country: How Evangelicals Have Become America's New Mainstream* (New York: Bloomsbury, 2006), 227.
4. Source lost in the internet ether, a good metaphor for the transitoriness of Contemporary Worship. Unfortunately, as it pains me to report such strangeness, I couldn't make this stuff up!
5. Gary Stern, "Episcopal 'U2-charist' uses songs in service," *USA Today*, November 14, 2006.
6. El-Faizy, *God and Country*, 68.

CHAPTER 12
THE NEW COMMUNION: MUSIC

1. Cf. David de Sabatino, *The Jesus People Movement: An Annotated Bibliography and General Resource*, 2nd ed. (Jester Media, 2003).
2. Richard Quebedeaux, *The New Charismatics* (New York: Harper & Row, 1983) 181.
3. Harold Bloom, *The American Religion*, 59.
4. *Rolling Stone*, June 6, 1985, 10.
5. Ibid.
6. *HM Magazine*, Issue 67, 34-35.
7. CCM Magazine, August, 1990, 10.
8. Harold Bloom, *The American Religion*, 202.
9. Harold Bloom, *The American Religion*, 207.
10. Samir Selmanovic, one such Emergent Christian, writes in an essay entitled, *The Sweet Problem of Inclusiveness: Finding Our God in the Other*, "Christianity's idea that other religions cannot be God's carriers of grace and truth casts a large shadow over our Christian experience." Pagitt and Jones, *An Emergent Manifesto of Hope*, 191.
11. Ferguson, *The Aquarian Conspiracy*, 366.
12. Gary Stern, "Episcopal 'U2-charist' uses songs in service," *USA Today*, November 14, 2006.
13. Brett McCracken, "100 Greatest Worship Songs of All Time," *The Search*, March 14, 2008 retrieved at http://stillsearching.wordpress.com/2008/03/14/100-greatestworship-songs-of-all-time/.
14. Margaret Talbot, "Red Sex, Blue Sex: Why do so many evangelical teen-agers become pregnant?" *The New Yorker*, November 3, 2008.
15. Miriam Williams, *Heaven 's Harlots: My Fifteen Years as a Sacred Prostitute in the*

Children of God Cult (New York: Eagle Brook, 1998), 8.

16. Ibid., 8-9.
17. Ibid., 14-17.
18. Ibid., 38-39.
19. Webber, *The Younger Evangelicals*, 191.
20. *Christian Post*, "S. C. Pastor," August 4, 2010. Retrieved from *Christian News*, "Megachurch Pastor Slams 'Normal' Churches," August 23, 2010.
21. Davies, *Romantic and Esoteric Tradition*, 96.
22. Quebedeaux, *The New Charismatics*, 182.
23. Kimon Howland Sargeant, *Seeker Churches: Promoting Traditional Religion in a Nontraditional Way* (New Brunswick, NJ: Rutgers University Press, 2000), 72.
24. Ibid., 72-73.
25. Charles Trueheart, "Welcome to The Next Church," *The Atlantic Monthly*, August, 1996, 44.

CHAPTER 13

THE NEW GOD: THE SELF

1. Ahlstrom, *A History of American People*, 1033.
2. Schuller, *Self Esteem: The New Reformation*, 25.
3. Ibid., 13.
4. Ibid., 13.
5. Ibid., 18.
6. Ibid., 106.
7. Ibid., 119.
8. Ibid., 79.
9. Ibid., 72.
10. Cited in Sargeant, *Seeker Churches*, 80.
11. Pamphlet for "Inward, Outward and Upward: Ministry That Transforms Lives," *A New Seminar for Church Leaders Featuring George Barna* (Ventura, CA: Barna Research Group).
12. Cited in Sargeant, *Seeker Churches*, 77.
13. "this [red] is 4 u," a pamphlet for The Church on Strayer, Maumee, OH.
14. Webber, *The Younger Evangelicals: Facing the Challenges of the New World*, 192.
15. Schuller, *Self Esteem: The New Reformation*, 45.
16. Ibid., 45-47.

CHAPTER 14

THE NEW INITIATION SACRAMENT: CONSUMER CHOICE

1. Warren Cole Smith, *A Lover's Quarrel with the Evangelical Church* (Nottingham, UK: IVP Books, 2009), 110-111.
2. Sargeant, *Seeker Churches*, 11.
3. "Where Do Teenagers Want to Go to Church?" *The Parish Paper*, February 2007,

edited by Herb Miller and Lyle E. Schaller.

4. The retort to this point will be that the Bible mentions each of these activities – song, dance, movement, and hand clapping – in such passages as Psalm 149. A sample from Psalm 149: "Let them praise His name with the dance; Let them sing praises to Him with the timbrel and harp. . . . Let the high praises of God be in their mouth, And a two-edged sword in their hand." (NKJ) In other words, if we take this literally, taking up the sword should also constitute part of our worship, something a true millenarian would surely endorse. However, more moderate spirits, in the tradition of ancient Christian worship, use discernment when applying biblical principles to worship. When feelings, fun, and sentiment revolutionize traditional theology because of worship practices – the very point I am arguing – it's time to apply a bit more discernment regarding Scripture than "what can we get away with given our unbridled Christian freedom?" Or else we may be dealing with a situation in which, yes, taking up the sword will be seen as worship.

5. "Building a Church for New Generations," 12th Annual Evangelism Conference, April 12-15, 1999, Joy Leadership Center.

6. Pamela Miller, "Big churches give the young their own way to worship," *Minneapolis Star Tribune*, March 23, 2007.

7. Sargeant, *Seeker Churches*, 71.

8. Ibid., 58-59.

9. Ibid., 59.

10. Anna David, "The New Face of Faith," *Details*, September, 2010, 156-159.

11. Harold Bloom, *The American Religion*, 37.

CHAPTER 15

THE EMERGENT CHURCH

1. Harold Bloom, *The American Religion*, 184.

2. Ibid., 185.

3. Cited in Sargeant, *Seeker Churches*, 6.

4. Pagitt and Jones, *An Emergent Manifesto*, 69.

5. Ibid., 61.

6. Ibid., 148.

7. Ibid., 228-229.

8. Ibid., 228.

9. Ibid., 143.

10. Ibid., 147.

11. El-Faizy, *God and Country*, 229.

12. Webber, *The Younger Evangelicals*, 193.

13. El-Faizy, *God and Country*, 228.

14. Webber, *The Younger Evangelicals*, 193.

15. Ibid., 195.

16. Pagitt and Jones, *An Emergent Manifesto*, 193

17. Ibid., 193.

18. Ibid., 66.
19. Mark Schulz, "Church Growth Study Has Faulty Premise About Culture," *JesusFirst*, Issue 19, May 2001, 3.
20. George Elerick, "The Miracle of Broken Sinew: An End to Missions," *TheOoze.com*, retrieved at http://theooze.com/culture/the-miracle-of-broken-sinew- an-end-to-missions/.
21. Ibid.
22. El-Faizy, *God and Country*, 231.
23. Pagitt and Jones, *An Emergent Manifesto*, 199.
24. "Willow Creek Repents?" *Christianity Today*, October 18, 2007, retrieved at http://www.outofur.com/archives/2007/10/willow_creek_re.html.
25. El-Faizy, *God and Country*, 230.
26. Pagitt and Jones, *An Emergent Manifesto*, 232.
27. Ibid., 106.
28. Matt Mikalatos, "Will the Real Jesus Please Stand Up? Conservative Jesus. Cool Jesus. Activist Jesus. Why we can't make God's son into our own image." *Relevant*, July/August 2012, retrieved at http://www.relevantmagazine.com /god/god-our- generation/will-real-jesus-please-stand.
29. El-Faizy, *God and Country*, 231.
30. Ibid., 232.
31. Ibid.

CHAPTER 16

NEO-EVANGELICALISM'S GNOSTIC ROOTS

1. Harold Bloom, *The American Religion*, 22.
2. Ahlstrom, *A Religious History of the American People*, 476.
3. Pagitt and Jones, *An Emergent Manifesto*, 62.
4. "Many Americans Say Other Faiths Can Lead to Eternal Life," *Pew Research: Research & Public Life Project*, December 18, 2008, retrieved at http://www.pewforum.org/2008/12/18/many-americans-say-other-faiths-can-lead-to-eternal-life/.
5. "Agnostic Southern Baptist Preachers," *Christian News*, December 6, 2010, 3. Citing "Atheist Ministers Struggle with Leading the Faithful," ABC World News, November 9, 2010.
6. Nancy Pearcey, *Total Truth*, 326.
7. Ibid., 326.
8. Ibid., 253.
9. Mark Noll, *The Scandal of the Evangelical Mind* (Grand Rapids, MI: William B. Eerdmans Publishing Company, 1995), 48.
10. Ibid., 123.
11. "Trend builds for house churches: Participants say they are more at home in cozy settings," *Toledo Blade*, Saturday, July 31, 2010.
12. Frank Viola and Geroge Barna, *Pagan Christianity: Exploring the Roots of Our Church Practices* (Tyndale House Publishers, 2002), 253.

13. Pamphlet for "Inward, Outward and Upward: Ministry That Transforms Lives," *A New Seminar for Church Leaders Featuring George Barna*.
14. Liddell and Scott, *Greek-English Lexicon*, 7th Ed., 844.
15. Phyllis Hodgson, *Three 14ᵗʰ-Century Mystics*, rev. ed. (London: Longmans, Green and Co., 1967), 9.
16. Berman, *Coming to Our Senses*, 148.
17. Dworkin, "The Rise of the Caring Industry."
18. Cited in Ahlstrom, *A Religious History of the American People*, 128.
19. Ibid., 460.
20. David P. Scaer, *Christology*, vol. 6 of *Confessional Lutheran Dogmatics*, edited by Robert Preus (Fort Wayne, IN: The International Foundation for Lutheran Confessional Research, 1989), 16.
21. Ahlstrom, A Religious History of the American People, 817.
22. Some might object that the abolitionist movement was an astounding success, in that the slaves were ultimately freed. Yet, the Civil War occurred toward the end of a wave of abolitionism in the Western world. Brazil was the last Western nation to abolish slavery in 1885, only 20 years after the end of the Civil War. The point is, American slavery's abolition was inevitable due to societal pressures begun, ironically, by Christian Medieval kingdoms and the Church – slavery continued in the twentieth century only in non-Christian lands. The eruption of fire and blood that was the American Civil War recalls millenarian, crusader fervor, the American parallel to the Jacobin movement in France. One wonders how things would be different had slavery run its course in America and come to an end a few decades later. One could hypothesize that race relations in America would be similar to those in countries where slavery ended peaceably.
23. "Willow Creek Repents?" *Christianity Today*, October 18, 2007.

POSTLUDE: GOD OUTSIDE HIS BOX

1. Gypsy Freeman, "An Attitude of Praise" *My Words His Message,* retrieved at http://mywordshismessage.wordpress.com/2010/08/.

✧ Index ✧

393

33366954R00250

Made in the USA
Charleston, SC
13 September 2014